MAIN LINE TO THE WEST

The Southern Railway Route between
BASINGSTOKE & EXETER - Part One
BASINGSTOKE to SALISBURY

by John Nicholas and George Reeve

Battle of Britain Pacific No. 34109 *Sir Trafford Leigh-Mallory* drifts into Salisbury with an Exeter - Waterloo relief in September 1964. Sid Nash.

IRWELL PRESS Ltd.

i

ACKNOWLEDGEMENTS

The authors have been particularly fortunate in the assistance received in the preparation of this book. Railwaymen who worked on the line include Barry Lake, Derrick Hopkins, Ron Grace, Peter Diaper, Graham Hatton, Reg Randell, Derek Clayton and Bill Trigg. A number of local people, who have had an interest in railways, include David Lindsell, Peter Yarlett, Rod Hoyle, Greg Gregory, Arthur Blake, Dr Keith Norris, of the Bourne Valley Historical Society, who has supplied much information about the Porton Military Railway and society reminiscences about the Porton area. Several collectors of railway timetables, locomotive and carriage working diagrams also assisted including Nik Pomfret, Roger Merry Price and Roger Whitehouse. Several have very kindly shared their previously unpublished railway research with us including Mick Hutson and Roger Hateley. Details of private owner wagons have been kindly supplied by Mr Ian Pope. We gratefully acknowledge the help John King and his staff provided from the Rail Track offices at Waterloo and the many photographers who assisted with the illustrations in this book, and the following volumes, and credited appropriately with their photographs. We would like to pay a particular tribute to the late Sid Nash who did so much, not only to assist us with this and many other projects, but the help and contribution he made over the years to the railway field. He is sadly missed. We would also like to give a special thanks to Barry Hoper of the Transport Treasury who gave open access to his vast collection of photos and a special thanks also to Eric Youldon for his help in checking the manuscript and many other matters.

BIBLIOGAPHY

LSWR, SR and BR records held at The Records Office, Kew
The London and South Western Railway Vols. 1, 2 , 3 R.A.Williams
Regional History of the Railways of Great Britain Vol.1 D.S.J.Thomas
Regional History of the Railways of Great Britain Vol. 2 H.P.White
The Longparish Branch Line Peter A.Harding
The Bulford Branch Line Peter A.Harding
Waterloo Ironworks L.T.C.Rolt
LSWR Engine Sheds (Western District) C. Hawkins and G. Reeve
Track layout diagrams of the Southern Railway G.A.Pryer & A.V.Paul
Signal Box diagrams of the Great Western & Southern Railways G.A.Pryer
Public & Working timetables London and South Western, Southern, and British Railways
South Western Circular
Southern Notebook
Southern Newsletter
Railway Magazine
Trains Illustrated
Railway and Travel Monthly
Southern Railway Magazine
Hampshire County Magazine
Live Rail
Kelly's Directories of Hampshire and Wiltshire

First published in the United Kingdom in 2004
by Irwell Press Limited, 59A, High Street, Clophill,
Bedfordshire MK45 4BE
Printed by Interprint

CONTENTS

INTRODUCTION TO VOLUME ONE

First proposals for a central main railway line from London to the port of Falmouth, through Salisbury and Exeter, came in the 1830s. The first section as far as Basingstoke opened in 1840 as part of the London & Southampton Railway, which in line with its plans for expansion, soon became the London & South Western Railway. The Bishopstoke to Salisbury Milford branch opened in 1847 but the route from London to Salisbury was indirect. A quicker and thus more direct route from Basingstoke was promoted and after delays following the Railway Mania the single track branch from Basingstoke to Andover was opened in 1854. It was extended to Salisbury Milford in 1857 and then to Salisbury Fisherton in 1859. The Basingstoke & Salisbury Railway is the subject of Volume One.

Although linked by the long distance through traffic each part of the line had many individual features. The Basingstoke & Salisbury Railway skirted Salisbury Plain, large areas of which were acquired at the turn of the century by the War Department who made extensive use of the line to transport troops and their equipment for manoeuvres. Soon double track was laid on the branch and trains carrying 500 or more men arrived in rapid succession from all over the country, with Salisbury shed contributing large numbers of locomotives and men. In 1902 the Andover Junction to Grateley section was equipped with the first automatic block signalling system in the country, and new pneumatic operation of both points and signals was installed at Grateley and Salisbury. At Andover Junction the main line was crossed by an important cross-country route from Cheltenham by the independent Midland & South Western Junction Railway. From Hurstbourne the Fullerton branch was constructed by the South Western to block the advance of the Great Western towards Southampton and at Porton a narrow gauge branch was built to Porton Down, to serve the army establishments. Local features included the Portals banknote paper mill, built adjacent to Overton station, and the wheat and barley agriculture of the region with grain stores and a flour mill at Andover. Sheep fairs at Overton and Salisbury, and just off the line at Stockbridge and Weyhill, generated many special trains. Military traffic has been a feature for a century, with traffic both in peace and wartime to many bases, and to this day to the military depot at Ludgershall.

The description in Volume One ends at Salisbury, a major traffic centre, and includes the development of Milford station, the city's terminus until 1859 and then a major goods station. Salisbury Fisherton station opened in 1859 with a single through platform but in 1878 a new Up station was opened in an inconvenient location making connections for passengers between trains difficult. In 1902 the station was extensively rebuilt to its present form, but in 1906 tragedy struck when an Up Plymouth boat train derailed at speed on the sharp curve to the east of the station killing 28 people. Salisbury also hosted one of the South Western's largest locomotive sheds with a wide variety of duties, Salisbury locomotives and men going as far as London, Exeter, Portsmouth and Bournemouth. Shortly after the Great Western converted its broad gauge Salisbury branch to standard gauge goods traffic was exchanged, initially a few wagons but soon by the trainload, particularly coal from South Wales. Large East and West Yards were provided to cope with the increasing freight traffic and in addition, with an increasing number of through passenger trains, the Great Western closed its own station all trains using the Southern establishment.

The Basingstoke & Salisbury railway escaped most of the closures of the Beeching era, although a few stations and most goods yards closed, along with the branches. Nurtured by the Southern Region it escaped the ravages west of Salisbury and by the 1980s began to prosper, particularly with long distance commuting to London. Network Southeast continued the good work of the Southern Region and in the 1990s implemented a complete route modernisation including new trains, station improvements and a new diesel train depot at Salisbury. This legacy was inherited by South West Trains who continued to work the line and provided more trains so that the line now enjoys its best passenger train service ever.

Standard Class 5 No. 73081 *Excalibur* **on an Up passenger train passes Battle of Britain Pacific No. 34063 229 Squadron just west of Battledown Junction. The Transport Treasury.**

Chapter 1
THE LINE DESCRIBED

Basingstoke station after re-building by the South Western in 1904. We are looking east towards London with Great Western station in the background. In the foreground are the Up local and Up main lines and to the right a train leaves the Down main platform. Dennis Cullum Collection.

In this first chapter we look closely at the West of England main line, concentrating mostly on the 1950s when the steam worked route was in its heyday. We start at Basingstoke, although our detailed description of the line begins at Worting Junction.

BASINGSTOKE

One of the first stations in Hampshire, Basingstoke soon became a major junction not only for the South Western's Bournemouth and West of England main lines but also an important interchange point for the Great Western's line from Reading. Such was the level of traffic that quadrupling of the main line from Waterloo through Basingstoke to Worting Junction was completed early in the twentieth century. Some prestige trains such as the *Atlantic Coast Express*, the *Bournemouth Belle* and Southampton Docks Ocean Liner Expresses such as *The Cunarder* sped though Basingstoke non-stop. A large number of semi-fast and stopping trains called and many started or terminated here. By the 1950s there were two daily long distance inter-regional trains calling at Basingstoke, from Birkenhead and York, both destined for Bournemouth West. Some local trains started at Basingstoke, often in the Down

bay platform, *en route* for Salisbury, Yeovil and, at one time, Alton – all were timed to connect with semi-fast trains from Waterloo.

In addition to trains starting or terminating at Basingstoke there were many long distance Southern freight trains together with inter-regional freights, many destined for Southampton Docks. Numerous wagons were transferred here, in particular off the Great Central. These had been routed via Banbury and Reading and then forwarded on scheduled services. A number of freights along our line originated in Basingstoke West Yard, to Overton, Andover and Amesbury among other places.

Locomotives allocated to Basingstoke shed, together with Basingstoke drivers, firemen and guards, worked trains along our line to Andover Junction, Bulford, Salisbury, Reading and Waterloo. Details of such locomotive workings appear in Chapter Ten In South Western days there was a daily Basingstoke to Fullerton Junction via Longparish goods train.

The section of the London & Southampton Railway between Nine Elms and Basingstoke station opened in 1839, the double track line opening throughout in 1840. The single track branch to Andover opened in 1854 and was extended to Salisbury in 1857. There was a short viaduct,

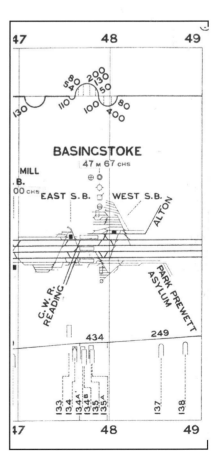

Just before the end of steam in 1967 drivers and firemen at Basingstoke shed with BR standard 4-6-0 No.73093. Back row Reg Hand (driver), George Arnald (foreman), Roy Porter (driver), Trevor Gosling (driver), Ron Grace (fireman), Cyril Warren (driver). Front row Jim Wilks (foreman), Tony Wiggins(fireman), Adrian Rowe (fireman), Ron Rood (foreman), Di Evans (driver). Ron Grace collection.

24ft high, just to the west of the station and on 23rd May 1856 a passenger, returning from the Portsmouth naval review, stepped on to the parapet and fell, fracturing an arm and leg. As we will see in Chapter Two, an accident report of 1858 illustrates the working practice of the period.

In 1848 the broad gauge Berks & Hants branch from Reading was opened to an adjacent terminus just to the north of the South Western station. Transfer of passengers between trains was straightforward enough but freight had to be unloaded and reloaded until the Great Western mixed the gauge to Basingstoke in 1856, the broad gauge here being abolished in 1869. The Basingstoke & Alton branch opened in 1901 and the Park Prewett Hospital branch opened in 1914.

The South Western and Great Western had their own passenger stations, goods yards, signal boxes, engine sheds and staff until the Great Western closed its own passenger station in 1932, its bay platform becoming part of the Southern station. Other facilities were amalgamated shortly after nationalisation in 1948. The Western Region engine shed closed and its locomotives and men transferred to the Southern Region shed; the passenger and goods stations were afterwards managed as one. Similar rationalisation took place at about the same times at Salisbury.

***

As intimated above, increasing traffic demands meant that by 1904 the South Western had widened its main line from Waterloo to Worting Junction to four tracks. Major changes were made at Basingstoke where the formation was extended to the south of the line. This involved sweeping away the previous station. New automatic block was installed on the main line and the pneumatic signalling was operated from new Basingstoke East and West signal boxes. There were new platforms, passenger station, goods and marshalling yards and a three road engine shed. Some of these features survive to this day, despite changes

In the early 1960s BR standard 4-6-0 No.75079 passes Basingstoke shed with an up Southampton line parcels train. The signals are operated pneumatically. The Transport Treasury.

Outside Basingstoke shed ex-LBSCR E5 class 0-6-2T No.32568, employed here on carriage and yard shunting, shortly before withdrawal in 1955. GER George Powell collection.

made for the Bournemouth line electrification completed in 1967, when the signalling was replaced by a Basingstoke panel box and the engine shed demolished.

In the 1950s Basingstoke was a quiet but substantial market town in the north of Hampshire. It had developed its own industries, including the factories of Thorneycrofts and Wallis & Stevens, both manufacturing road vehicles. The Basingstoke & Alton line closed, for the second time, in 1935 and was used for a number of films including *Oh Mr Porter*. However, a short section from Basingstoke was retained as a siding to Thorneycrofts works and remained in use until the 1960s. The well-known cricket commentator John Arlott was once asked the origin of his fine country accent, to which he replied *'When I was a young man everyone in Basingstoke spoke like this.'*

From Basingstoke to Worting Junction

From Basingstoke the quadruple track main line ran on a rising gradient of 1 in 249 on a straight alignment to Winklebury signal box. Here there was a gentle curve to the south-west of 170 chains radius and then again straight on a very low embankment through open countryside. Near Worting House the line crossed the old Roman road from Winchester to Silchester on bridge No.140

ROUTE MAP OF THE BASINGSTOKE and SALISBURY LINE

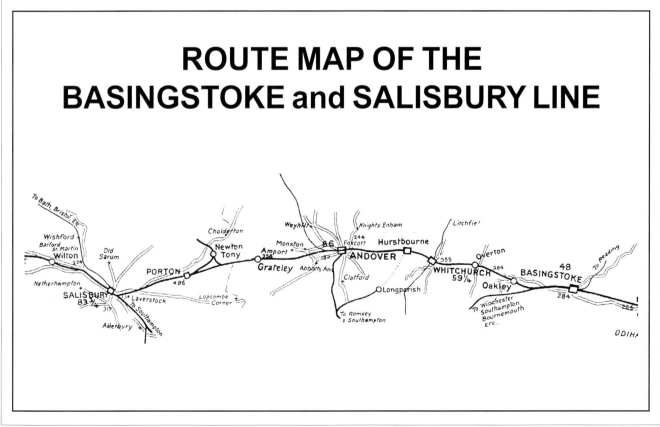

On 17th June 1959 Drummond T9 class 4-4-0s Nos.30338 and 30718 double head a troop special from Farnborough to Yeovil Town, for Houndstone Camp, on the Down main line at Winklebury, a mile or so west of Basingstoke. S.C.Nash.

and then on bridge No.141, the B3400 road from Basingstoke to Whitchurch and Andover. As with other under bridges on the quadruple track section, inspection from road level shows the brickwork of the original two-track bridge of 1839, with extensions on each side to carry the extra two lines.

Just before Worting Junction signal box, in a low cutting, a farm track was carried over the line on an iron deck span resting on brick abutments. Bridge No.142 was built in 1897 to replace an earlier bridge spanning the original two tracks, now just a footbridge.

WORTING JUNCTION
Chronology
Signal box (50 miles 37 chains from Waterloo) opened on new quadruple track from Basingstoke, with crossovers forming a junction between Southampton and West of England main lines, 30th May 1897.
Signal box closed, functions transferred to Basingstoke panel, 20th November 1966.
(The distances in miles and chains from Waterloo are taken from official railway records. However in recent years, with the benefit of modern technology, it has been found by Gerald Jacobs that there are some discrepancies in measurements, to the extent that the declared route mileage of Exeter Central from Waterloo is 30 chains greater than the milepost mileage.)

Description
Situated on the north side of the line, Worting Junction signal box controlled the junction between the Southern's two principle main lines, to Bournemouth and to Exeter, although it was not immediately obvious that it was a junction. Here the 50 miles of quadruple track from Waterloo,

which from north to south were designated Up Local, Up Main, Down Main and Down Local, were connected by trailing and facing crossovers to become Up Bournemouth, Up Salisbury, Down Salisbury and Down Bournemouth lines. There was also a trailing crossover between the Up and Down main lines which was used only when the civil engineers required a track to be taken out of use for Sunday maintenance. In the Down direction just in advance of bridge 142 was

the distinctive lattice post carrying four dolls with the four Down Home signal arms; from north to south there were: Down Main to Salisbury, Down Main to Bournemouth, Down Local to Salisbury, Down Local to Southampton. Here the Worting Junction signalmen regulated traffic on the two main lines, with block sections from Basingstoke West, or 'B', and to Wooton and Oakley.

Here, about 1897, the South Western had built a block of four terraced houses on the

Worting Junction signal box, shortly before its closure in 1966. R.M.Casserley.

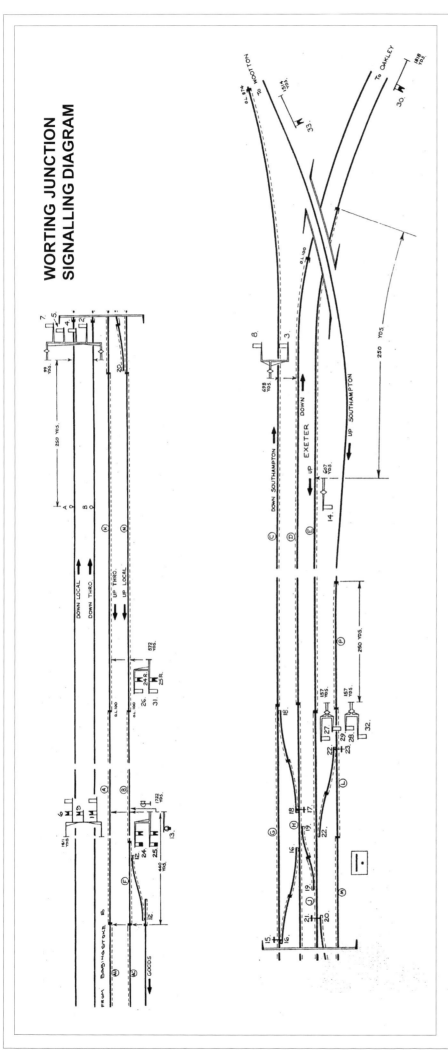

WORTING JUNCTION SIGNALLING DIAGRAM

north side of the line adjacent to bridge No.142, for its signalmen and permanent way men. Starting in the 1960s one of the residents, Mr Ron Grace, had made a splendid collection of Southern Region enamelled station name boards which were displayed in the garden for the benefit of passing travellers. When Ron moved here in 1962, as a railway lorry driver and later a fireman, the cottages were occupied by a guard, Mr Van Rooyen, a platelayer Mr Ned Oliver and a driver Mr Peter Conduct. Previously the cottages had been occupied by three signalmen and a lengthman; they had outside toilets and no bathroom, though they have long since been brought up to modern standards.

Worting Junction Today

In 1966, as part of the Bournemouth line electrification, new colour light signals controlled from the new Basingstoke panel were installed and electric point motors replaced the point rodding. The signal box and all the semaphore signals were removed. Basingstoke has expanded over farmland, so that today the western town boundary runs along the old Roman road crossed on bridge No.140. Between Basingstoke and Worting Junction the four tracks are very busy, often with up to ten trains per hour each way.

Worting Junction to Battledown Junction

The Up home signals for Worting Junction were passed. From Worting Junction signal box the four tracks ran in a south westerly direction, emerging from a shallow cutting on to a low embankment, still on a rising gradient of 1 in 249. The exception to this was the Up Bournemouth line which veered slightly away from the other three and ascended above them towards Battledown flyover (although of course the Up trains were descending). Before the flyover was reached a minor road was crossed on bridge No.143, a complex structure with the original double track bridge extended for one track to the south, but with a higher level extension to the north to carry the Up Bournemouth track.

BATTLEDOWN JUNCTION

Early documents, from the opening of the Andover line in 1854, refer to this original junction as Worting Junction but when the 'new' Worting Junction opened in 1897 almost ¾ mile to the east this location became known as Battledown.

Chronology
Double track main line opened 11th May 1840.
Junction to single Andover line opened 3rd July 1854.
Pointsman's Box provided 1857.
Line to Oakley doubled 24th December 1861.
First signal box opened circa 1865.
First signal box closed, second (51 miles 13 chains from Waterloo) opened, Up Southampton line carried over flyover, main line to Basingstoke quadrupled 30th May 1897.
Second signal box closed, third opened, layout changes 4th December 1904.

On 18th May 1963 Urie S15 class 4-6-0 No.30498, heads a heavy down freight for the Southampton line on the approach to Battledown flyover. The two tracks in the foreground are Up and Down Salisbury, whilst the Up Southampton line is on an embankment behind the photographer. R.C.Riley, The Transport Treasury.

All points removed, third signal box closed 18th January 1925; junction thereafter at Worting.

Description up to 1925

Battledown Junction was opened in 1854 for the new line to Andover, gaining its name from Battledown Farm fairly close to the line. The junction was originally operated by a signalman who pulled levers on the Up side adjacent to the points and cross-bar and disc signals.

Life got a little better for the pointsman in 1857, when a small hut was provided for him. On 11th May 1865 the South Western Officers' Conference decided to install Saxby & Stevens semaphore signals, not only here, but at the junctions at Woking and Weybridge. It would appear therefore that the first signal box was erected at this

time although full interlocking of the levers may have come later. On 31st March 1886 the South Western Traffic Committee approved plans to improve the junction here but took no action at that time.

'Flyover junctions', which form part of our modern motorway network, are no recent invention. The South Western installed its Battledown flyover in 1897 to eliminate conflicting train movements here

Battledown flyover in 1936 carrying the Up Southampton line over the double track Salisbury line. Reg Randell.

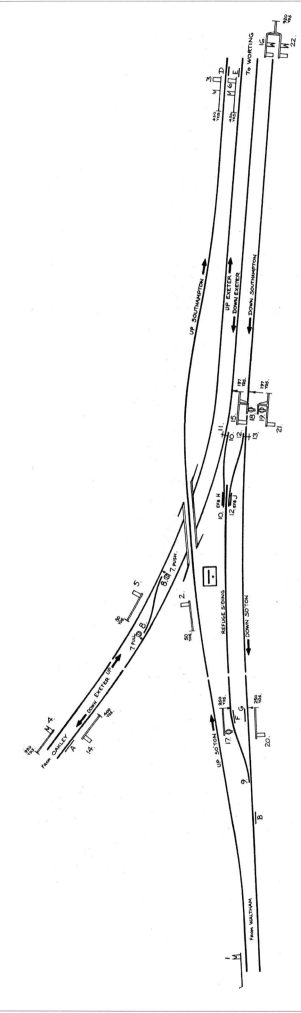

BATTLEDOWN SIGNALLING DIAGRAM 1898

over the increasingly busy junction between its two main lines.

Description after 1925

Battledown flyover was bridge No.143A and carried the Up Bournemouth line over the double track to Salisbury which diverged from the original Southampton line on a curve of 40 chains radius. The flyover consisted of a skew bowstring girder bridge carried on brick abutments. Adjacent to it were the Up distant signals for Worting Junction box, one for each route.

Leaving Battledown, the double track line ran level and straight almost due west through a shallow cutting. After half a mile the line passed under a minor road on a brick built bridge, No.144, and then passed on to an embankment. Here the line passed over another minor road on iron deck bridge No.145. The line entered a cutting and passed the Oakley Down distant signal. At milepost 52, bridge No.146 carried a footpath over the line. Shortly after another minor road, leading to Oakley church, crossed the line on brick built bridge No.147. The Oakley Down home signal, being just in advance the line, entered Oakley station.

OAKLEY

Chronology
Single track line opened 3rd July 1854.
Station opened April 1856.
Double track from Worting Junction opened 24th December 1861.
Double track to Whitchurch opened 1st June 1866.
Signal box (circa 52 miles 35 chains from Waterloo) opened circa 1875.
Goods yard closed 25th November 1963.
Station closed 17th June 1963.
Signal box closed 20th November 1966.

South Western Traffic Committee Minutes 1865-1895
The following extracts refer to various issues at Oakley station.
25th February 1858 A cheap clock is needed.
30th November 1871 Mr Fifield, station agent, requested that his daughter be appointed as telegraphist at 7/- per week. Recommended to Board.
9th November 1881. New crossover approved for £185 as requested by Engineering Committee.
27th September 1893. Approved small goods store at £70.
16th October 1895. The Engineering Committee had reported that on 7th and 9th September Sir Edward Bates' gamekeepers had been found ferreting for rabbits on the slopes of cuttings between Worting Junction and Oakley. This was referred to the company Solicitor.
1st February 1899. Approved building a carriage dock and removal of old wagon turntable at £32.
18th July 1900. LNWR wagon No.60317 was on fire at Oakley on the 8.20am down goods on 12th July, damage £15.
23rd February 1911. Alter gates at entrance for £89 as requested by Engineering Committee
23rd July 1914. Extend loading dock on Up side at £148.
23rd July 1914. The platforms at Oakley, which at present are low in one point, are to be made up to a uniform level and the sleeper crossing removed, for £45. The Traffic Officers'

An Up Southampton to Waterloo passenger train crosses the West of England main line on Battledown Flyover - the third signal box is seen clearly in the fork of the lines, dating this photograph between 1904 and 1925.

Conference wanted the dip abolished due to problems alighting from modern types of carriages.

In 1889 *Kelly's Directory* included East Oakley as part of the parish of Wooton St Lawrence, the whole of which in 1881 had a population of 996. The main crops were wheat barley, turnips, clover and hay. Oakley station had a telegraph office.

Wyndham Portal 1822-1905

Wyndham Portal, who for many years ran the family banknote papermaking business at Laverstoke Mill (described in the Overton section), lived at Malshanger House a mile or so to the north of Oakley station. In 1861, just seven years after this section of the line opened, he became a director of the South Western, stepped down through ill health between 1864 and 1871, was appointed

deputy chairman in 1875 and chairman between 1892 and 1899, before finally standing down again in 1902. He and his family were regular users of Oakley station and when on the Board he often chatted to the driver and fireman of his train, gave them newspapers to read and tried to persuade them to buy a few shares in the company. However in 1902 Wyndham Portal's son, Sir William Portal, took his father's seat on

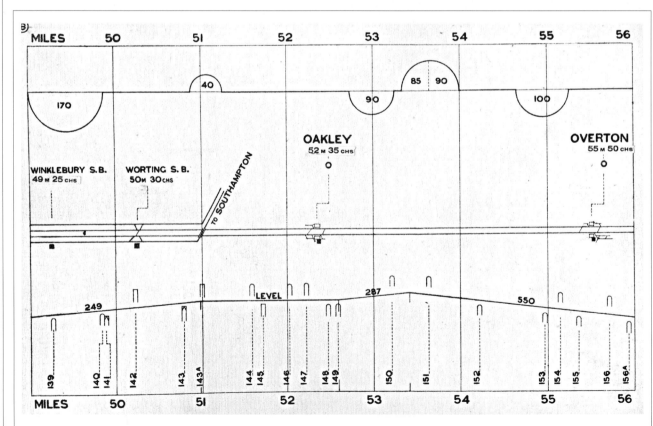

H15 class 4-6-0 No. 30521 on a Down goods train passing Oakley in 1962. Jim Davenport.

the board and from 1910 to 1922 was deputy chairman of the South Western. Sir William inherited the Portal's paper-making business and lived at Laverstock House near Overton.

Oakley Station

The station was apparently opened in 1856 with a temporary wooden building, replaced by a conventional building when the line from Worting was doubled in 1862. In the 1950s Oakley was a typical Hampshire village, a few houses spread out over a wide area with open fields between. It generated but limited traffic for the railway and had closed before the Beeching cuts of the 1960s. Photographs show the station surrounded by trees and fields with only one house in sight. It was located on a straight, level section of line running almost east to west between over bridge No.147 and under bridge No.148 which spanned the B3400 road.

The station layout was straightforward and similar to many others on the line. There were two trailing crossovers on the main line with the platforms between them, together with Up sidings east and west and a Down siding, all with trailing connections. 'Up Siding West' was also known as 'the coal road', where the odd wagon was unloaded.

The Down siding was essentially a refuge siding where a very short goods train or a few wagons could be berthed. Indeed in 1909 a typical short goods train, the 9.52am from Basingstoke to Fullerton, was booked to shunt at Oakley between 10.4am and 10.40am to allow the 8.50am Waterloo to Exeter express to pass. 'Up Siding East', which had trailing connections at both ends, served a small goods yard including a long

dock which at one stage incorporated a cattle pen and terminated in an end dock. The 1872 Ordnance Survey shows the signal cabin on the Up platform and a wagon turntable in the Up siding.

The station approach road led up from the B3400. The two storey station house on the Up platform was brick with a slated roof and three chimneys, with exceptionally tall pots. The building incorporated the Stationmaster's home as well as booking hall, booking office and waiting room. When Oakley station was opened in 1856 the platform was on the Down side. However, it was not until 1862, when the line was doubled, that the station house was constructed on the Up side to a design by Joseph Bull. It followed very closely the design of the station house at Overton, built in 1855. At the Down end was the signal box with an adjacent lamp room and wooden hut.

On the Down platform was a wooden waiting shelter and a square section telegraph post of South Western vintage. Quiet unusually for a station on a busy main line, there was no footbridge or subway, but passengers used a foot crossing instead between the platforms. These originally had a dip in the middle to enable passengers to step down, but this feature was removed in 1914. Passengers alighting from Down trains had the choice of two footpaths to leave the station, one up to the road adjacent to bridge No.147, and another down the line to the B3400 road near bridge No.148. At the west end of the station was a barrow crossing linking the bottom of the platform ramps. *In the goods yard was a cart weighbridge of 10 tons capacity with its office, near the loading dock, and a highway vehicle dock.(SR 1934)**

Traffic and Train Services

As can be seen from the table the passenger train service at Oakley was limited, reflected in the small number of tickets sold. There was some commuting, including schoolchildren, into Basingstoke and a little towards Whitchurch and Andover, with a few long distance travellers. Most Up trains went to Waterloo but some terminated at Basingstoke. The earliest Up train in 1909 was at 8.44am, advanced to 7.50am in 1947, which was early enough for a day's work in Basingstoke but not London. The busiest day was Friday, for Basingstoke market. Few people lived near the station and buses, introduced along the main road, proved more convenient. Boys travelling to and from Hilsea College used the station at the start and end of term and their luggage also came

* Taken from official Southern Railway Working Timetable Appendix

The brass LSWR hand bell at Oakley signal box. Shortly before the arrival of trains the signalman rang it to alert station staff. Peter Yarlett.

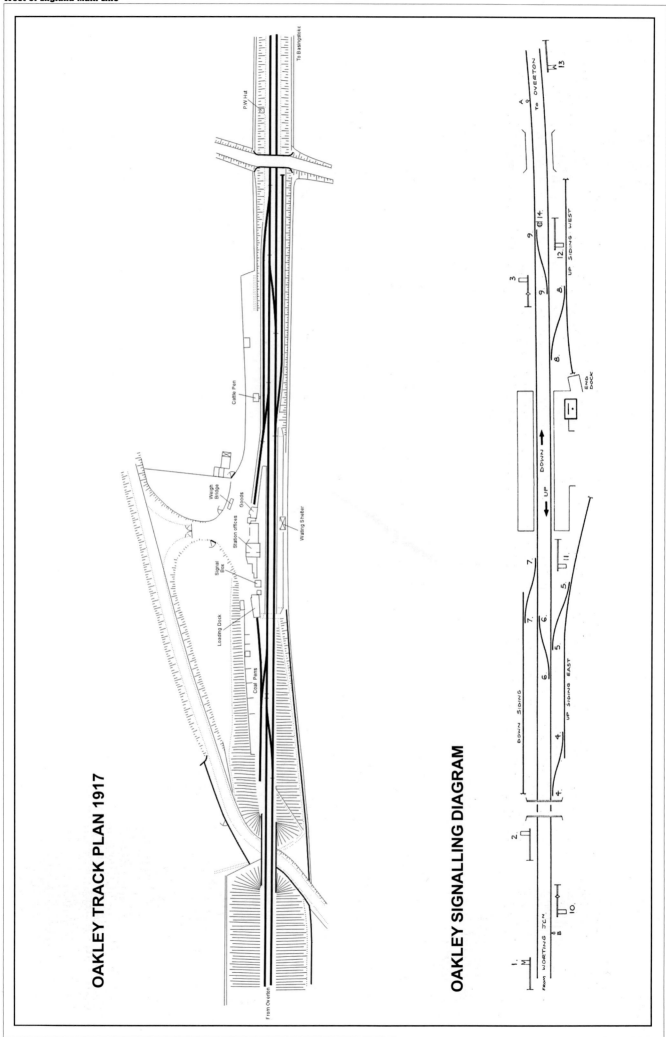

OAKLEY TRACK PLAN 1917

OAKLEY SIGNALLING DIAGRAM

Top left. On the last day of service 17th June 1963 Oakley station house from the station approach, still displaying a Southern Railway enamel sign. At the time of writing the house survives. Peter Yarlett.

Middle left. The interior of Oakley signal box in 1963 showing the polished levers, block instruments, bell pushes and release plunger, with illumination by Tilley lamp. Peter Yarlett.

Below. Oakley station buildings on the Up platform on the last day of service 17th June 1963. Peter Yarlett.

Up to the mid-1920s staff at Oakley comprised a Stationmaster and a couple of porters on early and late turns who between them ran the passenger station, selling tickets, dealing with telegrams and parcels, and giving departing trains the right away. They also dealt with the paperwork for the goods yard and assisted customers with the loading and unloading of goods. Porters' duties also included pumping water for use at the station from a well, lighting up the oil lamps at dusk and, on a weekly rota, replacing signal lamps. The Stationmaster was also responsible for the monthly station returns to the divisional office, but in later years this post was withdrawn and Oakley station was covered by two porters, supervised from Overton. There were three

Oakley station looking east in later years. Little had changed here over the stations lifetime apart from the crossing dip in the platforms being removed in favour of a wooden foot crossing at the Down end the oil lamps being replaced by Tilley lamps hung from the lamp standards at night. Dennis Cullum.

signalmen who normally covered the shifts in the signal box, assisted by rest day relief men who covered for days off, holidays and illness.

In 1871 the Stationmaster, then known as station agent, was Mr Fifield, in 1895 Mr Frederick William Laker, in 1915 Mr Frank Wills, and in 1923, Mr McGarry. From the mid-1920s the post of Oakley Stationmaster was abolished, and thereafter was supervised by the Overton Stationmaster who visited once a week to check the paperwork in the booking office and the train register in the signal box.

Oakley Today

Viewed from Bridge 147 the double track runs through the station site, past the overgrown Down platform and a wall on the Up side. The old station yard is thriving with various commercial premises and the

Oakley signal box in 1963, little changed since its construction about 1875. Dennis Cullum.

On 22nd September 1936 the Up *Atlantic Coast Express* headed by King Arthur class 4-6-0 No.782 *Sir Brian* with Nine Elms duty disc No. 8 passes a Down stopping train at Oakley. The footpath to the Down platform is to the left. H.C.Casserley

station house is in good repair and occupied. Since closure in 1963 extensive house building has taken place between bridges Nos.144 and 146 and southwards to East Oakley, straddling the Bournemouth main line. Oakley station as it was is inconvenient for this new population, although no doubt a case might be made for a new, better placed station on either of the two main lines.

From Oakley to Overton

Leaving Oakley station the line continued level and straight to the west, crossing bridge No.148 with three brick arches over the B3400. Almost immediately after bridge No.149 the line crossed over a minor road at Clarken Green next to the Red Lion Inn, later to become the Beach Arms. The line then began to climb gently at 1 in 287, passing first the Oakley Up distant signal then milepost 53 where the line curved

gently to the south on a 90 chains radius. The line entered a cutting near Deane Down Farm which was spanned by over bridge No.150 and curved gently to the north at first 85 then 90 chains radius. Towards the end of the cutting was over bridge No.151 at Deane and in the cutting, about halfway between these two bridges, the line reached a summit about 400 feet above sea level, 53.5 miles from Waterloo.

The gradient now became a very easy 1 in 550 down towards Whitchurch and Hurstbourne, first in the long cutting, then on a low embankment. Passing milepost 54 the line then crossed a minor road on under bridge No.152 near Ashe. In 1854 Capt. Tyler reported that there had been difficulties here when the bridge abutments had to be renewed. Here the reason for the falling gradient was revealed as the line passed close to the springs which form the source of the River Test near Ashe church, the line following the valley down to Whitchurch. Nearby was Ashe Park, home of William Portal (1755-1846), another member of the papermaking family.

Continuing down the Test valley the line curved gently to the south on a 100 chain radius

curve. Towards the end of the curve was under bridge No.153 over a track leading to Polhampton Farm. Milepost 55 was passed the line running into a cutting spanned by over bridge No.154 at Quidhampton with the Overton Down distant signal in advance of it.

Continuing downhill, now straight, the line ran over a road on bridge No.155 and entered Overton station.

OVERTON

Chronology
Single track line opened 3rd July 1854.
Station with single platform opened on down side January 1855.
Double track Oakley to Whitchurch, Up platform and waiting shed opened 1st June 1866.
Signal box (55 miles 52 chains from Waterloo) opened circa 1875.
Footbridge installed 1919.
Portal's Siding installed 1919.
Goods yard closed 14th September 1965.
Portals Siding closed about 1966.
Signal box closed 5th February 1967, trailing crossover operated from ground frame retained.
Station modernised with extended platforms 1993.

Up Passenger Trains departing Oakley station (weekdays)

1857	1867	1909	1947
4	5 + 1 request	9	6

Passenger Trains Oakley Weekdays Summer 1958

Train	Oakley dep.	To
6.33am Woking	7.43am	Templecombe
6.45 Salisbury	7.51	Waterloo
7.20 Waterloo	8.59	Salisbury
8.46 Salisbury	9.49	Waterloo
10.45 Basingstoke	10.54	Salisbury
9.3 Templecombe	11.7	Waterloo
10.54 Waterloo	12.26pm	Salisbury
11.54 Waterloo	1.24	Salisbury
12.58pm Salisbury	2.0	Waterloo
2.48 Basingstoke	2.57	Salisbury
4.48 Basingstoke	4.57	Yeovil Town
4.5 Salisbury	5.13	Waterloo
5.0 Waterloo	6.11	Yeovil Junction
5.15 Salisbury	6.20	Waterloo
5.39 Waterloo	7.15	Salisbury
6.54 Waterloo	8.42	Yeovil Town
8.44 Salisbury	9.42	Woking

Goods Trains at Oakley 1909

Train	Time at Oakley	Destination
9.52am Basingstoke	10.4 – 10.40am	Fullerton
3.10pm Fullerton	6.34 – 6.50pm	Basingstoke
3.55pm Exeter	8.10 – 8.23	Basingstoke

Freight Trains Oakley Weekdays Summer 1958

Train	Oakley arr.	Oakley dep.	To
7.45am B'stoke W/Yd	8.6am	8.26am	Andover Junction
4.3pm Overton	4.11pm	4.21pm	Basingstoke Up Yard

Overton station looking east in South Western days, with many features similar to Oakley, before the construction of Portals's Mill in 1919. The road van conveying banknote paper from Laverstock Mill to the Bank of England was loaded on to a carriage truck in the siding on the right. Colin Chivers Collection.

The LSWR Traffic Committee Minutes 1861-1921 contain the following references to Overton station:

3rd October 1861. Mr Wyndham Portal wants trains to stop at Oakley and Overton on Basingstoke Market days. The 3.40pm down Exeter to stop at Overton.

5th October 1876 The Officers Conference recommended a new siding costing £400. Approved

14th July 1883. As a result of a Directors Inspection it was recommended to erect a portion of old roofing on the up platform.

21st November 1883 The Civil Engineer, Mr Jacomb, suggested that the up platform be roofed over with old materials and new corrugated iron, for £40. (This explains why the up side shelter was longer than the original and has earlier supports)

9th July 1884. As a result of a Directors Inspection it was recommended to extend the west end of the down platform, and to provide a shelter at the west end of the up platform. To be done.

6th January 1892. As the result of a Directors Inspection the Engineer says that the road box shed, improvements to the booking office and waiting room will cost £187. The goods store and rebuilding of the coal store will be done for £82, but the station improvements were postponed.

3rd October 1894. As a result of a Directors Inspection approval was given for a siding and horsebox dock for £288.

26th June 1895. Agreed improvements to waiting rooms and office accommodation for £92.

11th December 1895. The above was confirmed, plus additional roofing on the down platform for £66. (a non standard style of canopy)

24th July 1919. Approved an additional siding for Messrs Portals mill, Portals to pay.

7th October 1920. Approved improvements to parcels office and waiting room accommodation for £270.

21st July 1921. The small goods shed is insufficient for traffic; approved extensions costing £100.

22nd May 1922. Approved installation of semi-portable overhead runway in goods yard, including rolled steel girder track with run of 25 feet, costing £169.

Overton 1870-1922

The Ordnance Survey of 1872 shows the double track main line, the Down Sidings East and West, and the single Up Siding before Portals Mill was constructed. The signal box on the Down platform is clearly identified, but apart from the Stationmaster's house there are no other buildings shown.

Kelly's Directory of 1889 described Overton as a large parish, formerly a market town, with the station half a mile from the village at Quidhampton. There had been four annual fairs but at that time only the July one survived, with 50,000 sheep and lambs sold. The chief crops were wheat, barley, oats and turnips, and the 1881 population was 1,443. Prominent citizens listed included William Wyndham Portal of Southington House and Melville Portal of Laverstoke, and the Stationmaster was Mr Henry G.Watts.

Overton in the 1950s

The little town stood at the intersection of the old turnpike road between Basingstoke and Andover, which later became the B3400, and another road running south from Kingsclere. It was the first town on the River Test, only a mile or so from its source at Ashe, but there was sufficient flow in the river for two water mills. The best known establishment at Overton of course was Messrs Portals paper mill which produced paper for banknotes, of which more later.

Overton Fair attracted sheep farmers and dealers from a wide area.

Overton station was built at Quidhampton, almost a mile along a minor road, to the north. It was on a straight length of line falling gently at 1 in 550 between under bridge No.155 in an embankment and over bridge No.156 in a cutting. There were crossovers at each end and two Up sidings to the west of the platforms both connected through a scissors crossing to Messrs *Portal's siding through a gate. The two were also connected by a crossover near the buffer stops which facilitated the running round of a short train and special trains of banknotes from Portal's. Portal's Siding at Overton was served by Down goods trains; available only for Portal's, there was a gate across the siding unlocked by a key held by the station master. (SR 1934)*

The inner of the two was designated the Up refuge siding which could hold an engine and 26 wagons. (BR 1960).

Coal and minerals were unloaded at the short Down Siding East; adjacent was a 10 ton cart weighbridge and office. The Down Siding West served a small goods yard with a loading dock, a 5 ton outside crane and a highway vehicle dock (BR 1960).

On the Down platform was the two storey station house, similar in many respects to that at Oakley, incorporating the station master's accommodation, booking hall, booking office and waiting room. There was a short platform awning and outbuildings, some wooden, served as toilets and stores. On the Up platform was a waiting shelter incorporating a small awning and at the west end the signal box, a small clapboarded cabin on a brick base. Adjacent was a corrugated iron lamp room. Originally the station was lit by oil lamps,

OVERTON TRACK DIAGRAM 1913

OVERTON SIGNALLING DIAGRAM

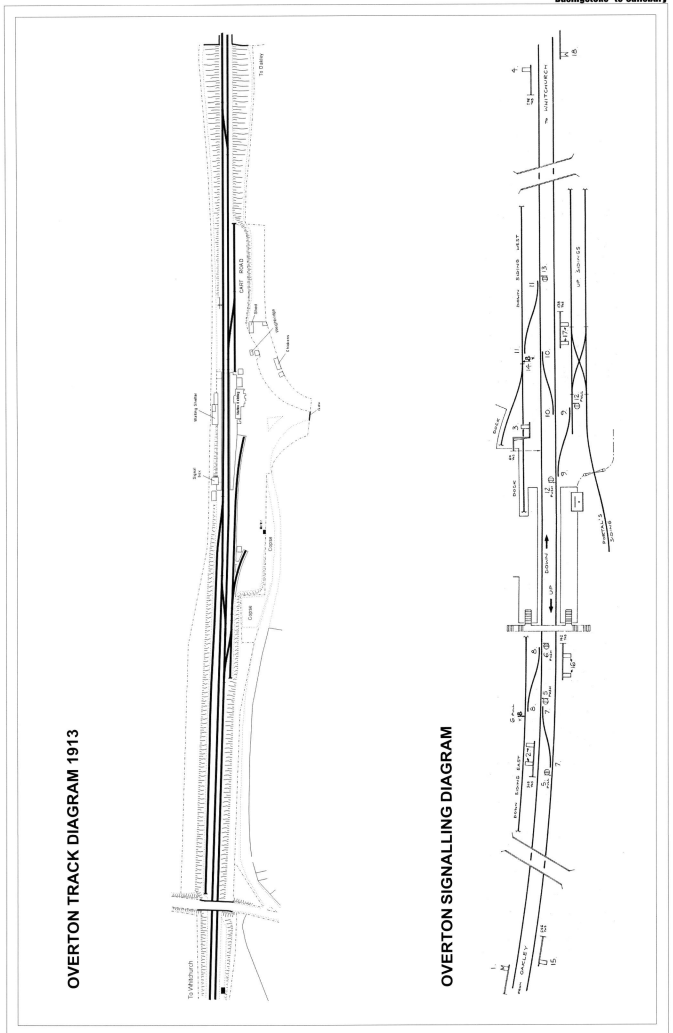

The exterior of Overton station in South Western days with horse drawn transport of the period. The station house, opened in 1855 a year after the line, is of similar design to Oakley seen on page 11. Dennis Cullum Collection.

but by the 1950s electric lighting had been installed.

At the eastern end the platforms were connected by a wooden barrow crossing which for many years was also used by passengers. In 1919, however, a lattice steel footbridge, No.155A, was provided. This also doubled as a crossing for a footpath to the new mill under construction at Portal's, the firm contributing a £350 for the extra staircases. Some sections of this footbridge apparently came from one at the east end of Yeovil Junction station declared redundant in 1915.

Portal's Mills

The upper Test valley proved to be very popular for waterpowered papermills. In 1712 Henry Portal, of Huguenot origin, established a papermaking business at Bere Mill on the River Test a mile or so to the east of Whitchurch, and in 1719 leased a second watermill another mile to the east, Laverstoke Mill, near Overton. From thereon six generations of the Portal family managed and developed the business. In 1724 Henry acquired an exclusive contract with the Bank of England for banknote paper. This was carted by wagon 12 miles north to Newbury, loaded onto a river barge and conveyed down the Kennett and Thames to the Bank of England in London. By the 1790s however, the paper went to London in regular deliveries in a 'waggon with six fine horses'.

In 1855 new buildings were erected at Laverstoke and in 1860 new counting machines were installed. In December 1867 the then owner, Wyndham Portal, was concerned that the police constables on duty at the mill should be armed and three dozen constables' staves were sent from Woolwich Dockyard to Overton station. In the 1880s paper was supplied also to the Banks of Scotland and Ireland. Up to 1922 coal, cotton rags used for papermaking, machinery and other supplies arrived by train at Overton station and were then carted to Laverstoke Mill about three miles away.

According to Portal's records, in 1853 the first delivery of banknote paper by train to the Bank of England was

Overton signal box about 1960, very similar to Oakley seen on page 12. Portal's Mill behind employed a substantial workforce, many of whom commuted by train. Dennis Cullum.

made by the London & South Western Railway. Apparently Basingstoke station was used initially but when Overton station opened the traffic would have been transferred here. More details appear in the South Western Traffic Committee minute of 30th December 1869: *'Letter from Secretary to Bank of England requesting alterations to the van which conveys the Bank Notepaper between Messrs. Portals mills and London. As the van was built at the cost of this company precisely as then required by the Bank of England and Messrs Portal, any alterations now desired can only be made by those parties or at their cost.'*

On 13th October 1897 the Locomotive and Stores Committee minute reads: '*Approved provision by the company of a new road van for Messrs Portal of Laverstoke Mill, Whitchurch, for the conveyance of their paper by rail, the cost of which is estimated at £80. To be constructed.'* Another minute of 4th March 1908 of the same committee read *'approved an additional road van being provided for conveyance of paper for the Laverstoke Mills, Whitchurch at cost £80'.* In 1908 a 21ft open carriage truck No.6308 was marked for use between Overton and Waterloo for banknote paper train.

It would appear that up to 1922, when Overton Mill opened, Portal's loaded the banknote paper into a specially constructed road van at Laverstoke Mill. After 1908 more than one van was available. It was drawn by horses to Overton station where, using the end loading dock in the goods yard, it was placed in a carriage truck for conveyance by train to Waterloo station. Here it was run off the truck and horses attached again

for conveyance to the Bank of England itself. This continued until 1916 when the printing plant was relocated nearby at the former St Lukes hospital in Old Street. No doubt appropriate security arrangements were made throughout the journey. In 1909 there was a 8.20am 'banknote paper train when required' from Overton to Basingstoke. From 1922 the loading was carried out within Overton Mill using Portal's private siding, the paper then being carried in box vans.

In response to the Munich crisis of 1938, the Bank of England constructed a 'shadow factory' on a site adjoining Overton Mill and station. On the outbreak of war the following year large numbers of Bank staff arrived at Overton and the 'shadow factory' commenced production. This continued throughout the war, although printing at St Lukes was also maintained. Chalets were built, many in the grounds of Hurstbourne Park, for 450 Bank workers who lived in Hampshire during the week and returned home for the weekend. The Bank built a social club for its displaced employees in Winchester Road Overton; after the war, when the workers returned to London, it was presented to the town where it remains in use as St Lukes Hall. In July 1940 Overton Mill had a narrow escape when bombs fell wide and failed to explode, one finishing up eight feet below the ballast on the main line. The factory was not so lucky in March 1941 when two bombs hit the building and exploded causing five casualties and killing two people in adjacent cottages. There was considerable damage and production was interrupted for three days.

By 1939 the number of 'cylinder mould papermaking' machines had risen to four, in

1949 to six, and in 1954 to seven, when Portal's were making banknote paper for no less than 66 different currency issues for delivery to 101 governments and banks all over the world. Overton Mill was now the largest of its type in the world. In 1956 the Bank of England moved its printing works from St Lukes to Debden in Essex so deliveries were transferred there. An aerial photograph taken about 1960 shows about a dozen open wagons in the siding. By the winter of 1966 there was a 3.25pm freight from Basingstoke to Overton, where it arrived at 3.50pm, shunted the sidings, and returned to Basingstoke at 5.20pm. Following conversion of the mill to electric power the coal traffic ceased and Portal's Siding was taken out of use and lifted about 1970. During the 1990s the Portal company became part of De la Rue, who at the time of writing operate the business.

Much of the information about Portal's Mill has been obtained from the book 'Portal's' by Sir Francis Portal.

Traffic and Train Services

Although not particularly convenient for the town centre, about 15 minutes walk away, there was a modest passenger traffic, into Basingstoke for work, shopping and school and Andover too, as well as some travel to London and elsewhere. Some employees of Portal's mill travelled to work here by train from other stations. Up to twenty used the first Up train which arrived at 7.34am in 1964 and more came on the first Down train at 7.46am. The earliest Waterloo arrival in 1947 was 9.20am and in 1964 it was 8.59am requiring a change at Basingstoke, which hardly encouraged daily commuting to

Overton station looking west about 1960. The runway crane erected in 1922 can be seen in the goods yard, and opposite are the points for the Up sidings leading to Portal's Siding. Dennis Cullum.

The station approach and exterior of Overton station in 1963. Portal's Mill can be seen behind. Not only the paper but banknotes themselves were produced here by the Bank of England as a wartime expedient. R.M.Casserley.

London. One senior Bank of England man, whose work had brought him here during the 1939-45 war, moved house to St Mary Bourne and commuted daily to London.

During the 1939-45 war extra passenger services ran to and from Overton for Portal's and Bank of England staff. In 1944 these comprised a 6.20am from Andover Town, reversing at Andover Junction to arrive at Overton at 6.55am, a 6.40am from Basingstoke arriving at 6.56am and a 4.54pm from Overton to Andover Junction. It would appear that the return journey from Overton to Basingstoke was by scheduled train.

Other traffic handled by passenger rated trains included churns of milk and horses, parcels and mails. There were several scheduled calls by milk and horse box trains. Boxes of watercress were forwarded from local growers, much of it on the 5.4pm Down train in a van destined for the Midlands via Templecombe and the Somerset & Dorset line.

Traffic at Overton goods yard was in general what might be expected for a small country town – coal, minerals for road building, bricks, tiles and timber for house building, seed, hay and other animal feedstuffs and fertilisers. The Overton coal merchant in later years was Wakefield & Sons who also had premises at Whitchurch. Traffic forwarded included grain and livestock, particularly after Overton Fair.

Goods trains calling at Overton were similar to those already described at Oakley, except for those with Portal's traffic only which ran into the Up Sidings. The locomotive would first enter Portals siding to bring out empty wagons. It then shunted ingoing wagons as far as the top of the slope

and from there onwards Portal's staff moved the wagons. The locomotive then ran round the wagons in the Up sidings and departed with its train when the road was clear.

Overton Fair attracted dealers from a wide area; some sheep came to Whitchurch GWR station and were herded about three miles along the road to the fair which was held in the town centre. For Overton Sheep Fair on 18th July 1914 a shunting engine and 100 cattle wagons were provided, which made up several sheep specials to Nine Elms.

On Boxing Day 1927 there was heavy snow and the 12.43pm train from Salisbury to Waterloo became stuck in a snowbound cutting towards Oakley. The 50 stranded passengers returned to Overton station where they were somehow accommodated until they could leave, the train departing for Waterloo at 3.5pm next day.

Signalling

The signal box, 3 miles 325 yards from Oakley box, was on the Up platform and had a closing switch. There were two crossovers, 270 yards on the Oakley side and 90 yards on the Whitchurch side. (SR 1934)

An 18 lever Stevens' frame, with no spare levers, and Preece 3 wire block instruments controlled the block sections to Oakley and Whitchurch. There were distant, home, starting and advance starting signals for both Up and Down trains. No less than three of these were mounted on tall posts with co-acting arms and one on a bracket – all to improve sighting for drivers. This was particularly important here because many trains ran through at speed. In 1914 Overton signal box was open between 7.0am and 10.35pm on weekdays, and on Sundays

between 8.30am and 1.0pm and 6.0pm and 8.5pm (or after the 7.35pm train from Basingstoke had cleared the section). The closing switch facilitated closure of the signal box when traffic was light, the section becoming Oakley to Whitchurch.

Staff

For many years the staff at Overton comprised the Stationmaster, two signalmen working alternate early and late turns, two porters also on early and late turns working on both the passenger and goods stations, and a team of platelayers under a ganger with their own length of track.

In 1862 the Overton Station Agent was Mr Chapman. In 1889-1895 the Overton Stationmaster was Mr Henry G.Watts, in 1915 Mr Luke Partridge, in 1923-1932 Mr Arthur Phillips, in 1934-1937 Mr J.L.Poate, in 1939 Mr W.H.J.Miles and 1948 Mr G.W.Mills. As we have seen from the mid-1920s the post of Stationmaster at Oakley was withdrawn and thereafter it was supervised by the Overton Stationmaster, who visited there once a week.

Overton Today

Although still in a remote rural location, more than a mile down a country lane from the town centre, the station today continues to serve Overton and district but in a different way than in the past. Almost all the features previously described have disappeared, although there is a crossover operated from a four lever ground frame behind the new platform, normally only used when single line working for engineering purposes is required on a Sunday. Where there used to be sidings to the west of the original station, both platforms have been more than doubled in length and raised to accommodate modern nine coach class 159 trains. Tickets are sold from a plastic orange pod on the Down platform during the weekday morning shift and a new footbridge has replaced the old No.155A. There is also a secure bicycle storage and glazed waiting shelters. Modern electric lighting mounted, on distinctive tall blue posts illuminates the whole station at night. Industrial units have been built on the old goods yard on the Down side.

Dominating the area Portal's paper mill remains, but with no railway connection. There are now three times the number of passenger trains than in steam days, all arriving at Waterloo in about an hour. Four get there before nine o'clock making Overton a very attractive town for London commuting.

Up Passenger Trains departing Overton station						
1857	1867	1909	1947	1964	1984	2002
4	5 + 1 request	9	7	8	14	21

Passenger Trains Overton Weekdays Summer 1958		
Train	*Overton dep.*	*To*
6.45am Salisbury	7.43am	Waterloo
6.33am Woking	7.52	Templecombe
7.49 Salisbury	8.31	Waterloo
7.20 Waterloo	9.5	Salisbury
8.46 Salisbury	9.40	Waterloo
10.45 Basingstoke	11.0	Salisbury
9.3 Templecombe	11.0	Waterloo
10.54 Waterloo	12.32pm	Salisbury
11.54 Waterloo	1.30	Salisbury
12.58pm Salisbury	1.54	Waterloo
2.48pm Basingstoke	3.3	Salisbury
4.5 Salisbury	5.5	Waterloo
4.48 Basingstoke	5.5	Yeovil Town
5.15 Salisbury	6.13	Waterloo
5.0 Waterloo	6.17	Yeovil Junction
5.39 Waterloo	7.21	Salisbury
6.54 Waterloo	8.48	Yeovil Town
8.44 Salisbury	9.36	Woking
8.54 Waterloo	10.46	Salisbury

From Overton to Whitchurch

Leaving Overton station the line continued almost straight, a little to the south-west on the north side of the Test valley, falling gradually at 1 in 550. Towards the end of the cutting at Overton the line passed under the B3051, Kingsclere Road bridge No.156, and the Down advanced starting signal. The line emerged on to an embankment where there were good views to the south over the valley and town. The line crossed culvert bridge No.156A, and passed the Overton Up distant signal and milepost 56. At Foxdown bridge No.157, provided for a minor road, marked the beginning of a long cutting where the line curved to the south on a radius of 400 chains. At Lynch another track crossed the line on bridge No.158 towards the end of the cutting. Here the line emerged again on to an embankment with two accommodation under bridges, Nos.158A and 159. There were views to the south towards Laverstoke House, residence of members of the Portal family, the Portal's Laverstoke Mill and the village.

Next came milepost 57 and another long cutting where there was a half mile stretch of level track with three over bridges towards the end. No.160 was a track to Home Farm and Nos.161 and 162 carried minor roads towards Freefolk where the descent continued at 1 in 345. Freefolk House was another residence of the Portal family. There was a brief section on level ground where the line curved to the north on a 130 chain curve before another cutting, spanned by bridge No.163 for a footpath near Priory Farm, and milepost 58. Emerging from this cutting, first at ground level and then on an embankment, there were views of the outskirts of Whitchurch to the south. The downhill gradient then eased to 1 in 550. On the embankment the line crossed occupation bridges Nos.165 and 166 near Berehill Farm, passed the Whitchurch Down distant signal, and curved to the north at 60 then 130 chains radius. The town now disappeared from sight as the line entered a cutting, passing first the Whitchurch advanced starting signal, then the Down home signal. At milepost 59 the line ran under the main Newbury to Winchester A34 road on bridge No.167. Constructed with a long arch in an arc from one side of the cutting to the other the line entered Whitchurch (North) station.

WHITCHURCH

Chronology
Station and single track line opened 3rd July 1854.
Double track from Oakley opened 1st June 1866.

Freight Trains Overton Weekdays Summer 1958			
Train	*Overton arr.*	*Overton dep.*	*To*
7.45am Basingstoke West Yard	8.34am	9.20am	Andover Junction
10.45am Salisbury East Yard	2.7pm	2.17pm	Basingstoke Up Yard
1.8pm light engine Andover Junct.	1.28pm		Stops
4.3pm Overton		4.3	Basingstoke Up Yard

Overton station in the 1960s; the buildings were demolished a few years later.

U class 2-6-0 No.31799 passes Overton on Saturday 26th July 1958 on a west country holiday train, with Portal's Mill behind. R.K.Blencowe Collection.

Double track to Andover opened 2nd December 1867.
Signal box (59 miles 19 chains from Waterloo) opened pre-1872.
Hurstbourne Loop platform opened June 1885.
First footbridge installed 1897.
Second footbridge installed 1923.
Renamed 'Whitchurch North' 26th September 1949 until 2nd October 1972.
Goods closed 7th June 1965.
Signal box closed 5th February 1967
Station modernised with extended platforms 1993.

The following extracts from the South Western Traffic Committee Minutes 1857-1909 deal with Whitchurch:
16th July 1857. Mr Horridge wants to raise a subscription to light Whitchurch Station Road. Mr Jackson to establish the cost of lighting the road by gas.
22nd September 1857. Facing points left open, leading to a siding. The Locomotive Committee reported that the engine on the 4.20pm down train hit a wagon and knocked off two buffers. The points-man was dismissed.
8th April 1858. Gas to be supplied to the station.
28th November 1861. Mr Temple and others want the station re-sited. The General Manager Mr Scott to report back.
12th December 1861. The re-siting proposal was found to be too expensive.
21st August 1862. The Board propose to re-site the station. Mr Castleman and Mr Portal to visit the new site.
4th September 1862. A petition of 61 persons opposes the re-siting proposal.
2nd April 1863. Extension of platforms discussed.
2nd August 1866. Proposal for a through crossing to the east of the station referred to Ways and Works Committee.

26th August 1869. Agreed provision of stable for horse to be kept there to shunt wagons and deliver goods and parcels.
25th April 1883. Mr Verinder asks for additional stables for horses, costing £45, to Engineering Committee.
19th March 1885. Improvements at the station in connection with the new Hurstbourne to Fullerton line approved – to Board and Engineering Committee.
2nd September 1885. Alteration to waiting shed on the up platform by closing the opening on one side and putting doors on the other opening, costing £10, to be done.
3rd August 1898. Additional sidings costing £859 approved.
1st February 1899. Cost of additional sidings now £1177 as no land to be taken from the Didcot Newbury & Southampton company.
7th October 1903. 30 sheep killed by a train on 19th September.
18th February 1909. New road to connect with the South Western approach road. Mr Spencer Portal to pay.

Whitchurch 1854-1922

When the station opened in 1854 Messrs. Wolfe set up premises for the sale of coal, artificial manure, oil cake and salt and shortly after, in 1856, the Whitchurch & District (Hants) gas company established its gasworks. *Kelly's Directory* of 1889 described Whitchurch as consisting of five streets all diverging from the Market Place. The population in 1881 totalled some 1,866 souls. The principal landowners included Earl Portsmouth, at Hurstbourne Park, and Mr Melville Portal of Laverstoke House. The main crops were wheat, barley, oats and turnips; the South Western Stationmaster was Mr Robert Murray. Local businesses which would have used the railway included:

Carrier - Henry Parker of Bell Street who travelled weekly to Andover, Basingstoke, Newbury and Winchester
Corn and coal merchant - John Butcher
Corn dealer - George Taplin
Baker and coal merchant - Joseph Webb
Watercress dealer - John Faulkner
Gas Works - in Bell Street, manager William Sackett
Silk manufacturer - James Hide of the Victoria Mill (water),
Millers - Henry Lloyd of Town Mills (water), Earle Wedge of Bere Mills (water),
Railway Hotel - Joseph Hodges
Whiting Works - manager John Leader
In later years there were also the Jam factory of J. Long and Goddards soap factory.

Whitchurch in the 1950s

The town lay at the intersection of the old turnpike road from Basingstoke to Andover (now the B3400) down the Test valley and the old Winchester to Newbury road (the A34, which in recent years has been replaced with a new dual carriageway road to the west). The South Western built its line about half a mile to the north of the town; the station was approached from Newbury Street and was located between the Newbury Road bridge No.167 and bridge No.168 which carried our line over the Great Western's Didcot Newbury & Southampton line.

An early 40ft to the inch plan, apparently the 1854 original plan updated to about 1867, shows the layout during doubling before the Up platform was built. An interesting feature is that the Down Siding West would have run into a goods shed, which might well have been to a similar wooden design as that at Andover. There is no other evidence of its existence so this goods shed, though obviously planned, seems not to have been constructed. An imposing brick goods shed *was* built, in 1864, by Thomas Budden for £648 10s, and was served by a spur from a wagon turntable. There were two wagon turntables serving spurs in the Down Siding West and one in the Down Siding East. The 1872 Ordnance Survey shows the double track main line through the station with the three short spur sidings radiating from wagon turntables on the Down Siding West. One ran into the new brick goods shed and there was a short spur from a turntable in the Up Siding East. It would appear that horses were then used to shunt wagons on these spur lines. The station house, Up side waiting shelter, signal box are all shown, and the Railway Hotel clearly identified.

Between the two trailing crossovers connecting the main lines were the two platforms, slightly offset from each other, and Down Sidings East and West. The two Up Sidings were reached by a trailing connection to the Up Loop, the Up platform having two faces. *By the 1950s the Up Loop had been reduced to a siding, then designated the Up refuge siding which could hold a locomotive and 70 wagons (BR 1960)*

The goods yard comprised the Down Siding East which incorporated a side and end loading dock and cattle pens. The Down Siding West incorporated two wagon turntables giving access to three sidings, one of which ran into the goods shed. In the goods yard were a wagon turntable and a highway vehicle dock. (SR 1934)

The South Western at first considered Whitchurch important enough for one of its most impressive station houses of the period, designed by William Tite and constructed by William Gue. It is a large and imposing two storey building similar to that at Andover, though a bit smaller. Opposite, at the entrance to the station approach, was the Railway Hotel. On entering, there was the conventional booking hall with waiting/ladies waiting rooms. There were more offices for staff and parcels and outside were toilets. An awning with a flat roof covered the platform for the length of the station building. To the east of the platform was the signal box and an adjacent lamp room.

Originally passengers crossed the line by the foot crossing but as traffic increased, after the opening of the Fullerton line in 1885, the South Western, in 1887, installed a wooden lattice footbridge, No.167A, at a cost of £200. This was later replaced with a steel girder version. On the Up platform was another substantial awning, this one with a curved roof, and also a small wooden waiting room. The awnings provided for the stations at Wherwell and Longparish were to a similar design and they all appear to date from 1885. For many years the station, and some signals, were illuminated by gas from the town gasworks but these were later replaced by electricity and oil lamps for the signals.

There were further changes for the opening of the Hurstbourne to Fullerton line in the mid-1880s. The Up platform was converted to an island and the Hurstbourne Loop signalled for use by Down branch trains but not Up, which had to use the main Up platform. The name Hurstbourne Loop appears in official South Western documents, although Fullerton Loop (see below)might have been a more logical description. To date no photographs of branch trains in the Hurstbourne Loop platform have come to light, so it appears to have been a bit of a white elephant.

The Didcot Newbury & Southampton Railway opened to Winchester in 1885 and passed under the South Western main line at bridge No.168. The Didcot company built its station, known in BR days as Whitchurch (South), convenient to the town centre but a mile from the South Western station making for difficult interchange of passengers or goods. The Fullerton branch, which ran from a bay platform here and connected with the Andover and Redbridge branch, was more or less constructed 'defensively' to prevent the DN&SR gaining access to Southampton via a loop from their line down to the South Western. More on this in Chapter 5.

Traffic and Train Services

Whitchurch, like most country towns and villages, was fairly self-contained and the townsfolk had little inclination or indeed the wherewithal, to travel. Passenger traffic therefore was modest – mainly season tickets to Basingstoke and Andover and shoppers, particularly on Wednesdays, for market day in Basingstoke. Until its closure in 1960 there was competition from the Great Western line, with its more convenient station, for similar travel to Newbury, the county town, Winchester or the largest shopping centre, at Southampton. There was some longer distance travel to Salisbury or London, although the earliest Waterloo arrival in 1964 was 8.59am after a change at

A complete view of Whitchurch North station from the Newbury Road bridge on 5th May 1965, with West Country class 4-6-2 No.34007 *Wadebridge* leaving with an up morning stopping train from Salisbury, then the westward limit of scheduled steam working. Peter Groom.

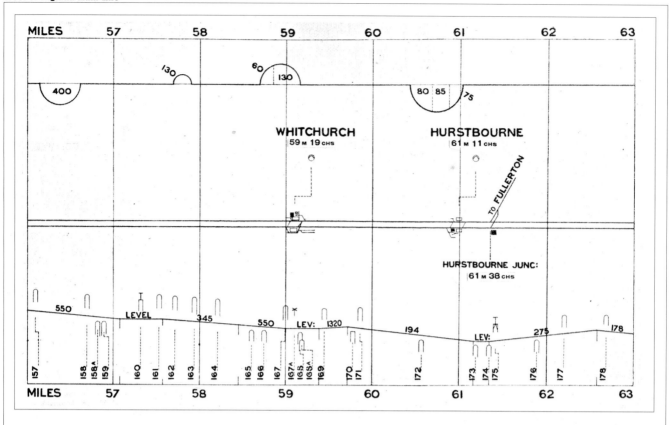

Basingstoke. In 1964 Chris Kerby paid £3 9s (£3.45) for his third class weekly season ticket No.97 between Whitchurch North and Waterloo. Some travelled daily by train from Whitchurch to work at Portal's Mill at Overton. The Fullerton branch service brought in a few passengers from the villages along the Test, some for the town, others for onward connections and in 1914-18 some passengers travelled from Whitchurch to Longparish to work in the Kynoch factory.

A well-known Whitchurch resident was Tom Denning. Born in 1899, Alfred Thompson Denning was the son of a draper who lived over the shop in Newbury Street, in 1889 listed as 'Godwin and Denning, Drapers'. Between 1909 and 1916 he commuted by train to Andover Grammar School, then studied law, and eventually reached one of the highest legal positions in the land, Master of the Rolls, as Lord Denning. He retained his Hampshire accent, and in 1960 returned to live at The Lawn, in Church Street, Whitchurch where he died just after his 100th birthday. He travelled by train regularly to the High Court in London as well as to Birkbeck College, University of London, where he held the position of President for many years. He was a well-known and respected resident and station staff and regular travellers knew him well.

There was of course a wide variety of small consignments received and forwarded by shops, households and businesses in the town. Occasionally a hamper, from one of the well known department stores in London, would arrive for one of the large country houses in the area. Traffic forwarded included watercress from the local growers for London and other markets. In the 1950s and 1960s a van for the Midlands, via Templecombe and the Somerset & Dorset line, was included in the 5.11pm Down

Proposed Loops at Whitchurch

passenger train and much of the watercress was sent by this service. Farmers forwarded so many churns that in 1888 the morning milk train to London was allowed 6 minutes for loading, the milk churn traffic continuing until bulk tankers from Devon and Somerset creameries took most of the business. There was also a moderate amount of horsebox traffic.

By 1909 there was also a 6.15am goods from Salisbury to Whitchurch, arriving at 9.29am, with the locomotive returning light to Salisbury at 10.10am.

There was also an unadvertised Mondays Only 12.20am from Waterloo to Salisbury which called at Whitchurch at 1.40am.

When two competing railway companies served a town it usually transpired that the first to arrive would have a well-established goods yard where many of the local traders already had premises, making it difficult for the newcomer. However, the Great Western on arrival at Whitchurch, could bring coal direct from the collieries in South Wales. The South Western of course had no direct access to coal mines which greatly disadvantaged it against the *arriviste* GW. As a result, after 1882, much of Whitchurch's coal went to the Great Western station where a number of merchants established themselves.

So traffic received at Whitchurch LSW amounted to general merchandise, a little coal, minerals for road building, bricks, tiles and timber for house building, fertilisers, seed, animal feedstuffs, supplies for the soap factory at the Andover end of the station, and some livestock. Traffic forwarded included general merchandise, wheat and barley in season, livestock (with a cattle special to Basingstoke market on Wednesdays recorded both in 1888 and 1909), jam from J. Long's factory, watercress, lettuce and cucumbers. None of it was outstandingly profitable. There was the inevitable competition with the Great Western on rates for London but the Southern route had the edge, getting to market early the following morning.

Fullerton Branch Services

Branch trains ran from Whitchurch to Hurstbourne on the main line, then to Longparish and Wherwell on the double track branch to Fullerton Junction on the Andover to Southampton line. It was a beautiful line serving the exquisite Test

WHITCHURCH TRACK DIAGRAM c1900

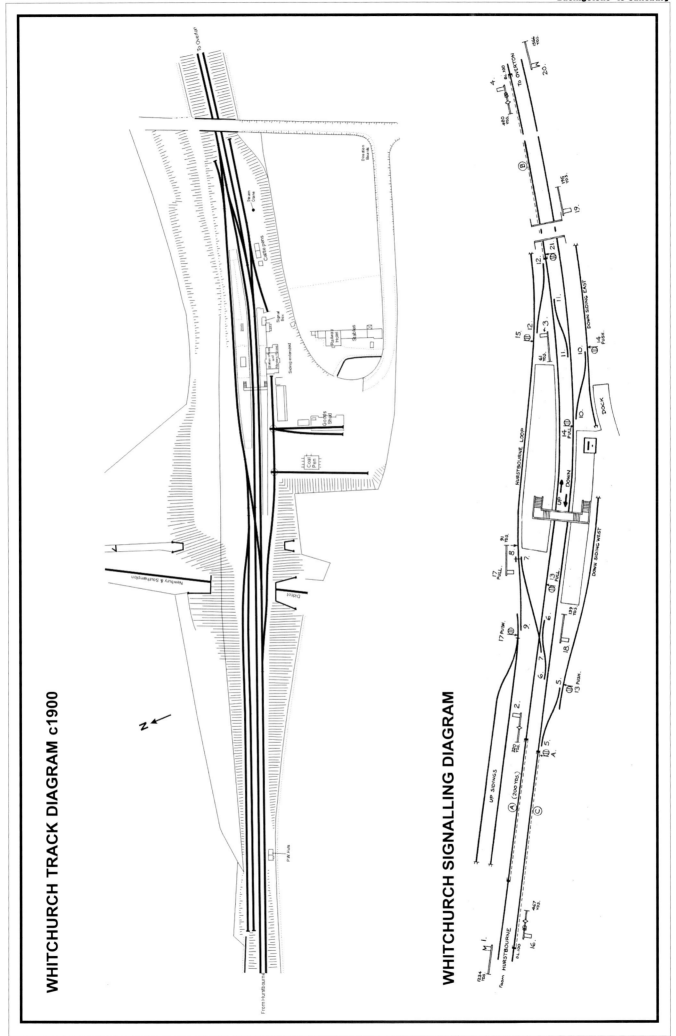

WHITCHURCH SIGNALLING DIAGRAM

The exterior of Whitchurch North station in 1962 showing the elegant building designed by William Tite. The only intermediate station on the line when it opened in 1854, it was similar to but smaller than Andover. H.C.Casserley

valley where, unfortunately, very few people resided. The 1888 timetable shows the branch service just three years after opening. There were five trains each way, one Up starting from Stockbridge and one running to and from Basingstoke. From footnotes to the timetable it appears that the locomotive was based at Andover shed with the coaching stock berthed at Fullerton.

By 1909 the passenger services were operated by railmotors, together with one goods train departing Basingstoke at

9.52am, returning from Fullerton at 3.10pm. By 1913 the service was down to four passenger trains each way, the best London train being the 2.10pm from Waterloo which connected at Whitchurch with a branch train arriving at Fullerton at 4.15pm.

During the 1914-18 war the firm of Kynock Ltd commissioned a wood distillation factory adjacent to a sawmill at Longparish station. More than 100 people were employed here, many of them resident

in Whitchurch, and a special train ran between the two stations for them.

By 1922 there were just three weekday branch passenger services, the first Up train leaving Southampton Town at 6.25am and running via Redbridge, Romsey and departing Fullerton at 7.29am to arrive at Whitchurch at 7.57am, making a connection to arrive at Waterloo at 10.1am. The best Down service was off the 5.0pm from Waterloo, connecting with the 6.46pm from Whitchurch giving a Fullerton arrival at

On 23rd March 1963 BR standard class 4-6-0 No.73002 crosses culvert No.168A to the west of the station to pass Whitchurch North with the 3.15pm Salisbury to Waterloo semi-fast train. S.C.Nash

On 7th April 1938 the Down *Atlantic Coast Express* headed by double chimney Lord Nelson class 4-6-0 No.865 *Sir John Hawkins* carrying Nine Elms duty disc No.7 emerges under the Newbury Road bridge (No.167) to pass through Whitchurch station at speed.

7.9pm, and terminating at Stockbridge. By 1924 this service, leaving Whitchurch at 6.50pm, had become a through train to Southampton Terminus. In 1913 the line was reduced to single track; passenger services were withdrawn in 1931 and the section from Hurstbourne Junction to Longparish closed completely in 1934. The goods service for Wherwell and Longparish was afterwards run from the Fullerton end.

During the 1914-18 war a number of trains, conveying both troops and munitions, ran along the line to and from Southampton Docks. Apart from these no evidence has yet come to light of any scheduled trains running between Basingstoke and Southampton via Whitchurch, the purpose for which the line was allegedly built. It seems more likely therefore that it would have been used only for diversions due to engineering work.

The layout at Whitchurch dictated that Fullerton branch trains had to use the Up main platform. Photographs show that the branch train was then berthed in the Down Siding East before departure from the Down platform; this was more convenient for passengers either from the town or alighting from Down main line trains. In South Western days the trains were formed by a couple of coaches hauled by a tank engine, replaced in the mid 1900s by a railmotor.

Surprisingly there is no evidence of a water supply for branch line locomotives at Whitchurch, which may explain its mid-day trip to Basingstoke. In Southern days the train usually consisted of a single carriage hauled by a tender locomotive, which had a greater water capacity.

Signalling

The signal box, 3 miles 993 yards from Overton box, was on the Down platform; it was not fitted with a closing switch so was open continuously. There were two crossovers, 71 yards on the Overton side and 160 yards on the Hurstbourne side. (SR 1934).

There was a Stevens frame with 20 levers, increased to 21 in 1898, with Preece 3 wire block instruments controlling the block sections to Overton and Hurstbourne, although BR Southern 3 position block instruments were installed in 1955 to Hurstbourne. The block sections were to Overton, or when it was switched out to Oakley, and to Hurstbourne, or when it was switched out to Andover Junction (East). There were distant, home, starting and advance starting signals in both directions and also a Down starting signal from the Hurstbourne loop platform from 1885, until it was converted to a siding in 1939.

Staff

A South Western period photograph shows the station master, a signalman and two porters, while another shows no less than seven staff with the Fullerton branch train, together with the driver and fireman on the footplate. As an important station on the line, Whitchurch had a Stationmaster living in the large station house in charge of a full staff. After Hurstbourne lost its Stationmaster in the mid-1920s it was supervised by the Whitchurch man who visited once a week to check the books and sign the train register in the signal box. There were two or three porters on early and late turns who were employed in the passenger station booking office selling tickets, dealing with the considerable telegraph and parcels traffic, loading parcels, milk churns, boxes of watercress and so on into the vans of passenger trains, and despatching trains. Porters were also employed in the goods shed and yard, shunting wagons with horses, loading and unloading all sorts of merchandise, making out wagon consignment notes, and invoicing customers. A collection and delivery service to and from the town and surrounding countryside was operated from the goods shed, first by horse-drawn wagon and later by lorry. The signal box was open continuously so required three signalmen, augmented by rest day relief men as required.

In 1871 the station agent, or Stationmaster, at Whitchurch was Mr Burn; his salary increased from £90 to £100 when he became responsible for the new siding at Hurstbourne but subsequently Hurstbourne had its own Stationmaster. In 1895 the Whitchurch Stationmaster was Mr Samuel A. Ockford, in 1915 Mr Alfred W. Eyres, in 1923-1927 Mr William H. Butler, in 1930-1934 Mr C. T. Waldren, in 1936-1937 Mr S. S. Towler, in 1939 Mr A. F. Wiles , in 1948 Mr A. G. Vince, and in the late 1950s Mr Gerald Sampson who later transferred to Gillingham in Dorset.

In the 1930s Mr Jim Chard was a porter at Whitchurch and after serving in the Navy during the war, returned as signalman. He also ran the local retained fire brigade and his brother Peter kept the Railway Hotel. Another signalman, in the 1960s, was Mr George Carter, who later worked in the booking office and also played in the

Up Passenger trains departing Whitchurch station (weekdays)

1857	1867	1909	1947	1964	1984	2002
4	6	9	8	8	14	21

Trains calling at Whitchurch March & April 1888

Time	Train	Origin	Destination
12.5am when required	6.0pm Goods	Exeter	Nine Elms
6.47 – 6.52am	6.20am Goods	Basingstoke	Salisbury
7.2	6.45 Pass & Goods	Salisbury	Waterloo
8.5 Weds Only	7.45 Engine + Van	Basingstoke	Whitchurch
8.22	8.22 Pass	Stockbridge	Whitchurch
8.27 Weds Only	8.27 Cattle	Whitchurch	Basingstoke
8.39	6.0 Passenger	Yeovil	Waterloo
8.45	6.25 Passenger	Waterloo	Exeter
8.52	8.52 Pass & Goods	Whitchurch	Fullerton
8.52 – 8.58	8.40 Milk Churns	Andover Jcn	Waterloo
10.35	9.0 Passenger	Waterloo	Exeter
11.10	10.45 Passenger	Fullerton	Whitchurch
11.15	11.15 Pass	Whitchurch	Fullerton
11.31	6.55 Passenger	Exeter	Waterloo
12.9 –12.10pm	11.45 Passenger	Fullerton	Basingstoke
1.9 – 1.10	12.45pm Pass	Basingstoke	Fullerton
1.53	11.45am Pass	Waterloo	Exeter
2.14	1.50 Passenger	Fullerton	Whitchurch
2.17	12.5pm Churns	Waterloo	Templecombe
2.34 – 2.36	10.15am Passenger	Exeter	Waterloo
2.40	2.40pm Pass	Whitchurch	Fullerton
4.36	1.5 Passenger	Exeter	Waterloo
5.12	4.20 Pass & Gds	Fullerton	Whitchurch
5.23 – 5.26	3.24 Churns	Waterloo	Salisbury
5.43	3.50 Passenger	Waterloo	Templecombe
5.55	5.55 Pass	Whitchurch	Fullerton
6.5	2.15 Passenger	Exeter	Waterloo
7.0 – 7.34	4.5 Goods	Salisbury	Basingstoke
7.43	5.50 Passenger	Waterloo	Salisbury
9.34	4.30 Passenger	Exeter	Waterloo
11.30 – 11.40	10.45 Goods	Basingstoke	Salisbury

Passenger Trains Whitchurch North Weekdays Summer 1958

Train	Whitchurch Nth dep.	To
6.45am Salisbury	7.35	Waterloo
6.33 Woking	7.58	Templecombe
7.49 Salisbury	8.25	Waterloo
7.20 Waterloo	9.13	Salisbury
8.46 Salisbury	9.34	Waterloo
9.3 Templecombe	10.52	Waterloo
10.45 Basingstoke	11.7	Salisbury
10.54 Waterloo	12.38pm	Salisbury
12.58pm Salisbury	1.48	Waterloo
2.48 Basingstoke	3.9	Salisbury
4.5 Salisbury	4.58	Waterloo
4.48 Basingstoke	5.11	Yeovil Town
5.15 Salisbury	6.6	Waterloo
5.0 Waterloo	6.24	Yeovil Junction
5.39 Waterloo	7.28	Salisbury
6.54 Waterloo	8.54	Yeovil Town
8.44 Salisbury	9.30	Woking
8.54 Waterloo	10.52	Salisbury

Freight Trains Whitchurch North Weekdays Summer 1958

Train	Whitchurch arr.	Whitchurch dep.	To
7.45am Basingstoke West Yard	9.30am	10.0am	Andover Junction

Whitchurch Town Band. Later in the 1960s a Mr Vaicaitis worked in the booking office; he was the last railwayman to live in the station house.

Whitchurch Today

Many features of the original passenger station were retained when the line was modernised. The main station house was restored to its former glory and the booking office is open every weekday morning, with access to the raised platform up a ramp. The wooden Up side buildings were also restored and on a recent visit there was a vase of newly cut flowers on the table in the waiting room. The platforms have been

raised and at the western end extended with concrete components to accommodate nine coach trains of class 159 units. Standard tall blue lamp posts provide excellent lighting for the station and outside the station house a splendid tall traditional lamp has been installed. The Railway Hotel remains on the station approach but opposite there are houses where the goods yard used to be. The car park is small by modern standards but for commuters there are now many houses within walking distance.

In its new role Whitchurch station has increased in importance. The 21 daily Up trains now provide a splendid service, particularly to London, the first Up train at 5.55am arriving at Waterloo at 6.57am, with four trains giving Waterloo arrivals before 9am. Consequently there is now considerable commuter traffic to London.

From Whitchurch to Hurstbourne

Leaving Whitchurch the line continued level and straight, almost due west, leaving the River Test which had turned to the south west. Now on an embankment, it crossed the Great Western line over bridge No.168. The line crossed a 'cattle creep' on No.168A and passed the Whitchurch Down advanced starting signal. Running into a cutting the gradient changed to an almost imperceptible 1 in 1320 upwards and passed under a footpath on bridge No.169. By the 1990s another bridge, No.169A, a wide concrete structure, carried the new A34 dual carriageway over the line. The line now emerged on to an embankment where it crossed a minor road on bridge No.170. It passed the Whitchurch Up distant signal and then, at the start of a long cutting, passed under a footpath on bridge No.171.

raised and at the western end extended with concrete components to accommodate nine coach trains of class 159 units. Here a long section of 1 in 194 decent began and passed the Hurstbourne Down distant signal. Emerging from the cutting the line passed over a minor road at New Barn Farm (bridge No.172) to swing gently to the south on a curve first of 80, then 85, then 75 chains radius, past the Hurstbourne Up advanced starting signal to Hurstbourne station.

HURSTBOURNE

Chronology

Up siding opened 1st August 1871.

Station and signal box (61 miles 2 chains from Waterloo) opened 1st December 1882.

Goods closed circa 1963.

Station closed 6th April 1964.

Signal box closed 15th June 1964.

The following relating to Hurstbourne have been gleaned from the South Western Traffic Committee Minutes:

29th July 1869. Mr George Lamb on behalf of Earl Portsmouth requested a goods siding near Newbarn Farm, west of Whitchurch. Request declined.

5th May 1870. The South Western approves the proposed arrangements for the siding.

13th July 1871. The siding to be under the charge of Mr Burn, agent at Whitchurch, with his salary increased from £90 to £100.

30th November 1876. Mr Jacomb to produce plans and an estimate for a station requested in a memorial to the South Western.

11th January 1877. The cost will be £1400. Mr Scott to tell the parties concerned.

15th May 1878. Received request for increased siding accommodation, costing £200.

30th May 1878. Board approves increased sidings.

30th April 1879. Mr Scott asked to find out on what terms Mr Beach M.P. will sell the siding to the South Western.

4th August 1879. Mr Backhouse of Whitchurch has asked for a goods shed at Hurstbourne – a further report is to be made. The Directors have raised the question of a passenger station – a plan is to be submitted and Mr Scott is to report back.

21st August 1879. Mr Scott is to negotiate with Lord Portsmouth about the South Western "absorbing" the siding.

17th October 1880. Proposals for a signal cabin at Hurstbourne siding to shorten the signalling block section between Whitchurch and Andover.

5th January 1881. The Engineering Committee produces a plan of the proposed signal cabin, to cost £365. Mr Scott recommends that negotiations are opened with Lord Portsmouth to acquire rights at the siding. Referred to the Board.

3rd November 1881. Mr Scott recommends the new station after an interview with Lord Portsmouth. The plans to be considered.

7th December 1881. Mr Scott will arrange the purchase of the siding from Earl Portsmouth. Mr Jacomb says the station will cost £2158.

5th January 1882. The Board agrees the new station at a cost of £2158.

23rd May 1883. The Engineering Committee reports that cost of a footpath on the up side of the line from the Hurstbourne road to the station will be £10.

5th July 1883. Local landowners request the South Western to build a line from Hurstbourne up the Bourne valley to Ibthorpe, Upton and Fosbury, but the Board declines.

15th April 1885. The Engineering Committee considers building four new cottages.

Whitchurch North station looking east after the removal of signal wires and point rodding in 1967 but before demolition of the signal box. Gas lamps are still in use. Peter Swift Collection.

Looking west through Whitchurch North station about 1960 showing the signal box, similar to Oakley and Overton, and the Up island platform with the outer face known as the 'Hurstbourne Loop' provided for Fullerton branch trains. The large wooden building behind the signal box was the Goddards soap factory, on a site previously occupied by a brick goods shed. Dennis Cullum

Whitchurch North in July 1963 with the Down pick-up goods shunting, probably the 7.15am Basingstoke West Yard to Andover Junction. The steel footbridge has replaced the wooden original, and on the right is the SCATS depot which received fertilizers and animal feedstuffs by train. H.C.Casserley.

22nd April 1891. Mr Taplin agrees to rent 12 acres of meadow near Hursbourne for the South Western's horses at £12 per acre per annum.

3rd October 1894. Following a Directors Inspection a road box store is to be built for £70.

3rd April 1895. The Engineering Committee agrees to a request from the Post Office for a wall letter box.

23rd June 1910. Local farmers request a cart weighbridge, but this is declined.

27th January 1914. The Traffic Officers Committee recommend a 15 ton cart

weighbridge for the very extensive agricultural traffic.

29th January 1914. Approval given for cart weighbridge costing £170.

Hurstbourne 1882-1964

To the south of the line here lay the extensive grounds of Hurstbourne Park with The Mansion at its centre, one of the country seats of the Earls of Portsmouth. Another of their estates was Eggesford House in North Devon, where the Fourth Earl had been a leading supporter of the North Devon

Railway opened in 1854. The Fifth Earl had been Chairman of the Devon & Cornwall Railway in the 1860s and had been ally to the South Western during its struggles west of Exeter. When the Sixth Earl asked the South Western to provide a siding to serve his new grain store on the valley of the Bourne Rivulet, the company was ready to oblige him and opened the siding in 1871. The station itself followed a decade later; the platforms and awnings were built entirely in wood but nevertheless lasted intact for 82 years and served the village of St Mary Bourne a mile up the valley.

The platforms were on a 75 chain curve on the top of an embankment which accounts for the wooden construction. There were covered steps up to each side but no subway or footbridge, the platforms being connected by sleeper crossings at each end. There were steps down the embankment to a field on the Down side. The approach led from the B3048 to the station building, on the Up side. This incorporated a booking hall and office and a covered stairway led to the Up platform. Adjacent was a shed and the Stationmaster's house. Opposite was a terrace of railway cottages, one occupant being Mr Ron Bundy, a 'travelling shunter'. In 1933 the Southern Railway had plans drawn up for a signal box on the Up platform under the awning but this did not materialise.

There were the usual two trailing crossovers connecting the main lines but the goods yard was built on level ground on the Up side at the Whitchurch end, with a Down refuge siding opposite. In the goods yard there were two sidings, one of which served

The Down *Atlantic Coast Express* hauled by Merchant Navy class 4-6-2 No.35030 *Elder Dempster Lines,* speeds through Whitchurch North in the early 1960s. T. Wright courtesy Peter Swift.

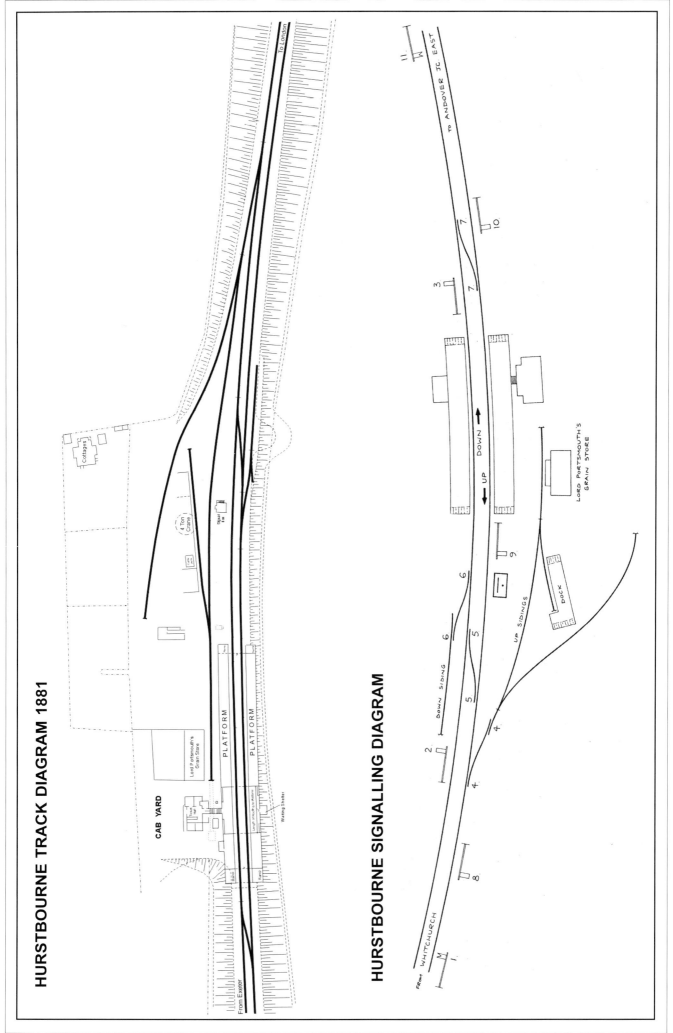

HURSTBOURNE TRACK DIAGRAM 1881

HURSTBOURNE SIGNALLING DIAGRAM

Hurstbourne station looking east in the 1950s. It opened in 1882 in response to requests from Earl Portsmouth at Hurstbourne Park. The platforms were constructed in wood, the line being partially on an embankment. Oil lamps are provided.

Earl Portsmouth's grain store, and an awkward connection from here led back into a side and end loading dock with cattle pens. *In the goods yard was a crane of 5 tons capacity, a 15 ton cart weighbridge and office, and a highway vehicle dock. (SR 1934).*

Traffic and Train Services

Hurstbourne station also served a couple of villages a mile or so away, St Mary Bourne up the valley and Hurstbourne Priors down the valley. Local passenger traffic was therefore limited, many villagers finding the road journey to Whitchurch or Andover more convenient. Some children went by train daily to Andover Grammar School, although buses took over in the 1930s. Only a limited number of main line trains called at Hurstbourne but the station did have a Fullerton branch service which made connections at Whitchurch. There were milk churns, a variety of parcels and boxes of

watercress from local growers; these went by van in the 1960s to the Midlands, via Templecombe and the Somerset & Dorset. As we have seen previously at Overton, during the 1939-45 war the Bank of England established a 'shadow factory' adjacent to Portal's Mill and to accommodate some of their 450 employees wooden chalets were built in the ground of Hurstbourne Park. Workmen's trains called at Hurstbourne, leaving Andover Town at 6.20am for Overton and returning from Overton at 4.54pm. This period probably saw the heaviest passenger traffic handled at Hurstbourne station.

In the goods yard some coal, minerals, fertilisers and animal feedstuffs were received. The main commodity forwarded was grain from Earl Portsmouth's grain store where it was held until a good market price was available. A by-product of the grain was of course straw which was baled and forwarded to the strawberry-growing region around Swanwick and Botley. Other

agricultural produce, such as hay and lettuce, were also forwarded. As at countless other such stations, the yard was shunted by the engine off the pick-up goods. In 1909, for instance, these were the 6.15am from Salisbury to Whitchurch, (booked to shunt 8.45 to 9.22am), the 9.52am Basingstoke to Fullerton goods (shunt 12.0 to 12.12pm) and the 3.10pm Fullerton to Basingstoke goods, between 3.56 and 4.30pm. The Up goods trains were required to shunt into the yard clear of the main line to allow other trains to pass.

Signalling

The signal box was 1 mile 1,488 yards from Whitchurch box and stood on the Up side at the Whitchurch end of the station. A closing switch enabled it to be switched out when not required. There was one crossover, 38 yards on the Whitchurch side (SR 1934).

However, there was a second crossover towards Andover, taken out in 1929 and re-

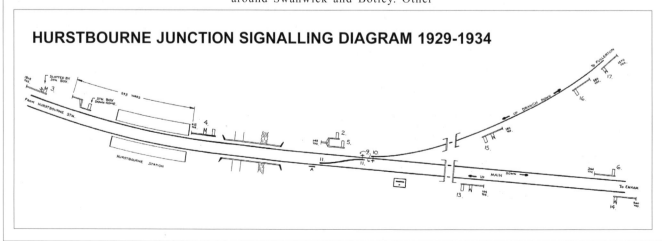

HURSTBOURNE JUNCTION SIGNALLING DIAGRAM 1929-1934

Hurstbourne station before closure looking west towards the viaduct. Standards for Tilley lamps, which provided more light from a glowing mantle, have replaced the original oil lamps with a wick. To the right are the covered steps down from the Up platform to the station building; there was also a footpath from the road to the Down platform.

instated in October 1934 when Hurstbourne Junction signal box was abolished. The box opened in 1882 and alterations to the signalling were made for the opening of the Fullerton line in 1885. There was a 12 lever Stevens' frame with Preece 1 wire block instruments for the sections to Whitchurch and Hurstbourne Junction boxes. In the Down direction were distant, home and starting signals, with the Hurstbourne Junction Down distant arm below the Hurstbourne home. In the Up direction there were two distant signals west of

Hurstbourne Junction, on the Andover and Fullerton lines respectively, together with home, starting and advanced starting signals. This left just four levers to operate the two crossovers and the Up and Down siding points. Even in South Western days the provision of two signal boxes within half a mile was something of a luxury so no doubt Hurstbourne signal box was switched out when not required, being opened up for goods trains shunting the yard. When switched out the block section became Whitchurch to Hurstbourne Junction by day

or Whitchurch to Andover Junction East by night.

After the closure of the northern end of the Fullerton line in 1934 Hurstbourne Junction box, on the Up side of the main line, was closed and all its points and signals removed, making the signalling at Hurstbourne station more straightforward with distant, home, starting and advanced starting signals in both directions. In June 1954 Hurstbourne station box was damaged by fire and put out of use but it was repaired and re-opened by October, when the Down siding had been taken out and Southern Region 3 position block instruments installed. After the closure of the goods yard in 1963 all points were taken out of use and the box closed in 1964. Photographs of the 1950s period show all signals pulled off indicating that the box was by then switched out for long periods.

Staff

A photograph of railmotor No.12 at Hurstbourne (the railmotor dates the scene between 1906 and 1910) shows no less than five railwaymen on duty, although two of them were probably the train crew. The Stationmaster here was responsible not only for the station but for the signal boxes at Hurstbourne Junction and St Mary Bourne. He also supervised the supply of coal and other stores, which arrived by trolley, until the service was abolished in 1934.

In 1895 Hurstbourne's Stationmaster was Mr Walter Hoare in 1915 it was Mr Horatio Lewis Taylor and in 1923 Mr Cobley, but by the mid-1920s the Whitchurch Stationmaster had taken over the duties, making a weekly visit to check

Up Passenger trains departing Hurstbourne station

1888	1909	1947
5 + 4 for Whitchurch	7 + 4 for Whitchurch	6

Passenger Trains Hurstbourne Weekdays Summer 1958

Train	Hurstbourne dep.	To
6.45am Salisbury	7.29	Waterloo
6.33am Woking	8.3	Templecombe
7.20 Waterloo	9.19	Salisbury
8.46 Salisbury	9.29	Waterloo
9.3 Templecombe	10.46	Waterloo
10.45 Basingstoke	11.11	Salisbury
10.54 Waterloo	12.43	Salisbury
12.58pm Salisbury	1.43	Waterloo
11.54 Waterloo	1.41	Salisbury
2.48 Basingstoke	3.14	Salisbury
4.5 Salisbury	4.51	Waterloo
4.48 Basingstoke	5.16	Yeovil Town
5.15 Salisbury	6.1	Waterloo
5.0 Waterloo	6.29	Yeovil Junction
5.39 Waterloo	7.33	Salisbury
6.54 Waterloo	8.59	Yeovil Town
8.44 Salisbury	9.25	Woking
8.54 Waterloo	10.57	Salisbury

Freight Trains Hurstbourne Weekdays Summer 1958

Train	Hurstbourne arr.	Hurstbourne dep.	To
7.45am Bas'ke West Yard	10.6am	10.40am	Andover Junction

In June 1960 King Arthur class 4-6-0 No.30796 *Sir Dodinas le Savage* of Salisbury shed 72B departs from Hurstbourne with the 2.48pm Basingstoke to Salisbury stopping train. Ron Grace.

BR standard class 4-6-0 No.73087 carrying Basingstoke duty disc No.251 with a Down passenger train at Hurstbourne in the early 1960s. Peter Swift Collection.

700 class 0-6-0 No. 30368 comes to grief whilst shunting some wagons at Hurstbourne. This unique scene was captured by Ron Grace in 1962.

on the books and to sign the train register in the signal box. In later years it would appear that the station was staffed on the standard Southern basis of two porter signalmen working alternate early and late turns, being responsible for all station duties. These

included sale of tickets and dealing with parcels in the booking office, operating the signal box when required, assisting with the loading and unloading of wagons in the goods yard and the associated paperwork. Rest

day relief men were provided to cover for staff vacancies.

Hurstbourne Today

From the B3048 road, which runs underneath the viaduct, the old approach

Hurstbourne's Down platform from a passing train shortly after closure. H.C.Casserley

Left. In early 1951 Hurstbourne viaduct had to be strengthened with concrete below track level. Single line working was introduced whilst the civil engineers worked first on one side then the other, making use of a narrow gauge tramway. Reg Randall Collection.

for double track, it had nine arches of approximately 40ft diameter and carried the line about 60ft above the level valley and stream below. The civil engineers carried out substantial renovation work on the viaduct in the 1950s; single line working was introduced for several weeks whilst first one line then the other was lifted to enable the tops of the arches and piers to be strengthened and waterproofed with concrete. On the embankment beyond it crossed a branch of the Bourne Rivulet on bridge No.174 and arrived at the site of Hurstbourne Junction.

leads up to the site of the station which is now occupied by J.Hirst, scrap metal dealers. It seems the only surviving building is one which originated as stables and a hay store. There is no evidence of the platforms – being wooden, they must have been swept away soon after closure. On the Up side of the line, spread across the valley, are now very extensive watercress beds run by Vitacress whose distinctive lorries distribute the cress which formerly went by train.

Hurstbourne to Hurstbourne Junction

Leaving Hurstbourne station the main line ran straight on the level out on to Hurstbourne Viaduct, bridge No.173, the most substantial engineering work on the line between Basingstoke and Salisbury. It spanned the B3048 road, which ran from Hurstbourne Tarrant to Longparish, and the adjacent Bourne Rivulet with its watercress beds. Constructed in brick and originally

HURSTBOURNE JUNCTION

Chronology
Signal box on the Up side (61 miles 38 chains from Waterloo) and junction with double track to Fullerton Junction opened June 1885.
Line to Fullerton Junction singled, but junction still double, 13th July 1913.
Junction altered to facing crossover and single lead to branch 15th December 1929.
Branch closed 29th May 1934.
Signal box closed 14th October 1934.

On 29th July 1939 *King Arthur* himself, 4-6-0 No.453, and always a Salisbury engine, crosses Hurstbourne viaduct with an Up mixed train of coaches and vans. The locomotive is approaching the station whilst the rear van has just passed the site of Hurstbourne Junction.

On 12th July 1969 an unidentified Warship heads a morning Waterloo to Exeter train over Hurstbourne viaduct near the road junction. Strengthening stanchions have been added to the viaduct. On the demolition of West Meon this became the highest viaduct in Hampshire. Rod Hoyle.

Description

Just off the end of Hurstbourne viaduct was the junction for Fullerton, originally a conventional double track junction (see earlier) but later reduced. Just beyond the junction were two over bridges carrying a track from Chapmansford Farm, No.175 over the main line and No.1 over the branch. In 1909 supplies of coal and stores to Hurstbourne Junction signal box were by trolley from Hurstbourne station.

Signalling

Hurstbourne Junction signal box, 806 yards from Hurstbourne box, was on the Up side at the Andover end of the junction and was fitted with a closing switch enabling it to be switched out when not required. After 1929 there was one crossover, 145 yards on the Whitchurch side. Although there were only three or four scheduled trains each way along the branch a variety of other trains used the line including passenger excursions, military and sheep specials running to special traffic notices

The signal box had a 17 lever Stevens frame but between 1885 and 1913 there were just two levers controlling the junction points, the one facing point lock in the Down direction and nine signal levers. In the Up direction on both main line and branch were distant and home signals, the latter just in advance of over bridges Nos.175 and 174 respectively. In the Down direction were distant, two junction homes and starting signals on main line and branch. Several of these signals were carried on the same posts as Hurstbourne station signals.

On the main line there were Preece 3 wire block instruments controlling the block sections to Hurstbourne (station) and St Mary Bourne signal boxes and Preece 1 wire to Longparish. When the branch was singled Tyers No.6 tablet instruments controlled the section to Fullerton. Hurstbourne Junction signal box was open whenever the branch was, which in 1888 was about 8am to 6pm and, in 1924, from about 7.15am to 7.15pm with long gaps between trains. It would appear, therefore, that it was possible to operate on one shift, or alternatively, one man during his shift could work both Hurstbourne station and Hurstbourne Junction boxes, walking the ten minutes or so between them, switching them in and out as required.

From Hurstbourne to Andover

From Hurstbourne Junction the line began to ascend for a mile on a gradient of 1 in 275 up from the valley, mainly in cuttings, with some parts at ground level. About half a mile west of Hurstbourne Junction the line passed under a lane carried on bridge No.176, passed Milepost 62, and then under a minor road bridge No.177 near Apsley Farm. This was approximately the site of St Mary Bourne signal box.

The site of Hurstbourne Junction in 1966 with the alignment of the abandoned Fullerton branch passing under branch bridge No.1 and the main line under bridge No.175, both carrying a track from the adjacent Chapmansford Farm. The signal box, closed in 1934, was on the Up side just behind the camera. H.C.Casserley courtesy E. S. Youldon.

ST MARY BOURNE SIGNAL BOX

Chronology
Signal box opened 1898.
Signal box closed circa 1915.

Description

On 6th July 1898 the South Western Traffic Committee agreed to build additional signal cabins at St Mary Bourne, Enham, Monxton and Newton Tony. These were intermediate block posts for Army manoeuvres carried out in August and September that year when, for several days, the boxes were open continuously.

St Mary Bourne box was about halfway between the boxes at Hurstbourne Junction and Enham and, according to a 1901 District Engineer's drawing, was about 62 miles 23 chains from Waterloo close to Bridge No.177. The box got its name from the small village of St Mary Bourne, a mile or two away up the valley of the River Bourne.

The 1909 Working Timetable stated that supplies of coal and other stores to St Mary Bourne signal box were by trolley from Hurstbourne station, indicating that it was supervised by the Hurstbourne Stationmaster. Following the 1909 traffic pooling agreement a number of such intermediate block posts were closed about 1915.

Signalling

It seems likely that the signal box had a Stevens frame of four levers to control distant and home signals in each direction. It would have had Preece block instruments for the sections to Hurstbourne Junction and Enham, and a closing switch. It would have been brought into use only at busy periods and switched out for much of the time when the section became either Hurstbourne Junction or Whitchurch to Andover Junction East. It seems likely that a man was sent from Hurstbourne to open the box when required.

At an early stage there had been an occupation crossing at St Mary Bourne which later fell into disuse; on 10th July 1895 the South Western declined a request to reopen it. Leaving bridge No.177, the line continued to climb at 1 in 275 to bridge No.178 near Lower Wyke farm. In 1854 Capt. Tyler reported problems with three arches of bridge No.178 but subsequently a single span bridge was built. Between these bridges, in a cutting through the chalk up to 60 feet deep, the line reached a summit before beginning a descent at 1 in 178 and passing milepost 63. From there the straight line continued a gentle descent at 1 in 178, now mainly on embankment with fine views of the countryside. In South Western days there were catch points on the Up main line to arrest the progress of any wagons breaking away from their trains. *Here there was an Up intermediate block signal 2 miles 566 yards from Andover Junction A box (BR 1960).*

This signal was normally off but was returned to danger by a track circuit whilst a train occupied the track to its rear. The line passed milepost 64, then crossed a minor road on bridge No.179 near Finkley Down Farm, started to curve towards the north on a 70 chain radius, and arrived at the site of Enham signal box.

ENHAM SIGNAL BOX

Chronology
Signal box (64 miles 48 chains from Waterloo) opened circa 1898.
Signal box closed 14th October 1934.

Description

On 6th July 1898 the South Western Traffic Committee agreed to build Enham signal box at a cost of £209. It was 3 miles 160 yards from Hurstbourne Junction box and was named after the village of Knights Enham to the north. It was on the Up side of the line and had a closing switch which enabled it to be switched out when not required. Like St Mary Bourne it was open continuously for several days during the army manoeuvres of August and September 1898. *There were no crossovers but there were catch points fitted in the Up line 550 yards towards Andover on a rising gradient of 1 in 178. (SR 1934).*

In 1909 supplies of coal and other stores for the box were sent from Andover Junction on the 6.15am Goods from Salisbury to Whitchurch. In Edwardian days the Andover Junction Stationmaster, who was responsible for the box, visited about once a month to check and sign the train register book, walking up the line, often with his daughter who picked flowers along the way. On 14th October 1934 both Enham and Hurstbourne Junction signal boxes were closed and replaced by the Enham intermediate block signal on the Up line only.

Signalling

Enham signal box contained a 6 lever Stevens frame for Up and Down distant and home signals, with two spare levers. There were no point levers. However, there were catch points provided on the Up line, on a gradient of 1 in 178 down all the way to Andover Junction. Preece 1 wire instruments controlled the block sections to St Mary Bourne or Hurstbourne Junction and Andover Junction East. When Enham was switched out the block section became Andover Junction East to Hurstbourne Junction during the day and to Whitchurch at night. It would appear that in later years a signalman was sent from Andover Junction to open Enham signal box when it was required during busy periods.

Leaving Enham signal box the line continued curving towards the north and then southwards on a curve of 80, and latterly 100 chains radius, passing the fixed distant for the Enham intermediate block signal. Walworth Bridge, No.180, crossed over a Roman road which ran from Cirencester and Fossbury Camp to Winchester. There were two railway cottages to the south of the line and in the 1950s one was occupied by the Hardy family. Walworth Farm was then about ¼ mile away to the south east. In recent years the area has become the Walworth Industrial Estate. The line passed the Andover Junction Down distant and milepost 65 and then, on a long embankment, crossed over five brick arch bridges. In rapid succession No.181 crossed a minor road from East Anton to Andover and No.182 a stream. No.183, 'Enham Arch', had a large arch for the main A343 Newbury to Andover road; No.184 came next, with a track and finally No.185 over the River Anton which ran through the town. To the south of Enham Arch there was a saw mill and to the north an engineering works. In the 1980s two more bridges were built to carry the line over new roads. The line now became straight and level, passed the post carrying the Andover Junction A home and B distant signal arms, under bridge No.185A which carried Daisy Dell footpath and then milepost 66, to arrive at Andover Junction station.

ANDOVER JUNCTION

Chronology
Andover station and single line from Basingstoke opened 3rd July 1854.
Single line to Salisbury (Milford) opened 1st May 1857.
Single track to Romsey opened, station renamed Andover Junction, 6th March 1865 Double track from Whitchurch opened 2nd December 1867.
Double track to Grateley opened 1st February 1870.
East Signal Box (66 miles 11 chains from Waterloo) opened 1882.
West Signal Box (66 miles 30 chains from Waterloo) opened 1882.
Train service to Grafton opened 1st May 1882, using temporary junction at Red Post.
Single track to Red Post and thence Grafton opened 19th November 1882.
Double track to Andover Town opened 1st January 1883
Signal boxes renamed 'A', 'B' in 1938.
Passenger service to Swindon and Cheltenham withdrawn 9th September 1961.
Passenger service to Romsey withdrawn 7th September 1964, station renamed Andover.
Andover Town line singled and downgraded to a siding 29th September 1964.
Goods service to Andover Town withdrawn 18th September 1967.
A and B signal boxes closed, ground frame into use, 2nd December 1973.
Goods shed closed circa 1983.

LSWR Traffic Committee Minutes 1854-1922 contain the following references to Andover:

8th June 1854 An engine shed is required at Andover

6th July 1854 Mr Beattie, the Locomotive Superintendent, complains to the Ways and Works Committee about the lack of an engine shed.

24th September 1857. The station agent wants a shelter on the up platform. The cover on the down platform at Walton station is to be removed and re-erected over the up platform at Andover. Referred to Ways and Works Committee.

16th October 1862. The engine, guards van and one carriage of the 1.25pm up train from Exeter delayed at Andover on 8th October 1862 due to the porter not being at the points in time to turn the train into the loop siding, the train being delayed for an hour and three-quarters.

9th July 1863. Agreed to build a sheep loading bank, referred to Ways and Works Committee.

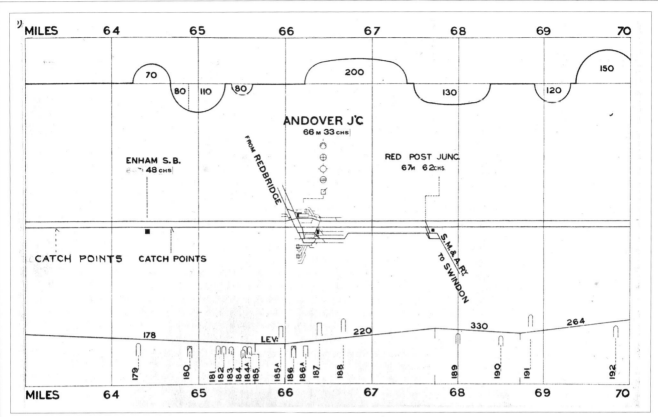

6th December 1866. Received complaint of the exposed state of the up platform waiting shed, the ends to be glazed.

22nd September 1870. Agreed that levers be covered cheaply.

7th September 1871. The Officers Committee recommended the building of an agents office costing £50.

24th April 1873. Locomotive Committee. Read report from agent reporting a fire in the roof of the engine shed on night of 15th April. The signalman to receive £2, and porters and other men 5s each for their exertions in putting out the fire.

13th July 1876. Mr Bainton, the agent, was admonished for not residing in the station house, and on 27th was ordered to sleep in the house.

11th January 1877. Agreed increased accommodation for timber traffic at a cost of £500. This was approved by the Board on 1st February 1877.

12th December 1877. Read report from agent concerning a traction engine consigned by Tasker & Co. to Mr Dugdale at Lymington, having been loaded at Andover Junction and damaged by falling off the truck. Postponed until next meeting.

Approaching Daisy Dell footbridge to the east of Andover Junction in July 1962 West Country class 4-6-2 No. 34006 *Bude* heads an Up afternoon stopping train, apparently the 4.5pm Salisbury to Basingstoke. The sidings to the left are on the site of the first two South Western engine sheds of 1854 and 1866. Behind them the Redbridge line curves away and in the distance a 'Hampshire' diesel-electric multiple unit waits in the bay behind the East signal box. Rod Hoyle.

On 14th May 1955 King Arthur class 4-6-0 No. 30779 *Sir Colgrevance* passes Andover Junction West signal box with Maunsell 3 coach set No.245, apparently a Waterloo to Salisbury stopping train. Behind the signal box is the top of the crane used in the saw mills in Millway Road. R.C.Riley, The Transport Treasury.

20th December 1877. Agreed to repair Taskers traction engine, and to fit the van trucks with improved scotches.

21st March 1878. Approved a new stable costing £250.

8th January 1879. The Revd. Johnson complained of no gentleman's waiting room. Plans and an estimate were drawn up, and approved on 2nd April to be done when convenient at a cost of £132.

18th September 1879. Approved station rooms costing £219.

20th January 1881. Approved a crane costing £280.

16th March 1881. Approved a temporary siding for Swindon Marlborough & Andover Railway building materials.

3rd January 1883. Approved an additional line to new engine shed costing £230.

25th April 1883. Approved the Engineering Committee plan for a refreshment room costing £280.

22nd November 1893 Approved provision of new porters room, the old one to be converted to a lamp room, for £80.

1st May 1895. Approved a coal siding at the coal stage costing £77.

11th November 1896. Approved General manager's request to enlarge the parcels office for £105.

27th September 1899. Report of fire on 8th July 1899 which destroyed the old engine shed and part of the coal stage. Postponed decision on proposal to build a new engine shed costing £510.

29th April 1903. Approved a short siding for repairing carriages and wagons for £92.

7th October 1903. Approved an urgent request from the Engineering Committee to widen the public road bridge to remove the reverse curve and stop complaints about running. Approved tender of £1100 from Eastwood and Swingler for the ironwork. [Bridge No.186]

16th December 1903. Approved Engineering Committee proposal for a new engine shed costing £2550, and new siding costing £2250.

16th December 1903. Approved Engineering Committee proposal for a footbridge costing £215 at the footpath crossing on the London side of the station used by schoolchildren.(Bridge No.185A, Daisy Dell)

27th January 1904. Accepted a tender of £917 from Humphreys & Sons for a corrugated iron engine shed.

7th March 1906. Reported that bridge No.186 shows signs of brickwork failure, the ironwork was to be secured.

10th October 1910. Approved Engineering Committee proposal for a lock-up in the goods shed costing £59.

Andover 1854-1948

When the railway arrived in 1854 Andover already had several established commercial enterprises including the Andover & Redbridge Canal. It was navigable between 1796 and 1859 and filled in to form the track bed of the Andover & Redbridge Railway opened in 1865. Tasker's Waterloo Ironworks had been established in 1815 in the Anna Valley and the Andover Gas Works, at the canal basin in 1838.

An Ordnance Survey of 1871 also shows steam sawmills and timber yards on the Down side of the line adjacent to the Millway Road bridge, identified in 1889 as the premises of Benjamin Hawkins. It had gone from the site by 1896. On the opposite side of the line, in 1871, was the 'South Western Works' with a well and engine house, though the 1896 map describes this as the Acre Iron Works, identified in 1889 as those of Watson and Haig.

Kelly's Directory of 1889 described Andover as an ancient municipal borough, with a population of 5,654 in 1881. There was a corn market every Friday in the Town Hall, a market for fat and store cattle at Bridge Street every Monday and a market for pigs, sheep, fat and store cattle on Fridays at the Masons Arms in Winchester Street. There was a sheep fair on 17th November and a wool fair commencing on the last Friday in June. Weyhill, with one of the largest fairs in the country, was nearby and contributed to Andover's prosperity.

The Stationmaster at Andover Junction was William James Hill and at Andover Town Christopher Schofield. Omnibuses ran from the Star & Garter Hotel in the High Street to the Junction station to meet every train. There was a long list of carriers who departed to no less than 27 destinations, ranging from nearby Abbotts Ann and Wherwell to more distant Marlborough, Newbury and Winchester. Some were

Andover Junction station in 1961. The original William Tite house of 1854 was similar to the design at Whitchurch (see page 24) but had five upstairs windows instead of three. To the left is the extension of c.1863 (one upstairs window) and then a further addition dating from 1879. R.M. Casserley.

served only on Friday afternoons after the markets, some on two or three days, and others daily.

Andover Station 1854-65

Andover Junction was for three years the terminus of a single track line from Basingstoke and subsequently the principal intermediate traffic centre after the line was extended to Salisbury. On 3rd July 1854 the South Western eventually opened its single track line from Basingstoke which parliament had authorised in 1846. In a rural location about a mile from the town centre, its terminus was simply laid out, with an attractive station house on the single platform. The first engine shed and turntable appeared soon after; a temporary construction, the shed was dismantled and re-erected at Basingstoke in 1858. The goods shed was moved here from Andover Road (now Micheldever) station and was of an unusual wooden design covering two tracks which were connected by wagon turntables. The initial service comprised a handful of trains, some mixed, to and from Basingstoke.

There was some enlargement of the station when the line to Salisbury (Milford) opened in 1857, including a passing loop serving an Up platform, which initially had no waiting shelter. The August 1857 train service consisted of four mixed passenger and goods trains between Basingstoke and Salisbury, augmented with two morning goods trains between Basingstoke and Andover. Only once in the day, at 7.15pm, did two trains cross on the single line sections.

Andover Junction 1865-1883

Andover station became Andover Junction with the opening of the Andover & Redbridge line in 1865, the new Andover Town station being more convenient for the town centre. A bay platform was provided for the new branch line, together with more sidings. All the routes remained single track. In 1867 Andover Junction had eleven trains to Basingstoke, nine to Salisbury and three to Redbridge and Southampton.

In 1867 and 1870 the single line sections to Whitchurch and Grateley were converted to double track. An 1870s period photograph illustrates the station at this period, apparently with the first signal box on the Down platform adjacent to the Redbridge bay buffer stops. Weyhill Fair produced much extra traffic to the extent that railway staff were paid gratuities for performing this extra work. However, on the arrival of the Swindon, Marlborough & Andover Railway from the north much of this was taken up when their Weyhill station opened. In 1877 the South Western Traffic Committee agreed to lengthen the Up platform by three carriage lengths and, in 1881, to lay in a siding for construction materials for the SM&AR.

An 1881 plan shows the double track main line with Up and Down platforms and the Southampton bay and siding. Also shown is the first signal box on the Down platform adjacent to the buffer stops of the Redbridge bay. The goods yard on the Down side boasted no less than four wagon turntables with numerous spurs, requiring the employment of shunting horses to move

wagons in the yard and goods shed. On the Up side was just one siding, opposite the goods yard, together with the new siding beyond the Millway Road bridge, as mentioned, for SM&AR construction materials.

Traffic on the main line had gradually increased and on the arrival in 1882 of the SM&AR a third independent track was installed, on the north side of the line, from Red Post Junction to a loop platform to the rear of a new Up platform. Through lines had also been added to the station which now boasted four tracks through the station in addition to the SM&AR single line. A subway was built at this time to link all the platforms.

In 1883 the line to Andover Town was doubled and Andover Junction station now reached its zenith. It would appear that the station house was extended about this time.

Andover Junction from 1883 to the 1960s

From 1883 Andover Junction was a principal station on the West of England main line, also served by the major north to south route completed between Cheltenham and Southampton in 1890. By the 1950s Andover Junction was little changed in many respects from the 1880s. Essentially all of the features on the south, or Down, side of the line were LSWR in origin whilst most of those to the north, or Up side, were added for the Swindon Marlborough & Andover Railway.

On 14th May 1955 King Arthur Class 4-6-0 No.30452 *Sir Meligrance*, leaves Andover Junction with Bulleid five coach set No.832 in carmine and cream livery. To the right vans stand outside the two-road goods shed. R.C.Riley, The Transport Treasury.

The station and its layout occupied about three-quarters of a mile between Daisy Dell footbridge, No.185A, and the Weyhill Road over bridge No.188. Between these were under bridge No.186 for Charlton Road. The subway between the two platforms was No.186A and the over bridge at Millway Road was No.187. In a cutting, bridges Nos.186 and 187 had originally been constructed in brick for a double track, like all the other bridges seen along the line, but when the alignment was widened for the Swindon Marlborough & Andover in 1882 they were altered. No.186, nearer the platforms, was rebuilt completely with two iron girder spans supported on brick abutments and central pier, the southern span crossing four LSWR tracks and the northern span three SM&AR tracks. The original No.187 bridge remained but a second brick bridge, wide enough for two tracks, was constructed to the north although in the event it was used by just the single SM&AR line.

From the footpath (bridge No.185A at milepost 66) the line rose for almost two miles at 1 in 220, initially straight but then on a very gentle right-hand curve of 200 chains radius. On the Down side, after footbridge 185A, there were the two (at some times three) Down Sidings on the site of the first engine shed and in the 1950s and 1960s were often used to store condemned wagons.

The Andover Town line curved in from the south forming a double track junction, the actual configuration changing several times over the years. Entrance to the bay platform was located here used by branch trains though there was no run-round. There was also a bay siding, taken out in 1930. Back on the main line the layout originally opened up to four through tracks with Nos.1 and 2 (Down) and 3 and 4 (Up) Main Lines, Nos.2 and 3 being through roads without platform faces. However, at some stage, possibly in 1917, the facing points for No.2 (Down) Main Line were taken out and it became a Down refuge siding instead, later designated Middle Siding East. Between the Bay and Down Main lines was Andover Junction 'A' signal box (East until 1938) and then the Down platform which incorporated the main station buildings.

At the end of the Down platform was the goods yard served by three trailing connections from the Down main line. The long Down siding ran under bridge No.187 almost as far as No.188; two tracks ran off it to the goods shed with another loop serving a loading dock with cattle pens. In the goods yard was a 10 ton crane and two highway vehicle docks; the goods shed had a 40cwt crane. In Victorian days there were a number of wagon turntables and spurs in the yard, with wagons moved either by horse or men equipped with pinch bars. At first sight this might seem to be a rather small goods yard for such an important town but much more freight was handled at Andover Town station goods yard, on the site of the Andover Canal basin where many traders already had their premises.

In the Up direction from Red Post Junction three tracks, the single SM&AR and the Up and Down LSWR, ran into Andover Junction on bridge No.188. To the north of the line were Nos.1, 2, 3, and 4 Branch Sidings and between the running lines two more, designated Up and Middle Siding West. Seven tracks ran under bridge No.187, to Andover Junction 'B' signal box (West until 1938) and the island platform. This was considerably offset from the Down platform; its southern face was the LSWR Up main platform and the northern face the branch or SM&AR Up and Down platform, although through trains from Cheltenham could also use the Up main.

To the north of the island platform were the No.2 branch road, later branch siding, which served as a run round and gave shunting access to the branch sidings and to both SM&AR* and LSWR engine sheds. It could also be used for through goods trains to Southampton. Behind this was another siding. Just behind the boundary fence a road ran from Charlton Road past extensive Saw Mills to Millway Road, where there was also the Acre Iron Works. By Southern Railway days the distinctive large white McDougalls Flour Mills were built adjacent to Millway Road by the yard, on the Down side.

There were speed limits of 20mph for Up trains through the junction to Andover Town, and 50mph in both directions on the

* *Became the MSWJR (Midland & South Western Junction Railway in 1884.*

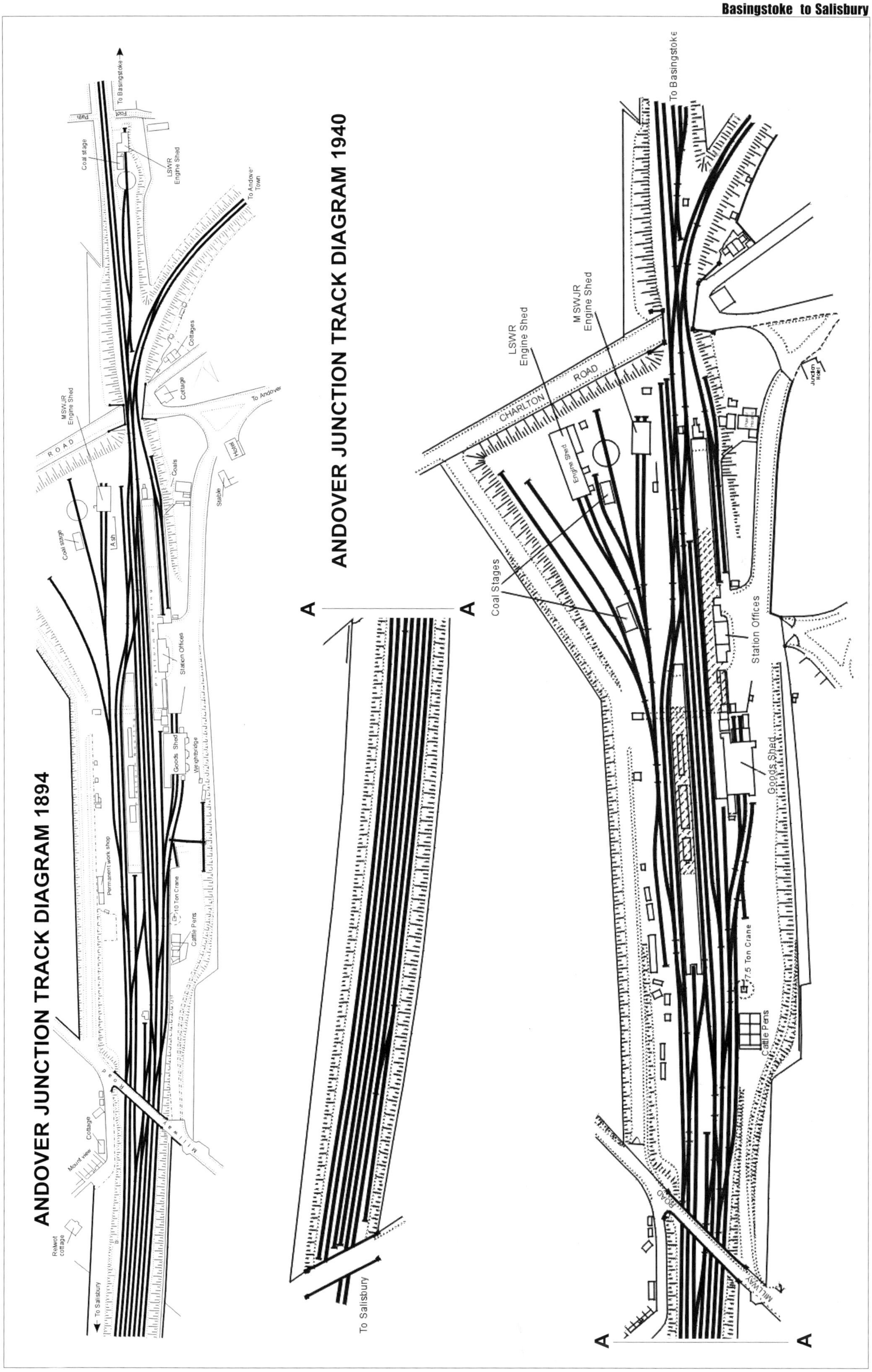

ANDOVER JUNCTION TRACK DIAGRAM 1894

To Basingstoke

Coal stage
LSWR Engine Shed
Shed
Foot
To Andover Town
MSWJR Engine Shed
Cottages
Cottage
ROAD
To Andover
Coal stage
Ash
Hotel
Stable
Coals
Coal stage
Station Offices
Goods Shed
Weighbridge
10 Ton Crane
Cattle Pens
Permanent way shop
Mount view Cottage
Relwot cottage
To Salisbury

ANDOVER JUNCTION TRACK DIAGRAM 1940

To Basingstoke

CHARLTON ROAD
LSWR Engine Shed
M SWJR Engine Shed
Engine Shed
Junction Hotel
Coal Stages
Station Offices
Goods Shed
7.5 Ton Crane
Cattle Pens
RAILWAY ROAD
A — A

A
A
To Salisbury

On 2nd November 1957 Merchant Navy class 4-6-2 No.35002 *Union Castle* of Exmouth Junction shed departs from Andover Junction on the 6.30am express from Exeter Central to Waterloo, a principal business train for west country passengers. S.C.Nash.

single line between Andover Junction B and Red Post Junction. The Up refuge siding could hold a locomotive and 55 wagons. (BR 1960)

The station approach ran from the Junction Hotel (demolished in the 1990s and replaced by a small housing estate) on the Charlton Road. The two-storey 1854 station house was similar to that at Whitchurch but was larger with five windows upstairs rather than three. Extensions later appeared, a two-storey on with three more upstairs windows and another of one storey. The station house had the original flat sloping awning of 1854 but the other platform awnings, built in 1882 on both sides, had arc roofs. On the Down platform, No.2, were waiting room, ladies and refreshment rooms, together with offices for parcels, porters, Stationmaster, inspectors, other railwaymen and a W.H.Smith's bookstall. The island platform had a long wooden building incorporating waiting and refreshment rooms together with toilets. Here the Up platform was No.3 and the MSWJR platform No.4.

During the twentieth century Andover Junction station, and all its South Western routes, came under the control of the Central District offices at Eastleigh, later transferred

On 19th October 1957 Merchant Navy class 4-6-2 No.35007 *Aberdeen Commonwealth* of Salisbury passes Andover Junction with the 1.0pm Waterloo to Plymouth and North Devon express. S.C.Nash.

to Southampton West. This became the Southern Railway Central Division until about 1930 when it was re-named the Southern Division. In 1948 the Basingstoke to Salisbury line was transferred, along with its branches, to the London West Division with offices at Woking; Andover Junction and Andover Town were transferred and Clatford, to the south of Andover, became the boundary with the Southern Division.

Edwardian Reminiscences

In 1899 Margaret Dudman's father, the Stationmaster at Botley, was promoted to Andover Junction and in 1978 her childhood reminiscences, about life at Andover, were published in the *Hampshire County Magazine*. The extensive family home, including four bedrooms, was upstairs in the station house, accessed from the Booking Hall through a door marked private. There was no bathroom so the family bathed in front of the kitchen range using rainwater from huge water butts. Porters carried scuttles of coal up the stairs for the family.

Outside the station there was a 'fly', driven by 'Mr Bob' and an open landau driven by Mr Sweetland, the proprietor of a livery stable in London Street. On 'Orphanage Sunday', boys and girls who lived at the South Western Orphanage at Woking arrived at Andover Junction by train. Accompanied by a brass band they were taken by local railwaymen to spend the day in their homes and a collection was made for orphanage funds.

Weyhill Fair, held during a week in October, was one of the biggest sheep fairs in the south of England and is mentioned in several Thomas Hardy novels. Early morning passenger trains brought crowds

of dealers to Andover, and up to forty horse-drawn vehicles took them the three miles to the fair.

The Stationmaster spent much time in his office on paperwork and conducting business over the new invention, the telephone. At the end of the platform was the lamp-room where porters filled oil lamps for trains and signals, although the station itself was lit by gas from the town. During the winter months porters filled the iron foot warmers which were in demand by first and second class passengers on cold days. In the parcels office there were sometimes puppies or calves, which could be made a fuss of or fed. A firm called Spiers and Ponds operated the refreshment rooms. Boys delivered luncheon baskets, ordered in advance by telegraph, to first and second class passengers on their arrival at Andover while other boys sold newspapers and magazines from W.H.Smith's bookstall.

On Sunday mornings there was sometimes a special treat when homing pigeons were released from their baskets, which had arrived by train. The Stationmaster, an important man in the town, often received gifts from regular travellers, including hares, rabbits, pheasants and, at Christmas, a goose or turkey, together with cigars, bottles of crystallised fruits, and fruit in brandy. Even so the Stationmaster had his own garden where he kept hens and grew a variety of vegetables, with asparagus a speciality

Traffic and Train Services

Passenger traffic levels at Andover Junction have always been 'steady'; there was always some travel to London, Basingstoke and Salisbury but long distance commuting

has increased greatly in recent years. Passengers came by train to work in shops and offices, and children to school, though passengers from the Southampton line usually used Andover Town station, which was more convenient for the centre. Apart from the usual local passengers there were often many soldiers travelling to and from the various barracks on Salisbury Plain, served by both Ludgershall station and the Tidworth and Bulford branches. Onward from Andover Junction some soldiers reached their barracks by scheduled or special bus services or by army lorry.

Until local bus services took over in the 1930s, schoolchildren travelled to Andover Junction to attend the grammar school, about 15 minutes walk away in the building now occupied by the town museum. In the 1950s pupils from Romsey, Mottisfont and Stockbridge used Test Valley trains, calling at Andover Town, also to attend the grammar school. On the morning of 13th October 1914 the boys arriving at Andover Junction, from Whitchurch and Hurstbourne, found a scene of devastation following a destructive goods train collision. Not surprisingly they had a good look at the scene and as a result were all late for school and caned as punishment. One of the boys concerned was a young Tom Denning who was destined to become one of England's senior judges.

In the early South Western period, there were more trains from Andover than Salisbury but that changed when the line was doubled. As traffic built up, the occasional West of England express ran non-stop through Andover but for a century most of the best Waterloo trains called after stopping at Woking and Basingstoke. Following the demise of the *Atlantic Coast Express* in 1964 all trains have since called

One of the many shunting mishaps that befell Andover Junction over the years. For more details on these unfortunate events see chapters Four and Five. Ron Grace.

Looking east along Andover Junction Up platform in 1956 with wooden goods shed to the right and wagons in the sidings adjacent to the engine sheds. The main features of this layout, including the subway date from the SM&AR opening in 1882. H.C.Casserley.

here. At Andover Junction there were usually other trains waiting for passengers on the Southampton and MSWJR lines but with a few honourable exceptions a wait of twenty minutes or more was required, which explains why the refreshment rooms on both platforms were well patronised.

The population of Andover has increased greatly since the 1960s and the improved train service has encouraged considerable commuting, not only to London, Basingstoke and Salisbury but into Andover itself.

Over the years the booking office also dealt with a considerable volume and variety of parcels and telegraph traffic. Parcels were received here for residents, shops, offices and businesses in the town and surrounding countryside. There were some milk churns originating at Andover but many more were transferred – in 1913 for instance no less than eleven MSWJR milk churn vans were scheduled for daily transfer to the LSWR at Andover Junction for onward transit to London. In 1932 Chapel River Press, who published *Kelly's Directory*, transferred their printing works from Kingston in Surrey to a purpose-built factory in Weyhill Road, Andover and forwarded considerable quantities of their publications by train. Local growers sent watercress to London and the Midlands, via Templecombe, on the 5.29pm Down passenger train. In the 1950s, Ron Grace recalls that a large can of cream from Andover Creamery was put on to the 3.40pm Up train for delivery to the Station Hotel at Basingstoke.

The 5.50pm from Waterloo was particularly well served by connections to Horsebridge, Tidworth and Bulford and it would appear that the 5.0pm from Waterloo had to shunt back into the Down Sidings to allow the 5.50pm to overtake it.

For a couple of years in the mid-1960s Peter Yarlett commuted between Andover Junction and Waterloo. Only a handful of men commuted to London at that time and he recalls that there was almost a club atmosphere on the 7.22am Up train to Basingstoke. Here they changed onto a Southampton train to arrive at Waterloo at 8.59am. Another commuter was Mr Fred Sayers, who worked for *Kelly's Directories* and regularly carried a large suitcase full of printing blocks between the works and London. About a dozen girls travelled from Andover to work at Portals Mill at Overton and more got on at Hurstbourne and Whitchurch. The return journey was by the 6.0pm Waterloo to Exeter express which arrived back at 7.21 and had full dining car and buffet facilities – this was 1964, when a nine day season ticket cost £3 17s 2d.

Working Timetable descriptions of West of England trains as, for example, 12.20pm Ilfracombe, were somewhat economical as they also included coaches from Plymouth Friary and often other termini. However, for our line these are West of England expresses; this issue will be addressed in Volume Two.

The Suez Mobilisation

When the Suez crisis broke in 1956 there was a rapid general mobilisation of reservists. Late one Sunday evening, starting about 9.20pm, the first of about six Down special trains arrived at Andover Junction carrying a total of more than two thousand servicemen returning to their bases in the area. The trains backed up the main line block to block, the locomotive lamps showing one waiting at the outer home signal and another at the Enham intermediate signal. Each train was unloaded and the carriages shunted into the sidings before the next could be admitted to the Down platform. More special trains were booked to run to the Bulford branch but had to wait outside Andover until the Down road was clear for them to pass through the station. The servicemen, with suitcases and kitbags, then waited in the station approach for transport to their bases.

Unfortunately, proper arrangements had not been made with the local bus company, Wilts and Dorset, for the transfer of these men to their camps and the local inspector, Arthur Blake, had to conjure something up. At very short notice he was able to rustle up twenty or so double deck buses, each of which could take about 50 seated and 8 standing passengers, with their crews from garages at Andover, Salisbury, Amesbury, Blandford and Pewsey. A further complication arose as the men were destined for nine different bases, the RAF at Andover, Upavon, Nether Avon, Boscombe Down, and the army at Barton Stacey,

Larkhill, Tilshead, Tidworth and Bulford. Each double-decker and crew made two journeys, the last train arriving at 2.20am and the last bus departing at 3.0am. The knock-on effect was that some services next morning had to be cancelled.

Southampton Line Services

Just two years after the line opened the 1867 timetable for 'Andover Junction, Romsey, Redbridge and Southampton' showed just three trains stopping at all stations in each direction over the single line, running via Blechynden to Southampton Terminus. By 1888 there were six similar trains but in 1893, the MSWJR inaugurated its through passenger trains between Cheltenham (Lansdown) and Southampton which initially included through Midland Railway carriages from York and to Sheffield. By 1914 there were three MSWJR trains each way between Cheltenham and Southampton, those from Andover calling only at Romsey and Southampton West (as Blechynden had become). This was in addition to six LSWR stopping trains to Southampton, of which two now ran via Eastleigh, and one to Horsebridge.

In 1914 main line connections at Andover Junction were of variable quality. The best Down trains were the 11.15am from Waterloo, which arrived at 12.46pm, connections leaving at 12.56 (fast) and 1.3 (stopping), the 5.50pm express arrived at 7.24 with a 7.32 connection to Horsebridge. Up trains were better with the 10.27am arrival from Eastleigh connecting into the 10.35am arriving at Waterloo at 12.8pm, the 4.30pm arrival from Southampton connecting into the 4.40pm arriving at Waterloo at 6.5pm, and the 8.37pm arrival

from Horsebridge connecting into the 8.51 arriving at Waterloo at 10.34pm. Other Southampton line trains required a wait of half an hour or more at Andover and, in some cases, the connection was into a main line stopping train.

By 1947 three trains per day ran from Andover Junction to Romsey, three to Eastleigh and one to Portsmouth via Southampton, together with two ex-MSWJR services to Southampton, one from Cheltenham and one from Marlborough. In 1964, the year the Andover to Redbridge line closed, there were sixteen trains, all formed by 'Hampshire' DMUs. Of these, thirteen ran to Portsmouth via Southampton, two to Portsmouth via Eastleigh, and one to Eastleigh. However, connections were poor with a wait of more than thirty minutes before departure towards Southampton; long enough for a leisurely cup tea in the refreshment room but otherwise unsatisfactory.

Trains arriving from the Southampton line could use the bay at Andover Junction which, at either ends of the period, was not a problem for a Hampshire diesel multiple unit or a South Western railmotor. However, without a run-round during all that time, a second engine was required to release the train engine. If available, a Southampton train could use the Down main platform and the locomotive could run round the train there, and shunt the coaches to the bay for the next departure. Through trains from Southampton to Cheltenham ran right across the junctions at Andover East signal box and used the

MSWJR platform, whilst trains from Cheltenham to Southampton could use either the branch or the Up main platform.

An interesting feature during the 1939-45 war was that every evening many of the documents used at the Central Division offices adjoining Southampton Central station were loaded into a train and sent to Andover for safekeeping, to return the same way next morning. No more details of this fascinating working have so far come to light.

When the first section of the Swindon, Marlborough and Andover Railway opened in 1882 there were four return trips between Andover and Grafton. By 1883, when the line opened in full, there were seven between Andover and Swindon, some including South Western through carriages between Southampton and Swindon. In 1891 the company had become the Midland and South Western Junction, extending three of

Up Passenger trains departing Andover Junction						
1857	1867	1909	1947	1964	1984	2002
4	7	14	13	14	21	31

its Andover trains from Swindon to Cheltenham (Lansdown), where it connected with Midland Railway trains. In 1892 MSWJR goods trains began to run to Southampton. In 1893 MSWJR passenger trains began to run between Cheltenham and Southampton hauled by LSW locomotives from Andover. MSWJR locomotives took over in 1894 and in 1898 there were five trains from Andover to Cheltenham, some originating at Southampton. A significant feature of the service was the provision of through coaches between Southampton and

A 1955 view of Andover Junction with a few wagons in the Down siding. The subway approaches sloped up underneath the open awnings on each side; the subway brick arch can be seen on the Down side opposite the wagons. R.C.Riley, The Transport Treasury.

A branch train, apparently the 7.40pm from Andover Junction to Eastleigh, hauled by L class 4-4-0 No.31775. It is on Eastleigh duty No.295 about 1952 and awaits departure from the Redbridge bay having connected with the adjacent Down main line train. Andover Junction A signal box and the lower quadrant starting signal are in the foreground and McDougalls flour mill in the background. Ron Grace Collection.

various stations to the north, including Birmingham and Manchester.

The best MSWJR trains were the two 'North Expresses'; in 1914 these left Southampton at 10.5am and 1.45pm and

called at Andover Junction at 10.56 and 2.34, where they connected with the 8.50am and 1.0pm expresses from Waterloo. They arrived at Cheltenham at 12.45 and 4.19pm, whence through carriages worked to

Birmingham and Manchester. In the opposite direction the two 'South Expresses', with through coaches from Birmingham and Manchester, left Cheltenham at 10.37am and 1.10pm and

On 24th May 1957 Merchant Navy class 4-6-2 No.35026 *Lamport &Holt* Line, of Exmouth Junction shed passes under Millway Road bridge (No.187) to arrive at Andover Junction apparently on the 7.30am Exeter Central to Waterloo service. McDougalls flour mill dominates the skyline, with MSWJR line tracks to the right. R.C.Riley, The Transport Treasury.

Passenger Train Services Summer 1914

Train	Andover Jcn arr.	Andover Jcn.dep	To
6.45 Andover Jcn		6.45	Southampton
7.0 Andover Jcn		7.0	Cheltenham
6.10 Waterloo	7.37	7.40	Torrington
7.38am Tidworth	7.59		
8.5 Andover Jcn		8.5	Tidworth
5.50 Yeovil	8.6	8.8	Waterloo
5.15 Cheltenham	8.20	8.25	Southampton
7.20 Southampton	8.33		
8.45 Andover Jcn		8.45	Cheltenham
6.35 Waterloo	8.56	8.59	Yeoford
9.6 Andover Jcn		9.6	Waterloo
9.12 Andover Jcn		9.12	Southampton
9.37 Salisbury	10.8	10.10	Basingstoke
9.5 Swindon	10.20		
9.26 Eastleigh	10.27		
8.31 Yeovil	10.31	10.35	Waterloo
8.50 Waterloo	10.37	10.39	Plymouth
10.5 Southampton	10.54	10.56	Cheltenham
10.23 Salisbury	11.7	11.9	Waterloo
11.22 Andover Jcn		11.22	Southampton
10.50 Basingstoke	11.29	11.31	Salisbury
12.20 Andover Jcn		12.20	Cheltenham
11.15 Waterloo	12.46	12.49	Exeter
10.37 Cheltenham	12.46	12.56	Southampton
11.10 Yeovil	12.56	12.59	Waterloo
1.3 Andover Jcn		1.3	Southampton
12.38 Salisbury	1.10	1.12	Basingstoke
12.30 Basingstoke	1.5	1.22	Salisbury
12.45 S'thampton	1.56		
1.12 Basingstoke	1.58	2.1	Salisbury
1.55 Fullerton	2.10		
1.0 Waterloo	2.27	2.30	Plymouth
1.45 Southampton	2.32	2.34	Cheltenham
2.20 Salisbury	2.44	2.47	Waterloo
2.47 Andover Jcn		2.47	Cheltenham
1.10 Cheltenham	3.1	3.3	Southampton
10.55 Torrington	3.29	3.31	Waterloo
2.35 Swindon	3.46		
2.10 Waterloo	3.57	4.0	Salisbury
3.17 Salisbury	3.59	4.1	Basingstoke
4.5 Andover Jcn		4.5	Tidworth
4.7 Andover Jcn		4.7	Southampton
4.10 Tidworth	4.28		
3.3 Southampton	4.30		
12.5 Plymouth	4.38	4.40	Waterloo
4.14 Southampton	5.6	5.10	Cheltenham
5.3 Salisbury	5.40	5.43	Waterloo
3.0 Cheltenham	5.55		
3.50 Waterloo	6.15	6.18	Plymouth
6.33 Andover Jcn		6.33	Southampton
5.0 Waterloo	6.53 waits until	7.35	Bulford
6.52 Fullerton	7.7		
6.2 Southampton	7.17		
5.50 Waterloo	7.24	7.27	Plymouth
7.32 Andover Jcn		7.32	Horsebridge
7.33 Andover Jcn		7.33	Tidworth
5.0 Waterloo	6.53 see above	7.35	Bulford
7.8 Basingstoke	7.45	7.48	Salisbury
7.50 Andover Jcn		7.50	Swindon
5.15 Cheltenham	8.24		
8.7 Horsebridge	8.37		
4.0 Plymouth	8.49	8.51	Waterloo
8.27 Southampton	9.44		
7.50 Templecombe	9.46	9.48	Waterloo
7.22 Cheltenham	10.5		
8.15 Waterloo	10.13	10.16	Salisbury

arrived at Andover Junction at 12.46 and 3.1pm. Here they connected with expresses reaching Waterloo at 2.35 and 4.48pm and arrived at Southampton at 1.48 and 3.54pm.

There were claims that the MSWJR/LSWR route from Cheltenham to London was quicker than the GWR route via Gloucester but the evidence suggests that such claims were overstated. For comparison, in 1922 the 6.0pm restaurant car express from Paddington arrived at Cheltenham at 8.55pm, and several others took about half an hour longer. The best LSWR/MSWJR time from London was about 25 minutes longer than the GWR and at Cheltenham the Midland's Lansdown station was less convenient for the town centre than the Great Western's St James.

After the grouping the Great Western concentrated on its own through services, such as that between Bournemouth and Birkenhead. The MSWJR line and services were downgraded, although one through coach remained between Southampton and Liverpool until 1939. Even so, passengers from stations at the south end of the line, particularly soldiers from Tidworth and Ludgershall, changed at Andover Junction for London trains.

It is interesting to note that the last timetable published by the Southern Railway in 1947 included two pages for GWR services between Andover Junction, Tidworth, Swindon and Cheltenham Spa. On weekdays there were two trains from Southampton to Cheltenham and from Andover, one each to Cheltenham and Swindon, two to Marlborough and three to Tidworth, making a total of nine MSWJR line departures from Andover Junction. Of the nine similar MSWJR line arrivals the two through trains to Southampton originated at Cheltenham and Marlborough.

Services declined even more when British Railways took over. In 1955 the Tidworth branch passenger service came to an end and in September 1958 the Andover Junction to Cheltenham service was reduced from three each way daily to just one. A few passenger trains still ran as far as Swindon, until finally abandoned in 1961.

From 1796, long before the railway arrived at Andover, some traffic reached the town by means of the Andover & Southampton Canal. As previously mentioned, it closed for construction of the Redbridge line which opened on its alignment in 1865. The basin was filled in and used as Andover Town goods yard and traders, already established here, simply transferred their travel arrangements from barge to wagon and didn't bother transferring their businesses to the yard at Andover Junction. The medium size goods yard at Andover Town incorporated a Shell Mex oil depot, stores for Cullen, Allen & Co., hay and seed stores for SCATS (Southern Counties Agricultural Trading Society) and coal storage for several merchants including Woods and Days. There were several private owner wagons operated by Andover businesses including Gosling & Bunie, recorded in 1926, Day & Co. of 61, Bridge Street, and the Andover Co-op which had eight 12 ton wagons, Nos.24-29, 31 and one other, supplied by the CWS Wagon Works,

Passenger Trains Weekdays Summer 1958

Train	Andover Jcn arr.	Andover Jcn dep.	To
1.15am Waterloo (Pass. & News)	2.31	2.34	Ilfracombe etc.
2.30 Basingstoke (Milk)	3.13	3.25	Yeovil Town
6.16 Salisbury	6.40	6.42	Portsmouth
7.0 Andover Jcn		7.0	Marlborough
6.13 Southampton Terminus	7.15		
6.45am Salisbury	7.16	7.19	Waterloo
7.25 Andover Jcn		7.25	Portsmouth
7.50 Andover Jcn		7.50	Cheltenham Ldn
6.33 Woking	8.11	8.14	Templecombe
7.49 Salisbury	8.12	8.13	Waterloo
6.53 Portsmouth	8.29		
8.42 Andover Jcn		8.42	Fareham
7.5 Swindon Junction	9.8		
8.46 Salisbury	9.17	9.19	Waterloo
7.20 Waterloo	9.27	9.32	Salisbury
8.32 Eastleigh	9.29		
9.45 Andover Jcn		9.45	Portsmouth
7.30 Exeter Central	9.57	10.0	Waterloo
9.0 Waterloo	10.27	10.29	Plymouth etc.
8.53 Portsmouth	10.29		
6.35 Exeter Central	10.31	10.35	Waterloo
10.42 Andover Jcn		10.42	Portsmouth
10.10 Southampton Terminus	11.0	11.5	Cheltenham Ldn
10.45 Basingstoke	11.19	11.21	Salisbury
9.53 Portsmouth	11.29		
11.36 Andover Jcn		11.36	Eastleigh
10.53 Portsmouth	12.29		
12.42 Andover Jcn		12.42	Portsmouth
10.54 Waterloo	12.51	12.54	Salisbury
8.15 Plymouth Friary	12.57	1.0	Waterloo
10.10 Cheltenham Lansdown	12.52	1.3	Southampton T.
12.40 Eastleigh	1.29		
12.58 Salisbury	1.29	1.33	Waterloo
1.42 Andover Jcn		1.42	Portsmouth
11.54 Waterloo	1.49	1.51	Salisbury
1.0 Waterloo	2.16	2.18	Plymouth etc.
12.53 Portsmouth	2.29		
2.45 Andover Jcn		2.45	Portsmouth
2.50 Andover Jcn		2.50	Swindon Town
2.48 Basingstoke	3.22	3.24	Salisbury
3.36 Andover Jcn		3.36	Southampton C.
1.53 Portsmouth	3.29		
3.15 Salisbury	3.39	3.41	Waterloo
3.0 Waterloo	4.18	4.20	Plymouth etc
2.53 Portsmouth	4.29		
4.5 Salisbury	4.36	4.40	Waterloo
2.0 Cheltenham Lansdown	4.37	4.42	Southampton T.
4.48 Andover Jcn		4.48	Eastleigh
12.20 Ilfracombe	5.16	5.18	Waterloo
4.48 Basingstoke	5.24	5.26	Yeovil Town
4.26 Southampton Terminus	5.29		
4.50 Southampton Terminus	5.41	5.43	Cheltenham Ldn
5.42 Andover Jcn		5.42	Portsmouth
5.15 Salisbury	5.47	5.51	Waterloo
4.49 Swindon Town	6.5		
5.42 Eastleigh	6.31		
5.0 Waterloo	6.37	6.39	Exeter Central
6.39 Andover Jcn		6.39	Portsmouth
2.20 Ilfracombe	6.46	6.48	Waterloo
6.0 Waterloo	7.20	7.22	Exeter
5.39 Waterloo	7.41	7.47	Salisbury
6.3 Portsmouth	7.43		
7.47 Andover Jcn		7.47	Portsmouth
5.25 Cheltenham Lansdown	8.24		
6.53 Portsmouth	8.32		
3.50 Plymouth Friary	8.35	8.38	Waterloo
8.42 Andover Jcn		8.42	Portsmouth
6.54 Waterloo	9.7	9.10	Yeovil Town
8.44 Salisbury	9.14	9.16	Woking
7.53 Portsmouth	9.29		
9.42 Andover Jcn		9.42	Portsmouth
8.53 Portsmouth	10.29	10.31	Salisbury
8.54 Waterloo	11.5	11.7	Salisbury

Peterborough between 1927 and 1935. Much of this traffic ran via Andover Junction and in later years all of it. In earlier years, there was traffic such as pig iron and coal to Tasker's Siding between Andover Town and Clatford, Messrs Taskers producing traction engines still to be seen to this day at steam fairs. As revealed in the 1877 Traffic Committee minutes earlier, Tasker's traction engines were loaded on to flat trucks at Andover Junction station by railway staff for delivery to customers.

Extra facilities were required for sheep and timber traffic. The latter was still extensive in the 1950s, much of it received for the timber yard on the Up side of the line. The large goods shed, with its two tracks, took a considerable amount and it required speedy handling. There were daily road van services from Nine Elms, Salisbury and Southampton conveying smaller consignments overnight for delivery next morning to customers in the town. On

Southampton Line passenger trains departing Andover Junction

1867	1888	1909	1947	1964
3	6	10	9	16

occasion more than one van was required. In 1909 no less than three Down fast goods trains from Nine Elms called in the early hours to detach these and other wagons at Andover Junction. In 1929 the Southern Railway agreed to provide a roof over a dead end siding at the west end of the goods yard and also to develop a railhead distribution centre. Four other stations were chosen with selected staff made 'canvassers' and provided with a car.

The area around Andover has a reputation for high quality barley ideal for malting, as well as wheat suitable for milling into flour. The goods handled here thus reflected this. In the 1960s a feature of the loading dock was the mobile Archimedes screw apparatus used for transferring grain between wagons and lorries. In season many wagons were received loaded with bags of fertilisers for distribution to local farms. These local farms also required a wide variety of agricultural machinery. Some was produced locally, at the Acre Iron Works off the Millway Road, and some from Taskers works. Raw materials, for the iron works and saw mills, also came by train.

In the 1960s it was reported that that the McDougalls mill, adjacent to the goods yard, produced about 75 tons of flour per day from the milling of about 100 tons of local wheat and that this traffic had been running for more than 50 years. At the McDougalls mill, cardboard boxes were filled with one and three-pound bags of self-raising flour for grocery shops all over the country. The boxes were carted to the goods yard where they were loaded into covered vans – eight to ten vanloads of flour were forwarded from Andover daily.

Barley for malting went to distilleries in Scotland and in season wagons loaded

Andover Junction shed in the 1950s with an ex-GWR 2-6-2T No. 5536 (used on the MSWJR line) and Drummond 0-6-0 No.30368 used for local freight work. Coaling by hand was hard and dirty physical work. George Powell.

with sugar beet were sent by local farmers to processing plants at places such as Kidderminster. The huge grain silo, a short distance down the line, had its own siding between 1943 and 1962. It was latterly operated by the Southern Counties Agricultural Trading Society (the 'SCATS'

mentioned earlier) and large quantities of grain were dealt with by both rail and road.

From 1943, when the new Red Post Junction opened, the normal arrangement for handling traffic between there and Andover Junction was that all Great Western trains originating or terminating at Andover Junction used the ex-MSWJR

single track. All trains to or from the Test Valley line and Southampton ran along the Southern double track main line and crossed to the Weyhill line at Red Post Junction. During and after the 1939-45 War the stiff 1 in 81 then 1 in 62 gradient, between Andover Town and Andover Junction, proved too heavy for some MSWJR line freights from

On 24th May 1956 T9 No.30117 arrives at the Down platform with the 6.39am goods train from Eastleigh, a regular T9 duty scheduled to arrive at 11.55am. When the lines are clear the T9 will pull forward to the Weyhill Road bridge, shunt back over the crossover to the Up line and then into the sidings. J. T. Rendell, The Transport Treasury.

On 1st September 1952 at Andover (the box is Andover Junction A) Merchant Navy class 4-6-2 No. 35001 *Channel Packet* arrives with the 5.0pm Waterloo to Yeovil Junction semi-fast. Drummond T9 class 4-4-0 No.30287 waits to leave with the 6.40pm to Eastleigh, substituting for the usual L1 class. H.C.Casserley.

Southampton. These heavy trains carried both troops and munitions and, once the war was at an end, bananas from Southampton Docks. An assisting engine was sent out from Andover Junction shed to Fullerton Junction where it was coupled to the rear of the goods train: *'The signalman at Andover Junction B must accept the train over the down main line to his down starting signal at which signal the train must be stopped and the assisting locomotive detached.'* After detachment of the assisting locomotive the train ran Down the Southern main line to Red Post Junction where it crossed over to the Weyhill line.

Freight Traffic after the 1960s

The connection to the Ludgershall branch by means of a trailing crossover from the Up line (operated by ground frame since

On 30th April 1928 Adams 460 class 4-4-0 No.0478 shunts wagons under the eye of the signalman in Andover Junction West signal box. H.C.Casserley.

1973) has been used by military traffic as and when required. Block instruments have been replaced by 'one engine in steam' arrangements.

The connection has also been used to gain access to what sidings still remain today in the area once occupied by the engine shed and for the occasional enthusiasts' special trains including those hauled by steam engines. On 10th August 1992 a van was derailed on to its side during shunting when points were wrongly set, a brake-down crane and crew coming from Eastleigh to put the vehicle back on the track. The ground frame was damaged by the derailed van.

On 17th September 1992 a goods train from Eastleigh to Dagenham via the Laverstock curve loaded with new Ford Transit vans was halted at Andover when an overheated axle box burst into flames. Two fire engines arrived and put out the fire but commuters were held up for an hour.

Although many stations lost all their freight traffic during the 1960s this did not happen at Andover. The small goods yard on the Up side was retained and the goods shed remained in use for sundries, or parcels traffic. Up to a dozen vans were recorded here in photographs up to about 1982 when the traffic eventually ended. At this stage Andover was a collection and distribution depot with consignments received for road distribution to customers over a wide area.

Vans ran to and from Basingstoke, Swindon and many other depots.

After the engine shed closed in 1962 the site was redeveloped but the sidings were retained. In May 1969 a large new warehouse was constructed for Shellstar and bags of fertiliser were delivered by train,

Goods & Milk Trains Weekdays 1909

Train	Andover Jcn arr.	Andover Jcn dep.	To
11.20 Basingstoke	12.3am	12.45am	Salisbury
9.58 Nine Elms	1.55	2.5	Salisbury
8.25 Exeter	2.40	2.55	Nine Elms
12.25 Nine Elms	3.13	3.30	Yeovil
1.0 Yeovil Jcn	5.0	5.20	Woking
3.0 Waterloo milk	5.24	5.29	Yeovil
CheltenhamMSWJ	5.48	6.3	Southampton
2.40 Nine Elms	6.3	6.30	Yeovil
4.0 Woking	6.45	7.10	Salisbury
6.15 Salisbury	7.30	8.30	Whitchurch
CheltenhamMSWJ	8.30	8.35	Southampton
6.19 Yeovil milk	8.42	8.51	Waterloo
7.47 H'bridge cattle W/O	8.27	9.15	Basingstoke
9.20 Andover Jcn		9.20	Andover Town
10.40 And'r Town	10.45		Andover Jcn
10.45 Andover Jcn		10.45	Bulford
9.32 Eastleigh	1.52pm		Andover Jcn
3.0 Andover Jcn		3.0pm	Eastleigh
1.55 Bulford	4.13		Andover Jcn
2.35 Wm'don milk	4.35	4.52	Salisbury
4.45 Andover Jcn		4.45	Clatford
3.55 Salisbury	5.21	6.10	Basingstoke
5.40 Clatford	6.5		Andover Jcn
5.15 T'combe milk	7.53	8.3	Waterloo
7.5 Southampton MSWJ	8.12		Andover Jcn
3.55 Yeovil	9.18	10.40	Nine Elms
7.16 Yeovil milk	10.8	10.17	Waterloo
9.10 Southampton MSWJ	10.15		Andover Jcn
10.0 Salisbury	10.45	11.20	Woking
8.48 Guildford	11.21	11.26	Salisbury

On 14th May 1955 U class 2-6-0 No.31634 of Basingstoke passes Andover Junction West signal box on an Up freight, possibly the 3.0pm Amesbury to Basingstoke. Framed under Millway Road bridge is the Andover Grain Silo, which had its own siding. R.C.Riley, The Transport Treasury.

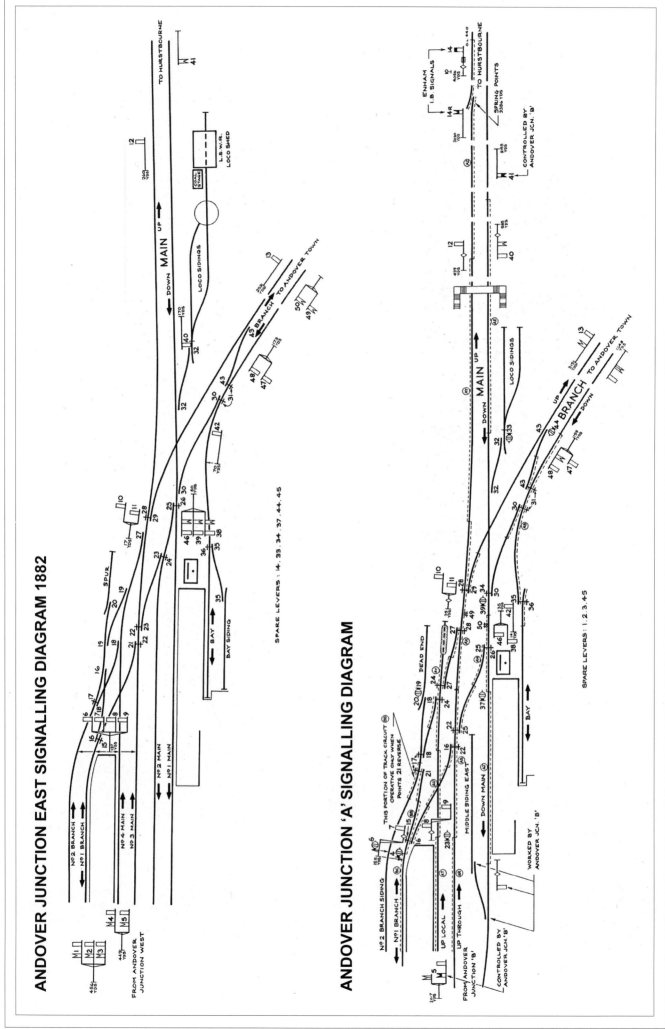

ANDOVER JUNCTION EAST SIGNALLING DIAGRAM 1882

ANDOVER JUNCTION 'A' SIGNALLING DIAGRAM

Freight Trains Weekdays Summer 1958

Train	Andover Jcn arr	Andover Jcn dep	To
3.27 Basingstoke West Yard	4.30am	4.45am	Salisbury West Yard
5.21 Plymouth	5.23	5.38	Feltham Yard
5.30 Basingstoke West Yard	6.26	6.46	Amesbury
8.15 Andover Junction		8.15	Swindon Town
8.55 Andover Junction		8.55	Andover Town
9.5 loco Andover Town	9.10		
6.48 Cheltenham	10.50	11.10	Redbridge
7.45 Basingstoke West Yard	10.50		
6.39 Eastleigh	11.55		
10.45 Salisbury East Yard	12.47	1.40	Basingstoke Up Yard
1.8 engine Andover Jcn		1.8	Overton
1.10 Andover Junction		1.10	Romsey
11.45 Beavois Park	1.10	1.30	Cheltenham
1.12 Salisbury East Yard	2.6	2.41	Basingstoke Up Yard
3.15 engine Andover Town	3.20		
9.10 Cheltenham	3.50		
2.48 Southampton Docks Q	4.10	4.15	Cheltenham
3.0 Amesbury	4.15	6.54	Basingstoke Up Yard
5.0 Andover Town	5.5		
6.10 Basingstoke West Yard	7.5	8.35	Plymouth
8.20 Cheltenham	8.3	8.50	Eastleigh

pallets being unloaded from the modern wagons by fork lift truck. This depot was later operated by UKF and then Kemira who received block loads from their plant at Ince and Elton in Cheshire. This finally succumbed with the demise of Speedlink in 1991.

Subsequently the land was sold to an international transport and distribution firm, Switch of Andover, and used as a depot for their large articulated lorry fleet. The sidings remained in situ and were used again by the newly privatised EWS rail freight company. On Wednesday 21ˢᵗ January 1998 six polybulk wagons were loaded with barley brought by lorry to the sidings and were then forwarded to Roseisle whiskey distilleries on the Burghead branch in Invernesshire. The contract for three trains a week lasted for ten weeks but was not renewed. A trial consignment of bagged fertiliser was conveyed from Great Yarmouth on 2nd December 1998 and further trains were operated on a weekly basis until 3ʳᵈ March 1999. The yard has subsequently been used for the storage of Railtrack plant.

Signalling

As we have seen, in 1862 a porter had to walk to the points to operate them but by 1870 the levers were in a frame and a box. A photograph of the 1870s shows the signal box to have been a weather-boarded structure, at platform level with no space for the interlocking which came later. Along the edge of the platform were three sets of point rodding and two signal wires. A surviving drawing of 1881 shows this box on the Down platform adjacent to the Redbridge bay buffer stops. The 'table of lever functions' shows 28 levers of which three were spare, there being Up distant, stop and starting signals, Down distant, stop, starting and advance starting signals, and Branch distant, stop and to main line stop signals. The Up stop and Down advance starting signals were mounted on opposite sides of one post to the west of the Millway Road bridge. Up and Down sidings had both point levers and point bolt levers.

The first signal box was replaced during the extensive enlargement of the station for the opening of the SMAR, two signal boxes, East and West, opening in 1882 and remaining in use with little major change until their closure in 1973. Andover Junction East signal box, 5 miles 435 yards from Hurstbourne box, and 1,247 yards from Andover Town box, was on the Down platform and was not fitted with a closing switch so was open continuously. There

Outside Andover Junction LSWR locomotive shed on 30ᵗʰ April 1928 are Adams 460 class 4-4-0s Nos.0470 with original boiler and 0473 with Drummond boiler, just months before their withdrawal. Although built in 1904 the corrugated iron clad structure is already under repair. The gentleman standing may well be the Running Shed Foreman, Mr Bull. H.C.Casserley.

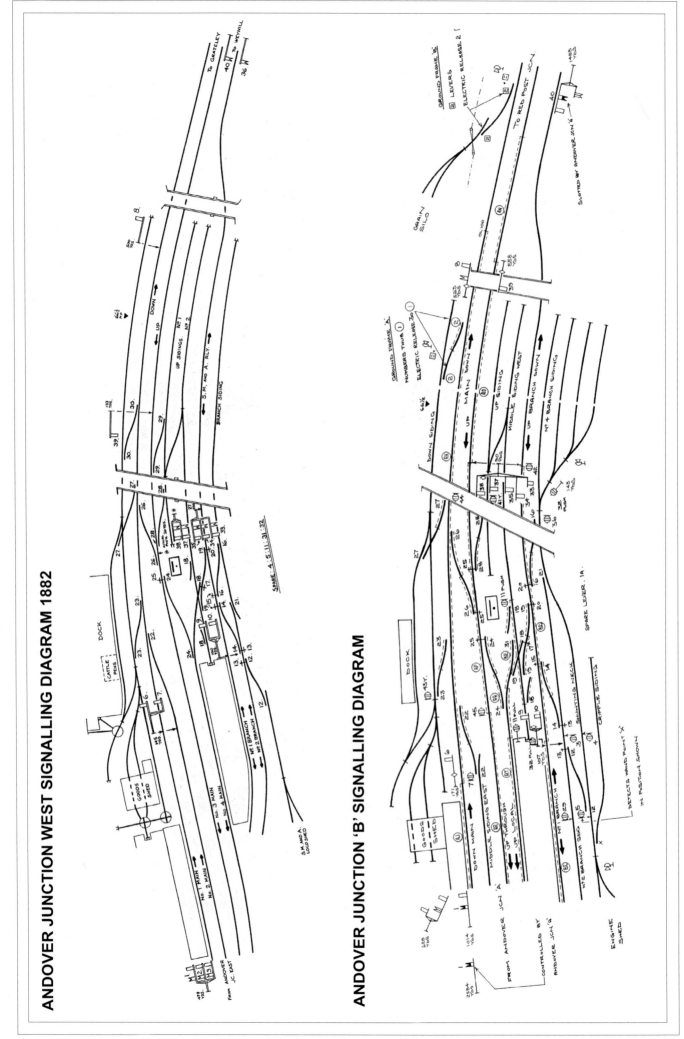

ANDOVER JUNCTION WEST SIGNALLING DIAGRAM 1882

ANDOVER JUNCTION 'B' SIGNALLING DIAGRAM

On 24th February 1952 Q1 class 0-6-0 No.33021 unloads permanent way materials on the sharply curved 1 in 62 branch down to Andover Town, the main line at Andover Junction is in the background. E.R.Morton.

were no crossover roads but there were catch points in the Up platform road, operated from the signal box, 34 yards on the Grateley side on a rising gradient of 1 in 220. Renamed Andover Junction A signal box in 1938 it was 5 miles 435 yards from Hurstbourne signal box.

Andover Junction A signal box had a Stevens frame of 50 levers, initially with Preece 3 wire block instruments on the main lines, replaced in the 1950s by BR 3 position instruments. On the branch to Andover Town and the MSWJR lines there were Preece 1 wire instruments. The complexity of the signalling arrangements can be seen from the diagrams which also show that some East box signals were slotted by the West box, and vice versa. The Andover East signalman essentially dealt with every train using the station on all four routes which required the box to be open continuously. When the connections to No.3 Down Main line were taken out in 1917, the points and signalling were simplified accordingly. Andover West signal box, 429 yards from the East box, was on the Up side at the Grateley end and was like East box open continuously. There was one crossover opposite the box. After 1938 the boxes were renamed, West becoming A and East becoming B.

It had 40 levers, originally with Preece 3 wire block instruments on the main line. These were replaced in the 1950s by BR 3 position block and Preece 1 wire instruments to A box on the MSWJR line. On the MSWJR single track to Red Post Junction, or Weyhill, Tyers No.6 tablet instruments were used. The signalling was complex with

several signals controlled by B box slotted by A box and vice versa. With the exception of trains terminating in the Southampton bay B box controlled every train through the station in conjunction with A box. However, B box had complete control of locomotive movements in and out of the engine sheds.

The B box also had two ground frames, on the Down main line. Ground Frame A was about 500 yards away and its two levers operated the points at the end of the Down siding.

It was electrically released by lever No.30 so that a porter, acting under the signalman's instructions, could operate the points. Similarly Ground Frame B, 32 chains away, operated the points for the Grain Silo Sidings and was electrically released by lever No.2. Both A and B boxes closed on 2nd December 1973 when control of the now much simplified layout passed to the Basingstoke panel.

Locomotives

Over the years Andover Junction was served by no less than four engine sheds. The first, temporary, shed and turntable appeared in 1854 when the station opened as a terminus; once the line opened to Salisbury in 1857 it was no longer required and was re-erected at Basingstoke in 1858. The turntable remained. Following the opening of the Redbridge line in 1865, the South Western paid William Gue & Son £511 1s 8d in June 1866 for building a new shed and coaling stage. This was apparently on the same site as the original of 1854 and adjacent to the turntable, in the V between the main line

and Redbridge branch. This second building was destroyed by fire in 1899, a fate often suffered by early wooden sheds; apparently the engine sidings remained in use until a new shed opened in 1904.

In the meantime a third engine shed had been built, this time for the Swindon Marlborough & Andover Railway for its opening in 1882. It was constructed at the end of the strip of land to the north of the South Western line and comprised a two road shed adjacent to the Up main line and a third track serving the coal stage and a 51ft turntable. Early SMAR locomotives were small tank engines but by the end of the independent life of the MSWJR most were 4-4-0s and 0-6-0s. The turntable was South Western property and they charged the SMAR and later the MSWJR one shilling to turn an engine. The shed, about 65ft by 35ft, had weather-boarded wooden sides and a slated roof with four smoke vents.

MSWJR locomotives and crews worked their own line and services over LSWR metals to Southampton via Eastleigh and Redbridge and would turn and take water at Southampton. MSWJR men from Andover shed knew both the routes to Southampton, often taking over from Cheltenham men here for the final leg of the journey but when a MSWJR excursion train ran to Portsmouth a South Western pilotman was beyond Eastleigh. There was a steady flow of MSWJR locomotives arriving at Andover with trains from Tidworth, Swindon and Cheltenham and locomotives came on shed for servicing before the return journey. In 1884 the SMAR allocated three small tank

Railwaymen outside the porters' room next to the goods shed at Andover Junction in the 1960s. Left to right Jerry Jerome (porter/shunter), George Adcock (porter), Cyril Gale (porter), John Lancefield (porter/shunter). Ron Grace.

engines here to cover two duties, in 1922 the MSWJR allocated five locomotives here, and in 1923 the GWR four. Details of the 1884 and 1923 locomotive duties are given in Chapter Ten.

The 'fourth' shed, a replacement for the one destroyed by fire, was authorised by the South Western board in 1903 at a cost of £2,550 and opened the following year. The new LSW shed was built on land to the north of what was now the MSWJR shed; it had two roads and was about 140ft by 35ft, built in corrugated iron on a steel frame, with two long sidings to the north, one

Railwaymen at Andover Junction Reg White (porter, left) and Jerry Jerome (porter/signalman). Ron Grace.

serving the coal stage. Locomotives of both companies used the 51ft turntable but an extra MSWJR siding was laid in behind their coal stage so that their coal wagons did not block access to the turntable. Later an awning was constructed over the coal stage and it appears that locomotives may have been coaled direct from waiting trucks. The two sheds were independent concerns in most respects, sharing the turntable and water supply. There were very harmonious relationships between the two companies and when they were short of stock the MSWJR often hired LSWR locomotives and coaches. In the 1906-1910 period two railmotors, for the Fullerton and Whitchurch service, were based at Andover and there were problems in keeping the passenger coach section clean within the dirty confines of a running shed.

Water was pumped from a well behind the East signal box to one (later two) tanks between the station house and the goods shed on the Down platform. There was a pump house at the bottom of the embankment and a coal shute enabled coal for the steam pumping engine to be delivered direct from a wagon in the bay siding.

At the station there were four water columns, with a further two at the engine sheds. The 'dual arrangements' at the engine sheds continued with the Southern and Great Western until early BR days when both came under SR management. The ex-MSWJR shed (sub to Swindon) closed in 1958 and the Southern one followed in 1962. In 1922 the

South Western allocated three locomotives to Andover, one for the Fullerton-Whitchurch branch, a second for the first passenger train to Southampton, and the third for station piloting, local goods trips to Andover Town, Clatford and Bulford. The Southern Railway Running Department returns of 1926 show 29 men employed at the shed, including ten pairs of drivers and firemen. By the 1930s it was a outstation of Eastleigh, with no allocation of its own.

In 1952 Andover Junction had five locomotive duties, two for T9 4-4-0s working on the Hampshire lines, two for ex-GWR 43XX 2-6-0s on the MSWJR route and one for a new BR class 2 2-6-2T between Ludgershall and Southampton.

Andover Junction men worked as far as Fullerton Junction, Horsebridge and Eastleigh, where they changed over with Eastleigh crews. One duty took them to Tidworth and back. Duty No.269 with a 43XX 2-6-0 took one Andover crew to Southampton Terminus and back on the 10.10am passenger to Cheltenham, relieved at Andover Junction by a second crew. These worked all the way to Cheltenham, returning with a freight.

Andover Junction men worked to and from Bulford, with a Basingstoke 700 class and with WR locos from Swindon and Cheltenham between Marlborough, Savernake, Romsey and Southampton. Western Region men from Swindon and Cheltenham worked through to Andover Junction but not beyond. Full details are given in Chapter Ten.

Later in the 1950s the SR duties were reduced when the 'Hampshire' DMUs took over the Stockbridge line and the branch from Fullerton closed. When the 'GW' shed closed in 1958 the few remaining locomotives and duties were transferred to the 'Southern' shed until final closure in 1962 although the 'GW' building remained in situ.

Final closure came as no surprise when it was announced in April 1962, following the dieselisation of the Southampton line and closure of the MSWJR to all services but the odd freight to Ludgershall. At this time the shed employed ten crews and a labourer for shovelling coal and ash. Twelve of the footplate staff were offered work at Basingstoke, Salisbury and Eastleigh after closure, on 18th June 1962.

Staff

As the principal station between Basingstoke and Salisbury Andover Junction had a substantial establishment of its own, together with supervisory and rest day relief men for the surrounding district. Up to the mid-1960s the Stationmaster was in charge of Andover Junction, but under the new managerial system the post became Station Manager.

In the passenger station there were booking office staff covering early and late turns with one on duty at quiet times and two, or even three, when the station was busy. The total complement of booking staff therefore was some five or six clerks. One or two porters handled parcels and a wide variety of small consignments, up to the size of milk churns, between platform and the luggage compartments of trains. Often such consignments had to be transferred between trains.

In the goods yard a number of porters were kept busy loading and unloading wagons, along with a goods checker and a number of delivery drivers.

Passenger and goods guards for both companies were stationed at Andover and shunters were required for all sorts of duties in the goods yard.

Both signal boxes were open continuously on a three shift system, so an establishment of about eight men was required, together with relief signalmen who could work not only the Andover boxes but many others in the area as required. A number of other staff were based at Andover Junction, including the area Permanent Way Inspector, gangers and their teams of platelayers, a team of Signalling and Telegraph maintenance linemen, a railway plumber and railway policeman. The Andover Junction Permanent Way Inspector supervised the main line track gangs from Whitchurch to Grateley stations. From Overton and above was in the Basingstoke area whilst below Amesbury Junction came under Salisbury. He also had responsibility for some of the branch in the direction of Kimbridge Junction.

We know that the Station Agent, Mr Verrinder, rose to become LSWR Superintendent of the Line in 1874. By 1876 the Andover Station Agent was Mr Bainton, who retired in 1882 when 80 subscribers held a dinner in the Star and Garter Hotel and presented him with 20 guineas, a gold watch and chain. In 1889 the post had become Stationmaster.

The incumbent was a Mr William James Hill in 1895, Mr Robert Murray in 1915, Mr E.Jerome in 1916-1925, Mr Owen 1925-1932, Mr William Ward, in 1932-1936 Mr H.Tate, from 1937 to 1940 Mr G.Voller and in 1948 Mr H.F.Rose. Andover Town always had its own Stationmaster, who for many years also supervised Clatford. Up to about 1930 Andover shed had its own Locomotive Foreman; in 1923-1927 this was a Mr Bull, but subsequently it came under the Eastleigh Running Shed Superintendent.

About 1960 the staff at Andover Junction included:
Stationmaster Mr Tom Elkins, who had replaced Mr Lester Whitmore
Station Inspectors Mr Jack Fleming, Mr Gus Gilbert
Booking Office staff Mr Jack Cornelius
Parcels Office staff Mr Bill Philimore, Mr Dowling
Ticket Collectors Mr Les Cook, Mr Cliff Parker
Porters Mr Williams, Mr Williams, Mr Adcock, Mr Crumplin, Mr Churchill, Mr Guyatt, Mt Tarbart
Signalmen Mr George Yates, Mr Bill Bendall, Mr Cyril Hawkins, Mr Allan Hawkins
Permanent Way Inspector Mr Ted Ireson
Permanent Way Sub-Inspector Mr Dan Carter
Permanent Way Timekeeper Mr Edward Yarlett

Guard Harry Wheeler in a 'Hampshire' diesel at Andover Junction. Ron Grace.

Passenger Guards 4 including Harry Wheeler and Walter Tull
Goods Guards 4 including Mr Ernie Newman
Travelling Shunter Mr Ron Bundy
Shedmaster Mr Minard Wigmore, who was a local magistrate
Drivers Mr Dick Pemble, Mr Dick Hawkins, Mr Dan Carter(junior)
Refreshment Room staff Mrs Bashford
W.H.Smiths bookstall Mr Charlie Gosling, who was with the firm for 48 years

As we have seen, the Stationmaster and his family usually lived upstairs in the station house but by 1960 the incumbent Mr Tom Elkins lived in Cross Lane opposite the station. One of the signalmen, Mr Hughes, lived in the station house itself. There was also a block of four railway cottages built by the South Western in Charlton Road, adjacent to bridge No.186. From 1968 the Andover 'Station Manager' was Mr Reg Twigg, until he was transferred to Salisbury in 1982.

Peter Yarlett's uncle, Mr Edward Yarlett, started as a toolboy on the Southern Railway and joined the Permanent Way Institution as a student member in 1932. He eventually became the timekeeper in the Permanent Way Inspector's office at Andover, finally retiring in 1982, aged 71. He sold the BR staff magazine in the Andover area, up to 130 copies a month. Mr Ernie Newman was instrumental in setting up the British Railways Staff Association, which had its clubroom in the Station Approach. He organised social events

including the 'Railway Kids' Christmas Party'.

Accidents

There were four major accidents at Andover Junction, all involving Up freight trains running into the rear of stationary trains but fortunately without loss of life. These occurred in 1914, 1916, 1929 and 1943 and are described in Chapters Four and Five respectively. On 1st December 1944 some wagons were derailed during shunting and the yard foreman, Mr Albert Henry Newman, was badly injured losing his left leg below the knee and three fingers, despite immediate first aid from railwaymen and staff from McDougall's Mill.

Andover Today

Since the 1950s much of Andover has changed, almost beyond recognition, as the town has expanded with many more offices and industries and more houses for the increased population. Complete new road systems have now been built and as a result it is almost impossible to detect the course of the first mile of the Southampton line from Andover Junction. New concrete bridges carry the line over the new Artists Way and Redon Way built in the 1970s.

Replacing the signal boxes in 1973, a 10 lever frame was opened near the site of B box to control the remaining connections, comprising a trailing crossover between the main lines and between the Up line and the MSWJR lines. Most Ludgershall goods trains run direct from Eastleigh to Andover using the Laverstock curve at Salisbury and

on arrival in the Up platform they shunt back into the sidings where the locomotive runs round before proceeding to Ludgershall. For the return journey to Eastleigh, via the Laverstock curve, the train departs from the Up platform across the trailing crossover to the Down line. When Ministry of Defence trains arrive in the Down direction, often from Didcot, they run through the station to halt clear of the trailing crossover, reverse over the crossover on to the Up main line and then pull forward over the trailing crossover to the MSWJR sidings. The return journey to Didcot requires no reversals.

The main station buildings have remained almost intact and have been refurbished, although those on the Up side have been reduced by about half. In 1985 there were 279 season ticket holders at Andover and 28,228 other tickets were sold. In the goods yard 68 loaded wagons were forwarded for Cornflow Ltd. and 310 loaded wagons were received for UKF fertilisers. In 1987 one of the town's major employers, TSB, contributed to the renovation of the station house and other buildings and this is recorded on a plaque on the Up platform, now No.1. The old clock with two faces on the Down platform, now No.2, had become unreliable and showed different times to those on the new digital clocks. In 1989 however, it was restored by staff of 34 Field Workshops REME Donnington. The goods shed and yard on the Down side have given way to a large car park. In 1993 the Down platform was extended at the west end and the Up platform at the east end, using standard concrete components. The levels were raised so that they can both now accommodate a nine coach class 159 multiple

The manager of W.H.Smith's bookstall at Andover Junction Mr Charlie Gosling, well known in the town and at his previous post at Templecombe. His son-in-law and daughter Ron and Jill Grace have greatly assisted the authors in researching this book. Ron Grace Collection.

Andover Junction permanent way gang and trolley in the 1930s with Ganger Mr Ted Yarlett wearing the trilby hat. Peter Yarlett Collection.

West of Andover Junction was the Andover Grain Silo Siding, brought into use in 1943. By the 1950s the silo was operated by SCATS (Southern Counties Agricultural Trading Society) which forwarded and received grain by rail. Here there were three running lines Up, Down, and (MSWJR) Branch with houses in the Avenue on the far side. In 1962 the Down evening stopping train was hauled by an unidentified Battle of Britain class 4-6-2 with McDougalls flour mill is behind the train. Rod Hoyle.

unit train. On the platforms, screens advise real time train details. The newsagent's kiosk on the Down platform, installed by W.H.Smith a century before, was gutted by fire in January 1995 but was subsequently replaced by a small shop in an old office.

Dominating the station area to this day is the tall white flour mill of Rank Hovis McDougall, served by road transport although the large articulated lorries arriving here have to carefully reverse into the loading bays from Millway Road. The timber yard to the north of the line has now become the premises of Jewsons, the builders' merchants, while Switch lorries drive down the road on the Up side of the line to their depot. The Junction Hotel and railway cottages in Charlton Road have been demolished, with a new Baptist Church built on the cottage site. For railwaymen the British Railways Staff Association remains in the Station Approach. In 2001 Andover won the national Station of the Year Award, reflecting both the structural improvements made and the highly motivated railwaymen and women, three working in the booking office and two on the platform. The staff include Moira Kellett in the booking office and Rob McDonald on the platform. The station comes under the Salisbury manager Kevin Whiting. The present weekday train service of 31 trains to Waterloo is the best ever, with times between 63 and 75 minutes depending on the number of stops. Although a couple of Wessex trains from Cardiff speed through non-stop, all South West trains call and there is an increasing level of travel to and from Andover.

ANDOVER SILO SIDING
Chronology
Ground frame (66miles 62 chains from Waterloo) and siding brought into use 28th January 1943.
Ground frame and siding taken out of use 17th September 1962.

Description
A short distance beyond the Weyhill Road bridge, No.188, on the Down side, was the large grain silo run by the Southern Counties Agricultural Trading Society, known as SCATS – as already mentioned above. Inside the siding gate the line split into two, connected at the end with a crossover. In 1945 it was reported that the siding received about twelve loaded wagons a day, mainly from Avonmouth or Salisbury, which were worked to Andover Junction. Here they were attached to a Down freight train which shunted them into the siding and took away the empties. On weekdays in summer 1958 the 5.30am freight from Basingstoke West Yard to Amesbury was scheduled to shunt Andover Grain Siding, when required, after leaving Andover Junction at 6.46am. The following is a BR notice from 1960: *'Silo Siding. This siding is on the down side between Andover Junction and Grateley with access by a trailing connection in the down line. The points are operated from a ground frame controlled from Andover Junction B signal box and the working is in accordance with electrical release lever control arrangements.'* The silo remains to this day, run by Banks Cargill, with all grain conveyed in and out by lorries using an access road

from Weyhill Road just to the south of the line.

From Andover Junction to Red Post Junction
For the mile from Andover Junction there were three tracks, the single MSWJR line to the north of the Up and Down main lines. The line was on a rising gradient of 1 in 220 on first a very gentle right hand curve of 200 chains radius, then left at 130 chains.

The Andover Junction B Up home signal was in advance of the Weyhill Road bridge No.188. Emerging from a cutting the line was at ground level near the Grain Silo Siding and then into another low cutting before reaching Red Post Junction. On 21st December 1922 the South Western decided to close a level crossing at Abbotts Ann if the tenants could use the stiles installed instead. Years later a footbridge was provided. By around 1970 a new concrete bridge, No.188A, had been built to carry the new A303 dual carriageway Andover Bypass over the line.

RED POST JUNCTION
Chronology
Temporary junction and first signal box (approx. 67 miles 70 chains from Waterloo) opened May 1882.
Third line from Andover Junction opened, as single line Andover to Weyhill, signal box and all points taken out of use 19th November 1882.
Loop siding on MSWJR opened 22nd October 1917.

On 14th May 1955 ex-GWR 2-6-0 No.5367 arrives at Red Post Junction with a freight on the double track MSWJR line. The locomotive slows to collect from the signalman the Tyers No.6 token for the single line to Andover Junction where it will terminate. The austere wartime signal box opened with the junction in 1943, the previous 1919 box and junction having been removed in 1936. R.C.Riley, The Transport Treasury.

Second signal box (67 miles 74 chains from Waterloo), MSWJR loop, and new junction opened 5th January 1919.
Junction taken out of use 19th September 1936.
MSWJR loop and all MSWJR points and signals taken out of use 27th September 1936, signal box controlling main line signals only.
Second signal box closed 4th April 1937.
New junction and third signal box (67 miles 68 chains from Waterloo) opened 5th September 1943.
Third signal box closed 1st September 1963.

1919-1937

There had been a temporary junction at Red Post for a few months after the SMAR opened in 1882. This was taken out and the SMAR, and later MSWJR, had a single line section of 3 miles 38 chains from Andover

Red Post Junction on 10th September 1961 with an S.L.S. Special from Birmingham hauled by No.7808 Cookham Manor. Sid Nash.

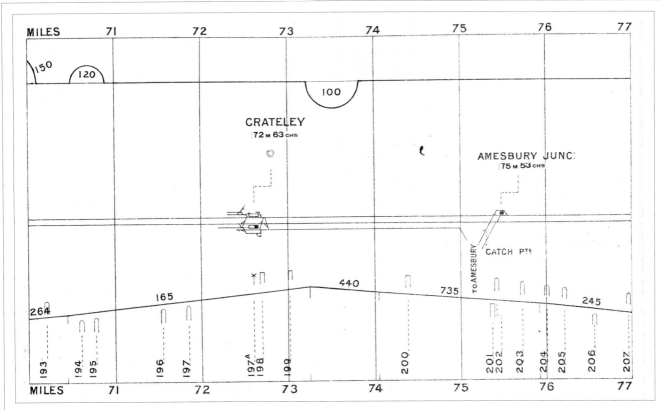

Junction to Weyhill diverging from the South Western here.

Between 1902 and 1919 this section of the main line, as far as Grateley, was controlled by the automatic pneumatic block signalling installed in 1902 and described in Chapter Four. There were six block sections each about a mile long protected by home and distant signals on a single post. During the 1914-18 war traffic on the MSWJR increased greatly to the extent that there were delays on this section. In 1917 a second signal box was installed to control a passing loop on the MSWJR and 1919 a junction with the LSWR. This box, built to the attractive standard South Western design of the period, was in the V between the two lines, with pedestrian access by a footbridge over the MSWJR. The layout comprised a pair of double junctions, one facing South Western Down trains the other MSWJR Up trains.

As an economy measure the junction was taken out of use on 19th September 1936 and on 27th September the MSWJR crossing loop was taken out too, the box closing on 4th April 1937. Now, for the time being at

On 14th May 1955 Urie S15 4-6-0 No.30504 passes Red Post Junction, apparently with the 10.48am Feltham Yard to Salisbury West Yard goods. The two tracks in the foreground are MSWJR with the two SR lines in the background. R.C.Riley, The Transport Treasury.

An imperfect but nevertheless interesting view of Red Post Junction towards the end of MSWJR services, in the summer of 1961. Ex-GWR 2-6-0 No.5306 and a three coach train approach the Junction signal box. At this stage all the points had been disconnected, there was single track working between Andover Junction and Weyhill. The signal box controlled only main line signals, the other arms having being removed. Rod Hoyle.

least, just the Southern two track main line and the Great Western single track branch diverged here.

Signalling 1919-1937

Red Post Junction signal box, 1 mile 653 chains from Andover West and 1 mile 1,685 yards from Weyhill box, was fitted with a closing switch which enabled it to be switched out when not required. There were no crossovers or catch points.

This LSW box had a 28 lever frame controlling the points for the double junction between the LSWR and MSWJR, the MSWJR loop and the signals. On the LSWR there were Up distant, outer home and inner home signals, and Down distant, home with two dolls carrying the junction arms and starting signals. On the MSWJR there were distant, home and starting signals in both directions, the Up home having two arms for the junction. On the main line there were Sykes' lock and block instruments and on the single line branch Tyers No.6 instruments, to both Andover Junction and Weyhill.

On 4th April 1937 two-aspect colour light signals were brought into use. These comprised Red Post Intermediate Down home and distant signals (controlled by Andover Junction West box) and Red Post Intermediate Up home and distant signals (controlled by Grateley box). It would appear that these four were the first colour light signals to be installed on the West of England main line. Full details appear in Chapter Five.

1944-1963

During the 1939-45 war there was again a great increase in traffic passing to the Great Western and a similar solution was implemented. Arrangements differed from 1919 in that this time the single line from Red Post Junction to Weyhill was doubled.

The new signal box was located to the north of the Great Western line and 270 yards nearer Andover than the 1919 box. This rather ugly box was built in brick with a flat roof to a standard austerity wartime design and was 1 mile 383 yards from Andover Junction B box. There was a 15mph speed limit in both directions through the junction for Ludgershall trains.

Signalling 1944-1963

The 1944 Red Post Junction signal box had a Westinghouse A2 frame with 22 levers. On the main line it controlled distant, home and starting signals, the Down home having two dolls with the junction signal arms. The

Great Western line signals were similar. Now only the Great Western line to Andover Junction West was single and was regulated with the Tyers No.6 instruments. The main line was controlled with Preece 3-wire block

About 1958 the fireman of an MSWJR stopping train to Swindon hands over the Tyers No.6 token for the single track from Andover Junction to the Red Post Junction signalman. Rod Hoyle.

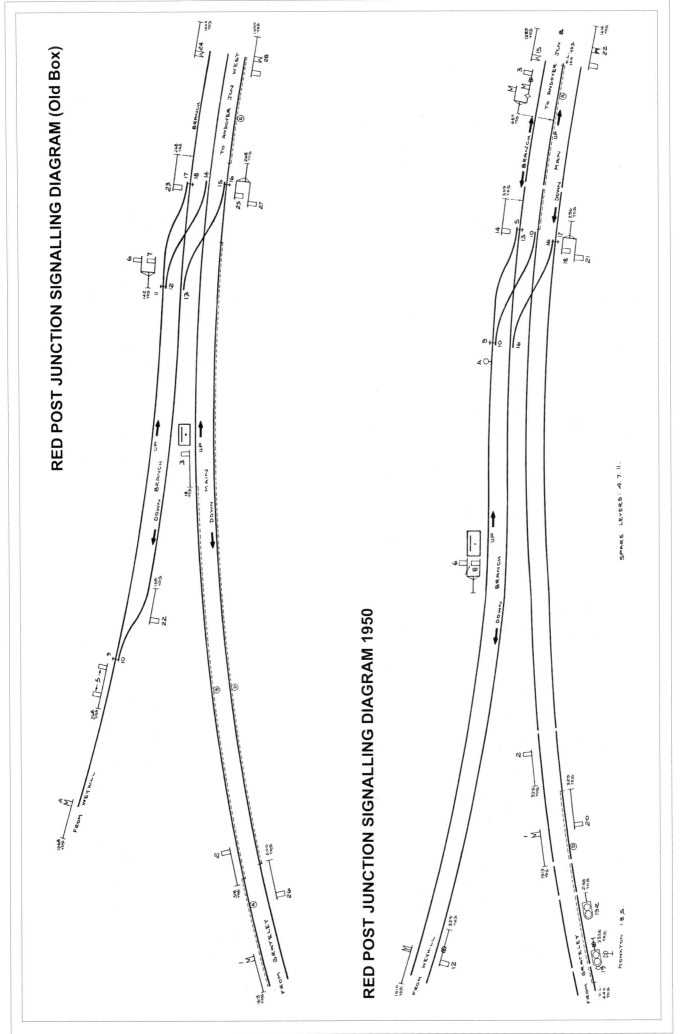

RED POST JUNCTION SIGNALLING DIAGRAM (Old Box)

RED POST JUNCTION SIGNALLING DIAGRAM 1950

Merchant Navy class No. 35016 Elders Fyffes heads west near Red Post Junction on 14th May 1955. R C Riley, The Transport Treasury.

instruments and the double track to Weyhill with Tyers' 3 position block. During and after the Second World War the box was open continuously and very busy indeed. It was later equipped with a closing switch, which enabled it to be switched out when the GW line was closed. As we have seen at Andover during this period, Great Western trains originating or terminating at Andover Junction used the single track former MSWJR line, whilst those to and from the Test Valley line used the Southern main line, crossing over at Red Post Junction. This changed on 28th August 1960 when the double track line to Weyhill was again singled and all the junctions again taken out of use. Red Post Junction signal box now ceased to control the Andover to Weyhill line but retained its signals on the main line. Prior to closure, on 1st September 1963, the box was little used and was switched out for long periods with all signals pulled to the off position.

From Red Post Junction to Monxton

On 10th September 1868 the LSW declined a request to build a station near Red Post for Weyhill Fair traffic. Leaving Red Post Junction the line now began to fall gently at 1 in 330 for about a mile curving gently on 130 chains to the south. On a low gradient the Red Post Junction Up home and Down starting signals were passed and at Milepost 68 the line crossed a minor road leading to Abbotts Ann near Little Park Farm on bridge No.189. The line continued through a low cutting and passed the Red Post Junction Up distant signal and emerged from the cutting to cross a valley on a straight alignment over Monxton Viaduct. A couple

of miles down the valley was the Waterloo Ironworks of Taskers, previously mentioned. Monxton Viaduct, No.190, comprised five spans of 40 feet and took the line over a minor road and Pillhill Brook, close to an old mill. Two railway cottages here were apparently purchased by the South Western from the contractor Thomas Brassey in 1856.

One of the Monxton cottages was occupied by Mr Henry Yarlett, one time ganger on the Southern Railway, up to his retirement in 1949 at the age of 70 years. Normal retirement at this time was of course 65 but his was delayed by the War. His grandson Peter has many memories of the cottages. One wall of the outside privy was a pier of the viaduct and the whole structure shook badly every time a train passed overhead, a very frightening experience for a five year old boy inside. The original water supply was hoisted up in a bucket from a well but in the early 1950s British Railways replaced it with a traditional cast iron pump. Waste water from both the house and the privy was discharged straight into the Pillhill Brook which ran through the garden. On his retirement, Henry Yarlett had to leave his cottage and live with his family in Andover. Today the railway scene at Monxton has changed little but for the construction of several more houses. Below the viaduct there are extensive watercress beds in the Pillhill Brook valley operated by Vitacress, something that was impossible in the earlier era of primitive sanitation.

As the line left the valley near Moxton village it started to climb again at a 1 in 264 gradient on a curve of 120 chains radius. The line ran into a low cutting behind the village here and bridge No.191 carried a

minor road over the line shortly after passing milepost 69. The line continued to climb steadily to the south at 1 in 264 and at the end began a long curve to the north at 150 chains radius. After a section at ground level it ran out on to a low embankment and passed over a country lane running south from Monxton on bridge No.192 and passed milepost 70. Near here was the site of Monxton signal box.

MONXTON
Chronology
Monxton signal box (approx.70 miles from Waterloo) opened 1898. Box closed 13th October 1901.

Description

On 6th July 1898 the South Western Traffic Committee decided to build Monxton signal box, at a cost of £209. Its purpose was to break up the long block section, 6 miles 40 chains, between Andover Junction West and Grateley. In August and September 1898 it was open continuously for several days dealing with traffic in connection with the army manoeuvres. It was closed in 1901 when the new automatic signalling of this section of the line was brought into use. A 1901 District Engineer's drawing shows Monxton signal box at about 69 miles 75 chains from Waterloo, adjacent to bridge No.192. The automatic signalling itself was taken out of use on 5th January 1919 when the second Red Post Junction signal box was opened.

In *The Railway Magazine* of June 1941 there was a photograph of the small box, a ground level weather-boarded cabin no more than eight feet square, and the following notes from the photographer the

Rev.H.M.Marshall: *'In 1898, when there was a review held on Salisbury Plain, Monxton box was opened to shorten the block between Andover Junction and Grateley. The signalman in charge told me that on the review day, when trains were running at intervals of a few minutes, Mr G.T.White, then Superintendent of the Line, LSWR, got out of a train which was being held, and ordered the signalman to pull off the signals and pass him through to the next section – a most reprehensible action. The signalman, I presume, had to report what had happened.'*

The article continued by recording that the LSWR often installed temporary block posts for use when traffic was heavy and, on the occasion of Queen Victoria's Diamond Jubilee in 1897, many were brought into use on the main line.

It would appear that Monxton signal box had a Stevens frame of at least four levers to operate distant and home signals in both directions. Preece 1 wire block instruments were in use between Andover Junction West and Grateley, and there was a closing switch so that the box could be normally switched out with the signals 'off' and opened up when traffic was heavy. It is likely that a signalman was sent from Andover Junction to operate the box when required and that the Andover Junction Stationmaster was responsible for its supervision and any supplies, such as coal for the stove.

In spring 1961 Schools class 4-4-0 No.30925 *Cheltenham* approaches bridge No.192 at Monxton with a Down afternoon stopping train. Note the photographer's bike. Rod Hoyle.

In the 1950s West Country class 4-6-2 No.34032 *Camelford* of Exmouth Junction, arrives at Grateley with the 10.1am stopping train from Salisbury to Waterloo. The two girder bridges were built for the widened trackbed when the Amesbury branch was opened in 1902, with signals regulating the junction here. Dennis Cullum

Apparently, during the 1950s, Monxton intermediate colour light signals were installed. Initially they were controlled from Red Post Junction signal box but after closure control fell to Andover Junction B. There was a Monxton Up intermediate block signal 3 miles 840 yards from Grateley and a Monxton Down intermediate block signal 1 mile 1,575 yards from Red Post Junction.

From Monxton to Grateley

On 23rd January 1913 the LSWR agreed to a request from Mr B. Hutton-Croft of Amport St Mary for 'game guards' or 'tabs' on telegraph wires. At a cost of £30 they ran for nearly one and a half miles between Andover and Grateley.

Leaving the site of Monxton signal box, and milepost 70, the line now ran into a long cutting and passed under an occupation bridge, No.193, in Sarson Wood. This appears to be the location of a collision in 1861 when, on the then single line, the Grateley Stationmaster was killed. For a few hundred yards there was a straight length of line which at the end curved to the right at 120 chains radius. The gradient now stiffened to 1 in 165 for the next three miles. The line was now on a low embankment and crossed two country lanes on bridges No.194, near Georgia Farm, and No.195 near Gollard Farm. From just in advance of milepost 71, for more than two miles, the line ran straight and rising on a gradient of 1

in 165 to a summit beyond Grateley station. There was an embankment more than a mile long here where the line crossed minor roads running east and south from Grateley village, on bridges Nos.196 and 197. The original brick arch of bridge No.197 was rebuilt with concrete beams and 13ft 6in headroom for road vehicles. Just to the south was Bridge House, an Edwardian property which may well have been erected by the railway. From the train there was an excellent view of Grateley village just to the north of the line but, sadly, more than a mile from the station. Grateley Down distant signal was passed followed by milepost 72; here the line ran parallel to a road, north of the line from the village, to a junction with the B3084 near the station.

GRATELEY

Chronology
Station and single line from Andover opened 1st May 1857.
Double track from Andover opened 1st February 1870.
Double track to Porton opened 1st July 1870.
First signal box (about 72 miles 64 chains from Waterloo) opened pre 1870.
Footbridge installed 1893.
First signal box closed, second signal box (about 72 miles 65 chains from Waterloo) with pneumatic frame, opened 20th July 1901.
Third line to Newton Tony opened 24th May 1902.

Passenger services to Amesbury commenced 2nd June 1902.
Mechanical lever frame replaced pneumatic frame 16/17 February 1921.
Public passenger services to Amesbury closed 30th June 1952.
Goods services to Amesbury closed 4th March 1963.
Goods yard closed 10th June 1963.
Signal box closed 2nd May 1968.
Station modernised 1993.

The following LSWR Traffic Committee Minutes relate to Grateley:
16th July 1857 Referred to the Ways and Works Committee a request from the station agent for the provision of an inn and siding.
13th August 1857. Approved the provision of a cart weighbridge, at Mr Smallbone's expense.
11th March 1858. Approved inn and stables costing £600, but the rent will be small.
1st November 1869. The Locomotive Committee reported that on 30th October 1860 the 9.0am down train hit a wagon in the siding too near the main line.
16th April 1863. Approved a small waiting shed on the Up platform,. The Ways and Works Committee to see if one of the two cottages, occupied by a platelayer, can be given up for a porter.
1st February 1866. Approved a cattle pen.
22nd September 1870. Agreed the levers to be covered cheaply.
11th April 1872. Agreed request from Archibald Scott, General Manager, to extend the Up Siding by 250ft.
12th July 1875. Agreed to replace old disc signals with new semaphore signals, but no new signal box was provided.

26ᵗʰ August 1875. Approved new loop siding.

7ᵗʰ July 1880. Considered a new bedroom to be added to the agent's house.

16ᵗʰ September 1880. Agreed the new bedroom costing £90.

14ᵗʰ July 1883. Following a Directors Inspection considered enlargement of the goods shed.

9ᵗʰ January 1884. Mr Jacomb, Engineer, quoted a price of £135 to enlarge the goods shed, which was approved, and referred to the Engineering Committee to carry out.

24ᵗʰ July 1895. Received a letter from Lt.Col.Sir Henry Wales about a proposed tramway or light railway to Amesbury or Stonehenge. A junction would be made between Grateley and Porton. If built the South Western would erect a station with exchange sidings.

Above. **Looking south across Grateley station about 1960 with the Amesbury branch platform in the foreground. From left to right are the goods shed, windmill to pump the station water supply, the station house, concrete footbridge and just in view the signal box. There was a similar windmill at Gillingham.**

Top right. **The Southern enamel sign about 1970 appears to have been used for target practice.** R.M.Casserley

23ʳᵈ June 1897. Approved proposal for additional bedrooms in cottages (all cottages with less than three bedrooms to get extra one), tender from Mr H.Barrow accepted.

22ⁿᵈ June 1898. Request from General Manager for additional sidings and to extend platforms for £2221 approved.

4ᵗʰ January 1899. Approved request from Salisbury Diocesan Committee for Welfare of Soldiers to place coffee stalls for a nominal rent.

23ʳᵈ May 1900. Alterations in connection with light railway costing £5598 were approved.

20ᵗʰ June 1900. Reported that four cottages were overcrowded and 'insufficiency of garden ground'. The Engineering Committee will report back.

17ᵗʰ April 1901. Lord Lawrence offered to abolish the occupation overbridge for £800 and allow him use of the adjoining level crossing for hunting purposes. A new bridge would cost £1415 – the offer to be accepted, and referred to the Engineering Committee.

9ᵗʰ July 1902. Approved four new cottages to the standard design costing £1071. These were urgently required, two for the Traffic Department, and two for the Engineering Department. Perry & Co. were proceeding under the District Contract.

29ᵗʰ September 1914. Reported that Locomotive No.584 ran into wagons left on the Up platform loop line whilst working the 11.50pm special empty goods train from Amesbury on 28ᵗʰ October 1914.

Grateley station looking east in early Southern days with a train of guns on flat wagons from the Amesbury branch behind an Adams locomotive. The original wooden footbridge was later replaced with an Exmouth Junction concrete example.

Grateley goods shed and station house looking west in the 1960s. Small consignments from road box vans were unloaded here whilst the train waited in the platform.

Description up to 1902

The *Kelly's Directory* of 1889 records that Grateley village had a population of 256 in 1881, that the principal landowners included Lord Lawrence and Miss Pickering and that the main crops were wheat, barley, oats, turnips, hay and clover. The Stationmaster was Mr Maurice Lovelock and that there was a telegraph office at the station. Local traders who had premises at the station included Albert Shearing 'miller (steam), corn, hay, straw and coal merchant', Alfred Tebbutt a coal merchant and George Harrrison of the Railway Inn.

Grateley station served a wide rural area including the Hampshire villages of Grateley, Over Wallop, Middle Wallop, Nether Wallop, and Cholderton just over the Wiltshire border. The single line opened in 1857 and Joseph Bull built the station house on a small platform, which on doubling of the line, in 1870, became the Down platform. A small waiting shed was provided on the Up platform. To the east of the station were Up and Down sidings with a small 1870s period signal box on the Down platform. The first Grateley road bridge, No.198, would have been of the conventional brick arch type seen elsewhere along the line.

An 1883 Ordnance Survey shows the double track Grateley station with Down sidings East and West, the latter with a wagon turntable and spur siding. On the Up side, opposite the station house, was a short siding to what appears to be a private compound and store. There was a pound for stray animals, the Railway Hotel and railway cottages, one house on the main road and a windmill (corn). For some years

passengers had to use a foot crossing until the South Western responded to a petition and installed, in 1883, a timber lattice footbridge at a cost of £200.

Grateley had a part in some of the army manoeuvres on Salisbury Plain in 1898. On Thursday 25th August that year it received the 1.15pm special train of hired transport from Waterloo. It was loaded with five vans on flat trucks, 21 horses in cattle trucks and eleven men in a carriage. Further trains arrived in the early hours on the Friday and Saturday. They carried between them 45 vans, 90 horses and 57 men. On the day of the grand review, on Thursday 8th September, eight special trains for spectators called in the morning and departed in the late afternoon but Grateley was less convenient than Porton for Boscombe Down where the event was held. Early in the morning on Friday 9th three trains departed, conveying troops, guns, horses and equipment to Colchester.

The War Department had purchased large areas of Salisbury Plain to the north of the main line in the 1890s and after the 1898 manoeuvres it was decided that better railway access was desirable. Grateley was chosen to be the junction for the Amesbury and Military Camp Light Railway, which opened in 1902; details of the promotion and construction of the line are given in Chapter Four.

A century ago railwaymen and signal engineers visited the isolated Grateley station to inspect the first pneumatic signalling installation and the first automatic block signalling in the country. Although the Grateley installation remained in use only between 1901 and 1921 other similar

installations on the South Western lasted until the 1960s. More on this in Chapter Four.

Description 1902-1965

The first two and a half miles of the Amesbury branch comprised a third track laid to the north of the main line, similar to the layout between Andover Junction and Red Post Junction. However, the bridges were rebuilt along this section and made wide enough for a fourth track if required. The original brick bridge, No.198, was demolished and replaced with a much longer bridge with steel girder sides resting on brick abutments. The layout was widened on the Up side with a loop and loop siding and a new signal box constructed on the Up platform.

Apart from the signalling, Grateley station changed little between 1902 and the late 1960s. The double track main line was dead straight, falling eastwards at 1 in 165 from a summit half a mile to the west. The Up platform was an island with the outer face serving a loop signalled for both directions. Facing and trailing connections underneath bridge No.198 made for very flexible use of the station. This was necessary because many of the services using the branch were special trains run to the requirements of the military authorities. These ran to and from a wide variety of destinations although some trains used the loop between Newton Tony and Amesbury Junction. There was a 15mph speed limit for Down trains through the junction for Bulford.

There were two Down Sidings East, with a crossover connection, from where there

Up Passenger Services departing Grateley						
1857	1867	1909	1947	1964	1984	2002
4	5	8	6	8	14	21

were two more sidings running back. One of these was extended in 1913 to serve the Marquis of Winchester's siding at the back of the goods yard. An agreement allowing this was terminated in 1930, part of it then being used for wagons for the wharf for Mr Shearing the coal merchant. The Down Siding West ran behind the platform to serve a long loading dock, which had cattle pens and a crane. *In the goods yard were an outside crane of 4 tons capacity and two highway vehicle docks. (SR 1934).* There was an Up Siding East and, also on the Up side (behind the bay platform) was a loop siding which served a second loading dock.

Access to the station was from the main B3084 road, which runs between Tidworth and the Wallops, with the Railway Hotel at the corner. The station approach ran gently downhill, through the station gate past the loading dock and to the modest station house on the Down side. This was a two storey brick building with extensions, providing accommodation for the Stationmaster and his family. On the platform were a waiting room and toilets and, in the absence of a conventional platform awning, a small area was covered by part of the roof. Adjacent to the station approach were four railway cottages, a necessary provision because of the remote location. The whole station area was dominated by a windmill, more than twice the height of the buildings. Constructed entirely in metal, it had a large diameter wheel at the top and was used to pump water from a well to a tank serving

several taps around the station, although there were no locomotive water facilities at Grateley.

On the Down platform was the goods shed and adjacent porters' room. There were a number of nondescript wooden buildings

in the yard used by local traders and others, including the local permanent way gang. In the 1920s the first wooden footbridge was replaced by a standard Exmouth Junction concrete example. The station and platforms were originally lit by oil lamps mounted on standard South Western posts but by the 1950s Tilley lamps on wires hanging from tall concrete posts had been installed. The island platform had the signal box and a small waiting shelter, built in 1863, which survived until 1969.

Passenger Trains Grateley Weekdays Summer 1958

Train	Grateley dep.	To
6.16am Salisbury	6.33am	Portsmouth
6.45am Salisbury	7.7am	Waterloo
7.20 Salisbury	7.43 arrival	Grateley (not advertised)
7.53 Grateley engine	7.53	Salisbury
6.33 Woking	8.25	Templecombe
8.46 Salisbury	9.8	Waterloo
7.20 Waterloo	9.42	Salisbury
9.3 Templecombe	10.22	Waterloo
10.45 Basingstoke	11.31	Salisbury
10.54 Waterloo	1.4pm	Salisbury
12.58pm Salisbury	1.20	Waterloo
11.54 Waterloo	2.1	Salisbury
2.48 Basingstoke	3.34	Salisbury
4.5 Salisbury	4.27	Waterloo
4.35 Salisbury engine	4.55 arrival	Grateley
5.19 Grateley	5.19	Salisbury (not advertised)
4.48 Basingstoke	5.36	Yeovil Town
5.15 Salisbury	5.38	Waterloo
5.39 Waterloo	7.57	Salisbury
8.44 Salisbury	9.5	Woking
6.54 Waterloo	9.20	Yeovil Town
8.53 Portsmouth	10.40	Salisbury
8.54 Waterloo	11.17	Salisbury

In 1964 Merchant Navy class 4-6-2 No.35024 *East Asiatic Company* of Nine Elms speeds through Grateley on a Down express, passing a rake of loaded coal wagons in the loop siding. Note the signal wires and point rodding to the left – this was installed in 1921 when the experimental pneumatic system was replaced. E.T.Gill.

GRATELEY TRACK DIAGRAM

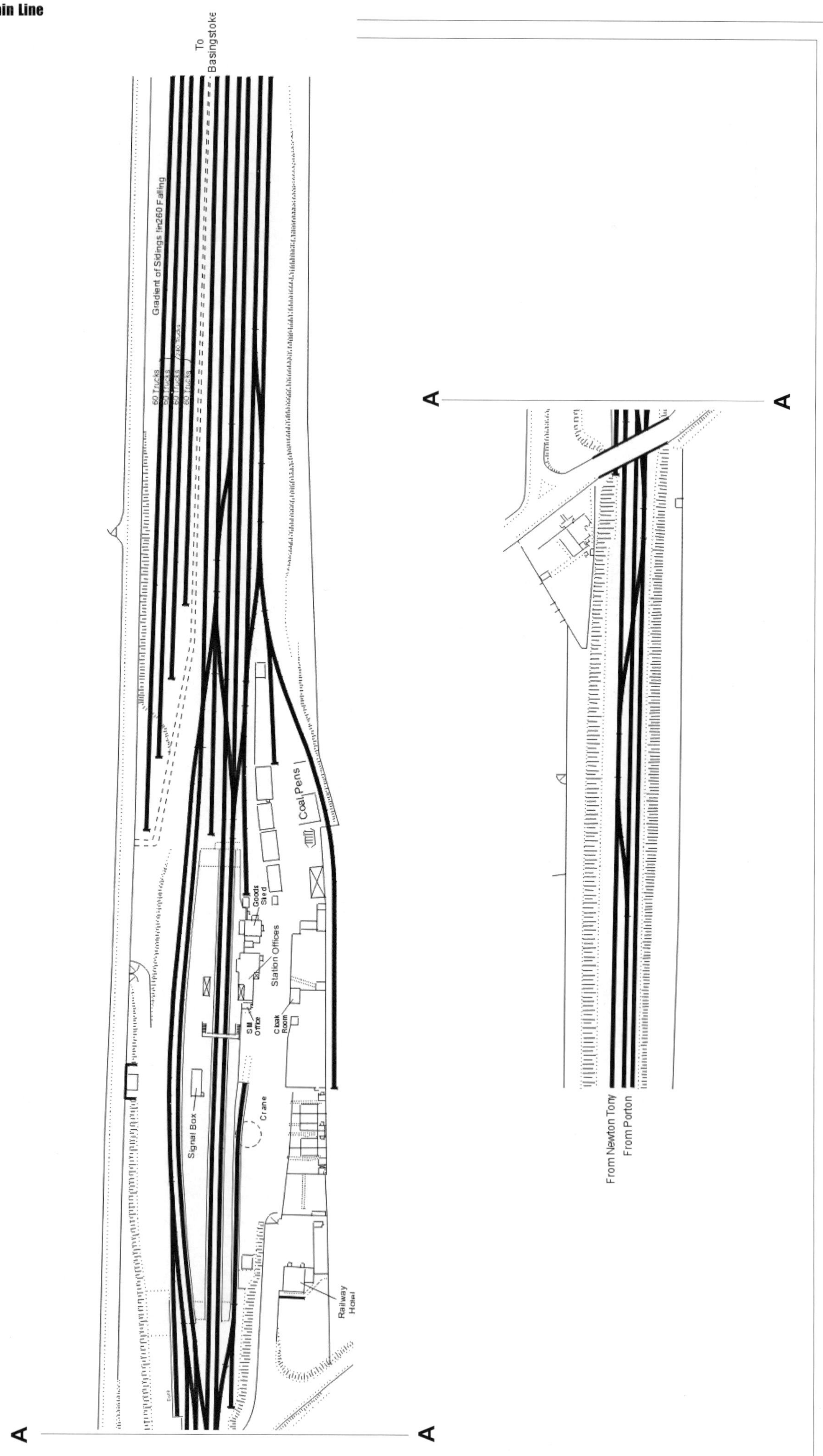

To Basingstoke

Gradient of Sidings 1in260 Falling

60 Trucks

Coal Pens

Goods Shed

Station Offices

Cloak Room

SM Office

Signal Box

Crane

Railway Hotel

A

A

A

A

From Newton Tony

From Porton

In November 1955, climbing up the 1 in 165 bank past the Down sidings at Grateley with the heavy 10.48am freight from Feltham Yard to Salisbury West Yard, is Urie S15 class 4-6-0 No.30498 carrying duty No.101. J.T.Rendell, The Transport Treasury.

Traffic and Train Services

Grateley station served a scattered rural community so traffic was limited, with about 40 passengers departing daily by the 1960s. There were a few passengers travelling to school or work at Salisbury, Andover or Overton and occasionally Waterloo. Some local children went to the grammar school at Andover and others to Salisbury and occasionally servicemen from local bases travelled to and from leave on a forces travel warrants. There was some parcels traffic received for local country houses, farms, businesses and customers in the surrounding villages. A grower at Nether Wallop four miles away forwarded boxes of watercress by passenger train as late as 1967.

Amesbury and Bulford Branch Services

The branch from Grateley to Amesbury, opened in 1902, was convenient for travellers from Amesbury to Andover, Basingstoke and Waterloo but inconvenient for Salisbury. In 1904 a new curve was opened at Newton Tony to connect with the main line in a westerly direction and most of the branch trains then ran direct to and from Salisbury, the branch passenger service being extended to

Goods and Milk Trains Summer 1909			
Train	Grateley arr.	Grateley dep.	To
6.15am Salisbury	7.3am	7.15am	Whitchurch
6.19 milk Yeovil Junction	8.31	8.32	Waterloo
8.20 milk Salisbury	8.41	8.43	Waterloo
10.45 Andover Jcn	11.0	11.30	Bulford
8.31 horsebox Yeovil	11.14	11.17	Waterloo
1.55pm Bulford	3.8pm	3.58pm	Andover Jcn
3.55 Salisbury	4.56	5.6	Nine Elms
5.10 Basingstoke	6.11	6.43	Salisbury

Bulford in 1906. Thus two years after its opening, the Grateley to Newton Tony section of the branch saw few scheduled trains. By 1909 there was one return passenger train between Bulford and Andover Junction via Grateley, a 5.0pm from Waterloo to Bulford but no return, and one goods from Andover Junction to Bulford and back. By Southern Railway days there were no public passenger services between Grateley and the branch, Amesbury and Bulford passengers for Waterloo having to change at Porton or Salisbury. The daily goods service continued.

The Grateley to Amesbury line was in regular use for troops, equipment and munitions for many years. Military traffic reached its peak during manoeuvres on Salisbury Plain and of course during the two world wars. The Salisbury to Bulford passenger service was withdrawn in 1952 and the curve it used at Newton Tony taken out in 1954. All services thereafter ran via Grateley until the complete closure of the branch in 1963. These services comprised two goods trains each way, one from Salisbury (reversing at Grateley) and one from Basingstoke. There were also troop

Freight Trains Grateley Weekdays Summer 1958			
Train	Grateley arr.	Grateley dep.	To
9.25pm stone Okehampton	5.29am	5.45am	Woking
5.45am Salisbury East Yard	6.15	6.40	Amesbury
5.30am Basingstoke West Yard	7.10am	7.25am	Amesbury
8.15am light engine Amesbury	8.40	8.42	Salisbury shed
10.45am Salisbury East Yard	11.59	12.32pm	Bas'stoke Up Yard
3.0 Amesbury	3.26pm	3.58	Bas'stoke Up Yard
9.45am stone empties Tonbridge	4.11pm	4.45pm	Exmouth Junction

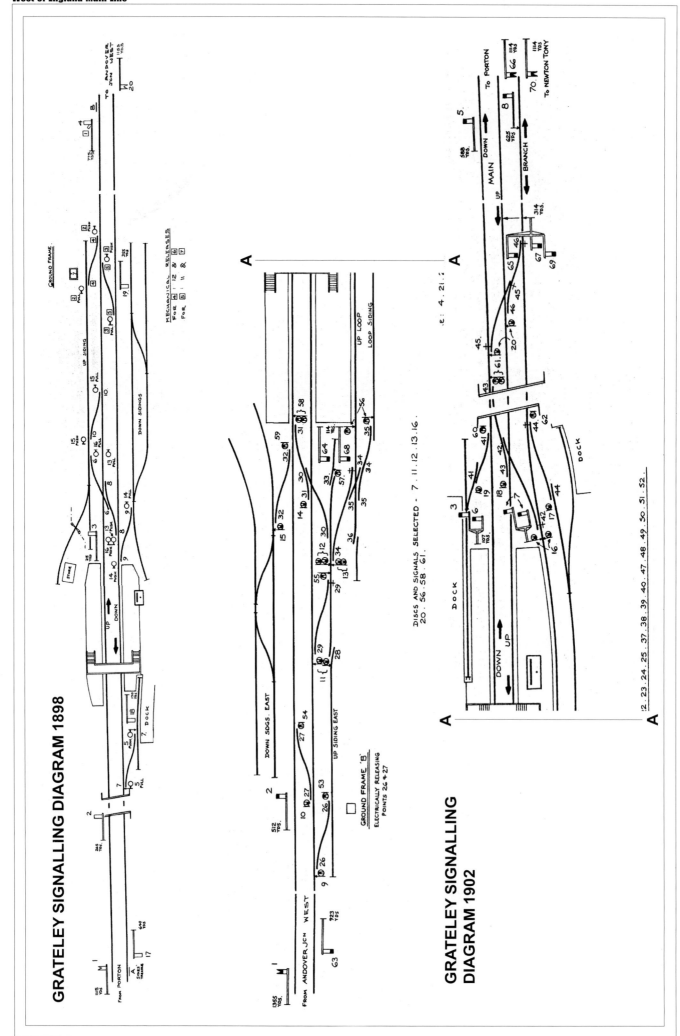

GRATELEY SIGNALLING DIAGRAM 1898

GRATELEY SIGNALLING DIAGRAM 1902

General view of Grateley station about 1955. The signal box was constructed in 1901 and controlled pneumatic points and signals using slides to open valves rather than levers. The section to Andover Junction West was controlled by signals automatically operated by track circuits, a world first, which merited press visits. The experimental system was replaced by conventional controls in 1921.

trains and a NAFFI train to Salisbury on some days. At one stage a through train ran on Sunday evenings from Waterloo to Bulford for servicemen returning after weekend leave. One weekend in 1956 there was a massive recall of army reservists for Suez which resulted in large numbers of full-length special trains from Waterloo, and elsewhere, running down the branch. It remained open day and night to receive them all and the returning empty stock.

After the opening of Idmiston Halt, sited between Amesbury Junction and Porton, in 1943 an early morning Salisbury to Idmiston and evening return passenger train ran for civilian staff going to work there. A tank engine hauled two or three red-painted non-corridor coaches which were berthed at Grateley during the day. The locomotive ran light to Salisbury and returned in the evening to take workmen home.

Goods Traffic

The public goods traffic handled at Grateley reflected the rural nature of the district. In the yard Messrs. Shearing had premises where they operated their business as merchants in coal, grain and fertilisers. Fertilisers arrived in weighty sacks in box vans and unloading them was heavy work for the station staff. Traffic received included coal, fertilisers and animal feedstuffs for local merchants, bricks, tiles, timber, cement and sand for house-building, roadstone for the Hampshire County Council and consignments of all descriptions. Sometimes there might be sufficient volume for a road van service from Salisbury or even Nine Elms. Traffic forwarded was more limited but included

some livestock for market at Salisbury or Basingstoke. There was also timber from local woods but the main business was in wheat and barley grown locally, as well as some straw used by strawberry growers in South Hampshire.

There was also, of course, a thriving military goods traffic – already touched upon above. Apart from troops and guns and the rest there were all manner of materials for the construction of various camps in the area, and the subsequent supplies of stores including coal, petrol, paraffin and foodstuffs. Much of this arrived by train where it was unloaded in the goods yard by military staff, or their civilian employees. It was taken away by horse-drawn vans and, later, by lorries.

The table shows a fair level of goods traffic. Several services called at Grateley for more than the ten minutes or so needed to shunt a few wagons in or out of the yard. The calls booked for Up milk and horsebox trains indicate a healthy level of business but the lack of traffic for corresponding Down trains meant that empty churns had to return using a Down passenger or goods train instead.

Signalling up to 1901

The first signal box on the Down platform, probably very similar to the Porton signal box, had a Stevens frame of 20 levers. There were distant, home, starting and advanced starting signals in both directions, the signal box controlling all station points with the exception of two crossovers at the Andover end of the Up Siding. These were too distant for direct operation from the signal box so a 7-lever ground frame was installed to control

them. Operated by a porter under the instructions of the signalman the ground frame was released by lever No.12 in the signal box. Sykes' lock and block instruments were then in use on the double track main line.

Signalling 1901-1921

A new box opened for the Amesbury branch line in 1901. It had 72 'levers' for the extended layout, although the ground frame at the Andover end of the Up Siding was retained. These were not conventional levers but 'slides', which opened control valves for the operation of points and signals, the pneumatic control system working at between 4 and 7lb per square inch. Some changes were made to the operation; for example, the first signalling diagram shows the Up distant signals from Porton and Amesbury to be controlled by levers 65 and 72, while a later diagram shows 66 and 70. Since this was the first pneumatic signalling installation in the country it is hardly surprising that modifications were required. Regulation of the single track branch to Newton Tony was by conventional Tyers No.6 instruments. However, this first installation proved to be expensive to maintain. When the new signal box at Red Post Junction opened in 1919 changes had to be made to the automatic block signalling between Andover and Grateley. The pneumatic signalling equipment at Grateley was replaced by a conventional mechanical frame over 16/17th February 1921. Some of the redundant pipes used for the pneumatic system remained in the box until its closure in 1968.

A group of railwaymen, many of them permanent way staff, outside Grateley signal box, probably in Southern Railway days.

Signalling after 1921

While the pneumatic 'frame' faced the running lines, the new 1921 mechanical frame was fitted opposite, facing the loop. The new Saxby frame was of the Stevens pattern and had 66 levers. The ground frame at the Andover end was initially retained but by 1940, along with the associated points, it had been removed. An architectural feature of the signal box was a bay window jutting out over the platform on the main line side. Its purpose may have been to ensure that the signalman could carry out his duty of observing the tail lamps of passing train. As can be seen from the diagram, the signalling at Grateley was complex, with many possible routes. The loop platform could be used for departures in the Up or Down direction of the main line but could only receive arrivals from the branch.

Grateley box was 4 miles 1,511 yards from Red Post Junction box and 2 miles 1,326 yards from Newton Tony Junction box. It was sited on the Up platform and had no closing switch. There were two crossovers, 148 yards on the Andover side and 170 yards on the Porton side.(SR 1934).

Staff

Just four years after the line opened the Stationmaster, Mr Tulk, was tragically killed in a shunting accident in 1861. Details of the accident and of the operation of Grateley station then are given in Chapter Two. From 1889 to 1895 the Grateley Stationmaster was Mr Maurice Lovelock, in 1915 Mr Herbert Lovelock, in 1923-1927 Mr Lewis Samuel Thatcher, in 1930-1932 Mr P.H.Corrick, in 1934-1937 Mr A.H.Trim, in 1939 Mr G.F.Davey and in 1948 Mr A.G.Loman. The post was latterly abolished, whereupon Grateley was supervised by the Porton Stationmaster. By the 1950s the staff comprised two senior porters working alternate early and late shifts carrying out a variety of duties. These included selling tickets in the booking office, dealing with parcels traffic in the goods shed,

assisting with the loading and unloading of wagons in the goods yard and attending to the station paperwork. Assistance was provided by the middle turn junior porter at Porton who came up on the 10.15am train and returned on the 1.30pm. During his part shift here his duties included issuing tickets in the booking office and changing the signal lamps. Grateley staff in the late 1950s included senior porters Mr Pat Britain and Mr Charlie Godalming and signalmen Bert Norton, Ginger Wilde and Johnnie West.

The signal box had no closing switch so was open continuously and was manned by three signalmen on a three-shift system. Rest day relief men covered the remaining work. There was also a permanent way gang based here to maintain the main line between Monxton and Amesbury Junction. Grateley at this time came under the supervision of the Porton Stationmaster who visited Monday to Saturday by train to check the books in the station office and sign the train register in the signal box. When this post was finally withdrawn the Andover Area manager took over.

Grateley Today

During the years of demise Grateley was reduced to an unstaffed station and the buildings demolished. However, in 1993 Grateley station was extensively rebuilt when the line was modernised. The double tracks were connected by a trailing crossover underneath bridge No.198 and is only used in emergencies or when one line is taken over by the civil engineers. It was removed during track renewals on 12th October 2002. The platforms were extended in length with concrete components and the levels raised for nine coach class 159 trains. During excavations to extend the Up platform at the west end a large number of metal pipes were unearthed, a legacy of the pneumatic signalling system taken out of use 70 years before. There is new lighting mounted on tall blue lamp posts, small modern steel and glass waiting shelters and a red plastic pod for a railwayman to sell tickets on weekday

mornings. The station is now the responsibility of the Salisbury Area Manager. The old concrete footbridge was replaced by a steel one recovered from Whimple station but it retains the LSWR bridge plate No.197A. It also carries two plaques reading: *Best Unstaffed Station 1994. Planted and maintained by Grateley W.I. in conjunction with South West Trains and Hampshire County Council* and *This footbridge was originally in use at Whimple Devon. It was re-sited here in March 1994 by British Rail Network South East and painted by volunteer members of the Andover and District Rail Enthusiast Society.*

The car park has been greatly extended so that it is now one of the largest on the line. With the improvements in the train service to 21 per day Grateley has become very popular with travellers who arrive by car from a wide area. Indeed, although the train service is not as good as that for Salisbury, the car driver can avoid the traffic in the city thus making Grateley a popular 'Parkway' station.

Grateley to Newton Tony and Amesbury Junctions

Leaving Grateley station under bridge No.198 the three track line continued dead straight in a cutting climbing at 1 in 165. A number of Grateley signals were passed at this point. First the Up home post, with three arms on separate dolls reading from left to right, branch to loop, branch to Up main and Up main and the two Down advanced starting signals on separate main and branch posts. Finally came bridge No.199 carrying a minor road at Palestine with the two Grateley Up distant signals in advance of it and milepost 73. Bridge No.199 was similar to No.198, the original brick arch having been replaced in 1901 by a long steel girder bridge on brick abutments but this time spanning all three tracks. Just beyond bridge No.199 came the summit of the line. From here it was downhill all the way to Salisbury, initially at 1 in 440 and in steam days the crews of Up trains, particularly heavy freights, could look forward to some easier work from here on.

The line curved very gently at 100 chains radius to the south and for the next four miles took up another straight alignment at ground level just to the south of the old Roman road. It passed milepost 74, the downhill gradient easing to 1 in 735, and then passed under bridge No.200 at Hampshire Gap, entering Wiltshire. Bridge No.200 was similar to Nos.198 and 199. The three tracks continued for another three quarters of a mile until the Amesbury branch curved away to the north at the site of Newton Tony Junction. Since the 1939-45 war land to the south of the line has been taken over by the Ministry of Defence and now exhibits a tall security fence emblazoned with warning notices. By the 1950s, of course, Newton Tony was simply the junction for the branch. Milepost 75, however, is appropriate at this stage to consider the junction arrangements a century ago.

GRATELEY SIGNALLING DIAGRAM FROM 1921

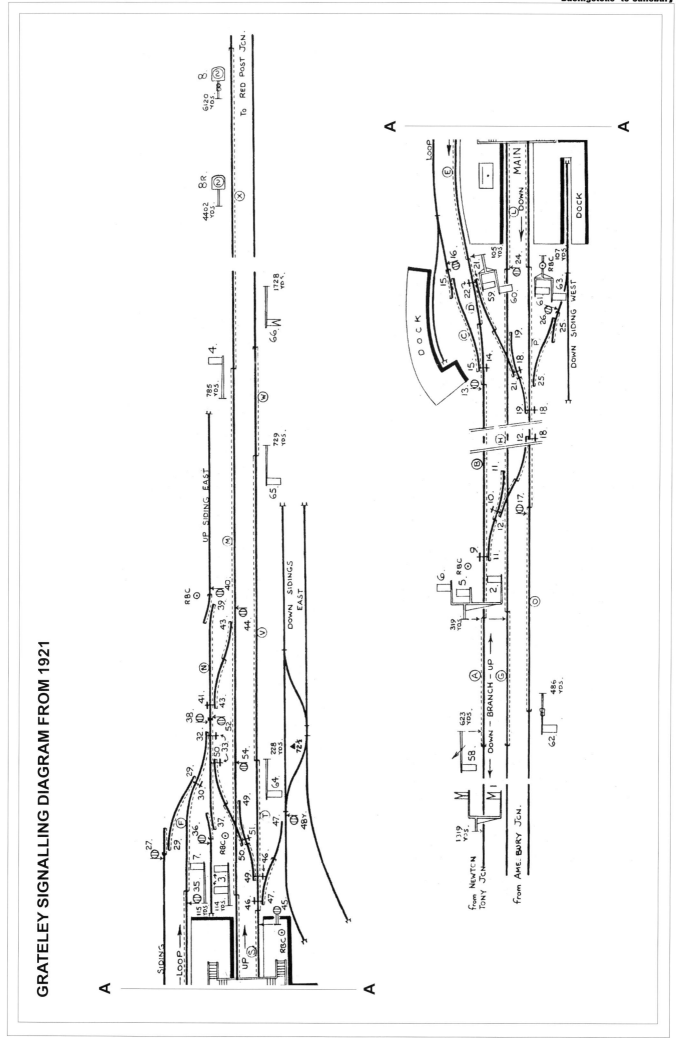

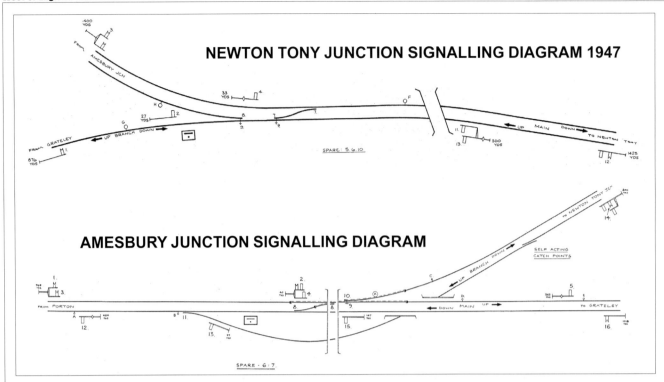

NEWTON TONY JUNCTION SIGNALLING DIAGRAM 1947

AMESBURY JUNCTION SIGNALLING DIAGRAM

NEWTON TONY JUNCTION

Chronology
First Newton Tony signal box (75 miles 42 chains from Waterloo) opened August 1898.

First signal box closed, second Newton Tony Junction signal box (75 miles 1 chain from Waterloo) and junction for contractors opened 1899.

Second signal box closed, third Newton Tony Junction signal box (approx. 75miles 10 chains from Waterloo) and junction opened September 1901.

Third line from Grateley opened 24th May 1902.

Third signal box closed, junction abolished, leaving independent third line from Grateley to Newton Tony on the branch May 1904.

A fourth Newton Tony Junction box on the Amesbury branch was opened in May 1904.

Third line from Grateley to Newton Tony closed 4th March 1963.

Description and Signalling 1899-1901
On 6th July 1898 the South Western Traffic Committee decided to build four intermediate signal boxes of which Newton Tony was the most expensive at £232. The others were costed at £209 and were sited at St Mary Bourne, Enham and Monxton. By this date the South Western had already applied for a Light Railway Order to build the Amesbury branch, which may have been a consideration when designing the box, thus accounting for the slightly higher price. It was open continuously for several days to deal with the extra traffic for the 1898 army manoeuvres.

The second signal box on the Down side was opened to provide access for the contractors building the branch to Amesbury and contained a 12 lever frame. There was a main line trailing crossover together with trailing connections from both lines on to what was then the contractor's siding. There were distant, home and starting signals in both directions on the main line, with connections to the contractor's siding controlled by ground signals. Quite possibly this was an old South Western box and frame of the 1870s, installed on a temporary basis until the branch was opened and a more permanent junction and box provided.

Description and Signalling 1901-1904
The third Newton Tony Junction signal box opened on the Up side in the V of the

Looking east over the site of Amesbury Junction after its closure in 1954, the signal box being re-named Allington, with bridge No.202 and signalmen's cottages beyond. The line from Amesbury burrowed under the main line and climbed round the back of the signal box to connect to the Down main line. Opposite the signal box was a facing connection from the Up main line to Amesbury. The branch was double track. Colin Chivers Collection

On 26th June 1952, two days before withdrawal of passenger services, 700 class 0-6-0 No.30317 with a single coach forms the Bulford to Salisbury train as it passes under bridge No.201 carrying the main line. In the distance is the windmill supplying water to railway cottages at Newton Tony. A.C.V.Kendall courtesy Peter Harding.

junction in 1901 and was much more substantial. There was now a conventional double track junction from the main line to the branch, which started as a double track and very soon became single. There were also connections between the third line from Grateley station to both the branch and the main lines.

It had a 37 lever frame to control the layout with distant, home and starting signals in each direction, some being junction signals. On the double track main lines to Grateley and Porton, Sykes' Lock and Block apparatus was in use while the single track lines to Grateley and Newton Tony station were regulated by Tyers No.6 tablets. An interesting feature here was that the branch

crossed the old Roman road, the Portway, and a level crossing was provided with levers 36 and 37 working the gate stops and bolts. A wheel in the signal box operated the gates. During its short life this was a busy box dealing not only with the main line traffic but also the branch and the level crossing.

When Amesbury Junction opened in 1904 Newton Tony Junction closed. All the points and signals were taken out of use and the branch level crossing reduced to an occupation crossing, the junction simply becoming a point of divergence between the double track main line and the single line branch. Confusingly, another Newton Tony Junction signal box opened, this one half a mile away on the branch itself. Here at this

remote location a pair of railway cottages were constructed by the South Western. As at Grateley a windmill was installed to pump water from a well.

Near the site of the divergence the main line passed Amesbury Junction Down distant signal. The double track continued straight downhill at 1 in 735, passed the Amesbury Junction Up starting signal and crossed the Up Amesbury branch line on iron deck bridge No.201.

AMESBURY JUNCTION
Chronology
Junction and signal box (75 miles 53 chains from Waterloo) opened May 1904. Branch to Newton Tony closed 10th October 1954. Signal box renamed Allington 25th September 1955. Signal box closed 20th January 1964.

Description
As soon as it was realised that most of the public passenger traffic on the Amesbury branch was to and from Salisbury, a direct double track connection was laid in at the Junction. At this time, 1904, the South Western was in the process of installing flyovers and burrowing non-conflicting junctions along its main line from Waterloo so one was installed here too. The extra expense could certainly not be justified by the public trains but it did help cope with the heavy military traffic. On 7th October 1903 the South Western approved a contract with Messrs. Braithwaite and Kirk for the ironwork for the dive-under bridge for £344.

The junction was laid in adjacent to bridge No.202, which carried a country lane between the village of Newton Tony and Tower Hill over the line. After Tower Hill had been taken over by the Ministry of Defence the bridge became redundant and

This official LSWR view of Amesbury Junction was taken on the opening of the double track loop between Newton Tony Station and Amesbury Junction in 1904 and shows the occupation crossing. To the left can be seen the Up side branch line which dived under the main line, in the background, and connected to the Down side (see left). The track in the middle of the photograph is the Down branch and leaves the Up side main line just out of view.

IDMISTON TRACK DIAGRAM 1947

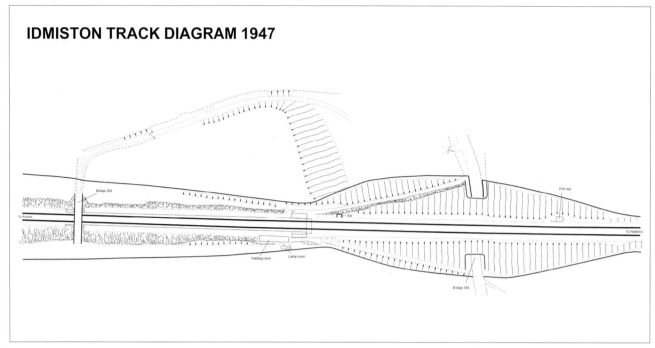

was later demolished. The connection to the branch from the Up main line was just to the east of bridge No.202, whilst that from the branch to the Down main line was to the west with the weather-boarded signal box in the V between them. Adjacent to the box was a lamp room. An extra bridge, No.1 on the branch, had to be provided for a lane over the branch as it climbed up at 1 in 45 from under bridge No.201 to the level of the main line. On the Up side of the main line at this point, adjacent to the bridge, was a pair of two storey cottages built by the LSW for signalmen. Water was drawn from a well. Two signalmen worked early and late turns, assisted by rest day relief men as required. The box was supervised by the Grateley station master who visited regularly and signed the train register book. In 1909 coal and other stores for Amesbury Junction were sent from Grateley on the 7.15am Coal Empties from Nine Elms to Salisbury.

Signalling

Amesbury Junction signal box was 2 miles 1,577 yards from Grateley box and 257 yards from Newton Tony Junction box on the branch. It stood on the Down side and had a closing switch which enabled it to be switched out when not required. There was a trailing crossover, 72 yards on the Grateley side.

The box had a 16 lever frame for the junction points and signals. On the main line there were Up and Down distant and home and starting signals, the Up distant and home posts having two dolls, for main line and branch. There were also distant and home signals for trains from the branch and, confusingly, Up branch trains joined the Down main line, and vice versa. Sykes' Lock and Block instruments were in use on both the main line and branch. Amesbury Junction box was normally open whenever the branch was, in essence for two daytime shifts. When the branch closed at night the box was switched out, the double track section becoming Grateley to Salisbury Tunnel Junction or sometimes Porton.

BR standard 4-6-0 No.73162 passes Idmiston Halt with a Padstow to Waterloo relief train on Saturday 12th September 1964. A remarkable train, because the Western Region had axed all such scheduled services the previous week. S.C.Nash

However, during busy wartime periods the box had to be open continuously.

After closure of the branch in 1955 the box was re-named Allington and almost all the levers taken out of use. The summer 1958 timetable showed the 4.5pm Salisbury to Waterloo passenger train stopping at Allington 'when required to set down staff'. The four remaining levers operated distant and home signals in each direction, the box remaining in use at busy times such as summer Saturdays until its closure in 1964. The tall security fence to the south of the line remains to this day.

From Amesbury Junction to Idmiston

Leaving Amesbury Junction the line continued straight downhill at 1 in 735 alongside the Portway, passing the Amesbury Junction Down starting signal. For more than a mile the line ran in a low cutting spanned by bridge No.203. This carried a farm track over the line with the Amesbury Junction Up distant signal with its two diverging arms in advance of it. Next in the cutting the downhill gradient stiffened to 1 in 245, milepost 76 was passed and bridge No.204 carried another farm track over the line at Allington Farm. Next came bridge No.205 carrying another track over the line and at the end of the cutting the line ran out on to a low embankment. From here to the north were fine views over the valley of the River Bourne, which the line was to follow all the way to Salisbury. On this embankment the line crossed over another track on bridge No.206 and again entered a low cutting. Here the Porton Down distant signal was passed in advance of a farm track carried over the line on bridge No.207.

Idmiston Halt Up platform. Peter Swift Collection.

Milepost 77 followed. Out of sight to the south was the extensive MOD complex at Porton Down, the only road access being through bridge No.208. Emerging from the cutting on to an embankment the line passed over a road on bridge No.208, close to the small village and church at Idmiston. Here the line ran into a cutting and arrived at Idmiston Halt.

IDMISTON HALT

Chronology
Halt (77 miles 50 chains from Waterloo) opened 4th January 1943.
Halt closed 9th September 1968.

Description

As we have seen, during the 1939-45 war a number of War Office establishments were built to the south of the line. Although Porton station was only three-quarters of a mile away, the Ministry wanted passenger facilities here for its service personnel and the large number of civilians who came to

Up Passenger trains departing Idmiston	
1947	1964
5 main line	6 main line
+7 to Bulford	

Looking west at Idmiston Halt opened in 1943 for men employed at Porton Down and a workmen's train, carrying about 100 men from Salisbury, was provided. A porter walked Up the line from Porton to sell tickets at the small booking office on the Down platform. Bridge No.209 spans the deep cutting where there were occasional landslips. R.K.Blencowe.

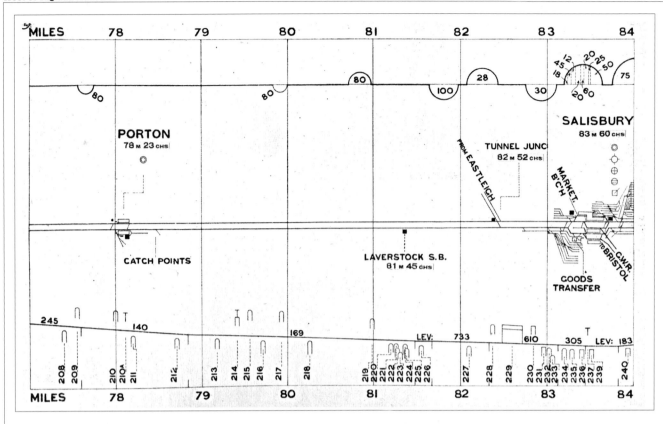

work daily on the base, particularly from Salisbury. The platforms were constructed from standard components supplied from Exmouth Junction concrete works and could take up to about six coaches. A small concrete building on the Down side served as waiting room and booking office and tall concrete posts carried electric lights. At the east end of the halt was a barrow crossing; public access to the platforms was by means of paths up from the road adjacent to bridge No.208. There was another path, through a gate on the Down platform, leading to the Porton Down military base, where local military police might well be in evidence at appropriate times.

For some years a workmen's train ran from Salisbury to Idmiston Halt for the army base. In 1943 this left at 8.28am arriving at Idmiston Halt at 8.41am; continuing empty to Grateley, the three-coach set was berthed in the yard and the tank engine returned to Salisbury. The tank engine returned to Grateley in the afternoon and collected the coaches, to form the 6.15pm from Idmiston Halt back to Salisbury. The service continued into the late 1950s when the (by now) two coach train could be packed with more than 100 passengers. When the hours of work on the base changed the train service did not, so many workmen used the local Silver Star bus service instead.

Although a halt, Idmiston was staffed for much of the day in conjunction with nearby Porton station. The early turn junior porter opened up the booking office in time to turn on the lights and sell tickets for the first trains, the 7.2am and 9.2am Up and the 8.27am and 9.54am Down. This was in the 1960s. In between trains, two or three times during his shift, the porter walked or cycled along the cess to Porton station to cover other duties there. Idmiston's junior porters were usually aged between 16 and

17, between school and national service, so an older late turn porter had to turn off the lights after the last trains, the 9.0pm Up and 9.26pm Down by 1964. Sometimes older men were employed part-time on this duty, including Mr Harold Diaper, Mr Ernie Steel and Mr Charlie Hatcher. Friday afternoons were very busy in the booking office when up to twenty soldiers might arrive for hand-written travel warrants for weekend leave, departing on the 5.28pm to Waterloo. When Barry Lake was the porter on duty here in the mid-1960s he could hear the noise made by contractors as they dismantled the Amesbury branch after its closure.

Traffic and Train Services

Service warrants aside, few locals used the trains, the Silver Star bus to Salisbury running through the village proving more convenient for many. The bus was also preferred by many servicemen going on weekend leave. As can be seen from the table, most of the passenger trains serving Idmiston Halt were those between Salisbury and Bulford and were convenient for the civilian staff, although the main line trains were usually more useful for servicemen and women going on leave in the London direction.

Once the Bulford trains were withdrawn, both Idmiston and Porton had a minimal train service, unattractive to passengers, and both closed in 1968.

Idmiston Today

After closure the concrete platform components were recovered for use elsewhere. Today, multiple units speed through Idmiston where there is practically no evidence that there was ever a halt at all, except for the overgrown path leading up

from the road below to the site of the Up platform. The tall security fence remains on the south of the line and just under bridge No.208 is an entrance to the army base.

From Idmiston to Porton

Leaving Idmiston Halt the line ran into a cutting spanned by bridge No.209, which carried a farm track over the line. The four miles of dead straight track, almost all the way from Grateley, was interrupted by a gentle curve to the south of 80 chains radius the line slowly diverging from the Portway. In the steep-sided cutting, the Porton Up advanced starting signal was passed, followed by the Down home signal. There was a ground frame here, in a weather-boarded shed, on the Down side. It controlled a trailing crossover, the line running under bridge No.210 at milepost 78 and entering Porton station. The high security fence to the south of the line continued. On the Up side, just above bridge No.210, were four railway cottages. It was here, on 6th January 1959, that several hundred tons of chalk and soil, loosened by frost and rain, slipped down and covered the tracks for a couple of hundred yards. Fortunately the Porton ganger Cecil Chandlers was able to notify the signalman who set all his signals to danger, in time to stop an Up train. It took two days to clear the line, the cutting strengthened during the work with bags of sand/cement.

PORTON

Chronology
Station and single line from Andover opened 1st May 1857.
Double track to Salisbury (Tunnel Junction) opened 1st June 1868.
Double track from Grateley opened 1st July 1870.

Porton station and Porton Down in June 1967 shortly before closure, with the original oil lamps replaced by standards for Tilley lamps. John Scrace.

Signal box (approx. 78 miles 24 chains from Waterloo) opened circa 1870.
Goods yard extended April 1899.
Footbridge installed 1902.
Military 2ft gauge line circa 1916 to circa 1946.
Goods yard closed 10th September 1962.
Signal box closed 2nd May 1968.
Station closed 9th September 1968.

The following LSW Traffic Committee Minutes refer to Porton:
30th March 1865 Agreed to Officers Conference request to improve the loop line by removing a siding.
22nd September 1870. Approved proposal for a small signal cabin to cover the levers on the up platform.
5th September 1878. Approved as necessary small wooden stables costing £18 10/-

13th October 1880. Approved Officers Conference request for two cottages.
30th July 1887. A medical allowance was made to the Stationmaster, after an assault by a signalman, who was imprisoned.
23rd July 1890. Received a request from the Amesbury Board of Guardians for extra sidings costing £1400.
15th October 1890. Declined request of 23rd July.
3rd February 1892. Approved new down platform waiting shed, the old one to be removed to other site as a porters room costing £6. (A new one would cost £71)
20th January 1897. Approved additional crossover costing £360.
3rd February 1897. Agreed to raise and extend platforms for £250.
23rd June 1897. Approved additional bedrooms in cottages (those with less than

two bedrooms to get extra one). Tender from Mr H.Barrow accepted.
22nd June 1898. Approved the General Manager's recommendation for additional sidings and extended platforms for £2900.
4th January 1899. Agreed to request of Salisbury Diocesan Committee for Welfare of Soldiers to place coffee stalls for a nominal rent.
22nd October 1908. Approved cattle pen costing £50.
24th April 1909 Agreed to shorten a siding and make a cart road round the back of it, costing £24.
4th October 1917. Agreed additional accommodation for Stationmaster.

Kelly's Directory of 1889 did not include Porton in its own right but as part of the parish of Idmiston. The 1881 population was 235 and the chief crops were wheat, barley and oats. The Porton Stationmaster was Frederick Compton. The Railway Hotel was constructed subsequently, in 1899.

Army Manoeuvres and Grand Review 8th September 1898

Porton station played a significant role in the transportation of ten's of thousands of men and equipment at this time and will be covered in detail in Chapter Nine.

Bourne Valley Historical Society Reminiscences

The Bourne Valley Historical Society archives include reminiscences of Jim Parsons who worked at Targett's Farm in Porton for 49 years, from about 1900. He recalled the six railway cottages and station house incorporating the waiting room, which was always very smart and had a good fire.

Porton station looking east with the principal buildings on the Up platform. Comparison with page 67 shows the station house to be of similar design to Grateley - both opened in 1857. In the distance is bridge No.210 (used by the Porton Military Railway) and beyond, the LSWR staff cottages. Peter Swift Collection.

PORTON TRACK DIAGRAM 1907

PORTON SIGNALLING DIAGRAM

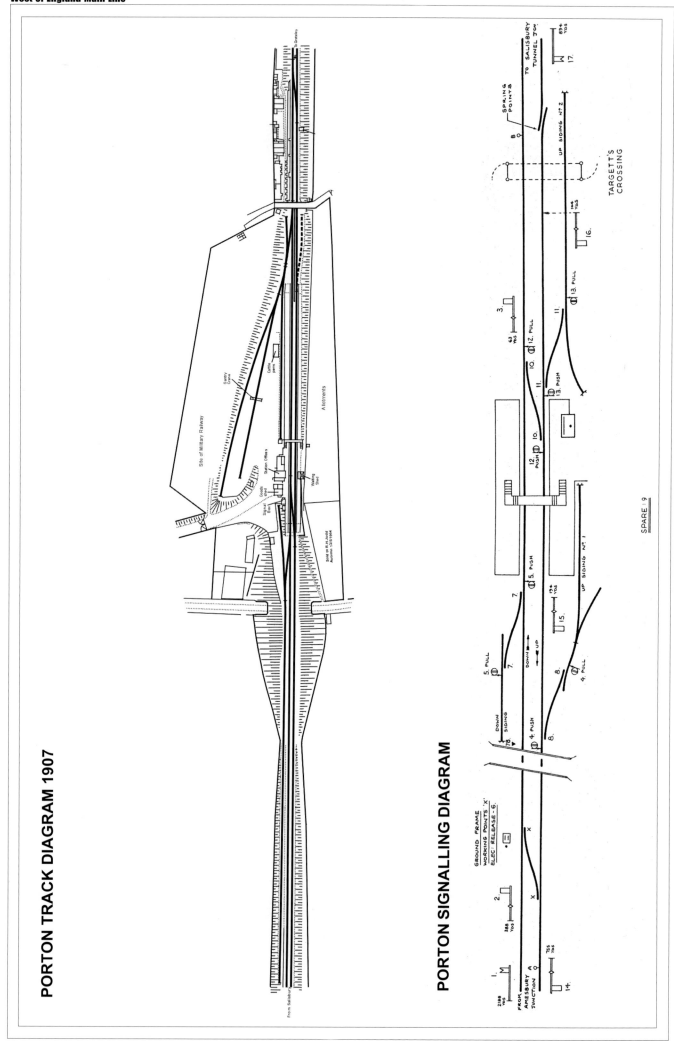

Porton station looking down the 1 in 140 bank towards Salisbury in BR days. Douglas Thompson, courtesy Peter Swift.

Many local residents took the train into Salisbury for shopping or visiting and mothers were allowed to travel in the guards van with babies still in their prams. London newspapers arrived on the Down train about 6.30am and local boys delivered them in the district; the evening papers were similarly delivered. Milk from five farms was sent to the station in churns, which were loaded on to the Milk Train at 4.30pm for transit to the South Down Dairies at Wimbledon. Heavy sacks of corn weighing 2½ cwt from local farms were loaded into box vans and artificial manure arrived in wagons for local farms. The busy goods yard was used by four local coal merchants and cattle were unloaded here for a farm at Boscombe. During the 1939-45 War American troops unloaded fuel at Porton station for their camp at Cusse's Gorse, which later became a prisoner of war camp. Jim remembered that the Americans were very good to the village children.

Norman Lake lived in Porton High Street for many years, his father having worked on the construction of the Amesbury branch at the turn of the century. He recalled that Mr Tompkins, a local farmer, took churns of milk every day to the station. He remembered the Porton Camp Light Railway conveying workers arriving by main line train to the camp. There was the viaduct bridge over the lane and he remembered the little wagons used for coal, timber, animal foodstuffs, scrap metal, bricks and cement. The workers rode in covered carriages, which at the weekend were left just over the main railway bridge near the railway cottages and were a great attraction for the village children. Norman's son Barry started work at Porton station and still works on the railway. Barry has kindly supplied much information for this and other sections of the book.

Description

When the line opened in 1857, Porton was regarded as the station for Amesbury, only some four miles away by direct road and track until it was blocked by the construction of Boscombe Down airfield. The small village of Porton lay in the valley of the River Bourne, off the main A338 road but on the Portway.

The station was constructed on the gentle hillside between overbridge No.210 in a cutting and underbridge 211 on an embankment and was originally a small wayside station with a passing loop. After the line was doubled there were just a couple of sidings on the Up side, one to the east serving a loading dock, a refuge siding to the west and a couple of trailing crossovers. However, as we have seen already, in the 1890s the War Office purchased much land on Salisbury Plain; it required good railway facilities and until the Amesbury branch was opened Porton station had to suffice.

In 1899 the platforms were greatly extended to the east, an enlarged goods yard was laid in on the Up side and a Down siding provided. About 1916 a narrow gauge (60cm) line was built by the army from the goods yard up on to Porton Down, and this remained in use until the late 1940s. It

Porton station in 1950 with footbridge No.210A and oil lamps.

On 6th August 1956 BR standard class 4-6-0 No.73112 departs from Porton with a stopping train for Salisbury. Note the Down starting signal with repeater arm and points for the Up refuge siding. J.T.Rendell, The Transport Treasury.

brought considerable traffic through Porton station and is described later.

From the village the station approach passed the Railway Hotel just outside the station gate. At one stage the Railway Hotel was badly damaged by fire – no doubt the fire brigade had difficulty in obtaining enough water – but it was subsequently re-built. All the main station buildings were grouped together the Up side. The two storey station house, built by Joseph Bull in 1857, incorporated the Stationmaster's accommodation with public access through a door into the booking hall and out on to the platform. As at Grateley, there was no conventional platform awning but a small area sheltered under part of the roof of a single storey section. A waiting room and toilets completed the facilities. Moving down the platform there was a coal store, a pump house with adjacent well and a goods shed with a sliding door on the platform. Towards the west end was the signal box, a weather-boarded cabin on a stone base. In 1902 the South Western installed the steel girder footbridge, No.210A, at a cost of £200. Before this passengers had used a barrow crossing opposite the signal box. On the Down platform was a small wooden waiting shelter with an awning, built in 1892. For many years the station was lit with oil lamps on ornamental posts but towards the end these were replaced with Tilley lamps.

Opposite the station house was the lamp room, by the entrance to the goods yard. Here there were three sidings. One, behind the platform, served a long loading dock, which included a cattle pen. Between 1917 and 1953 the two sidings to the rear flanked the narrow gauge sidings of the Porton Camp line, although their layout did change. In a long loop, with a section over a timber trestle viaduct, the Army's 60cm line crossed the main line by means of bridge No.210, previously erected for a farm track. To the east of this were three pairs of railway cottages and some sheds, their water coming from an adjacent well. In the yard there was a 2 ton crane and a vehicle dock. There was also an Up refuge siding which could hold a locomotive and 40 wagons.

Traffic and Train Services

Local passengers mainly used the service to Salisbury, for the shops, offices and factories there. Porton and district was in Wiltshire, so children attended the Bishops Wordsworth and Godolphin grammar schools and others in Salisbury, in contrast to those from Grateley in Hampshire who went to Andover.

Up Passenger trains departing Porton

1857	1867	1909	1947	1964
4	4	7	6	8
			+ 7 to Bulford	+ 7 to Bulford

Passenger Trains Porton Weekdays October 1947

Train	Porton dep.	To
6.45 Salisbury	6.55am	Waterloo
7.20 Salisbury (not ad'tised)	7.31	Grateley
7.50 Bulford	8.15	Salisbury
5.40 Waterloo	8.38	Templecombe
7.10 Yeovil Town	8.52	Waterloo
8.55 Salisbury	9.4	Bulford
7.20 Waterloo	9.51	Salisbury
9.40 Bulford	10.4	Salisbury
11.10 Salisbury	11.20	Bulford
9.30 Waterloo	11.42	Salisbury
11.52 Bulford	12.16pm	Salisbury
1.0 Salisbury	1.11	Waterloo
10.54 Waterloo	1.14	Salisbury
1.8 Salisbury	1.17	Bulford
1.51 Bulford	2.16	Salisbury
2.56 Salisbury	3.5	Bulford
1.30 Waterloo	3.47	Salisbury
4.0 Salisbury	4.11	Waterloo
3.55 Bulford	4.20	Salisbury
5.15 Salisbury	5.25	Waterloo
5.19 Grateley (not advertised)	5.32	Salisbury
3.30 Waterloo	5.50	Salisbury
5.43 Salisbury	5.54	Bulford
6.26 Bulford	6.49	Salisbury
7.55 Salisbury	8.5	Bulford
5.39 Waterloo	8.6	Salisbury
8.38 Salisbury	9.2	Salisbury
8.55 Salisbury	9.6	Woking
7.30 Waterloo	10.0	Yeovil Town
9.55 Salisbury	10.4	Bulford
8.54 Waterloo	11.11	Salisbury

Goods and milk trains calling at Porton Summer 1909			
Train	Porton arr.	Porton dep.	To
6.15am Salisbury	6.32	6.47	Whitchurch
6.19 Yeovil Junction Milk	8.18	8.21	Waterloo
8.20 Salisbury Milk	8.30	8.31	Waterloo
8.31 Yeovil Horseboxes	11.2	11.4	Waterloo
3.55pm Salisbury	4.12	4.40	Basingstoke
2.25 Wimbledon Milk	5.16	5.18	Templecombe
5.15 TemplecombeMilk	7.28	7.31	Waterloo

Freight Trains Porton Weekdays Summer 1958			
Train	Porton arr.	Porton dep.	To
10.45am Sal.E.Yrd	11.1am	11.43am	Basingstoke Up Yard

The train service, particularly to Salisbury when the Bulford trains augmented the main line, was quite generous for a village of Porton's size. Salisbury was also an attraction for service personnel having a day or evening out from their camps. There was also a considerable passenger traffic, both service and civilian, on the Army railway between the station and the camp.

Almost all of these passengers in turn arrived or left Porton by main line train. Just after the First World War, in 1919, there was a daily 7.16am workmen's train from Salisbury, returning from Porton at 4.50pm, for civilians employed by the War Department.

Passengers between the Bulford branch and main line stations to Waterloo were sometimes advised to travel via Porton. For example in 1947 three trains to, and two from Bulford, had advertised Waterloo connections via Porton.

There were other connections, were via Salisbury using fast main line trains which did not stop here. Three of these connections were very tight with just four minutes between booked arrival and departure times but timekeeping on the Southern was usually good and branch trains could be held to maintain an advertised connection.

However, Porton was not the best station for a lengthy wait between trains, although a convivial visit to the Railway Hotel might be fitted in.

Other passenger rated traffic included a wide variety of parcels received for villagers, local farms and various army camps. Traffic forwarded included some milk churns and other agricultural produce. Parcels traffic received for the army included canned ice containers, the size of tea-chests, small animals such as mice in cages and other animals such as dogs and goats. These were supplied in addition to other similar animals reared in the Chemical Defence Establishment's own farm. The Establishment sent a vehicle to collect them. Up to closure the station staff at Porton made use of a book of South Western paper tickets for miscellaneous traffic such as bicycles. On occasion a horsebox arrived, often on the rear of the 4.5pm passenger train from Salisbury to Basingstoke. On leaving the platform the train halted just beyond the bridge and the horsebox uncoupled to run back under gravity into the yard where the horses were unloaded in the dock behind the platform.

Public goods traffic at Porton resembled that at other stations on the line. Two coal merchants had premises in the goods yard,

Messrs Lanham and Hart. Incoming traffic included coal, bags of cement in box vans, steel girders, timber, roadstone for Wiltshire County Council, some fertiliser and animal feedstuffs in box vans. When steel girders arrived they were unloaded using a runway crane (see track diagram) but it was hard physical work. When fertiliser arrived the heavy bags were unloaded from box vans onto a lorry, sent up from Salisbury Milford Goods station for onward delivery to local farms. Some general merchandise was received and consignments for Porton were unloaded from vans. Traffic forwarded included hay for animal fodder and straw for use in the strawberry fields of South Hampshire. These bulky loads were piled high onto open wagons, and roped and covered with two tarpaulins, carefully secured for a safe journey. Sacks of corn were also loaded for transit to the docks at Poole.

When new army camps or air force bases were being constructed, almost all the materials came in by train. For a full description see the military railway section. Wagons were unloaded in the goods yard by army civilian staff or by the army and taken away by lorry or, if for Porton Camp, transferred to the narrow gauge wagons.

By the 1950s Porton goods yard was served by the 10.15am freight from Salisbury to Basingstoke, which arrived about 10.30am; by 1958 (see table) it ran about thirty minutes later. The locomotive first shunted into the sidings any wagons for Porton, which had been marshalled at the rear of the train. It would then shunt the couple of box vans (known as road boxes) of small and medium sized consignments from Milford Goods, to the goods shed on the Up platform. Here the consignments for Porton were unloaded, with the locomotive still coupled up. When this had been completed the locomotive would return to the goods yard with the two road boxes, couple them to the rest of the train along with any outgoing wagons, and depart when the line was clear. At this time the long Up Siding West was sometimes used for the berthing of a long rake of coal wagons.

Occasionally Down military special trains arrived to shunt the yard, using the run-round provided by the two crossovers. Only the West crossover was operated by the signalman; when the East crossover was required a porter operated the ground frame in conjunction with the signalman, using bell codes.

Much of the goods dealt with at Porton was for the military camps in the area – often a complete train (or more) laden with all sorts of equipment. During World War Two Cusses Gorse Camp, towards Great Durnford, housed American troops and, later on, Italian prisoners of war. During the build-up to D-day American troops were based at camps at Winterbourne and off the Winterslow Road – segregated camps for white troops and 'negroes'. In the 1940s special trains of Warflat wagons carrying tanks were loaded and unloaded. Army land rovers went to and from Winterbourne Camp on flat wagons, chocked and roped securely.

The embankment and trestle viaduct for the 60cm gauge Porton Military Railway under construction in 1917, adjacent to the LSWR buffer stops at Porton station. To the left is the station approach road leading up from Porton village in the Bourne valley. Col.Crossley courtesy Keith Norris.

DES 0-4-0Ts Nos. 130, 1030, 11 and 12 outside the Porton Down shed of the 60cm gauge Porton Military Railway in November 1917. Col. Crossley, courtesy Keith Norris.

The Porton Military Railway

In 1916 the Army acquired much of Idmiston Down for what became the Royal Engineers Experimental Station, Porton, intended to develop defences against chemical warfare. The War Department subsequently purchased much of the land to the south of the line in the 1920s. By the end of the war, in 1918, the camp had accommodation for a thousand men and extensive facilities. As recounted earlier, the only road access to Idmiston Down was the lane under bridge No.208 and when heavy equipment arrived at Porton station it was almost impossible to cart it to the base. Accordingly, in 1917, the army decided to build a 60cm gauge railway from Porton station to the base, using materials from its closed factory at Henbury.

The narrow gauge tracks commenced in the goods yard between the South Western sidings, laid in 1899, and curved right round to climb behind the yard, partially on a trestle viaduct. Here there were more sidings before the line climbed up and over bridge No.210 and out on to the downs. One 'main line' ran to Porton Camp where there was a complex of sidings serving all the principal buildings and another south-west to the Trench Mortar Experimental Station near the aptly named Winterbourne Gunner. The track layout and the buildings served changed considerably over the years but at its peak

there were more than four miles of 'main line' and miles more of sidings.

At Porton station a 3 ton steam crane was installed for transferring goods from the standard gauge to the narrow gauge wagons. This crane had three long fixed members in the form of a triangular pyramid with a long metal lattice jib. Originally bridge No.210 had been constructed to carry nothing heavier than a farm cart, so before the railway was laid over the top it was strengthened with half inch steel bars and a 'mattress' of six inches of concrete.

Almost all the construction materials arrived by train at Porton goods yard, starting with timber for the trestle viaducts, steel rails, sleepers, track spikes and ballast. The steam crane, steam locomotives and wagons of various types also arrived by train. As construction of the camp got under way material could be transferred to narrow gauge wagons, for transit to the various sites. Once the camp became established a wide variety of supplies were carried – coal and coke, food of all descriptions, guns and ammunition, furniture and fittings. Passengers were also carried between Porton station and the camp. The greatest number on the line in one month was 18,663 in December 1918, when 1,434 tons of freight was also transported. The volume of traffic was such that in June 1918 a plan was drawn up for a standard gauge line. The plans came to nothing but it would have commenced with a trailing connection to the Down Main line, curving through a semicircle into the camp on a grade of 1 in 80.

By 1919 the line was operated by five steam locomotives, one petrol engine, some 150 wagons (from small tipper trucks to 8 ton bogie wagons) and six passenger carriages. At the camp there was an engine

DES 0-4-0T No.12 with a construction train in January 1918, on the trestle viaduct curving round Porton station goods yard. Col. Crossley, courtesy Keith Norris.

arrive at Porton station about 10.30am, the train comprising a rake of empty skips with a couple of flat wagons. The train returned to the camp about 12 noon with skips loaded with coal, together with consignments for the camp which had just arrived on the Up main line goods carried on the flat wagons, the return uphill journey taking about 30 minutes.

The little railway remained in use until the late 1940s when coal deliveries were transferred to a Salisbury coal merchant who supplied the camp by lorry. Much of the information about the Porton Military Railway has come from an article written by Mr K.P.Norris in a publication of the Industrial Railway Society.

Signalling

The original signal box equipment at Porton included a Stevens frame of 13 levers and Sykes' lock and block instruments. In both directions there were distant, home and starting signals, with the addition of an Up advanced starting signal to control the departure of Up goods trains from the yard.

shed and workshops where some of the wagons were built. After the Armistice and demobilisation, traffic decreased significantly, and the steam locomotives were replaced by petrol engines.

Porton Down was the official name for the establishment here but was known by locals as 'Porton Camp'. It employed large numbers of civilian staff who greatly outnumbered the military. As the camp changed so did the railway. Passenger services continued until 1937 when the Silver Star bus services based inside the camp replaced them. At Porton station the Southern Railway replaced the steam crane with a runway type crane of two tons capacity and 20ft maximum height. It ran on its own rails and spanned three tracks, two standard gauge and one narrow gauge. It was operated manually, requiring hard physical effort by the men working it. When the Microbiological Research Unit was built in 1948 a new narrow gauge branch was laid down for the construction work. In the late 1940s a narrow gauge train, driven by Mr Arthur Roberts and Mr Jack Pope, would

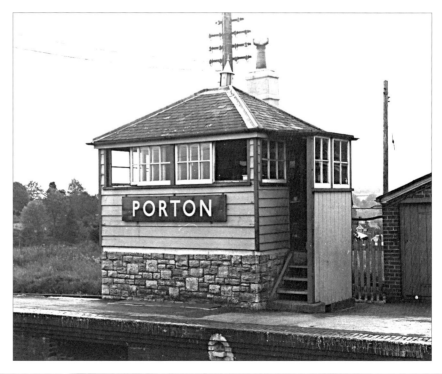

An unidentified West Country class 4-6-2 climbs Porton bank past the signal box on 6th August 1956. J.T.Rendell, The Transport Treasury.

Lever No.5 released the 4 lever ground frame at the Grateley end, which controlled the east crossover.

In April 1899 the layout was extended and this required an extra 4 levers in the frame, bringing it up to 17. The layout then included a Down siding but this was taken out in 1924. Closing switches enabled both Amesbury Junction and Porton to be switched out at night when there were no Bulford branch trains, the block section becoming Grateley to Salisbury Tunnel Junction. However, at night when there was heavy military traffic on the branch, or any at Porton station, the box remained open.

Porton signal box, 2 miles 1,147 yards from Amesbury Junction box, was on the Up platform on the Grateley side. There were two crossovers, 353 yards on the Grateley side, worked from a ground frame opposite the box. There were also catch points on the Up line, 730 yards on the Salisbury side on a rising gradient of 1 in 140.

Staff

In 1889 Mr Frederick Compton was the Stationmaster at Porton, in 1895 Mr Charles Fanner, in 1915 Mr Robert Francis Nobbs, during 1923-1927 Mr Charles L.Farbrother, from 1930 to 1932 Mr A.G.Carter who then moved to Seaton Junction, in 1934-1937 MrA.G.Hill, in 1939 Mr F.G.Carden, in 1945 Mr Gillingham, and in 1948 Mr R.I.Hunt.

For its first forty years, Porton was a quiet country station and staffed as such. With the first half of the twentieth century, as already seen, it became very active with military traffic and the Stationmaster was a

busy man. After 'Porton Camp' opened in 1943 he was also responsible for Idmiston Halt. By the 1950s the Stationmaster was assisted by three porters, one a junior who assisted on a variety of duties. As we have seen, some of the porters' shifts at Porton were spent at Idmiston Halt or Grateley on some similar duties. The porters worked one of three turns, early from about 7am starting at Idmiston, middle from about 9am involving some work at Grateley, and late from about 2pm finishing at Idmiston. One of the porters had passed as a porter-signalman who worked the signal box between signalmen's shifts.

The water for the station was pumped by hand from a well, as part of the porters' daily duties. In the 1940s this was performed daily by the early and late turn porters and the junior at the change of shift around 2.0pm. Pumping was effected by turning an enormous vertical wheel. About five feet in diameter, the four men and boys made light work of the task in hand. There was always more water required on Mondays after the Stationmaster's family had had their weekend baths. A windmill, as at Grateley, would have been most welcome.

The porters spent considerable time in the lamp room filling various lamps with paraffin and trimming their wicks. They replaced the oil lamps for signals on a weekly rota, the Up distant being the furthest away, the Down distant by then being a colour light. They were also responsible for lighting the Tilley lamps at dusk and extinguishing them after the last train. In the goods yard they assisted with checking incoming wagons and departing wagons. Much of work in the yard, transferring loads etc.,

was carried out by army staff, both soldiers and civilians. However, at busy times extra railway staff from Salisbury and elsewhere were sent to Porton to assist the local men.

Porton signal box was manned by two signalmen working alternate early and late turns, with a porter-signalman for an hour or so in between, assisted by rest day relief men. During the war considerable overtime was necessary to cope with all the traffic.

When Peter Diaper left school and started at Porton as one of the two junior porters in 1945, the Stationmaster was Mr Gillingham. The signalmen were Mr Ernie Light and Mr Tom Coombes (succeeded by Mr Wally James) and two porters, Mr Harry Demain and Mr Bob Grace. Later Peter became a porter and, after national service, a porter-signalman until leaving to become a guard at Salisbury. Mr Harry Selway was the village carrier; he ran 'a navy blue van' and there were two coal merchants. These were Mr Hart, who delivered with two horse and carts and Mr Harold Annetts who had two lorries.

By the late 1950s the Stationmaster was a Mr Steadman; signalmen Ernie Light was still there while the others by then were Mr Terry Fower with relief signalman Mr Peter Barlow and porter-signalman Mr Peter Witt. The porters were Mr Derrick Hopkins, Harry Selway and relief porter Mr Tony Kite. By the 1960s one of them was Mr Barry Lake and the signalmen were Mr Derrick Hopkins and, still, Ernie Light. Mr Steadman lived in the station house, the station cottages being occupied by a retired railwaymen. Water for the cottages was drawn by hand from a well. There was a permanent way gang based at Porton under ganger Cecil Chandlers, maintaining the line between Amesbury Junction and Winterbourne. Their supervisor, Bill Cancel, would use train or a bicycle to visit the gang wherever they were at work. *We would like to thank Mr Barry Lake, Mr Derrick Hopkins and Mr Peter Diaper for providing much information about Porton, Idmiston and Grateley stations.*

Porton Today

The goods yard was closed in 1962 and the station and signal box in 1968. Subsequently all the station buildings and railway cottages were demolished; a bungalow has been built in the light railway yard and the whole station area has become the Porton Garden and Aquatic Centre. Although the Railway Hotel has become the Porton Hotel the inn sign still has a green painted locomotive! A Wilts and Dorset bus service runs along the country lanes serving Idmiston, Porton and Gomeldon villages and in recent years there was an unsuccessful petition requesting the re-opening of the station. Multiple units speed through the empty site passing automatic colour light signals in each direction.

From Porton to Laverstock

Leaving Porton station the double track main line, and long Up siding, ran out over an embankment from where there were good views to the north over the small village and Bourne valley. Bridge No.211 carried the line over a country lane and continued straight to the south-west, falling on a 1 in 140 gradient. From here on there were occasional views to be had of the spire of Salisbury cathedral. The Porton Up home signal was passed followed by the buffers of the Up siding and the Porton Up distant

signal. To the south there were views through the fence of the army facilities at Winterbourne Gunner Camp – back in the 1920s these included the branch of the narrow gauge line. To the north was the meandering Bourne valley.

The line ran on to a long low embankment to Gomeldon bridge, No.212, carrying the line over a country lane. The gradient then eased to 1 in 169 and milepost 79 was passed followed by bridge No.213 which carried the line over a country lane at Winterbourne Gunner. The line entered a long low cutting near Winterbourne Dauntsey, passing under iron bridge No.214 and masonry bridge No.215 which carried footpaths from the village to army camps on the south of the line. The line passed on to an embankment and over a lane on bridge No.216. The line now ran into a cutting behind the village of Winterbourne Earls, spanned by bridge No.217 carrying a farm track. It turned a little to the south at 80 chains radius and passed milepost 80. On 11th January 1912 the LSWR declined a proposal for a halt at Winterbourne.

The line was now on a low embankment and crossed a farm track near Hurdcott on bridge No.218. The A338 main road ran alongside the line which curved slightly to the right at 80 chains radius. The road gradually gained height until crossing the line on bridge No.219 before milepost 81 near Ford, the road negotiating sharp bends on each side. Here, at Broken Cross, a railway cottage was built by William Gue & Son in 1857, for £190.

Emerging from the cutting the line ran out on to an embankment a mile long across the Bourne valley and passed the Tunnel Junction Down distant signal. Along this stretch were a number of small bridges. First

was No.220 for a minor road, No.221 for a stream, No.222 for the River Bourne, No.223 a culvert and 224 for another stream. No.225, St Thomas Bridge, crossed over the main A30 London Road and No.226, Bishopsdown Bridge, gave access to the water meadows. Near bridge No.225 was the site of Laverstock signal box. Although closed in 1930 it is appropriate to consider it here in our 1950s description.

LAVERSTOCK SIGNAL BOX

Chronology
Signal box (81 miles 45 chains from Waterloo) opened circa 1885.
Signal box closed 16th December 1930.

Description

On 10th December 1884 the South Western Traffic Committee approved a recommendation from a Mr Verrinder for an extra signal section 'to prevent detention to trains' between Porton and Tunnel Junction, costing £642 including two cottages. Laverstock signal box was perched on top of the embankment on the Up side of the line near the A30 road bridge, No.225. It was designed to ease the increasing traffic demands by shortening the block section, of more than four miles, between Salisbury Tunnel Junction and Porton. In the 1888 timetable an Up express train was allowed six minutes for this block section but a stopping goods train twelve minutes, due to the stiff grade. No doubt there were occasions when Up trains were held at both Tunnel Junction and Salisbury station waiting for a preceding train to clear Porton. After Laverstock box opened, Up main line trains could quickly clear Tunnel Junction and trains from Salisbury to Southampton and Poole could proceed without delay.

Approaching Laverstock on Saturday 31st July 1965 BR standard 4-6-0 No.73111 on the 2.13pm Exmouth/2.27pm Sidmouth to Waterloo, during the last summer of the service following the 1964 Western Region timetable changes. To the rear of the train are the Tunnel Junction signals. S.C.Nash.

In the late 1930s Lord Nelson class 4-6-0 No.851 *Sir Francis Drake* in Bulleid livery emerges from Fisherton Tunnel with the Up *Atlantic Coast Express*.

It would appear that Laverstock box was a wooden cabin with a small lever frame, probably of no more than six levers, to control distant, home and possibly starting signals in both directions, rather like Enham box near Andover. The Laverstock Up distant signal arm was on the same post as the Salisbury Tunnel Junction Up starting signal. There are no crossovers recorded. The block sections to both Porton and Salisbury Tunnel Junction were regulated with Sykes' Lock and Block instruments. It would appear that there was a closing switch and that this box was switched in at busy periods. In 1909 supplies of coal and other stores for Laverstock box came from Salisbury on the 5.30am Friday Goods from Salisbury to Bulford. Closing in 1930, the role of Laverstock box was taken over by an intermediate block signal, which was also controlled by the No.4 lever for the Up

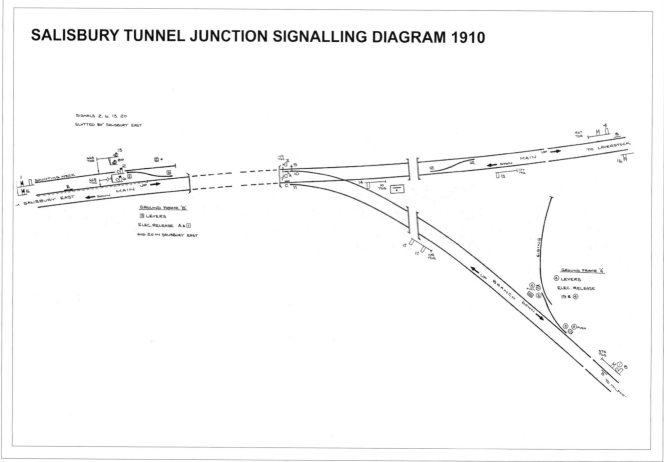

SALISBURY TUNNEL JUNCTION SIGNALLING DIAGRAM 1910

advanced starting signal for Salisbury Tunnel Junction. The two signalmen's cottages built about 1885 survive at the time of writing, at the side of the line on the A30 road near St Thomas Bridge.

There was an Up intermediate block signal 1 mile 66 yards from Tunnel Junction, and a speed restriction of 50mph for Down trains between 81 miles 67.5 chains and 82 miles 33 chains, on the approach to Tunnel Junction. (BR 1960).

From Laverstock to Tunnel Junction

The line, first level then falling at 1 in 733, continued south-west straight along the embankment. To the north was the main A30 London road with houses built along it, whilst to the south were splendid views over the water meadows of the River Bourne across to the village of Laverstock. The line curved gently to the left at 100 chains and passed milepost 82. The Tunnel Junction Down outer home and Up starting signals were passed as the line ran behind the houses in Cheverall Avenue. It crossed a track leading to the water meadows and Laverstock on bridge No.227, nowadays used by children cycling to school at Laverstock, and turned sharply to the right to commence a tight curve of 28 chains radius with a 50 mph speed restriction.

At this point the original embankment for the line, opened in 1857, continued on a gentle curve to the south to its terminus at Salisbury (Milford). After a couple of hundred yards its path was resumed with the tracks of the Salisbury to Eastleigh line. This short length of track was taken out of use in 1859 when the main line from

Andover was diverted from Salisbury (Milford) to Salisbury (Fisherton Street). As the main line rounded the sharp curve it passed under bridge No.228 which carried the A30 road over the line, the double track Eastleigh line curving in from the left at Tunnel Junction. Both routes opened in 1859.

TUNNEL JUNCTION

Chronology
Single line from Andover to Salisbury (Milford) opened 1st May 1857.
Original line closed, double line Salisbury (Milford) to Salisbury (Fisherton Street), and single line from Porton converging at Fisherton Junction opened 2nd May 1859.
Signal box opened circa 1865.
Double track Porton to Salisbury (Fisherton Street) opened, 1st June 1868.
Drummond's Siding and ground frame opened 1st March 1901.
Drummond's Siding and ground frame closed 5th December 1933.
Signal box (82 miles 43 chains from Waterloo) closed 17th August 1981.
Laverstock curve opened, to complete triangle between Laverstock North and South Junctions, 21st August 1981.

Description and Signalling

The South Western Traffic Committee approved the provision of two 'cottages for pointsmen' at Tunnel Junction on 18th September 1862. On 26th October 1865 it further approved an Officers Committee request to install a 'brick house to replace a wooden hut for the protection of pointsmen at Tunnel Junction'. On 30th June 1869 Stevens & Sons were paid to supply and fix new signalling apparatus at Salisbury Tunnel

Junction. From this, it would appear that Tunnel Junction signal box opened with the line to Fisherton Street on 2nd May 1859. The replacement brick signal box was built in 1865-66 and fitted with a Stevens' lever frame in 1869, although it would not have had the full interlocking required in the 1871 and 1873 Acts. It may be added here that on 18th February 1885 the South Western declined a 'memorial' (a sort of petition) from local worthies for a station at the east side of Tunnel Junction. The two signalmen's cottages were constructed adjacent to the A30 road with a footpath leading down the back garden to the signal box.

The brick-built Tunnel Junction signal box was one of the oldest and smallest on the South Western. It was, to say the least cramped, leaving little room even for a table for the train register. A hinged flap folded down from the wall but fouled the pull of several levers. The signalmen's lockers and a small wash basin were in the porch outside. By 1910 it contained a Stevens frame of 19 levers to control the junction points, trailing crossover and signals. In the Up direction the distant and home signals, with junction arms on separate dolls, were to the west of the tunnel sharing posts with Salisbury (East) signals. Here too was ground frame B, electrically released by a new lever A, to control the exit points from Salisbury East Yard. These new works came into use in 1910. On the Down main and Up branch lines approaching the junction were distant and home signals. The routes to Laverstock and to Salisbury (East) were controlled with Sykes' Lock and Block instruments and to Milford Junction by Preeces' 3 wire block.

On the Down branch there was a 4 lever ground frame A, with electrical release by

On 3rd April 1965 West Country class 4-6-2 No.34022 *Exmoor* brings the 10.54am Waterloo to Salisbury stopping train under London Road bridge (No.228) and past Tunnel Junction signal box. The signalmen's cottages are to the right. S.C.Nash.

Top. A Southern Railway view of 14th September 1944 through Fisherton Tunnel from Tunnel Junction. Civil engineers have 'raked out' the ballast in preparation for renewing the turnouts with rail and sleepers already delivered to the site. This is just a couple of months after D-Day and the track has taken a pounding from heavy wartime traffic. Reg Randell.

Middle. A subsequent photograph of 12th October 1944 looking from the tunnel to Tunnel Junction after completion of the relaying. The wooden hut next to the signal box appears to be a temporary structure, no doubt greatly appreciated by the engineers involved. Reg Randell.

Bottom. Salisbury Tunnel Junction signal box in 1966. Dating back to 1856-6 with later modifications, this was one of the South Western's earliest signal boxes. Signalmen found it very cramped inside. John Scrace

lever No.19, which controlled the points for a long refuge siding. Known as Drummonds Siding this was essentially the track of the main line between 1857 and 1859. It ended at buffer stops adjacent to, but without connection to, the Porton line. In 1933 the siding and ground frame were abolished.

As we have seen when Laverstock signal box closed in 1930, there were some changes made to Tunnel Junction signalling. In 1950 Ground Frame B was abolished and the points worked from Salisbury East box. From the late 1960s the semaphore signals were replaced by colour light signals and, when the box closed in 1981, control of the signalling passed to the new Salisbury panel established in the station building.

In 1909 coal and other stores for Tunnel Junction signal box were sent from Salisbury on the 9.20am Goods from Salisbury to Wimborne, on Fridays. There were speed limits of 50mph for Up trains through the junction between 82 miles 33.5 chains and 82 miles, and 20mph for Up and Down trains to Alderbury Junction by 1960.

Tunnel Junction signal box was 4 miles 465 yards from Porton box and 1,606 yards from Milford Junction box, on the Down side at the Porton end of the tunnel. It was not fitted with a closing switch. There was a crossover opposite the box. Tunnel Junction box was one of the busiest on the line with, usually, more trains on the Eastleigh branch than on the main line. It was open continuously, worked by three men on shifts round the clock together with rest day relief men with a high level of training assisting as required.

Tunnel Junction Today

At the time of closure of the signal box in 1981, a single track was laid along the original 1857-1859 formation, between what became Laverstock South and Laverstock North Junctions, to form for the very first

Milford goods station in July 1939 with Salisbury cathedral in the background. It had been the city's first passenger station, in 1847, and was converted for goods when Fisherton opened in 1859. The old station platform now serves as a loading dock; three tracks run into the extended goods shed beyond.

time a triangular junction east of the city. This has proved to be a very useful route from Southampton and Eastleigh to Basingstoke, used by both passenger and freight trains diverted due to engineering work and goods trains between Eastleigh, Andover and Ludgershall.

From Tunnel Junction to Salisbury (Milford)

As we have seen, all trains from Andover to Salisbury in the 1857 to 1859 period ran to Salisbury (Milford) station, which subsequently became the principal goods station for the city. From Tunnel Junction the double track line curved sharply to the south with a 20mph speed restriction in both directions. It ran along the embankment, constructed in 1857, which became the eastern boundary of the city, with views over the allotments and water meadows of the River Bourne. From Tunnel Junction the line first rose at 1 in 627 past milepost 96 (the mileage via Eastleigh), then fell at 1 in 569 and latterly at 1 in 1093. Crossing over the Salisbury to Laverstock road there was now housing on both sides of the line, which passed under two bridges carrying the streets above. The line fell at 1 in 265 curving sharply to the left, with a speed restriction of 40mph in both directions. The line now arrived at Salisbury (Milford), with the ancient Milford Junction signal box near milepost 95, 1607 yards from Tunnel Junction, and sidings to the west of the line. Here the main line fell at 1 in 265 towards Eastleigh.

SALISBURY (MILFORD)

Chronology
Double track line from Bishopstoke opened for goods 27th January 1847.
Bishopstoke line opened to passengers 1st March 1847.
Single track line from Andover opened 1st May 1857.
Spur to Salisbury (Fisherton) opened, Milford closed to passengers, 2nd May 1859.
Signal box (21 miles 53 chains from Bishopstoke) opened pre-1868.
Milford (Goods) closed 21st August 1967.
Signal box closed 1st January 1968.

LSW Traffic Committee Minutes relating to Milford:
7th April 1859. Agreed that Milford station should close to passenger trains from 1st May when Fisherton Street opened.
29th December 1859. Considered provision of a house for the station agent.
8th October 1868. Agreed that Milford Junction signal box to be fitted with interlocking for points and signals.
8th April 1869. Instructions published giving details of new signals at Milford Junction, the standard signals being semaphore signals.
21st September 1869. Accounts Journal. J. Bull paid to enlarge and erect signal box at Milford Junction.
17th August 1882. Board had approved the provision of a goods shed costing £300, from Engineering Committee.
9th October 1889. Approved request from General manager for the provision of a larger 10,000 gallon water tank at Milford, to ensure a better supply for cleansing cattle wagons, etc., costing £70.

7th July 1897. Approved the provision of a new 10 ton crane costing £250, to replace the old one which was broken.
3rd August 1898. Approved the conversion of the disused engine shed into a transfer shed costing £200.
22nd May 1922. Agreed to close Milford Junction signal box at night and on Sundays.

Salisbury's First Station

Milford terminus opened in 1847, just off the Southampton Road; it covered a fair amount of ground, though the passenger arrangements were limited. There was just one platform, about 350 feet long, but it could easily cope with the original four or five passenger trains daily from Bishopstoke. In 1855 the Stationmaster was Mr Thomas Frederick Hayward and the clerk to the goods department Mr Samuel Davis. In 1857, ten years after it first opened, the station became busier with the opening of the direct line from Waterloo through Andover. In August 1857 Salisbury Milford had four mixed passenger and goods trains each way to and from Basingstoke, together with nine trains to Bishopstoke or Southampton – seven passenger and two goods.

Basingstoke line trains could not run directly into Milford but instead ran past the entrance to the station and then reversed back into the platform – similar to the arrangement for Up trains at Dorchester well into British Railways days. Possibly a pilot engine was used to draw trains back into the platform; if this were so, presumably it would be necessary too, in turn, to draw out the Andover line trains. The single platform was home to the station offices,

In the 1960s Ivatt 2-6-2T No.41320 shunts next to Milford Goods signal box, with part of the original engine shed visible behind the locomotive. The sharply curved double track main line to the right follows the alignment of the original 1857 single track line from Andover to Milford; trains from Andover ran past the junction then shunted back into the terminus. Paul Strong.

waiting rooms, refreshment room and a W.H.Smith bookstall. Unfortunately a fire, on 27th March 1858, destroyed many of these ('within an hour') but temporary replacements were provided for the next year until Fisherton Street station opened and Milford closed to passengers on 2nd May 1859.

Much of the original Milford site was given over to the goods shed, engine shed and sidings. The former was very large, in brick, with three tracks running through; the engine shed was similarly in brick but with two roads. Both buildings had slated roofs. An early feature here was the extensive coal traffic on which the South Western had a monopoly until the Wilts Somerset & Weymouth branch opened to Fisherton Street in 1856, linking the city more directly with far off coalfields.

The 1889 *Kelly's Directory* recorded that the Agent to the Goods Department at Milford Hill was Edward Knight. Carriers included E.Goddard & Co. of 35, Milford Street who collected consignments in the city up to 4.0pm daily to be taken by the railway for delivery next morning in London. Goods collected in London by 5.0pm were delivered in Salisbury next morning. Chaplin & Co. of Milford Street were agents for the South Western and J.C.Wall of 22, Milford Street was agent for the great Western.

A Twentieth Century Description

The *Southern Railway Magazine* in 1934 described Milford Goods thus: '*The Milford Goods Station presents a scene of great*

activity at certain times, notably on market days, when as many as 40 wagons may be loaded during one afternoon. The yard is well able to deal with sudden influxes of traffic on its 17 roads, all of which bear names instead of the more usual numbers, due to the remaining features of the old passenger terminus equipment. It is rather unfortunate, however, that owing to the slope of the ground wagons will roll out of every road except one, unless braked, so it is anything but a gravity yard. The capacious goods shed becomes a transfer shed between 10pm and 6am, wherein about 45 wagons are dealt with nightly to enable next day deliveries to be given with 'smalls' *between stations on the Western and Eastern Divisions. There are a dozen coal pens for unloading coal through the bottom of trucks and special provision has been made for handling large timber, a 10-ton crane and wide loading docks assisting in the dispatch of this and similar awkward loads. The July wool traffic is always a considerable event, ten days being required to clear the effects of a sale, but apart from such exceptional times the everyday work of the yard includes the sorting of about 250 vehicles, so that although Milford station may have lost some of the glory of former days it has lost none of its utility.*'

There was a 10 ton crane outside at Milford, a 30cwt crane in the goods shed, a truck weighbridge 20ft long of 30 tons capacity, a 20 ton cart weighbridge, two highway vehicle docks and a locomotive water column (SR 1934). Salisbury Milford regularly dealt

with both long distance and local traffic. An example of the former appears in the 1939 Working Timetable – a vacuum fitted 'road box' from Manchester to Milford Salisbury was attached at Basingstoke to the 7.24am passenger train from Waterloo to Salisbury. At Salisbury it was detached to be worked round to Milford. This was a scheduled daily working, and although not recorded, there would have been a balancing working back to Manchester.

About 1960 Milford Goods was described further in the *Salisbury and Winchester Journal*: '*Every evening a trainload of wagons pulls out of Milford goods station – part of Salisbury's work in speeding up railway goods deliveries throughout the country. The wagons are bound for a minimum of 32 different destinations and without fuss or hitch have been quietly loaded with assorted consignments during the day. Some of the goods came by rail into the West yard early in the day, some were of local origin, but in a matter of hours they have been loaded expeditiously and are now on their way, probably to be delivered the next day.*

'*During the night the wagons will be shunted on to other trains, but early next morning a new line of wagons will have taken their place at Milford. These are all independently braked vans so that trains can reach speeds equal to those of crack expresses, as they roar through the night.*

'*There are many intriguing facts to be learned in the goods station by those who are railway-minded. For instance, at the sorting shed will be seen strange-looking*

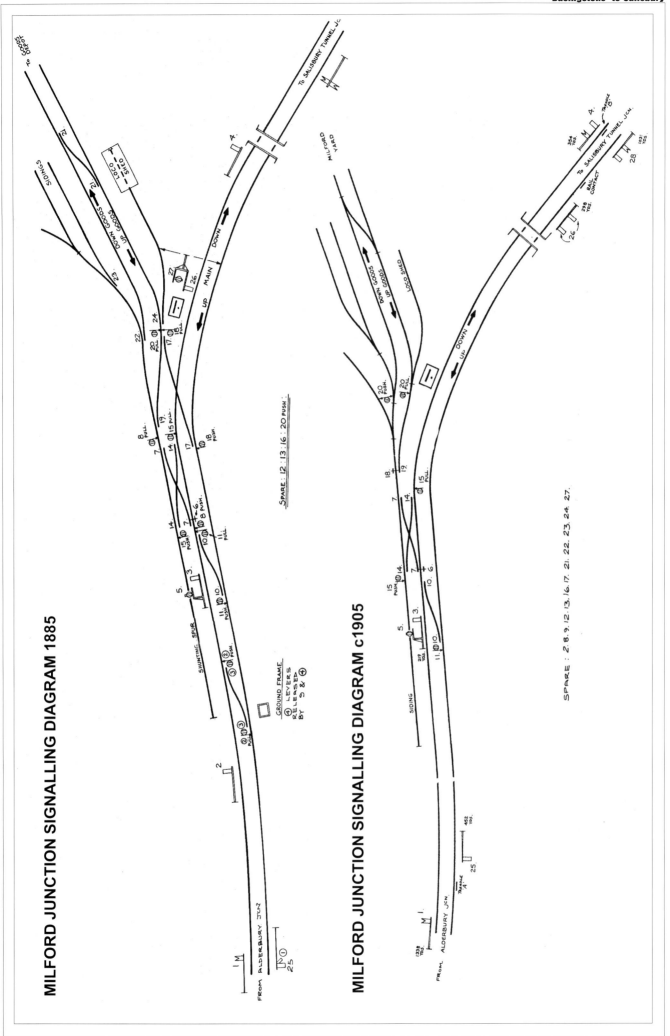

MILFORD JUNCTION SIGNALLING DIAGRAM 1885

MILFORD JUNCTION SIGNALLING DIAGRAM c1905

Milford Goods signal box from a passing train. As 'Milford Junction' it was fitted with interlocking in 1868. It was another very early signal box externally similar to Southampton Tunnel Junction. R.M.Casserley

and thinks that, in Salisbury traffic conditions, this is indeed a feat.

'He tells how one of them recently arrived at the College of Further Education to be asked by the headmistress if he could do anything with the boiler. Water had been cut off, the feed tank was dry and the fire was roaring under the boiler. The door to the boiler house was locked and the pressure was mounting. The driver kicked in the door, drew the fire and opened the safety valve. All in a day's work – but a letter of appreciation from the College is greatly prized.

'Milford is a cleansing point for cattle trucks, and last year was the first station on the South Western system to load barley in bulk – some 300 tons – into a goods wagon.

'The two goods yards at Salisbury handle nearly 40,000 tons of coal a year (apart from railway requirements); and last year dealt with 86,327 wagons, forwarded 56,442 consignments, and received 115,195, all dealt with quietly and with such an absence of fuss that the public could never guess that activity of this volume is being accomplished.'

The main line from the Eastleigh direction continued to the buffer stops, the line diverging to the north on a sharp curve. Between the main lines was a trailing crossover, and on the bridge over the River Bourne, a scissors crossing between the Down main line and the goods station.

As indicated in the *Southern Railway Magazine* and *Salisbury and Winchester Journal*, the freight traffic handled at Milford was of two types, transfer and local. For the Southern, Salisbury was an interchange station between three main lines, two branches and the Great Western. In the era when practically all merchandise travelled by rail, many consignments were fairly small and could not justify the provision of a wagon to itself. Such merchandise, often known as 'smalls', was loaded into a single van at a country goods yard, or loaded into a scheduled 'road van' ('road vans' were ordinary box vans, often vacuum braked) service and conveyed from a wide area on scheduled goods trains to Milford. Here the vans were unloaded and the merchandise transferred for forwarding to their destination. As we have seen, some of the smaller stations between Basingstoke and Salisbury, such as Porton and Grateley, had small lock-up goods sheds on the platform. They were specifically for consignments loaded to, or unloaded from, passing road box services.

As lorries gradually took over from horses the area covered by Milford extended beyond the city. Sometimes when heavy bags of fertilisers arrived at Porton station a lorry was sent out from Milford to deliver to local farms. Although the small goods yard at Wilton continued to deal with full loads, such as wagons for the local coal merchant, much of the collection and

trolleys looking something like Anderson air raid shelters on wheels. Goods are put into these, the corrugated iron keeping them dry in wet weather. To one side is a wide aperture, so that the trolley can be drawn alongside the appropriate wagon and the goods loaded directly in. These trolleys are said to be peculiar to Milford station.

'In contrast, there is a new piece of railway equipment, a powerful diesel driven heavy duty forklift which can haul up and place in position goods up to seven tons in weight. It was in great demand at the station recently for hauling equipment for the Royal Counties Show, all of which passed through Milford goods yard. Coal, still handled in traditional ways, passes through the yard by thousands of tons a year.

'The old passenger station – it opened in 1847 and has been closed for passenger work for more than 100 years – has little of the original left. There is a length of the old platform and the weighbridge office is all that is left unchanged, although the signal

box and old engine sheds, adapted and repaired, are still there. The engine shed is now a capacious store and holds many of the paper products of the Bowater group for distribution locally.

'The Goods Agent – a fine old railway title – is Mr F.Barton. He can introduce you at Milford to many real old railwaymen still working after nearly a half-century of service. It seems that old railwaymen today emulate old soldiers in that they never die, because Mr Barton says that the traditional loyalties of these men make them better employees than many of the newer generation who work only at a job – providing they can be hired at all. He looks forward to the next generation of railwaymen, who, under the modernisation scheme, will give a new loyalty to their service.

'His van drivers are a source of pride, too. Some of them have driven innumerable years without a single accident; one has driven horses and motors for 26 years without getting as much as a scratched wing,

Signalman Mr Dusty Miller on the steps of Milford Goods signal box about 1959. Maurice Bethell.

both forwarded and received for a large number of customers in the city.

There were many domestic coal merchants in Salisbury, several of whom had their own private owner wagons, although several of these used the Great Western goods yard. Those listed at Salisbury included:-

Bird, F. & Co. Ltd (of Radstock) 146, Fisherton Street 20 wagons 12 tons, 1924.
Blew, V.J. wagons supplied by Gloucester RC&WW 1903.
Building Material Co. (Salisbury) Ltd, 1926.
Hinxman, A.&Co. 146, Fisherton Street 1926.
Read & Sons. Large company with many Gloucester RC&WW wagons.
Read, John Gloucester RC&WW 1913.
Read & Westmoreland Gloucester RC&WW wagon.
Shepperd, J.&Son Gloucester RC&WW wagon.

For Salisbury market, in 1939, there was extra activity with the Yeovil goods arriving at 10.19am instead of 1.21pm, cattle trains to Salisbury at 5.40pm and Portsmouth at 6.3pm and associated light engine movements.

Signalling

For the first few years, after 1847, the points, cross-bar and disc signals would have been controlled on the ground by railway policemen but later the levers were concentrated in one place. Judging from its location the original Milford Goods pointsman's box was erected after the opening of the Andover line in 1857. In 1869 the box was apparently rebuilt and enlarged using parts of the original pointsman's box; in 1868 the South Western installed interlocking. It would appear that the box was open continuously, until in 1922, when the South Western decided to close it at night and on Sundays. However, since Milford Goods was open 24 hours a day, including the night-time transfer work, it would appear that a shunting engine was provided within the goods station limits for much of the time. Architecturally it was similar to the old box at Southampton Tunnel Junction but its foundations shifted so that the cabin floor sloped down from the door at one end to the fireplace at the other.

In 1869 Messrs. Saxby and Farmer enlarged and erected a Milford Junction signal box. The 1934 *Southern Railway Magazine* stated that it had a 28-lever Dutton frame dating from 1895 with Sykes' locking. Owing to the fact that most of the points in the old terminus had been disconnected, it recorded, many of the levers

Goods Trains at Milford Weekdays Summer 1909

Train	Milford arr.	Milford dep.	To
3.14am Southampton	4.38am	4.55am	Salisbury
4.40 Salisbury	4.49		Milford
5.56 Salisbury	6.5	6.14	Portsmouth
6.30 Salisbury	6.39		Milford
6.0 Eastleigh	7.19	7.38	Salisbury
5.30 Branksome'	8.53	9.8	Salisbury
9.20 Salisbury	9.29	10.10	Wimborne
7.37 Eastleigh	10.30	10.45	Salisbury
11.19 Salisbury	11.28		Milford
11.35 Salisbury	11.44		Milford
11.50 Milford		11.50	Bournemouth W.
12.20pm Milford		12.20pm	Bevois Park
7.0am Yeovil	1.21pm		Milford
1.33pm Milford		1.33	Salisbury
4.42 Milford	Engine	4.42	Salisbury
5.10 Salisbury	5.19		Milford
7.10 Salisbury	7.17 Engine		Milford
4.51 Wimborne	7.42	8.23	Salisbury
7.45 Milford		7.45	Southampton

Freight Trains Milford Summer 1958

Train	Milford arr.	Milford dep.	To
4.15am Salisbury East yard	4.25am	Stops	
5.15am Salisbury West Yard	5.29	Stops	
7.55am Salisbury West Yard	8.29	11.20	Wimborne
10.7am Salisbury East Yard	10.16	Stops	
8.51am light engine Milford		8.51am	Salisbury
12.15pm Milford		12.15pm	Eastleigh
9.47am Eastleigh	12.39pm	Stops	
4.21pm Salisbury East Yard	4.31	Stops	
5.24pm Milford		5.24pm	Salisbury West Yard
5.59 Milford		5.59	Salisbury East Yard
3.35pm Wimborne	5.35	9.50	Salisbury Fisherton
6.35pm Wimborne	8.38	9.25	Salisbury East Yard

delivery was carried out by Milford lorries and drivers.

Milford was the Southern's principal goods station for the city, although some freight was dealt with at Fisherton Street and several traders had premises served by the Market House branch. Although there was competition from the Great Western, several coal merchants had their premises here from the very start, including Clarke &

Lush who had offices and their lorry fleet here. There was heavy traffic in minerals for road building, bricks, tiles, cement, sand, timber, pipes and sanitary goods for house and other construction work – livestock too, for both market and local abattoirs. Agricultural machinery, fertilisers and animal feedstuffs were also handled. There was a large volume of smaller consignments

were out of use and painted white. However, more recently George Pryer notes that Milford Junction signal box had a Stevens' frame of 28 levers, of which 5 were push and pull. *The box, 1,607 yards from Tunnel Junction box, was on the Down side of the line and had a closing switch. There was one crossover 178 yards on the Alderbury side. (SR 1934).* When the box was switched out the section was usually Tunnel Junction to Dean and traffic was regulated using Preeces' 3 wire block instruments.

Staff

There was a high number of staff at Milford Goods station, including checkers, goods clerks, shunters, lorry drivers and a numerous porters. As we have seen, work inside the goods station transferring loads carried on right through using three shifts. All the other activities, including signalling, required at least two shifts,. There was also a permanent way gang based here.

With dates of appointment the Milford Goods Agents were:

1847	**Thomas Hayward**
(Stationmaster and Goods Agent)	
1862	George Holmes
1872	Edward Knight
1892	William Davis
1900	William Wort
1919	George Vigar
1930	Arthur Carter
1938	William Bist
1949	William Sparks
1952	John Brazier
1957	Freeland Barton
1965-67	Ernest Ebdon

Milford Today

After closure on 21st August 1967 the remaining goods traffic at Milford, in particular coal, was transferred to the former Great Western station at Fisherton Street. The site was cleared and redeveloped as a modern industrial and commercial estate and little now remains of Salisbury's first station. The only clue from a passing train is the sharp curve in the track at what was Milford Junction. On the corner of Blakey Road the Railway Inn remains.

SALISBURY

Nature made the ancient city of Salisbury one of the most important transport crossroads of Wessex. The River Avon running south from Pewsey to the sea at Christchurch is joined by the Bourne flowing south-west from Grateley, the Wylye south-east from Warminster and the

Top left. A group pose on BR standard 2-6-0 No.76067 on the 'under the tank' road at Milford Goods about 1959; left to right the fireman, a checker, Head Shunter Bethell, Driver Blake and, below, Shunter Williams. Maurice Bethell Collection.

Middle left. At about the same period Head Shunter Bethell uncouples wagons in the long Milford Goods headshunt, while the Milford permanent way gang attends to the main line. Maurice Bethell Collection.

Bottom left. By the 'straight road' at Milford Goods around 1959 are, top row left to right: Driver N. Harris, Driver S. Guyat, Head Shunter Bethell, Driver Bevis, Head Shunter D. Judd and, below, Checker Collins, Shunter J. Williams and the fireman. Maurice Bethell Collection.

Emerging from Fisherton Tunnel on 3rd April 1965 is U class 2-6-0 No.31790 with the 10.24am Basingstoke to Salisbury, with Bulleid set 819 leading. Behind the train are the Up starting signals for Tunnel Junction, one pair for the main line and the other for the shunting neck exit of Salisbury East Yard. S.C.Nash.

Nadder east from Tisbury. The valleys carved through the chalk downlands became natural communication routes, and four of the five valleys radiating from the city accommodated a railway.

Almost immediately after passing Tunnel Junction the line from Basingstoke entered structure No.229, Fisherton Tunnel, 443 yards long, and ran underneath the northern suburbs of Salisbury from the valley of the River Bourne to that of the Avon. It emerged, passed below bridge No.230 (carrying Marlborough Road) and continued on a long left-hand curve, first in a cutting then on a long embankment. Here the line ran along the backs of the houses in Hamilton Road and eventually passed over Castle Street Bridge, No.231, and its pedestrian subway. The original 1859 Castle Street bridge had been an elegant lattice girder structure resting on brick abutments carrying two tracks but it was replaced in 1898 by a substantial plate girder bridge. Latterly, in 1910, a third track was added on the Up side as an extension of the East Yard. This was carried on a longer plate girder bridge spanning both the road and the pavement, making bridge Nos.231 a very complex construction. The elegant 1859 bridge was moved a few yards down the adjacent Nelson Road to carry the road over the River Avon, for many years a toll bridge, just upstream of bridge No.232.

On the long embankment the line curved with the houses of Nelson Street to the north and here was a headshunt for the East Yard. The main channel of the River Avon and its footpath were crossed on bridge No.232 and a brick arch bridge, originally constructed

for a double track, was subsequently widened to take two more.

Next along the embankment came bridge No.233, originally constructed in timber. As Fisherton Viaduct it was rebuilt with three brick arches in 1868 for a double track, but was later widened on the Up side to carry two or three more as the East Yard sidings fanned out from here. Originally the bridge carried the line over a branch of the River Avon but in the 1970s, in conjunction with the building of the new Salisbury Bypass Churchill Way West, the watercourse was diverted. Two of the arches were utilised for a dual carriageway road from the bypass to the large new central car park created on former water meadows between the main railway and the line of the Market House branch. After bridge No.233 on the Up side was the extensive Salisbury East Yard with some 20 sidings and, to the north of the yard, the huge Dunns Farm Seeds warehouse, which at the time of writing (2003) is being converted into apartments. On the Down side was a fan of five carriage sidings and a long brick-built culvert, bridge No. 234. This took the multiple tracks over another watercourse and culvert No.235, for another stream subsequently diverted. The line curved now to the right over Fisherton Street Bridge, No.236, an iron deck bridge carrying four tracks over one of the principal city streets and into Salisbury station.

Chronology
Great Western station and single track broad gauge line from Westbury opened 30th June 1856.
South Western double track line from Milford, Salisbury & Yeovil single line

to Gillingham, and Fisherton Street station opened 2nd May 1859.
Salisbury & Market House branch opened circa 1860.
Line to Wilton doubled 2nd September 1861.
Nos.1 & 3 signal boxes into use c1869.
Great Western line converted to standard gauge 25th June 1874.
South Western to Great Western connection into use, No. 2 box opened, February 1878.
New up platform opened 19th August 1878.
Station re-built 1901/1902.
Nos 1 & 2 signal boxes closed, East & West boxes (83 miles 22 chains & 83 miles 60 chains from Waterloo) opened November 1902.
Great Western passenger station closed 12th September 1932.
Market House Railway closed 1st July 1964 .
Great Western main line and signal box closed, Westbury trains diverted via Wilton Junction, some sidings retained 27th October 1973.
East & West signal boxes closed, Salisbury panel opened 19th August 1981.
Network South East diesel multiple unit depot opened 1993.

Traffic Committee references are as follows:
3rd May 1860. The footbridge connecting the two stations is unfinished and is to be completed.
9th January 1862 the locomotive 'Rufus' had collided with a first class carriage and van being moved from a siding by a porter.
6th February 1862. The General manager, Archibald Scott, requested ticket collecting platforms, referred to the Ways and Works Committee as necessary.

SALISBURY TRACK DIAGRAM 1859 - 1878

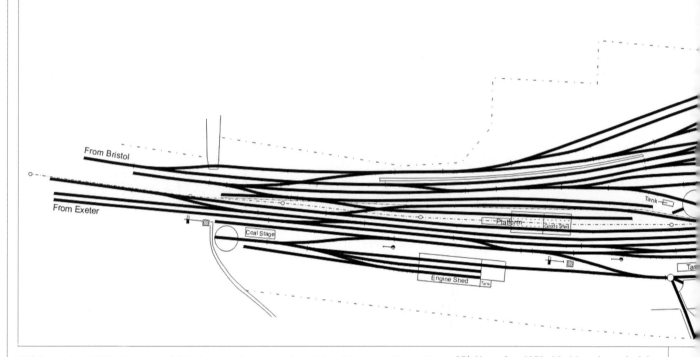

From Bristol

From Exeter

Coal Stage

Platform

Goods Shed

Engine Shed

Tank

Tank

Tank

10th December 1863 Mr Davis of Salisbury recommends a siding on the Market branch for Mr Williams, Maltster, for rent. To Ways and Works Committee for action.

30th July 1868. Following a runaway wagon incident agreed that the Market House branch be strengthened to allow an engine to run over it.

3rd December 1868. The Officers Committee recommended a small brick signal cabin at

the west end, and the old wooden box to be moved to the middle points, to be done for safety.

22nd March 1877. Following a Board meeting with the Mayor and Corporation the advertisements on Fisherton Street bridge are to be removed.

23rd August 1877. The Board approved station improvements costing £11,540. (A new up platform)

27th November 1878. Mr Mann has asked for a siding on the Market House branch, to cost £120 under agreement.

4th August 1886. Agreed to a drinking fountain to be provided by public provision.

23rd November 1892. A large iron grating had been thrown from Salisbury Tunnel on to the engine of the 8.54pm up passenger train on 21st November. The grating was the property of the water company. A £20 reward was to be offered.

11th July 1894. Agreed to remove iron sheeting under Fisherton Street bridge due to noise caused by trains, and to make provision to stop water drips.

29th May 1895. Accepted tender from Cleveland Bridge Co. to renew ironwork for Castle Street bridge, costing £410, referred to Engineering Committee.

17th February 1897 agreed to allow the Salisbury tramway to terminate in the station yard, but this was not built.

Salisbury 1859-1878

The Great Western branch to Salisbury opened in 1856 to a fine Brunel medium-sized terminus with an overall roof covering the two platforms and four tracks. A goods yard lay to the north and an engine shed to the south, with space beyond for a rather restricted station for the forthcoming LSWR line. The station was owned by the South Western, the Salisbury & Yeovil commencing 23 chains west of Fisherton Street bridge. Developments in the 1859-1878 period are covered in Chapter Two.

In 1959, exactly 100 years since its opening, the original William Tite station building at Salisbury Fisherton, in use as a large and busy parcels office, with the red brick 1902 extension behind.

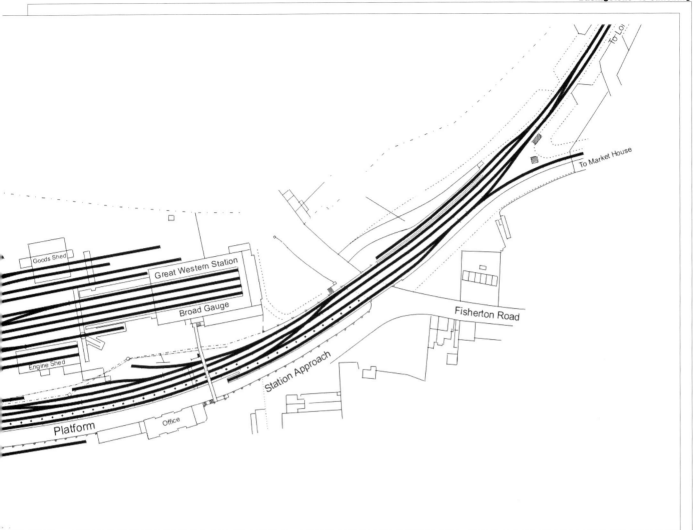

Our one sided Fisherton Street station, was opened in 1859, worked by the South Western who also leased the Salisbury & Yeovil. It consisted of a glass-roofed platform nearly 800 feet long, serving the Down line, together with the Southampton bay, essentially the familiar Nos. 4 and 6 platforms of today.

The two storey station building incorporated booking hall, booking office, waiting room, refreshment room, railway offices and, upstairs, the Stationmaster's accommodation. A footbridge from here connected with the Great Western station a little further to the west. This LSWR building, the part of the station nearest to Fisherton Street, was constructed in brick later rendered with stone window and door dressings and was converted to parcels and other offices in the 1902 re-building.

The glazed roof, or veranda, covered not only the platform but also the Down track. Beyond was a middle siding and then the Up line. Between the South Western Up line and the Great Western station were sidings, a transfer shed with broad gauge and standard gauge tracks on each side of a central platform and the GW engine shed. A ticket platform was built in 1862, on the embankment to the east of the station, and Down South Western trains thenceforward halted there first. After tickets had been inspected the train would draw into the station itself, using the single through platform. Up South Western trains usually

ran along the Up main line past the station to the ticket platform and then reversed into the main platform, which was long enough to accommodate two trains of the period.

This station catered for passengers on the Waterloo, Exeter and Bishopstoke lines and also, from its opening in 1866, the Wimborne line, although most of the goods traffic remained at Milford. In October 1867 there was a total of 33 weekday trains departing from Salisbury station, of which 21 were passenger trains.

These comprised five passenger and three goods trains for Basingstoke and London, five passenger and four goods for Yeovil and Exeter, seven passenger and two goods for Bishopstoke and Southampton. There was also three transfer goods to Milford and three passenger and a goods & passenger for the Wimborne, Dorchester and Weymouth line. Connections were made between the South Western and the Great Western lines. Some were good, such as the 10.50am Express from Waterloo which arrived at Salisbury at 1.13pm in time for the 1.30pm train to Wimborne, and the 1.30pm Express from Exeter which arrived at Salisbury at 4.18pm, just in time for the 4.23pm to Bishopstoke and Southampton.

Until 1874 the Great Western line was broad gauge and there was no physical connection between the two railways until 1878. Previous to this any goods were physically transferred between broad gauge and standard gauge wagons inside the

transfer shed located between the two stations. Here a central platform was flanked by two tracks, one of each gauge. A crane was provided but no doubt there were the occasional problems, well-chronicled at other stations where the gauges met.

1878-1902

The single through platform was an operational bottleneck until 1878 when an Up platform was opened on the north side of the line beyond Fisherton Street bridge. The Up platform was 683 feet long and rather narrow but it also had an Up bay. To reach the booking offices from the Up platform, which were on the Down side, passengers walked down the station approach into South Western Road and crossed Fisherton Street. From here there was a choice between walking under the line along Fisherton Street and up an approach road north of the line, or a path south of the line and through a subway, to the new platform buildings. These were single storey and wooden with a short awning, incorporating booking office, waiting and refreshment rooms, toilets and other offices. For Salisbury residents this was no great inconvenience but for those changing from trains arriving at the original station of 1859 it was particularly irritating. This straddled station brought particular complaints from passengers changing from the Wimborne line who had a walk of a quarter of a mile for the London train but they had to put up with it

Salisbury station in 1973. In 1902 these buildings were constructed in red brick, resulting in this large and spacious booking hall and office. Beyond are refreshment room, waiting room and toilets with offices above. John Scrace.

until the station was completely re-built in 1902. More details of these developments appear in Chapter Four.

Salisbury 1889

Kelly's Directory records that the 1881 population of the city was 15,870 within the parliamentary limits. There were four newspapers, including the *Salisbury and Winchester Journal* published on Saturdays. The South Western Stationmaster was Samuel Davis and the Great Western George Hirons. Omnibuses operated to and from the White Hart, Angel and W.Goddards in Milford Street to the stations to meet every train. The handsome and commodious Corn Exchange, erected in 1859, had its own railway – see later. The corn market was held every Tuesday and there was a cheese market on the second Thursday of the month.

1902-1970

The modern Salisbury station came into being in 1902 with the opening of Nos.1, 2, 3, 5 platforms, now providing two through platforms in each direction together with the Up and Down bays. All three platform areas were now connected by a subway, bridge No.239. The covered footbridge, No.237, at the Up end was retained and improved, though it was later removed by the Southern Region, in 1956. To facilitate this enlargement the GW engine shed was demolished and the connection from the Great Western moved to the west. This enabled some of its passenger trains to use the South Western platforms 1 and 3. So popular was this arrangement that in 1932 the Great Western shut its passenger station altogether. Unfortunately, during the 1902 rebuilding a sharp curve at the east end of the station, of 8 chains radius, was introduced and in 1906 proved the catalyst in the tragic accident in which 28 people lost their lives. Full details of the 1902 re-building and the 1906 accident are given in Chapter Five.

In the 1950s Waterloo to Exeter and many other Down trains called at platform 4. Here locomotives were changed or took water, often to be followed out by a Down stopping train waiting in the bay platform 5. Platform 2 served trains to Waterloo, often preceded by Up locals which terminated here and then quickly moved to sidings beyond. Platforms 1 and 3 were used by Western Region trains from and to Westbury, Bristol or Cardiff and some terminated here. Many, however, changed locomotives and went forward to Southampton, Portsmouth or Brighton. The Up bay platform 6, which in 1902 had been extended over the Fisherton Street bridge, was often used for local trains to Bournemouth, Southampton and Amesbury and the workmen's train to Idmiston Halt. Salisbury station could be

The two Down platforms, Nos.3 to the right and 4 to the left in 1911 with the original 1859 station building on the left. Above the barrow crossing is the footbridge which extended right across to the Great Western terminus. RegRandell.

operated in a very flexible manner for Southern trains but Western trains were obliged to comply with greater discipline because of layout restrictions. Vans or through coaches were often shunted off one train on to another.

Between the West Yard and the No.5 bay platform were several Down sidings served by side and end loading docks, used for carriage trucks, horse boxes, vans and other vehicles conveyed by passenger trains. To the east of the No.6 bay platform was a set of five carriage sidings, equipped with narrow platforms for the use of carriage cleaners and with flexible hoses for filling carriage water tanks. Near the entrance to the carriage sidings was an iron water tank mounted on a grey stone tower. Water was pumped up to the tank from the stream below to water columns, lavatories and various taps in the station, labelled not for drinking.

Salisbury East Yard comprised some fourteen sidings connected to a very long loop on the north side, on a wide embankment between Fisherton Street Bridge and Fisherton Tunnel. The East Yard was originally laid out in April 1878 with some five sidings, with six more added in 1902, and further extensions in 1940/1. Part of the 1878 Up platform was converted to a milk dock and a 1930 photograph shows a rake of milk vans being loaded with churns brought in by motor lorry. In 1944 a further siding was added at Dunn's Farm Seeds warehouse and a cattle dock on the north side. These East yard sidings primarily accommodated and re-marshalled Up goods trains, both Southern Region from the Exeter line and Western Region from the Westbury line.

After berthing trains in the sidings the locomotives ran back through the station to the engine shed for servicing. After any necessary re-marshalling locomotives arrived from the shed to take their goods trains up the main line to Nine Elms, Feltham Yard, Bulford and other destinations – to Eastleigh, Southampton, Wimborne and Poole. Many trains leaving the main line at Tunnel Junction were scheduled to call at Milford Goods to transfer wagons from main line services.

In Fisherton Street there was a gateway and metalled road into the East Yard, running between two of the sidings where wagons were unloaded into road vehicles. Opposite the end of platform 6, were end and side loading docks used for horse boxes, carriage trucks and other vans. Before 1902 this location had been occupied by the old Up platform. At the East Yard entrance was a substantial three storey building; in earlier days it served as F.Bird & Co.'s coal and coke office but latterly was used as a Royal mail sorting office, conveniently located for the transfer of mailbags to and from trains.

Salisbury West Yard comprised about five long sidings to the south of the line on the west side of the station and performed a similar function to the East Yard.

The Salisbury & Market House Railway

At the Castle street end of Salisbury Market Square, behind its elegant Bath Stone façade, was the spacious Market House opened in 1859 initially for trade in corn, cheese and wool. The short railway ran from the new station down to ground level and past a timber yard, saw mills and malt houses behind Fisherton Street. There were several sidings, the branch crossing several watercourses before terminating inside the Market House. Unseen from the outside, railway wagons ran to within a few yards of the Market Square. Initially they were horse-drawn, until a runaway in 1868, whereupon the branch was strengthened for locomotives.

There was considerable goods traffic on the Market House line, which diverged from the end of No.6 bay. Apart from the Market House itself, by 1900 there were sidings serving Messrs. Main & Sons, Frederick Griffin & Co. steam saw mill (later run by Annie Eugenie Hale and Thomas Wright) and Williams (Maltsters) Ltd.. The siding into the Market House itself was closed by about 1918, although the sidings still served the Salisbury Electric Light Co and, later, the CEGB small power generating station. Before final closure in 1964 the Market House line served the CEGB coal yard, Associated British Maltsters, Building Materials Ltd. and Main & Son.

Subsequently the whole area was redeveloped. Behind the Bath Stone frontage in the Market Place is now Salisbury Library, where some of the research for this book was undertaken. All the industrial premises have been swept away to be replaced by the Playhouse Theatre, the Maltings Shopping Centre and no sign of the railway remains apart from a couple of bridges used by pedestrians or traffic into the adjacent car park.

Southern Railway 1934

The extract below is taken from the Southern Railway Regulations for 1934.

'Salisbury Station. All trains, both Down and Up, must stop at this station.

Exchange of goods traffic.
Goods trains will be worked direct to the SR sidings at the Porton end of Salisbury station by the GWR engines and staff.

On arrival of the train at the sidings, the Examiner must commence the examination of the wagons at once, and any wagons marked as unfit to travel to destination must be shunted out by the GWR engine and the SR staff; any wagons so marked must be taken by the GWR engine, van and Guard to the GWR yard, or worked to the 'cripple' siding in the west yard by SR engine and staff as arranged by the Examiner.

Trains will be worked to the GWR sidings by SR engines and staff. On reaching the GWR sidings the Examiner will commence the examination of wagons at once, and any wagons marked by him as unfit to travel to destination must be shunted out by the SR engine and GWR staff; any wagons so marked must be taken by the SR engine, van and Guard to the SR sidings for the necessary repairs to be carried out there.

Loaded wagons in coal trains arriving from the GWR which are carded for repairs but are fit to travel, and allowed to travel their destination, will, when returned in the empty coal trains to the GWR sidings, be shunted out by the GWR engines and staff, and dealt with by that Company.

Exchange of through passenger trains or vehicles.
Through trains from the GWR will be worked by that Company's engines and Guards to the SR Up local platform, and through trains from the SR to the GWR will be taken forward from the SR Down local platform by the GWR engines and Guards.

Through vehicles, other than complete trains, must in each case be pushed into the Up local platform line in charge of a Shunter, who must remain with them until they are removed by an engine of the Company to which the transfer is made, and he will be responsible for placing a red lamp at each

Bridge No.3 on the Salisbury and Market House branch took the line over the River Avon straight into the Market House on the right.

Seen from bay platform 6 on 4th July 1959 U class No.31809 arrives with a long train from Portsmouth to Cardiff, which will run into platform 3 where a Western Region locomotive will take its place. To the right is the East signal box of 1902 with its wartime replacement flat concrete roof, and diverging at the platform end is the Market House branch. To the left is the milk dock, built on the site of the 1879 up station, and beyond the very busy East Yard. Peter Barnfield.

end of the vehicles during darkness, fog or falling snow.

The Inspector or Station Foreman on duty must personally supervise the transfer of all through trains and vehicles with passengers in them, and adopt any necessary precaution for safe working.

Shunting of vehicles on up trains
Whenever an Up passenger train has vehicles attached which require re-

marshalling or shunting at Salisbury the Guard, or rear Guard if there be more than one, of the train must inform the Station Master at Tisbury, if the train is booked to stop there, exactly what is required, and the position of such vehicles on the train, so that the Station Master at Tisbury may advise the Station Master at Salisbury, and so avoid any delay to the train at Salisbury.

Should such trains not stop at Tisbury the information must be given by the Guard

to the Station Master at the last station where the train is booked to stop.

Station Masters must be careful to obtain from the Guard and advise the Station master at Salisbury, complete information.
Market House Branch
The following engines are restricted from working over this branch:- 330-335 inc., 443-478 incl, 482-524 inc, 736-755 inc, 763-806 inc, 823-837 inc, 850-865 inc, 900-914 inc and 1816, 0-8-0 shunting tank engines of the Z class and all engines fitted with 8-wheeled tenders.'

Despite the locomotive restrictions on the branch on 16th December 1930 Z class 0-8-0T No.957 collided with another locomotive, Adams 4-4-0 No.564, whilst hauling two wagons from the Up yard to the Market House branch. There was a speed limit of 10mph between East and West boxes and through the junction to the Westbury line.

Great Western Station Closure
On 12th September 1932 the Great Western closed its Salisbury passenger station and all its passenger trains thereafter used the Southern platforms 1 and 3, although through trains between Cardiff, Bristol and Portsmouth had been using these platforms since 1902.

Shortly after nationalisation, in June 1949, the former GW engine shed was closed and its allocation of both men and locomotives transferred to the Southern

On 10th October 1956 T9 class 4-4-0 No.30702 shunts in Salisbury's platform 1, possibly stock of an Up stopping train terminating here. Over the wall is the old GWR station then used for goods only. Derek Clayton.

Looking west through Salisbury station in July 1959 with Down trains in platforms 3 and 4. The straight platforms 1 and 2 contrast with the sharp curved exit where the tragic 1906 derailment took place. On the right is the original 1856 GWR terminus. Peter Barnfield.

shed, although the building remained for many years housing stored locos.

On 2nd April 1950 the former GWR line from Westbury south to Salisbury was transferred to the Southern Region. All that now remained of the GWR station was the goods depot, which remained open. From time to time it was used for the storage of rolling stock used for exhibition trains.

On 28th October 1973 a new double track junction was laid in at Wilton, initially under the control of Wilton South signal box, and all trains to or from Westbury used the Southern line as far as the new Wilton Junction. Many of the remaining tracks at the Great Western station were lifted. However, there was a railway resurgence here in the early 1990s when the site was completely redeveloped as the new maintenance depot for the Network South East class 159 diesel multiple units. More about this is covered in **Chapter Nine**.

Connections at Salisbury

Apart from good connections between Exeter main line expresses and stopping trains which followed them, other connections were variable. By 1922 there were a handful of through services. There was a 9.53am Portsmouth to Plymouth, an 11.20am Brighton to Ilfracombe and Cardiff, and corresponding return workings.

Arguably the best years for connections between six routes at Salisbury was between 1932 (when all Great Western trains started to use the Southern station) and 1952 when the Bulford branch service was withdrawn. In South Western days, apart from expresses between Waterloo and the West

of England, almost all trains started or terminated at Salisbury.

The 1947 times illustrate the gradual build-up of the joint Southern and Great Western through services with five trains from Portsmouth to Bristol or Cardiff and four in the opposite direction. Although the train ran through, locomotives were usually changed at Salisbury with an average of sixteen minutes allowed for the purpose. In contrast, the Waterloo to Exeter expresses were allowed only about five minutes for locomotive changes, some less. Indeed the description of the 8.55am from Portsmouth, which arrived at Salisbury at 10.41 and left

39 minutes later at 11.20 as a through train seems rather optimistic. There was enough time to leave the station and go shopping in the city! Likewise the coaches of the 11.30am from Brighton, which arrived at 1.58pm, had to wait 45 minutes until leaving at 2.43pm after joining up here with the 12.50pm from Waterloo. Some of the regular passengers on this service were sailors using the through coaches from Portsmouth to Plymouth who regularly took advantage of the delay for a convivial visit to one of the hostelries close to the station. In contrast the Plymouth to Brighton train was allowed just four minutes for a locomotive change.

In platform 1 on 21st May 1957 is T9 class 4-4-0 No.30730 carrying Salisbury duty No.450. The train is the 8.10am from Bristol brought here by a Western Region locomotive, replaced by the Southern engine, to become the 10.37am to Portsmouth. In 1952 this had been a U class duty. H.C.Casserley.

SALISBURY WEST SIGNALLING DIAGRAM

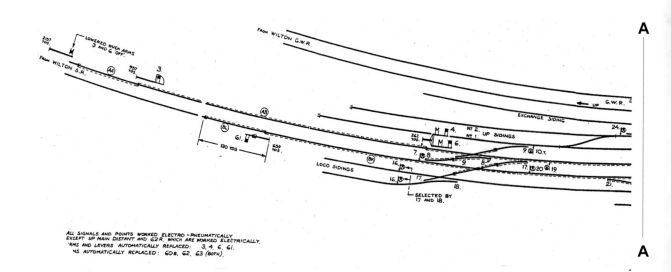

SALISBURY EAST SIGNALLING DIAGRAM

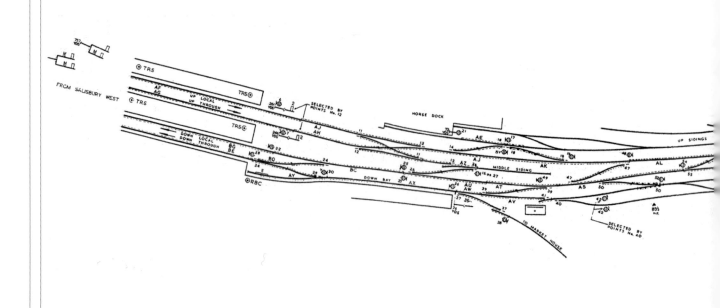

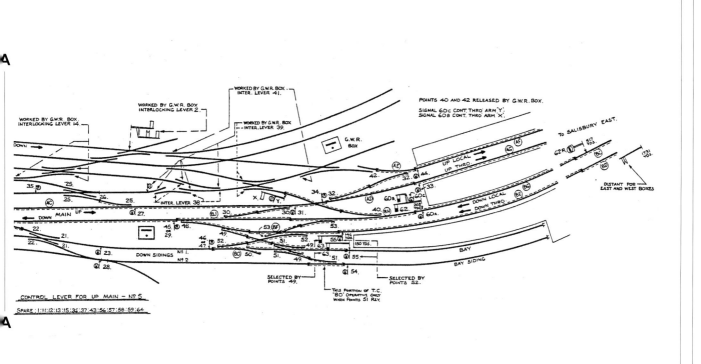

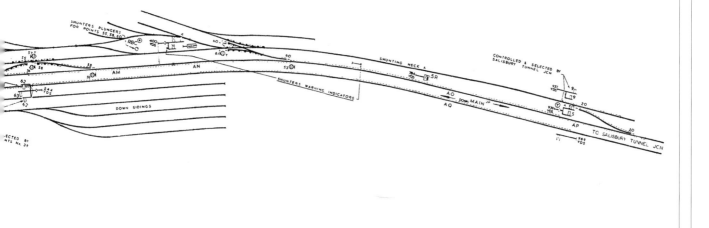

Traffic and Train Services					
Up Passenger trains departing Salisbury					
1867	**1909**	**1947**	**1964**	**1984**	**2002**
6	20	15	19	21	32
	+ 7 Bulford	+7 Bulford			

The night trains were not run principally with passengers in mind. The 11.10pm to Eastleigh arrived there at 11.48pm, with a Waterloo connection leaving at 1.29am. Alighting from the 10.30pm from Waterloo to Dorchester at 12.33am at Eastleigh there was the 1.55am to Yeovil Town. These two trains serving Salisbury ran to a route and schedule required for the Post Office and consisted of vans of mailbags, vans with other merchandise and the odd coach

Drummond T9 class 4-4-0 No.113 arrives at platform 6 on 19th July 1924 with the 4.25pm stopping train from Portsmouth, consisting of South Western non-corridor stock. H.C. Casserley.

WR *Grange* class 4-6-0 No.6849 *Walton Grange* awaits departure with a Bristol line train in platform 3 on 24th May 1957, while an M7 0-4-4T shunts in platform 1. Bulleid set No.445 in platform 5 will later form a stopping service on the Yeovil line. H.C. Casserley.

Passenger Train Service Weekdays October 1947

Train	Salisbury arr.	Salisbury dep.	To
155pm Eastleigh	2.36am	2.48am	Yeovil Town
1.25am Waterloo	3.18	3.24	Plymouth
3.35 Salisbury		3.35	Yeovil Town
3.50 Salisbury		3.50	Dorchester
6.45 Salisbury		6.45	Waterloo
7.15 Salisbury		7.15	Bournemouth
7.25 Salisbury		7.25	Cardiff
7.52 Salisbury		7.52	Portsmouth
8.0 Salisbury		8.0	Ilfracombe
8.10 Salisbury		8.10	Waterloo
6.48 Bournemouth	8.19		
5.45 Bristol	8.25		
7.50 Bulford	8.26		
6.0 Portsmouth	8.30		
7.10 Yeovil Town	8.33	8.40	Waterloo
8.55 Salisbury		8.55	Bulford
7.31 Basingstoke	8.48	9.30	Templecombe
7.42 Bournemouth	9.11		
8.48 Semley	9.18		
7.29 Portsmouth	9.19	9.35	Bristol
9.25 Salisbury		9.25	Bournemouth
7.30 Exeter	9.45	9.50	Waterloo
10.0 Salisbury		10.0	Portsmouth
7.20 Waterloo	10.2		
9.16 Templecombe	10.8		
9.40 Bulford	10.13		
8.10 Bristol	10.24	10.32	Portsmouth
11.10 Salisbury		11.10	Bulford
8.55 Portsmouth	10.41	11.20	Cardiff
9.0 Waterloo	11.1	11.5	Plymouth
11.15 Salisbury		11.15	Yeovil Town
10.0 Bournemouth	11.39		
10.45 Basingstoke	11.52		
5.56 Plymouth	11.54		
10.34 Portsmouth	12.20	12.50	Bristol
11.52 Bulford	12.25		
10.50 Waterloo ACE	12.33pm	12.36pm	Ilfracombe
8.15 Plymouth	12.36	12.40	Waterloo
12.45pm Salisbury		12.45	Exeter
12.55 Salisbury		12.55	Bournemouth
1.0 Salisbury		1.0	Waterloo
10.40 Bristol	12.53	1.2	Southampton
1.8 Salisbury		1.8	Bulford
10.54 Waterloo	1.24		
10.30 Cardiff	1.28	1.38	Portsmouth
11.30 Brighton	1.58	2.43	Plymouth
11.20 Exeter	2.10	2.20	Waterloo
1.51 Bulford	2.25		
12.50 Waterloo	2.39	2.43	Plymouth
10.0 Plymouth	2.44	2.48	Brighton
1.18 Bournemouth	2.55		
2.56 Salisbury		2.56	Bulford
10.15 Ilfracombe ACE	3.0	3.4	Waterloo
3.5 Salisbury		3.5	Exeter
2.45 Basingstoke	3.57		
4.0 Salisbury		4.0	Waterloo
2.33 Portsmouth	4.12	4.20	Bristol
2.36 Yeovil Town	4.26		
3.55 Bulford	4.29		
2.50 Waterloo	4.42	4.46	Ilfracombe
12.15 Ilfracombe	4.46	4.50	Waterloo
4.52 Salisbury		4.52	Cardiff
5.0 Salisbury		5.0	Templecombe
5.5 Salisbury		5.5	Portsmouth
5.15 Salisbury		5.15	Waterloo
5.20 Salisbury		5.20	Bournemouth
4.5 Yeovil Town	5.42		
5.43 Salisbury		5.43	Bulford
4.48 Basingstoke	6.0		
6.20 Salisbury		6.20	Waterloo
4.47 Bournemouth	6.22		
4.35 Portsmouth	6.51		
4.32 Bristol	6.46	6.53	Portsmouth
6.26 Bulford	6.58		
5.0 Waterloo	7.8	7.13	Yeovil Town
5.35 Portsmouth	7.21	7.35	Cardiff
4.35 Cardiff	7.37		
6.0 Waterloo	7.49	7.52	Exeter
7.55 Salisbury		7.55	Bulford
4.35 Exeter	8.2		
8.5 Salisbury		8.5	Yeovil Town
3.45 Plymouth	8.9	8.15	Waterloo
5.39 Waterloo	8.17		
8.28 Salisbury		8.28	Portsmouth
8.34 Salisbury		8.34	Bournemouth
8.55 Salisbury		8.55	Waterloo
8.10 Templecombe	9.3		
7.17 Portsmouth	9.6		
8.38 Bulford	9.13		
7.43 Bournemouth	9.26		
9.55 Salisbury		9.55	Bulford
7.10 Bristol	9.57		
10.15 Salisbury		10.15	Eastleigh
8.50 Basingstoke	10.10	10.18	Yeovil Town
9.39 Eastleigh	10.31		
8.45 Bristol	10.46		
4.40 Plymouth	10.52	11.10	Eastleigh
8.54 Waterloo	11.21		

for those travelling through the night. The 1.25am from Waterloo was the West of England newspaper train with a couple of coaches to Plymouth added for public use. Later this service blossomed to include more through coaches, to Ilfracombe, Bideford and Padstow.

Many of the 1947 features continued little changed up to the end of the summer 1964 timetable. However, by then the Bulford service had been withdrawn and almost all of the Portsmouth line trains were 'Hampshire' DMUs which terminated at the bay platform 6. The service of five trains from Portsmouth to Bristol or Cardiff and four in the opposite direction continued but there were only limited delays at Salisbury. Later service developments are covered in Chapters Seven and Eight.

Signalling up to 1902

The first reference to be found to signalling at Salisbury is contained in a minute of the LSW Officer's Committee dated 3rd December 1868, to a 'small brick signal cabin' at the west end and an old wooden box to be moved to the middle points. It would appear that by then at least some of the point and signal levers had been concentrated in early signal boxes, including one at each end of the station.

From about 1878 to 1902, Salisbury had three signal boxes. No.1 was on the Down side in the V between the main line and the Market House Railway. No.2 was on the Up side opposite the main station buildings and controlled the transfer shed siding and the 1878 connecting siding to the Great Western. No.3 was on the Down side at the west end of the station, adjacent to the engine shed.

Signalling after 1902

The new station layout was brought into use in November 1902. There were two new signal boxes, Salisbury East and Salisbury West, both on the Down side, each containing a 64 'lever' frame. There was also a ground frame of eight levers at the end of the East Yard. This was the South Western's second installation of pneumatic equipment after Grateley the year before. However, whereas the Grateley installation of 1901 was replaced just twenty years later, in 1921, the Salisbury 1902 signal boxes lasted for 79 years until 1981 when the new panel took over their functions.

Originally both boxes had pneumatic control and operating systems working at 7lb psi and 15lb psi respectively but by the 1950s the East Box was converted to electro-pneumatic with electric control of the pneumatic operating system. The 'levers' bore little resemblance to a conventional lever frame where levers had to be pulled with considerable strength and skill. In the pneumatic box the 'levers', like Grateley, were slides which moved with little effort to open and close the control valves. A fuller description is given in Chapter Five.

Salisbury East was 1,616 yards from Tunnel Junction box on the Down side at the Porton end and had no closing switch.

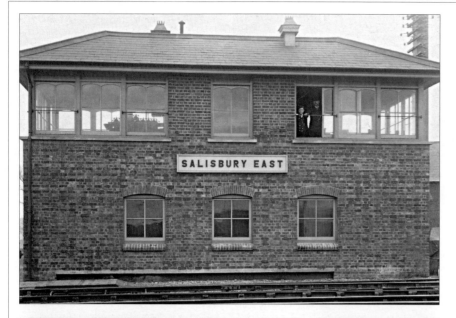

by 'lever' No.20 until 1950 when the points were directly operated from the box. Regulation of the four platform lines with Salisbury West was by bell block.

Salisbury East dealt with all movements in and out of the East Yard where engines were changed on almost every Up freight train both from the West of England and from the Great Western. Up expresses also changed engines here so there was a regular flow not only of trains but also light engines to and from the shed. It also covered the Market House branch and the Down sidings used to berth carriages.

Salisbury West was 755 yards from Salisbury East and 150 yards from Salisbury GWR, on the Down side at the Wilton end and had no closing switch. There were two crossovers, 83 yards on the station side and 230 yards on the Wilton side. The double track to Wilton was originally regulated by Sykes' lock and Block instruments, replaced about 1935 by SR 3-position instruments, whilst the double track to Salisbury GWR was controlled by Spagnoletti Block.

Salisbury West controlled the double track junction linking the Up and Down local lines, serving platforms 1 and 3 only, with the Great Western box only 150 yards away. The box dealt with all Down freight trains, which called either in the West Yard or in the Great Western exchange siding to change locomotives. It also dealt with all locomotive movements in and out of the shed.

When the Southern Region took control of the Western Region lines the old GW box

There was one crossover, 60 yards on the Porton side. Sykes' Lock and Block instruments regulated the line to Tunnel Junction and the Up signals in advance of Fisherton Tunnel were operated from Salisbury East but slotted and selected by

Tunnel Junction. The Salisbury East man normally obtained acceptance of Up trains from Tunnel Junction before departure from the station so that a clear road was always available. A ground frame of 8 'levers' at the Up end of Salisbury East Yard was released

1899 SIGNALLING DIAGRAM OF SALISBURY 'A' BOX TAKEN OUT OF USE IN 1902 FOLLOWING THE INTRODUCTION OF ELECTRO-PNEUMATIC SIGNALLING

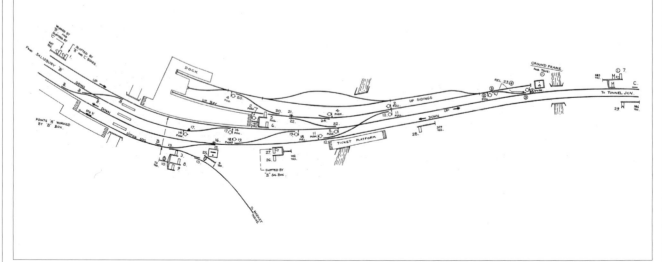

On 7th August 1965 Battle of Britain class 4-6-2 No.34089 *602 Squadron* departs from Salisbury past the West signal box with the 10.12am Brighton to Plymouth train. It had repleced a failed Warship diesel. S.C.Nash.

became Salisbury 'C' and the whole station operating as one entity.

All Westbury line passenger trains worked into the Southern station and their locomotives now used the Southern shed. The main role of Salisbury 'C' therefore was to regulate the block working of trains to Wilton North and Salisbury West respectively and the shunting of the former Great Western goods yard. This latter role became more important after the closure of Milford Goods when the surviving local traffic was transferred here. The traffic handled was mainly coal, for a number of merchants including Clarke & Lush, Voce and Reads.

Staffing

Until the railway management changes of the mid-1960s the post of Stationmaster at Salisbury was one of the most senior and sought-after on the South Western and Southern. He was responsible for not only Salisbury station itself but also Milford Goods and the signal boxes in the area. He was assisted by a number of Foremen and by Inspectors based here who covered a wider area.

The dates of appointment of Salisbury Stationmasters were as follows

1847-62	Thomas Hayward
1862	Samuel Davis
1892	Edward Knight
1899	George Lawrence
1914	Jasper Larcombe
1926	Frank Gabriel
1929	H.J.Towning
1931	George Roberts
1939	Thomas E.Sluman
1947	George Fryer
1952	Stanley Stanbridge
1957	Ivor Gilmore
1959	Maurice Booker
1962	Sydney Cooney
1966	Alan Child (Station Manager)
1968	Richard Faisy (Station Manager)
1984	Anthony J.Thomas (Area Traffic Manager)

Large numbers of railwaymen and women were employed in the station itself including booking office and parcels office staff, ticket collectors, porters, refreshment room attendants, drivers of collection and delivery vehicles horse-drawn in earlier years but lorries later. All the signal boxes in the area being open continuously there was a large number of signalmen. The locomotive department is dealt with separately but there were also large numbers of shunters, goods guards, and passenger guards required to operate the trains. There were also Signalling and Telegraph staff and several permanent way gangs based here, together with railway policemen, plumbers and other tradesmen who maintained railway property and equipment.

Between 1864 and 1899 the South Western had seven District Superintendents to assist the Superintendent of the Line. No.5 District covered the Basingstoke, Salisbury and Yeovil lines with Mr Davis of Salisbury as District Superintendent and Mr Deverill as District Inspector. It is believed that at one stage the District Superintendent's office was in a villa in Churchfields Road. There were re-organisation with seven districts reduced to four in 1899 and to three in 1912. Salisbury now came under the Central District with offices first at Eastleigh and then at Southampton and in the 1930s being re-designated the Southern District which included the West of England Main line between Worting Junction and Salisbury. However, in 1948 the main line from Basingstoke to Salisbury and branches were transferred to the London West Division with offices at Woking. The boundary with the Western Division was between Salisbury and Wilton, whilst the boundary with the Southern Division was between Milford and Alderbury Junction.

Salisbury Today

During the 1960s and 1970s many of the railway facilities at Salisbury contracted, although the passenger station with its six platforms remained almost unchanged. Adjacent to the Down bay platform 5 just one siding remained, with a large car park covering the old Down yard. Opposite the Up bay platform No.6 the East Yard remained with the new British Railways Staff Association building on the old horse dock, together with the Down sidings opposite, but saw little use. A few sidings remained in the Great Western station.

Although passenger train services on the Exeter line were drastically curtailed, as we shall see in **Volume Two**, those to Waterloo

On 29th August 1964, the penultimate summer Saturday for scheduled steam-hauled Waterloo to west of England expresses, Merchant Navy class 4-6-2 No.35025 *Brocklebank Line* at Salisbury platform 4 with the 3.0pm Waterloo to Ilfracombe and Plymouth express. Driver and fireman were changed and they, together with shed staff, trim coal on the tender and top up the water using the high pressure locomotive water crane. Stephen Derek.

a wide area, interfacing with the signal box at Gillingham and power boxes at Eastleigh, Basingstoke and Westbury. There was an office for the Locomotive Running Foreman and rooms for guards and drivers who book on and off duty here. Upstairs are offices for the Area Manager, permanent way and other railway staff.

In the late 1980s Salisbury station and the Waterloo to Exeter passenger train services came under the new Network South East and almost immediately the new corporate image was established with red lampposts and seats. Regional Railways took over the Cardiff and Bristol to Portsmouth services and soon new, more frequent, DMUs replaced locomotive hauled trains. A new DMU depot was built on the site of the Great Western station as part of the total route modernisation completed in 1993, the new class 159 units replacing the ageing and unreliable locomotives and coaches. During the privatisation of the railways, in the mid-1990s, the franchise for all the routes from Waterloo including the Exeter line was awarded to the Stagecoach Group. They operated as South West Trains and the Cardiff and Bristol to Portsmouth line being operated by Prism Group as Wales and West Trains, and more recently, as Wessex Trains.

For the railway passenger train services have increased greatly. In 2002 there were 32 weekday departures for Waterloo one of which runs via Southampton and twenty departures on the West of England line although only ten of these go all the way to Exeter, or beyond to Paignton or Plymouth. There are 28 weekday departures for the Southampton line with many going on to

gradually increased and the through services between Cardiff, Bristol and Portsmouth built up steadily. Up to the late 1980s most passenger trains on all routes were locomotive hauled, although the Hampshire multiple units continued in use. Most of the considerable freight traffic ran between

the Westbury and Eastleigh lines with a small number on the Andover line and no regular freight on the Exeter line. The offices in the station building were adapted to meet changing needs. Much of the parcels office was taken to accommodate the new Salisbury signal panel, which now controls

The west end of Salisbury station in June 1962 with the shed in the left distance. Station pilot M7 0-4-4T No.30021 is on the right, light Pacific No.34062 *17 Squadron* arrives with an up train and 34068 *Kenley* stands on the shed road. J.T. Kirke, The Transport Treasury.

On 4th July 1959 Battle of Britain class 4-6-2 No.34052 *Lord Dowding* on duty No.491 runs towards Salisbury platform 2 with an Up train past the conventional ex-GWR signal box. The layout here can be clearly seen with ex-GWR arrivals only able to use platform 1 and departures platform 3, with LSWR pneumatic mechanisms for semaphore signals, ground signals and points. Peter Barnfield.

Portsmouth and some to Brighton and 30 for the Westbury line with many going on to Bristol and Cardiff. The passenger station has been modernised and is a very attractive and busy 'travel centre'.

SALISBURY ENGINE SHEDS

During the railway era at Salisbury there have been no less than six engine sheds, four constructed by the South Western, two by the Great Western, and a further depot, for DMUs, built by Network Southeast. The two Great Western sheds are incidental to us so are included only where relevant to the story.

Chronology

First South Western shed opened at Milford 1847.
First Great Western shed opened at terminus 1856.
First South Western shed at Milford closed, second shed at Fisherton Street opened 1859.
Third South Western shed, additional to second shed, opened 1885.
First Great Western shed closed, second opened to west of terminus 1899.
Second and third South Western sheds closed, fourth shed to west of station opened December 1901.
Second Great Western shed closed, locomotives and men transferred to Southern shed 1949.
Southern shed reduced to signing on point July 1967.
Southern shed completely closed, signing on point transferred to station, 23rd February 1969.

Network Southeast DMU depot opened 1993.

South Western Traffic Committee Minutes are detailed and extensive:
29th May 1846. Approved an order by Mr Gooch, Locomotive Superintendent, for the Engineering Committee for a 34ft locomotive turntable from Messrs. Lloyd Foster & Co.
18th November 1858. The location of the new engine shed to be agreed between Mr Beattie and Mr Errington, representing Locomotive and Ways and Works Committees.
2nd March 1859 Agreed to build an engine shed costing £1600, referred to Ways and Works Committee to be done.
27th June 1861. Approved building of two cottages, for the locomotive and carriage foremen, on ground between the engine shed and turntable, referred to ways and Works Committee for completion.
26th June 1862. The cottages had been built, and rents are to be paid
30th May 1870. The Locomotive Committee found that the locomotive shed was too small, and on 10th February ordered that it be enlarged to hold two more locomotives. The shed has doors at one end only, doors are needed at both ends. Referred to Locomotive Superintendent, Mr Beattie, and the Locomotive Committee.
16th January 1901. Accepted a tender of £1649 from Patent Shaft & Axletree Co. for a 55ft turntable, also at Guildford. Referred to Engineering Committee.

First Shed at Milford 1847-1859

The first South Western shed was at the Milford terminus, opened with the branch from Bishopstoke in 1847. It was brick built with a hipped and slated roof. It was about

150ft long and 38ft wide and had two tracks – and so could accommodate about ten locomotives of the period, many more than were required to operate the initial train service. In an adjoining building were stores, mess-room and workshop, topped by a cast-iron tank providing the locomotive and station water supply. There was a 34ft turntable on an adjacent siding. As traffic and train services gradually increased so did the use of the shed, in particular in 1857 when the line from Andover opened. Milford shed closed when Fisherton Street opened in 1859. Subsequently the turntable and one track through the shed were removed. The building was eventually converted to a transfer shed, the water supply retained and enhanced for goods station use, as well as a standpipe for locomotives shunting the yard.

Second Shed at Fisherton Street 1859-1901

The shed opened on the Down side to the west of the station in the summer of 1859. It had three roads and was built in brick, about 120ft long and 50ft wide with a slated gabled roof. A surviving photograph shows a structure very similar to the contemporaneous sheds at Yeovil and Exeter. At the country end was a 60ft coal stage and a 45ft turntable, which could accommodate the Beattie 2-4-0s and small 0-6-0s of the period. The water tank was mounted above a small office and stores on the south side of the shed. There were inspection pits both outside and inside the shed on all three tracks, which terminated

A general view of Salisbury shed from a passing train in May 1956, host to both SR and WR locomotives. K.Pullen, Transport Treasury.

in the shed. The running roads, Nos.1 and 2 could accommodate about three locomotives each inside while No.3 road, on the south side, was used primarily for lifting and repair work. There were shear legs inside and a small siding outside provided for locomotives awaiting attention.

Steadily increasing traffic hauled by larger locomotives meant that the shed was soon too small for the work covered. It was lengthened by 40ft to accommodate two more locomotives and the northern No.1 road extended through a doorway to serve as a loop. A middle doorway for No.2 road was also built but this track was not extended until a few years later. By the late 1870s the coal stage had been extended to 160ft and No.2 road extended to become another loop. More offices, stores, mess-room, latrines and a workshop were added to the southern wall of the building. The 45ft turntable had been replaced by a 50ft one which could turn the latest 4-4-0 and 0-6-0 South Western engines.

By the early 1880s the LSW in the west had reached Devonport and many other towns bringing an ever-increasing volume of traffic through Salisbury. The result was that the original 1859 shed, with its 1870 extension, was again inadequate for the locomotive requirements and more facilities were required. The *South Western Gazette* records a conversation between Mr Verrinder, Mr Fisher and the Western District Contractor, James Brady, on the difficulty of finding the extra space and the expense involved. When pressed Brady suggested *'Put another storey on the present shed.'*

Third Shed at Fisherton Street 1885-1901

The third shed was built as an addition to the second, not as a replacement. It was squeezed into the remainder of the land between the station and Churchfields Road, and its proximity alarmed the residents of the substantial villas with gardens backing on the River Nadder on the other side of the road. The South Western undertook 'all reasonable precautions' to minimise both noise and smoke but of course the residents remained unhappy.

The third shed opened in early 1885, 200ft long and 50ft wide, constructed in wood with a slated roof. Again there were three roads, all with inspection pits; this more than doubled the Salisbury shed provision. The layouts of both sheds were linked at both ends and no new offices or stores were required. Now all the land between the main line and Churchfields Road was used up with no room for further expansion. When the fourth shed opened in 1901 these two were demolished and the area used for the West Yard, which incorporated extensive carriage berthing sidings and a freight sidings. As far as the residents of Churchfields Road were concerned this was an improvement, of sorts.

Fourth Salisbury Shed 1901-1969

In 1899 the GW built a new three road engine shed to the west of the terminus, enabling its old two road shed to be demolished for station improvements and expansion. The South Western also acquired more land, for a new shed appropriate for modern

demands. This lay further to the west, on the Down side of the main line between Ashfield Road subway (bridge No.240) and Cherry Orchard Lane bridge, No.241. Ashfield Road bridge was widened several times eventually carrying twelve South Western girder spans and four Great Western spans supported on its brick abutments. Although each span could carry a track not every one did. Cherry Orchard Lane bridge was a conventional brick arch, a few yards from the similar Great Western bridge; each carried a double track.

The fourth, and last, South Western shed was single ended with ten roads about 300ft long and 160ft wide. At the end of the shed adjacent to Cherry Tree Lane were offices for the timekeepers, locomotive foremen, fitters, a mess-room and stores. Between the shed and the main line were more sidings where locomotives could take water, coal from the elevated coal stage, sand and turn. Beyond the turntable was a long building for stores and a dormitory topped by a huge 100,000 gallon water tank. The water for the station and new shed came from the local Fisherton Onger and Bremerton Water Co. and the Salisbury Urban Sanitary Authority, who charged 3d per 1,000 gallons in 1901. There were no less than twelve locomotive water columns, eight in the station and four in the shed yard. The water pressure was unusually high to allow two locomotives of a double-headed train to speedily refill their tenders at the end of the platform. Consequently locomotive crews used the Salisbury water columns somewhat gingerly.

The lines from Salisbury to Waterloo, Exeter and Eastleigh were always worked by the most modern and largest locomotives, which required to be turned at Salisbury for the return trip. The first turntable in 1901 was a standard South Western 55ft one, which could easily accommodate the Drummond 4-4-0s with their bogie tenders. By 1905, however, the larger 4-6-0s arrived and although turned here there must have been many problems with balancing. A 65ft example had been installed in 1925 and this could cope with all the larger locomotives using Salisbury including Lord Nelsons, and later, Pacifics. Finally, in 1956, a 70ft turntable arrived.

The *Railway Magazine* of 1904 reported…
'*Salisbury at the present day is one of the most important locomotive depots on the line, no less than forty-two engines being stabled there. All the regular main line trains between London and the West of England change engines in each direction at Salisbury, so that a large staff of modern express locomotives is necessary to cope with the traffic, and in addition power had to be provided for many local services such as trains to and from Southampton, Portsmouth, Wimborne and Bournemouth, etc., together with short journey goods trains to those points and Andover and Basingstoke. Some of the latest and largest express locomotives designed by Mr Dugald Drummond, the railway's chief mechanical engineer, are now stabled at Salisbury, and work between that station and Exeter or London.*

'*Consequent on the large increase in the traffic and numbers of trains run, combined with the rebuilding of the passenger station etc the shed at Salisbury was found quite insufficient to provide accommodation for the large number of engines required to be stationed there, and in February 1900 the* directors of the railway decided to erect a new running shed to accommodate fifty engines, which was brought into use in December 1901, the site occupied by the old building being also required in connection with the station improvement scheme…the building, as will be noticed, consists of five spans, excellently arranged to provide good and sufficient space and light for all purposes connected with washing out and repairing of engines for duty etc. The walls are of brick and the pits bricked at the sides, with concrete floors and all are drained. Only two of these pits are utilised for washing out, eight hydrants being provided for that purpose, and these are specifically drained for rapidly carrying away the large quantity of water used in this operation. Each pit is provided with six electric light connections, and lamps are fitted with flexible tubes, so that light can be thrown on an engine standing in any position in the shed. The building itself is lighted by means of twenty large arc lamps with incandescent burners round the walls.*

'*The crane or hoist, worked by hand power, for lifting or repairing engines, changing wheels, etc is of modern type and can be easily moved from one end of the shed to the other. At one end of the building are situated the offices, cabins, stores and fitting shop. All necessary running repairs to the engines stationed at Salisbury, as well as to those working to the station, are carried out by the mechanical staff attached to this depot, about fifty four men and boys.*

'*In all respects the locomotive depot at Salisbury may be considered as thoroughly up to date and a model of modern requirements and management. The London and South Western Railway had recently erected a new shed at Eastleigh, Hants, of* similar design but bigger dimensions, and new engine sheds at Basingstoke and Andover etc have been or are being completed. The shed was thus a splendid addition to the London and South Western Locomotive Running Department and remains one of the company's most important and strategic depots.'

A feature of major running sheds was the steam breakdown crane but at this time Salisbury was not so equipped. Three steam breakdown cranes, from Nine Elms, Eastleigh and Exmouth Junction were required to clear the wreckage of the tragic accident at Salisbury in 1906 and later on Salisbury shed gained one of its own. The Southern Railway Running Department returns for 1926 showed a total of 310 men employed at Salisbury shed, which included 94 pairs of drivers and firemen.

In 1947 Salisbury shed had an allocation of 83 locomotives comprising
0-6-0T: 237, 279
0-4-4T: 10, 13, 41, 127, 243, 361, 675
0-8-0T: 957
0-6-0: 315, 317, 355, 690, 691, 3441
4-4-0: 117, 122, 285, 288, 310, 312, 314, 382, 388, 389, 405, 421, 432, 709, 715, 721, 727, 729
0-4-2: 652, 654
2-6-0: 1612, 1618, 1626, 1630, 1636, 1846, 1848, 1872, 1873
4-6-0: 330, 331, 332, 333, 334, 335, 448, 449, 450, 451, 452, 453, 454, 455, 456, 457, 475, 476, 744, 745, 746, 747, 748, 828, 829, 830, 831, 832
4-6-2: 21C6, 21C7, 21C8, 21C9, 21C10, 21C148, 21C149, 21C150, 21C151, 21C152

A fine view of ex-LSWR locomotives out of use at Salisbury shed on 18th April 1932 with Stephenson Clarke coal wagon No.5392, C8 class 4-4-0s Nos.292, 299, A12 class 0-4-2 No. 652, M7 0-4-4T No.133, C8 class 4-4-0s Nos 298, 296. H.C.Casserley.

Outside Salisbury shed on 26th September 1946 is King Arthur class 4-6-0 No.449 *Sir Torre*, still in wartime black livery. R.C.Riley, Transport Treasury.

Ransomes and Rapier steam breakdown crane No.37S of 36 tons capacity.

At this time on the SR Western Section only Eastleigh (126), Exmouth Junction (125), Feltham (95) and Nine Elms (114) had a greater allocation but unlike many others, Salisbury had no sub-sheds.

On arrival at the shed either the locomotive crew themselves, or a preparation and disposal crew, took the engine to one of the two coal stage roads, one on each side of the coal stage, where water columns were provided for filling the tanks. Here the tender or bunkers were filled by the coalmen using the traditional wheeled tubs. Ash was shovelled out of the smoke-box and the engine turned if required; it would then move off along the next road adjacent to the shed

In 1949 one of the first manifestations of nationalisation was seen when the Great Western shed on the other side of the line was closed and its locomotives and men transferred over to 'the Southern' although it was still used for many years as a stabling point.

Full details of the 1952 Engine Workings are given in Chapter Ten but they took Salisbury footplate crews as far as Waterloo, Exeter, Portsmouth, Bournemouth, Amesbury and Eastleigh together with shorter journeys, shunting Milford Goods, East and West Yards and transfer freights. Salisbury shed always had its own Running Shed Foreman, based in an office overlooking Cherry Orchard Lane. In 1923-1927 this was Mr Gower, in 1930-1937 Mr G.Churcher, in 1939 Mr R.M.Barton, and in 1948 Mr G.Shears.

Salisbury shed lost its steam duties in 1967, although dead steam engines were berthed here before being towed to South Wales for scrapping. The locomotive yard was taken out of use on 31st March 1969, drivers then signing on and off duty at the passenger station.

SALISBURY GUARD DUTIES

The guards at Salisbury station covered a wide variety of duties. Mr Peter Diaper transferred from Porton station in 1955 to become a guard at Salisbury. For the next decade or so there were some 50 guards at Salisbury station working in six links for both freight and passenger trains. These included trains to the Great Western at Westbury and beyond, to Bournemouth, Eastleigh and Portsmouth, which with a few exceptions are beyond the scope of this volume. Salisbury guards booked on and off duty at an office in the main station buildings on platform 4, other guards being based at Basingstoke, Andover, Templecombe, Yeovil and Exeter.

Guards started in the freight links with the local goods trains between Salisbury East Yard and Milford Goods where traffic was heavy and justified several daily trips. There were also local freight trains shunting the sidings at all stations to Wimborne, Eastleigh, and Templecombe. The Salisbury to Bulford goods continued to run at this stage but after the closure of Amesbury Junction the train ran to Grateley, where the locomotive ran round before joining the branch. The Salisbury to Wimborne freight started from, and finished, at Milford Goods so after booking on at Salisbury station the guard walked across the city to take charge of his train. The 10.15am Salisbury East Yard to Basingstoke freight included a couple of road vans containing general merchandise from Salisbury (Milford) and this train shunted the small goods yards from Porton to Oakley too.

Salisbury guards worked a freight to Feltham yard, which departed about 9.0pm, and returned with the 11.58pm freight from Feltham to Exmouth Junction Sidings, arriving at Salisbury station at 4.35am. Salisbury train crews also worked some of the stone trains loaded at Meldon Quarry, as well as the returning empty trains. They ran light engine to Wilton where they collected a rake of twelve vacuum-braked empty ballast hoppers and brake van, departing about 8.30pm, calling at Axminster for examination, and then Sidmouth Junction just after midnight, where crews were exchanged outside the signal box. Ten minutes were allowed for this exchange with the Exeter men, who had worked a loaded ballast train from Okehampton. On arrival back at Salisbury at 4.30am, yet another crew relieved.

With promotion to passenger guard there were numerous stopping passenger train duties to various destinations including Templecombe, Yeovil Town, Basingstoke, and Waterloo. Traffic handled by guards in the luggage compartment included mailbags, parcels of all descriptions, bicycles, passenger luggage in advance, dogs and pigeon hampers. Salisbury guards worked as far as Exeter Central but until the new timetable in September 1964 were not passed to work down to Exeter St Davids. Salisbury guards worked the Up 'Atlantic Coast Express' which left Exeter Central at 12.30pm, as far as Salisbury.

A Salisbury driver and guard worked the first Up passenger train of the day, a 'Hampshire' DMU, which left at 6.14am

Drummond L11 class 4-4-0 No.411 and an Adams 0395 class 0-6-0 at Salisbury shed on 30th April 1928. The coal stage arrangements were typical of the larger LSWR sheds. The turntable lies behind the coal stage. H.C. Casserley.

for Andover Junction, thence to Portsmouth. The last Down train from Andover Junction on the Redbridge line, on Sunday 6th September 1964, the 9.1pm to Portsmouth, was worked by Driver Fred Coffin and Guard Peter Diaper.

An unusual working involved the 3.17am train from Salisbury to Weymouth. The locomotive, three coaches and train crew, awaited the arrival to the 1.15am newspaper train from Waterloo to Plymouth, which eventually arrived at 2.57am. Two or more loaded vans, for Weymouth and Yeovil Town, were detached from its rear. The Weymouth train shunted from the bay platform to couple up to one of the newspaper vans and then departed, calling at every station where the guard put out the newspapers on the deserted platforms for collection by local newsagents. Locomotive crews were changed at Wimborne but the guard worked right through to Weymouth, the train travelling by the little used 'Old Road' between Broadstone Junction and Hamworthy Junction. Arriving at Weymouth at 5.35am the guard then took charge of the 7.37am 'Royal Wessex' express to Waterloo; coaches were attached for Bournemouth West and a vacuum brake test had to be carried out at Bournemouth Central. On reaching Southampton the Salisbury guard worked back to Salisbury.

Some guards' turns were mixed traffic duties such as that covering the 4.50pm restaurant car express from Salisbury to Waterloo, which had originated at Plymouth. After disposal of the train at Waterloo the guard travelled as a passenger to Vauxhall and then walked to Nine Elms goods station. Here he took charge of the prestigious fast overnight freight train, the 'Tavy', the 10.15pm Nine Elms to Plymouth. The train was restricted to 50 express fitted wagons, including the large bogie 'gondola' brake van and was hauled by a light Pacific to a tight non-stop schedule. It arrived at Salisbury station at 12.4pm where the crew were relieved by Exeter men, who then ran non-stop to Exeter Central.

The line described continues in Volume Two.

Nine Elms Merchant Navy class 4-6-2 No 35019 French Line C.G.T. slips at Salisbury as she leans into her Down Waterloo - Exeter express in November 1955. J T Rendell, The Transport Treasury.

The newly constructed platform at Basingstoke station in 1904.

CHAPTER TWO
THE BASINGSTOKE-SALISBURY RAILWAY TO 1878

BEFORE THE RAILWAY

Transport links in the area go back to the Romans who constructed the Portway, a road from Silchester, north of Basingstoke, to Old Sarum, which was abandoned in the thirteenth century for the new city of Salisbury. The South Western line from Basingstoke to Salisbury was built a little to the south of the Portway, and for several miles west of Grateley, almost alongside it. In some respects it might be argued that the Romans determined the route of the railway! A major construction project completed between 1220 and 1266 was Salisbury cathedral, using stone carted from quarries at Chilmark and Purbeck stone brought up the Avon by barge.

In our region a number of river navigations and canals were made in the eighteenth century, starting with the Kennet Navigation between Reading and Newbury, which opened in 1723. Soon after the canal opened banknote paper from Henry Portal's Bere Mill, near Whitchurch, was carted about twelve miles to Newbury Wharf and thence transported by barge to the Bank of England in London. The waterway grew in importance with the development of the national canal system and the opening of the Kennet & Avon Canal to Bath in 1810. A pamphlet of the period recorded barge traffic from all over the country to Newbury Wharf, and also by land carriage, almost daily, to Andover, Salisbury and Southampton. Further to the east of our region the Basingstoke Canal opened in 1794

from the River Wey Navigation, connecting the town to the national canal system.

A more local undertaking was the Andover & Redbridge Canal promoted at a meeting at the Star and Garter Inn, Andover on 4th August 1788. One of the leading promoters was William Steele Wakeford, an Andover banker. Robert Whitworth, the Engineer, had first surveyed the course in 1770 and his surveys were revised for an 1789 Act authorising work which commenced in 1790, the canal opening about 1796. It was 22 miles long, rose to a height of 179 feet from sea level and terminated at Bridge Street basin in Andover. The canal passed through 24 locks and was financed by 350 shares of £100 each and another £13,000 in loans. It had no connection with the national canal system; instead, cargoes were transferred from sea-going ships at Redbridge into canal barges. Inward cargoes included coal, building materials, fish and general merchandise, while some agricultural produce and timber went out. During 1842-46 stone from Normandy was brought up the canal for the construction of St Mary's church at Andover.

The Andover & Redbridge canal did not pay its shareholders a dividend but it played an important role locally in the establishment of trade and industry before the railway arrived. The Andover Gas Light & Coke Co. established its gas works adjacent to the canal basin in 1838, with supplies of coal brought up the canal. Several merchants

dealing in coal and other commodities established their premises at Andover canal basin. Just outside Andover in the Anna Valley a country blacksmith, Robert Tasker, established his Waterloo Iron Works in 1815 and acquired land adjacent to the canal for a private wharf. Tasker & Sons used the canal to bring in iron from South Wales, transferred from sailing ships to barges at Redbridge. Robert Tasker became a shareholder in the canal. An 1859 waybill for £1.10s.1d details the shipment of 6 tons of iron from Redbridge to Clatford, the journey taking two days.

The Andover & Redbridge Canal continued in business after the arrival of the railway from Basingstoke in 1854 but in 1859 was purchased for £25,000 by the Andover & Redbridge Railway. After the required three months notice, it terminated the navigation rights on 18th September. Subsequently part of the canal was filled in to form the track-bed. When the line opened in 1865 the canal basin had become Andover Town station so the businesses already there were now served by the railway and Tasker's Wharf became Tasker's Siding at Upper Clatford.

There were a number of turnpike roads constructed during the seventeenth century, the closest to our line running from Basingstoke to Salisbury through Overton, Whitchurch and Andover, with others linking these towns to Winchester, Southampton, Newbury and beyond. Wealthy passengers travelled by coach along

The original Basingstoke station, opened by the London & Southampton Railway in 1839, and demolished about 1900 during the widening of the line.

these turnpikes while a limited amount of goods traffic was conveyed by wagon, most towns and villages being almost self-sufficient at this time. Coaching inns had been established at many of these small towns and remain in modified form to this day.

The Approach of the London & Southampton Railway

The London & Southampton line opened to Basingstoke on 10th June 1839, when coach services to the South West commenced at Basingstoke station in connection with the trains from Nine Elms terminus. The line opened throughout on 11th May 1840, putting Andover on the railway map; to be more precise Andover Road station was opened, about eleven miles from the town near the village of Micheldever. The road from the town to the station was improved and incorporated a new section cut through the chalk of Bere Hill on the outskirts, passing under the 'Ladies Walk' which was carried over the new road by means of an iron bridge constructed from components cast in Tasker's Waterloo Ironworks. A livestock auction market was established at Andover Road station, and the firm of Wolfe had stores here for their business in coal, artificial manure, oil cake and salt. For the next fourteen years the Andover and Whitchurch areas were served by coaches and carts from Basingstoke and Andover Road stations.

THE BISHOPSTOKE AND SALISBURY RAILWAY 1847

Salisbury's first railway was a branch from Bishopstoke (now Eastleigh) by way of Romsey.

Board of Trade Inspections 1847

Capt. J.Coddington made his first inspection of the line on 24th February 1847 and made a very detailed report, which is here summarised. The first notice of opening had been made in November 1846 but there had been some slips in cuttings through clay soil which had caused delays. The quality of many of the bricks used in the construction of bridges was indifferent and one over-bridge had been damaged by subsidence. He was also concerned about the strength of a wooden viaduct at Romsey. The permanent way comprised double T pattern rail in 16 feet lengths, weighing 72lb per yard, each length set in four chairs spiked to transverse sleepers, resting on ballast two feet deep. The report ended:

'There are three intermediate stations at all of which as well as at the terminus, booking offices, waiting rooms and platforms have been erected; they are all provided with fixed signals both for day and night.

'The line is to be worked by the stock of the London & South Western company whose property it is. The staff has been selected from the servants of the old line, where their places have been supplied by new hands.

'In conclusion I have to report that this line is incomplete in the following respects. The centres have not been removed from

One of the high embankments was at Clerkengreen, just west of Oakley station, with a high bridge over the minor road. John Nicholas.

two of the bridges, which prevents me from being in a position to report on their stability. In the cuttings where the slips have occurred, the removal has not been finished and the slopes trimmed, though enough has been done to protect the line from danger on their account.

'The line, which was sanctioned by Parliament as a single line, has however been laid double, and about a mile of the second line is not laid, nor the cutting at the point sufficiently opened out to admit of it.

'About 2 miles of permanent way have not been sufficiently adjusted to admit of high speed, but I am of the opinion that if the precautions I have above recommended be enforced, the line may be opened for the conveyance of passengers without danger to the public.'

In fact Captain Coddington returned to the line and reported on 1st August 1847 that the four points of concern were now resolved and that the half mile of single track in a deep cutting near Salisbury had now been widened to take double track.

Opening from Bishopstoke to Salisbury

The South Western's Bishopstoke to Salisbury line opened to goods traffic on 27th January 1847, the first train consisting of some wagons laden with coal for distribution to the poor! On 1st March the line opened to passengers. The line terminated at Salisbury in the extensive Milford station, situated conveniently for the city centre off the Southampton Road. Prior to this, at the General Election on 25th January, the electors of Salisbury had chosen their new member of parliament, William Chaplin, who was also Chairman of the South Western Railway.

The *Salisbury and Winchester Journal* reported the opening in detail. On Monday 1st March the first train started for London at 6am carrying only a few passengers but the church bells rang throughout the day and the arrivals and departures were witnessed by large numbers of spectators. In the evening there was a public dinner in the White Hart, presided over by the Mayor G.Fulford Esq. Amongst the speeches it was pointed out that the railway

In 1854 the only intermediate station was this handsome building at Whitchurch designed by William Tite. John Nicholas.

The major structure on the line in 1854 was Hurstbourne viaduct, built for a double line of rails. John Nicholas.

would facilitate the rapid despatch of men and munitions for the army and that coal and salt could now be carried to both the city and the countryside around at far lower cost than that before. In 1847 John Marshall & Co. advertised their business in best Wallsend coals at the Milford station, and in 1854 the Great Western Coal Co. was advertising its business from depots at Salisbury, Romsey and Winchester. The initial train service of four or five passenger trains a day gave a best journey time of 3 hours 50 minutes from London, changing at Bishopstoke.

THE BASINGSTOKE AND SALISBURY RAILWAY, AUTHORISED 1846

By the time the South Western had extended its line in 1848 from Nine Elms to Waterloo the distance to Salisbury (Milford) via Bishopstoke was about 95 miles. As far back as 1839 Salisbury civic leaders had sought a direct line to London, and in 1845 Andover civic leaders put their case to the South Western. On 13th August 1846 Royal Assent was given for the South Western Basingstoke & Salisbury Extension Act for a line from Basingstoke to Salisbury, at an estimated cost of £700,000 for the 35 miles. The line authorised ran from Wooton St Lawrence to Salisbury (Milford), with a branch to Salisbury (Fisherton Street) to meet the Wilts Somerset & Weymouth branch authorised from Westbury, with three years allowed for construction. The new direct line would reduce the Waterloo journey by about twelve miles, to eighty-three. The South Western had promoted the line and would raise the capital itself by the sale of new shares.

The South Western acquired the land for the construction of a double track line but the price had exceeded that estimated and other costs had also risen. The prestigious railway contractor, Thomas Brassey, was engaged to carry out the work but by July 1847 there was sufficient concern, regarding security and theft at the site, for Brassey to arrange for the swearing in of some of his best men as special constables. By August four men were appointed to wear Hampshire Constabulary uniform at the South Western's expense. As the depression following the 'railway mania' deepened all railway companies, including the South

Western, found difficulty in raising capital. By December 1847 the board limited expenditure on the line to £3,000 a month. Work was concentrated on the section between the junction with the Southampton main line at Battledown and Andover in the hope that the section could open in May 1849 as authorised. However, by October 1848 despite local protests, the South Western had run out of money and suspended all work. Cuttings, embankments and bridges, some completed, lay abandoned awaiting better times. Powers for construction in the 1846 Act having expired, the South Western Act of 26th June 1848 extended these powers until 1850, but again the necessary capital could not be raised.

It may be added here that the broad gauge Berks & Hants line from Reading was opened to Basingstoke on 1st November 1848. The gauge on this branch, together with the broad gauge line through to the Midlands, was mixed so that standard gauge Great Western goods trains could run right through to Basingstoke, and thence by South Western to Southampton as from 22nd December 1856.

BASINGSTOKE TO ANDOVER

LSWR shareholders were by now deeply embroiled in arguments about either a coast line via Dorchester or a direct line to Exeter. The Basingstoke to Salisbury works had fallen further into disrepair so disillusioned local people took matters into their own hands. On 22nd November 1851 a meeting of local landowners at Andover decided to promote the Basingstoke & Salisbury company to take over and complete the abandoned South Western works. Although their Bill failed standing orders in parliament on 7th February 1852 the South Western again engaged Thomas Brassey to complete a single line as far as Andover for a price of £74,000.

On 4th August 1853 the London & South Western (Basingstoke and Salisbury) Act was passed and required the completion of the line to Andover within a year and to Salisbury within three years. Failure to comply would automatically result in the suspension of LSWR dividends, an indication of parliament's exasperation with previous South Western delays. As soon as the Act was passed Brassey's men were able to resume work on the earthworks and bridges abandoned five years previously.

Board of Trade Inspection 1854

Before the railway could open to the public the Board of Trade was required to carry out an inspection. The first report is shown in full, with its standard format of presentation but in subsequent reports the standard opening and closing paragraphs are omitted.

'London 21st June 1854
'I have the honour to report, for the information of the Lords of the Committee of Privy Council for Trade, that I have this day inspected the portion of the London and South Western Railway extending between Worting and Andover, in compliance with

Between Hurstbourne and Andover the long cutting with steep sides through the chalk at Wyke was up to 52 feet deep and spanned by several bridges. John Nicholas.

the instructions contained in your letter of the 14th instant.

'This portion is 15 miles in length, from the junction with the main line of the L&SWRy near Basingstoke to the town of Andover, and it is intended to prolong it to Salisbury. It is laid with a single line, but land has been purchased for a double line throughout, and many of the works were originally constructed for a double line. The rails are 16 feet in length, and weigh 80lbs per lineal yard; the sleepers are of larch and Scotch fir, and are generally of small size, so much so, in some cases, that the chairs have not a full bearing upon them, even under the joints; they are placed at intervals of 3ft 6in when next to the joints and otherwise at a distance from each other of 4ft 6in; they do not appear to be of a shape well adapted for packing. The ballast is scanty in some parts, and is not of the best description, consisting altogether of chalk mixed with flints.

'The embankments and cuttings are considerable, the former attaining in one case to 85 feet, and the latter to 52 feet. Some portions of some of the embankments have been formed for several years, but in other embankments the work is recent; and the surface of these latter which are almost entirely composed of chalk must be expected to sink considerably in the course of traffic; the slopes also will require, in places, to be improved, before the embankments can be considered as altogether in a satisfactory condition.

'Having regard to all the circumstances above stated, I cannot but consider that there would be considerable risk, if it were attempted to convey heavy traffic, at high speeds, over this line, and I think that, at all events, until the embankments shall be well consolidated, the speed of trains should not be permitted to exceed 20 miles an hour.

'There are 15 bridges under, and 19 bridges over the railway, constructed of brick and flint, of spans varying from 6 to 47 feet, in the case of one of the under

bridges, situated at 3 miles and 28 chains from the fixed point [this appears to be bridge No.152 at Ashe] and under an embankment 62 feet in height, it was found necessary to renew a portion of the abutments about a month since, and the shape of the arch has suffered from the weight of the super incumbent chalk, and I would recommend that it should be carefully watched; at the Wick Bridge, situated at 11 miles 32 chains from the fixed point [this appears to be bridge No.178 in the deep cutting at Wyke] and crossing over the line with 3 spans of 30 feet on the square, and 31 ft 6in on the skew, the centres, though stated to have been eased, had not been removed, the arches having only just been turned, and the railway was made for this reason slightly to deviate from its proper line at this point; but as regards the other bridges above alluded to, I believe them to be substantially constructed.

'There are two bridges under the railway composed of cast iron flat girders upon brick abutments, all of the same pattern, and the span being in each case 20 feet on the square and 22ft 6in on the skew. I estimate the breaking weight of these girders at 64.7 tons in the case of a weight applied in the centre, and the distributed breaking weight for each bridge would therefore be 258.8 tons, which, considering the weight of the heaviest engines now employed on the L&SWRy, 28 tons, appears to be amply sufficient. As the greatest deflection that I obtained from any of these girders, by passing a tank engine over them weighing 24 tons, did not amount to 3/16 in, I have every reason to consider them to be sufficiently strong.

'At the Worting Junction, I have recommended that the levers for working the points and signals shall be so arranged that they may all be on one side of the line, in order that the signalman may not be compelled to cross the line – as he would be at present – when it becomes necessary for him to work two of the levers. I have also requested that chock-blocks should be

placed in the junction siding, and on all the other sidings throughout the line.

'At Whitchurch station, a distant signal is required in each direction, and at Andover station, a distant signal, and a small quantity of fencing are required.

'I have not yet received a copy of the rules by which it is proposed to work the single line.

'For the several reasons above stated, I am of opinion that the opening of the portion of the L&SWRy extending between Worting and Andover, would, by reason of the incompleteness of the works, be attended with danger to the public using the same.

I have the honour to be Sir Your obedient servant.

H.W.Tyler Capt.R.E.'

The South Western wanted to open the line as soon as possible: 'London & South Western Railway
Engineers Office
Waterloo Station
23rd June 1854

Dear Sir
I beg to report that in accordance with the request which you made when inspecting the Basingstoke and Andover line on 21st inst. The following works have since been executed viz:- The levers of the auxiliary signals and points at the Worting Junction have been removed from the Down to the Up line side, chock-blocks have been placed on the sidings at the Junction, the Whitchurch and the Andover stations, and on the East side of the Andover station all the centres have been removed from the three arch bridge at Wick, and the road straightened. The arches at Wick are now perfect radius.

'The engine also has been engaged in taking ballast to those parts of the permanent way, where a sufficient quantity

TRACK DIAGRAM OF OAKLEY BEFORE DOUBLING

had not been laid at the time of your inspection.

I am, Dear Sir, your obedient servant Mr Strapp
Capt. Tyler Board of Trade'

Capt. Tyler reported again on the same day, 23rd June 1854:
'In reference to my report of the 21st instant on the subject of my inspection of the portion of the London & South Western Railway extending between Worting and Andover, I have now the honour to enclose a certificate from the Engineer of the line, of the completion of all the requirements therein enumerated and also a letter from the Secretary of the L&SWRy company stating that it is intended at present to run trains at a speed not exceeding 20 miles an hour, and that only one engine shall be at work on the single line at a time.

'Under these conditions, I have the honour to report, for the information of the Lords of the Committee of Privy Council for Trade, that I am of opinion that the portion of the L&SWRy extending from Worting to Andover may be opened without danger to the public using the same.'

From Capt. Tyler's report it would appear that the bridges carrying the line over roads and rivers originally constructed for double track were completed during the 1846-48 period before the money ran out. An example would be the eight-arch Hurstbourne viaduct which appears to have been constructed originally for a double track. Inspection of other under-bridges shows evidence of subsequent doubling; indeed some of those constructed underneath the high embankments might better be described as road tunnels rather than bridges. The heaviest excavations were in the Wyke cutting to the west of Hurstbourne viaduct, about two miles long and up to 50 feet deep. Much of the material excavated here was used for the long embankment to the west into Andover. The above 1854 report omits details which might be expected to be found in later reports, in particular any mention of Hurstbourne viaduct. The only stations mentioned are at Whitchurch and Andover.

However, Capt. Tyler was clearly less than impressed with the permanent way. Forced by Parliament to complete the line the South Western had kept expenditure to a minimum. The sleepers appear to have been obtained from local woods and ballast comprised chalk dug from the cuttings; neither were sufficient for a high quality permanent way. On 8th July 1854 the *Salisbury and Winchester Journal* reported the opening of the line:
'*LONDON AND SOUTH WESTERN – OPENING OF THE BASINGSTOKE AND ANDOVER BRANCH*
The above branch of the London and South Western Railway was opened for general traffic on Monday. Its inauguration took place on Saturday, upon which occasion Mr Brassey, the contractor of the works, invited the whole of the officers connected with the South Western Company, and a large party

Monxton viaduct. John Nicholas.

of friends, to a splendid dejeuner at Andover. A special train, conveying the party, left Waterloo at half-past twelve, and arrived at Basingstoke in due course, where several gentlemen from Southampton, Portsmouth, Dorchester, &c, joined. The train reached Andover in something less than three hours from Waterloo, and its arrival was duly welcomed by the good folks of the ancient borough. The company immediately adjourned to an extensive marquee, tastefully fitted up in an adjoining field, where a splendid collation, supplied by the Messrs. Wolfe, of the Star Hotel, greeted keen appetites after a long but interesting ride. The chair was taken by Mr Tite, the celebrated architect, who was supported by the Mayor and Town Clerk of Andover, Charles Pressley Esq.(stamps and taxes), and by several gentlemen of the town and neighbourhood. Mr Brassey occupied the vice chair. None of the directors was present, the whole of them being obliged to attend a board meeting, of some importance, in London. The usual loyal and other speeches appertaining to the occasion were given, and after spending an extremely pleasant afternoon, and partaking of the lavish hospitality of Mr Brassey, the company departed by special train, which reached London about half-past nine.

'This branch, it will be remembered, was commenced some six or seven years ago, with an intention of carrying it on to Salisbury, but in consequence of the panic of 1848-49, and the extraordinary pressure of monetary matters, it was deemed advisable by the directors to defer the completion of it until the present time. The line has cost an immense amount of money, not in consequence of any engineering difficulties, but simply from the deep and long cuttings through solid hard chalk, for which this part of the kingdom is celebrated. Some of these cuttings are of extreme depth and length; while, on the other hand the embankments are very steep and high, being in many places nearly 50 feet. At present there is only a single line of narrow gauge laid down, which will, no doubt, meet all the requirements of

passenger and goods traffic; but sufficient land has been reserved to lay another when necessary, and all the bridges are constructed to admit of an additional line. The country from Basingstoke to Andover is purely of an agricultural character, and there is only one station the whole distance of 18 miles, and that is Whitchurch, a small town of no pretensions to trade whatever. The traffic consequently cannot be expected to be remunerative; but when the extension of the line is completed to Salisbury, and then on to Yeovil, thus opening the great trading districts of the west, the reverse may be anticipated. The contract for completing the rail to Salisbury has been taken by Mr Brassey; and from what Mr Crombie, the solicitor to the company, intimated in his speech yesterday at the dejeuner, it will be finished and opened to the public in less than two years from the present time.'

This was not the first or last time that South Western directors had diplomatically absented themselves from the opening of a new line which they had been compelled to open – the board itself was deeply divided. The disparaging mention of Whitchurch in the *Salisbury and Winchester Journal* suggests that its Salisbury editor was unaware of the town's silk and banknote paper mills. Thomas Brassey was a very busy railway contractor – just a week later on 12th July there were celebrations at Barnstaple when a procession and dinner for 760 people were held to celebrate the completion of 31 miles of the North Devon line built by Brassey.

'In 1854 from their premises at Andover Road station Messrs. Wolfe advertised that they had opened depots at Whitchurch and Andover stations for their business in coal, artificial manure, oil cake and salt. Incidentally Andover Road initially retained its name; it was not until February 1856 that it became Micheldever station. The stations at Oakley, Overton and Hurstbourne did not appear immediately in the timetable.

ELEVATIONS OF OAKLEY STATION

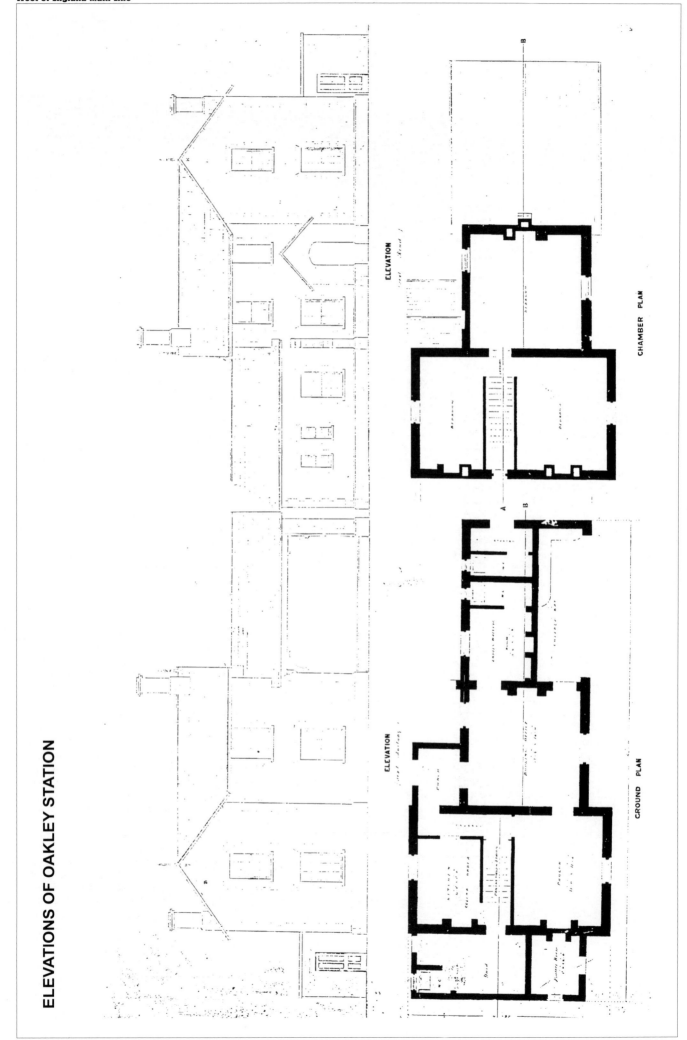

LSWR TRACK DIAGRAM OF OVERTON

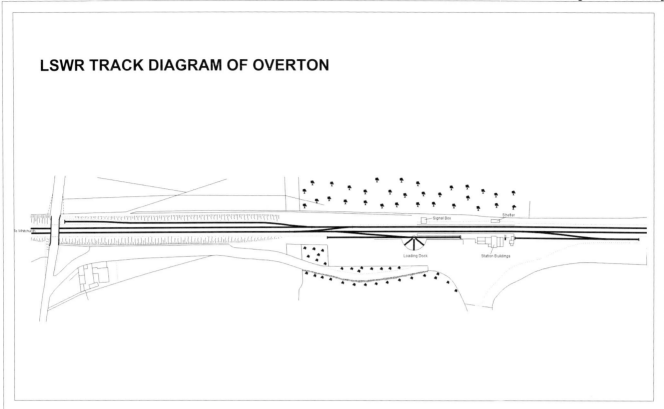

'The fine station house at Whitchurch and the larger one at Andover were constructed by William Gue to the design of William Tite, architect of many South Western stations. The stations were equipped with clocks from John Walker, 5 ton cranes from Dunn & Hattersly, weighing machines from H.Pooley & Sons, and signals of the early cross bar and disc type.

W. Gue was paid for a number of works at Andover station including the installation of an 'engine house' for £101 in December 1854. This was taken down and re-erected at Basingstoke for £90 in 1858. The contractor then built a new engine shed and coaling stage, apparently on the site of the engine house at Andover, for £511 in 1866 just after the opening of the Andover & Redbridge line.

OPENING OF OAKLEY AND OVERTON STATIONS
As we have seen, when the line opened in July 1854, the only stations were Whitchurch and Andover, built to similar designs. Oakley and Overton stations opened within a couple of years; the station houses were similar in design though very different from Whitchurch and Andover. At this time no Board of Trade inspection was

ELEVATIONS OF OVERTON STATION

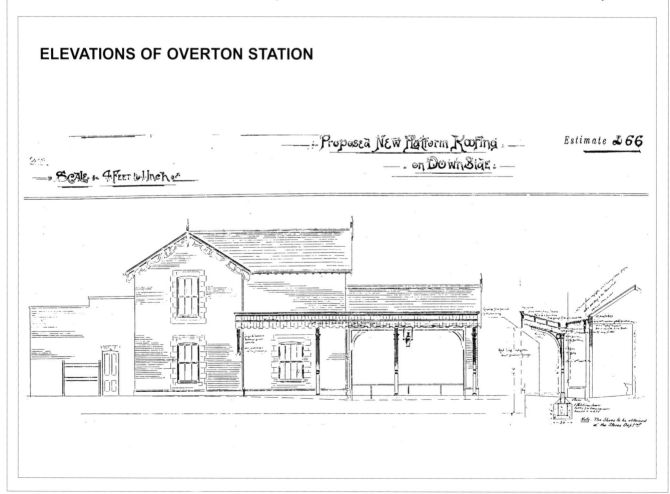

required for new works on a line previously inspected. Bradshaw's timetables in August 1854 include Overton station but none of the four Andover branch trains called. By January 1855 Overton was open with all three trains calling. It was built by D.Nicholson & Son, who were paid a total of £1,500 between November 1854 and April 1855. It had a single platform, station house with station offices, a siding or two and signals of the cross bar and disc pattern of the period.

According to Bradshaw, Oakley station was first opened near Clerkengreen in April 1856 with one of the three trains calling and another on request. However, the accounts show that less than £200 was spent on the Oakley station building, much cheaper than Overton, which suggests that the first station was a temporary wooden building. When the line from Worting Junction to Oakley was doubled in 1862 a new station building was erected by Joseph Bull, for some £1,000, on the new Up platform. Hurstbourne station was opened much later, in 1883.

THE ANDOVER TO SALISBURY RAILWAY 1857

On 14th August 1855 the South Western Consolidation Act included powers to extend construction of the line to Salisbury for another two years. Brassey was still the contractor and the line to Salisbury (Milford) opened on 1st May 1857. To cut costs all the works were executed for a single line only, apart from over-bridges and a viaduct at Monxton.

Board of Trade Inspection 1857

Col. Yolland made his inspection of the new line and reported on 17th April 1857:
'I have this day inspected the extension of the London and South Western Railway from Andover to Milford near Salisbury ...that the portion of the main line inspected commences at Andover, at 15 miles 47 chains from the junction with the main line at Worting, and ends at 31 miles 30 chains, together with a branch line, leaving the main line at 31 miles 30 chains leading to a junction with the Bishopstoke and Salisbury line at Milford near Salisbury, a total distance of 16 miles and 67 chains. [Note - the branch line ran from what is now Laverstock North Junction.]

'The whole is laid single throughout on the 4ft 8½in gauge, with loop sidings at Andover, Grateley and Porton, but the land has been purchased, and the over bridges and the viaduct have been constructed for a double line; the under bridges have however only been constructed for a single line.

'The width of the line at formation level is 15 feet in the cuttings and 18 feet in the embankments, and a 6 feet space between lines is kept where there are sidings. The permanent way is laid with double headed rails, in lengths of 16 feet, averaging 80lbs per lineal yard, resting on transverse sleepers placed at 3ft 6in distance on each side from the joint sleeper, and 4ft 6in between the intermediates. The sleepers are of Larch and Scots Fir and Beech, the latter

The deep cutting at Idmiston, originally built for a single line but spanned by a bridge for double track.

being creosoted – the dimensions are 9ft x 10in x 5in or 9ft x 8in x 6in.

'A portion of the line is laid with ordinary chairs of 32lbs weight for the joints and 23lbs for the intermediates; the other part of the line about 7 miles in length is laid with a modification of Adams patent brackets weighing 53lbs for each joint, and making a very efficient fish joint. The chairs are fixed to the sleepers with oak treenails in some parts, and with iron spikes in others; the rails are fixed to the chairs with oak keys. The ballast is of chalk and flint, 2 feet deep. The fencing is in good order.

'Some of the embankments are heavy and will require to be carefully watched after heavy rains. There are 21 over and 19 under bridges, the whole of these with two exceptions are built of brick, cement and mortar, or of brick, flint, cement and mortar – the two exceptions are two trussed over bridges for foot passengers – the whole of these are well and solidly built and of sufficient strength – there is a slight crack in the side wall of one of the under bridges, but it does not appear to be of any importance.

'There is one viaduct (the Monxton) of 5 segmental arches of 40 feet span, built in brickwork and mortar and the piers turned in cement, while the wing walls are built in brick and flint in mortar. It

appears to be very well built and sufficiently strong.

'The whole of the line runs through a chalk district, and in some parts the chalk is exceptionally hard, and is scarped almost vertical.

'Stations have been erected at Grateley and Porton, and they are properly protected by signals and distant signals. In making my inspection I noticed the following requirements:-

1. The distant signal on the branch to Milford, now at 330 yards from the junction, should be moved to a greater distance as there is a falling gradient of 1 in 314.

Service at Andover August 1857
Weekday Train

Time at Andover	Train	From	To
1.30am	12.25am Goods	Basingstoke	Andover
2.45am	2.45am Goods	Andover	Basingstoke
7.20am	6.30am Goods	Basingstoke	Andover
7.45am	7.45am Goods	Andover	Basingstoke
9.2am	8.20 Pass & Goods	Salisbury	Basingstoke
10.11am	9.27 Pass & Goods	Basingstoke	Salisbury
11.57am	11.15Pass & Goods	Salisbury	Basingstoke
1.9pm	12.23Pass & Goods	Basingstoke	Salisbury
3.22pm	2.40 Pass & Goods	Salisbury	Basingstoke
5.2pm	4.20 Pass & Goods	Basingstoke	Salisbury
7.15pm	6.33 Pass & Goods	Basingstoke	Salisbury
7.15pm	6.30 Pass & Goods	Salisbury	Basingstoke

Weekday Train Service at Salisbury (Milford) August 1857

Time at Milford	Train	From	To
6.10am	6.10am Passenger	Salisbury	Southampton
7.20am	5.30am Goods	Southampton	Salisbury
8.20am	8.20 Pass & Goods	Salisbury	Basingstoke
8.25am	7.0 Goods & Pass	Southampton	Salisbury
9.10am	9.10am Passenger	Salisbury	Bishopstoke
10.30am	10.30am Passenger	Salisbury	Southampton
10.54am	9.27 Pass & Goods	Basingstoke	Salisbury
11.4am	9.45am Passenger	Southampton	Salisbury
11.15am	11.15Pass & Goods	Salisbury	Basingstoke
12.40pm	11.25am Passenger	Southampton	Salisbury
1.30pm	12.0 Goods & Pass	Bishopstoke	Salisbury
1.52pm	12.23Pass & Goods	Basingstoke	Salisbury
2.12pm	12.35pm Passenger	Southampton	Salisbury
2.20pm	2.20pm Passenger	Salisbury	Southampton
2.40pm	2.40 Pass & Goods	Salisbury	Basingstoke
3.0pm	3.0pm Goods	Salisbury	Bishopstoke
4.30pm	4.30pm Passenger	Salisbury	Southampton
4.35pm	3.30pm Passenger	Southampton	Salisbury
5.15pm	5.15pm Goods	Salisbury	Bishopstoke
5.45pm	4.20 Pass & Goods	Basingstoke	Salisbury
6.5pm	5.12pm Passenger	Bishopstoke	Salisbury
6.25pm	6.25pm Passenger	Salisbury	Southampton
6.30pm	6.30 Pass & Goods	Salisbury	Basingstoke
7.58pm	6.33 Pass & Goods	Basingstoke	Salisbury
8.30pm	7.30pm Passenger	Bishopstoke	Salisbury
9.40pm	9.40pm Passenger	Salisbury	Southampton

2. A pair of facing points are both moved from the main line at the station at Grateley and placed on the loop siding.

3. Some facing points at the station at Andover, required while that place constituted a terminal station, are to be removed from the main line.

The Engineer promises that these requirements should immediately be attended to, but until they have been completed, I am of the opinion that, by reason of the incompleteness of the works, the opening of the extension of the London and South Western Railway from Andover to Milford near Salisbury for traffic cannot be sanctioned without danger to the public using the same.'

This was followed four days later by a second report, on 21st April 1857:

'...I have received from the Engineer stating that the requirements pointed out in my report of 17th have now been completed ...and that sanction for the opening may now be given, provided that it is clearly understood that only one engine in steam be admitted upon the several portions into which the line may be divided at one and the same time.'

On 2nd May 1857 the *Salisbury and Winchester Journal* reported as follows:

OPENING OF THE BASINGSTOKE AND SALISBURY RAILWAY

'This important link in the South Western scheme for a direct railway to the West of England was opened for passenger traffic yesterday – lessening the distance between London and Salisbury by 12 miles, and opening up a new and important agricultural district hitherto unsupplied with facilities for railway locomotion.

'The line from Basingstoke to Andover – about 16 miles – has been worked for nearly three years, and the extension of this branch to the city of Salisbury – about 17 miles – constitutes the new railway. The line traverses throughout the chalk formation – the prevailing geological peculiarity of this district of England. Without presenting any remarkable engineering difficulty, it has some rather heavy earthworks, which have been admirably executed by Mr Brassey, the eminent contractor. The surface of the country is chiefly sheep-downs. There are only two stations on the new line, Grateley and Porton; but Weyhill, the scene of the great agricultural stock fair, and the town of Amesbury, are served by it, and a large accession of traffic to the mother railway is anticipated from the extension. The face of the country traversed is picturesque, and there are some interesting historical associations connected with the vicinity. Soon after leaving Andover the village of Abbot's Ann is passed, remarkable as the scene of George the Fourth's marriage with Mrs Fitzherbert, which took place at Red Rice, a curious old family mansion formerly belonging to the Pitt family. The river Test meanders through the valleys of this district, and adds much to the beauty of the landscape. Amport Hall, the ancient seat of the Winchester family, now in the process of rebuilding, is next approached, and presently

Grateley station, overlooked by Quarley hill, on the summit of which is an old Roman encampment, commanding an extensive prospect of 20 miles in every direction. The 'Hampshire Gap', a long ridge covered with trees and brushwood, here forms a natural division between the counties of Hants and Wilts, shortly after entering which Porton station – the point of connection with Amesbury – is reached. The country continues remarkably picturesque – thenceforward to Salisbury, at present entered over the Bishopstoke line, but the new railway will hereafter have a station at Fisherton, on the other side of the city.

'A large party interested in the undertaking left London at eleven o'clock in the morning, in order to test the undertaking, and afterwards, on the invitation of Mr Brassey, to dine in this city. The dinner was served up in admirable style by Mr Jones, of the White Hart, and about 60 gentlemen were present. Mr Lacey, the Hon. Ralph Dutton MP, and Col. Luard represented the Directors of the London and South Western Railway, the former presiding. Sir Charles Fox and several other engineers of eminence were present, and Mr Brassey (who was himself detained on the Continent) was ably represented by Mr Ogilvie and Mr Tomline. The Mayor of Salisbury, Mr Pain, Mr Jacob, and other influential gentlemen of the district, joined the party at the White Hart. The former proposed 'Success to the New Railway', and the latter, in responding to his own health, mentioned as a remarkable fact, reflecting great credit on Mr Brassey's conduct of the works, that, although acting as a magistrate in the neighbourhood, not a single case arising from misconduct on the part of the workmen had arisen during the construction of the railway.

'Mr Crombie, the secretary; Mr Scott, the general manager; Mr Strapp the engineer; and Mr Young, the company's superintendent, accompanied the party. Mr Godson was prevented being present by pressure of business. The return train left Salisbury at six o'clock, and ran into Waterloo station at half-past nine.

The single line from Andover served new stations at Grateley and Porton, running down the valley of the River Bourne. From the village of Ford the line ran along a long embankment some 3 miles long and more than 20 feet high above the water meadows past Laverstock and thence to the east of the city to join the Bishopstoke branch just outside its Milford terminus. Much of the material used for the construction of this long embankment had been excavated from deep cuttings between Grateley and Porton and carted several miles to build up the embankment. This was Salisbury's third railway line, the broad gauge Wilts Somerset and Weymouth branch to its Fisherton Street terminus having opened on 30th June 1856. Salisbury (Milford) remained the South Western's station for two years, until on 2nd May 1859 the line was extended to Fisherton Street, Milford closing to passengers but retained for goods. Wagons in transit between West of England main line goods trains and Salisbury (Milford)

were conveyed either by trip workings or by other goods trains scheduled to call there.

As was often the case with early railways the Salisbury (Milford) terminus had not been built with a view to conversion into a through station. Any westward extension of the running lines would have gone through the water meadows and very close to the cathedral, spoiling the view made famous in John Constable's painting. The line from Basingstoke curved sharply to join the straight Bishopstoke branch just outside the terminus, requiring all Basingstoke trains to reverse from the junction just outside, in a similar way to Up trains reversing into Dorchester station for many years. The station had enjoyed extensive facilities, including a large goods yard, goods shed, engine shed and turntable. There was a wooden train shed and the usual offices, refreshment rooms, bookstall and so on but on 27th March 1858 there was a fire and all were destroyed within an hour. Salisbury (Milford) remained the city's principal goods station for both the South Western and Southern until its closure in 1967.

AUGUST 1857 TIMETABLE
In August 1857 there were four weekday and two Sunday mixed passenger and goods trains each way between Basingstoke and Salisbury (Milford), together with two more goods trains each way between Basingstoke and Andover. The only place where trains were scheduled to cross on the single line was at Andover, just once daily at 7.15pm. Overton and Oakley were now open, although some trains called at the latter only by signal. In contrast there were nine trains each way along the double track line between Bishopstoke or Southampton and Salisbury, which indicates that most Salisbury traffic was then routed via Bishopstoke rather than Andover.

EXPLOSION AT BASINGSTOKE 1857
On 11th October 1857 Beattie 'Saxon' class 2-4-0 No.139 *Lombard* was working a heavy Southampton to Nine Elms goods train and was detached for servicing at Basingstoke shed. A good fire was burning in the firebox when the boiler suddenly exploded killing both crew. Debris killed a horse 300 yards away. The Board of Trade Inspector found that the safety valves had been screwed down on the climb up from Winchester with the inevitable tragic result.

The following month, on 17th November 1857, sister locomotive No.138 *Vandal* was hauling a Salisbury to Nine Elms cattle train which called at Andover to take water. Steam was seen coming from the base of the boiler so the fire was thrown out and the boiler left to cool, but about ¾ hour later there was a subdued explosion, fortunately this time without injury.

ACCIDENT AT BASINGSTOKE 1858
On 22nd December 1858 there was a collision between two trains at Basingstoke. Capt. George Ross made his investigation on behalf of the Board of Trade and reported on 14th January 1859 in lengthy terms, here abridged.

The original Salisbury Fisherton station of 1859, designed by Sir William Tite. John Nicholas.

The information given in the report on the mode of train operation is very valuable. Public timetables of the period give times of arrivals and departures but omit details of when a change of train was required at a junction station.

OPENING OF SALISBURY (FISHERTON STREET) STATION 1859

The original 1846 South Western Basingstoke & Salisbury Extension Act, and subsequent Acts, authorised extension of the line at Salisbury from Milford to Fisherton 'near the proposed station of the Wilts Somerset & Weymouth Railway'. On 7th August 1854 the Salisbury & Yeovil Railway Act received the Royal Assent for its line 'commencing at or near the authorised terminus of the Basingstoke & Salisbury line'. The line authorised in 1846 was to cross Fisherton Street on the level; however, fortunately for posterity Salisbury Corporation objected and in 1857 a South Western Bill proposed changes to both the alignment and levels. The Salisbury Railway and Market House company objected to the Bill on the grounds that it would adversely affect their line authorised in 1856. This resulted in clauses to protect their interests inserted in the Act which gained the Royal Assent on 10th August 1857.

For three miles from Worting Junction Basingstoke was approached on a falling gradient of 1 in 249, easing to 1 in 434 through the station. Trains from Salisbury and Southampton were timed to arrive at Basingstoke nearly together and were there formed into one train to proceed to London.

As usual the 11.20 train from Salisbury arrived first and the engine detached. It then shunted the carriages 100 yards back along the main line into a siding, properly protected by signals, to allow the Southampton train into the station. Special regulations demanded that engine drivers 'stop before arriving at the Basingstoke station until a caution signal is shown'. But that day there was whistling from the approaching Southampton train giving notice that it was beyond control of the driver. The driver and fireman of the Salisbury engine endeavoured to re-attach the carriages so that they might draw them ahead but despite their action a collision took place with much damage to the Salisbury carriages and injury to some of the passengers. Fortunately many of the Salisbury passengers had left the carriages and were waiting on the platform for the arrival of the Southampton train.

Isaac Purser, driver of the Southampton train with nine years experience on the line, had checked his speed at Worting Junction to enable a Down Salisbury train to pass. The Southampton train comprised thirteen (four wheel) carriages well filled with passengers; luggage took up four vans and part of two carriages. The rails were very greasy in unfavourable weather conditions, with chalk in the ballast on the incline, preventing proper action of the brakes. A strong wind was also blowing. The only brakes available on the train were on the tender and the two brake vans, a normal arrangement at this period.

Driver Purser was held responsible for the accident finding that he was going too fast for the conditions.

There were recommendations for the provision of a reversing siding nearer the station, the distant signal to be moved out another 200 yards, that the Salisbury engine

should not be uncoupled from its train during shunting and that another carriage, with Newall's brake, be attached to the Southampton train. However, such accidents continued to occur from time to time until the introduction of the automatic vacuum brake in the 1870s.

The railway bridge over Fisherton Street, Salisbury. The first 1846 Act had authorised a level crossing, but fortunately Salisbury Corporation negotiated a bridge instead. John Nicholas.

This was the original railway bridge over Castle Street, Salisbury, supplied by Joseph Butler in 1857. In 1898 it was replaced by a girder bridge, and the original used nearby for a road over the River Avon. John Nicholas.

Another clause in the 1857 Act defined the boundary between the South Western and the Salisbury & Yeovil lines as a point 23 chains west of Fisherton Street bridge and that the station should also be west of Fisherton Street. The South Western again employed Thomas Brassey to build the line. It comprised a double track from Milford to Fisherton, with the single line to Basingstoke diverging at what became Tunnel Junction. There was no rail connection with the adjacent broad gauge station, now belonging to the Great Western who had taken over the Wilts Somerset & Weymouth railway, although a footbridge connecting the two was provided for

'The chairs are fixed to the sleepers with iron spikes and wood trenails and where the latter are used on curves a spike is driven through the trenail. The rails are fixed to the chairs by oak keys.

'The sleepers are of larch and scotch fir creosoted, dimensions 9ft long x 10in x 5in or 8ft 6in x 8in x 6in, the distance from the joint sleeper to each adjoining sleeper being 3ft 6in and 4ft 6in between the intermediates. The ballast is of chalk and flint 2 feet deep.

'There are 3 over and 5 under bridges. Two of the former are of brick with the arch built in cement, and the remainder in mortar, and the third is a footpath bridge in timber with brick abutments. Two of the under bridges are of brickwork, two have brick abutments with cast iron girders, one arched and the other straight and the fifth has brick abutments and wrought iron girders having a span of 35 feet on the square and 42ft 8in on the skew [Fisherton Street bridge.] *The whole of these bridges are well constructed and sufficiently strong – the strain per square inch of section on the wrought iron bridge being less than 4 tons. There are two viaducts on these lines, one of brick 23 yards in length and the other in timber 62 yards in length; both are substantially constructed and amply strong.*

'There is a tunnel 440 yards in length lines throughout with brick built with greystone lime and free from water. The workmanship appears to be very good.

'These lines are in good order and I had only occasion to suggest that a small indicator should be put up to show the signalman at the junction that the facing points which are at some distance from his box, were open or shut to the proper line, before he lowered the junction signals for a train to proceed to Salisbury (Fisherton) station. These facing points are placed at too great a distance for this junction signalman to attend to, so that another man will be required at the junction, and the clock was not up at the Fisherton station.

'The Resident Engineer promised that both these requirements should be attended to without delay. It will however in my opinion be necessary that an engine turntable should be erected at Fisherton station (Salisbury) if local trains are to be run at any time between Salisbury and Basingstoke or Salisbury and Gillingham station on the Salisbury and Yeovil line, so that the engines may be turned. If the London and South Western Railway company intended only to run through trains between Basingstoke and Gillingham, no turntable is necessary at Fisherton station

and their Lordships sanction for the opening of the line may be given on this condition.

'If the Railway Company will not bind themselves not to use local trains, between either of these places I have named, then, I am of the opinion that by reason of the incompleteness of the works, their Lordships sanction for the opening of these lines cannot be given without danger to the public using the same.'

Col. Yolland next reported on 26th April:

'I beg to state that as the London and South Western Railway are willing to bind themselves not to run local trains between Fisherton station Salisbury and Gillingham station on the Salisbury and Yeovil Railway there will be no necessity for insisting upon the erection of an engine turntable at Fisherton station, and I am of the opinion that their Lordships may give their sanction for the opening (of) the new lines between Milford and Fisherton stations at Salisbury.'

Salisbury Fisherton Station 1859-1878
The new station, much of which survives to this day, was to the west of the Fisherton Street bridge. To reach it from the other side of the city the South Western built a triangular formation at Laverstock, abandoning the original 1857 line (which Col. Yolland did not mention in his report). From Laverstock a new line ran through Fisherton tunnel, thence on a long embankment over water meadows to the north of the city, and curved sharply into the new station across Fisherton Street bridge. On this long embankment the line crossed over roads and watercourses by means of bridges, later replaced. Fisherton Viaduct was originally constructed in wood but in 1868 was replaced with a more substantial brick structure. The elegant lattice iron-work of Castle Street bridge, supplied by Joseph Butler & Co. in 1857, was again rebuilt this time with a plate girder structure in 1898.

The modern railway map of Salisbury came into being on 2nd May 1859. To the west the Salisbury & Yeovil line, worked by the South Western, opened to Gillingham and to the east the South Western's own trains, from both Basingstoke and Bishopstoke, ran direct through Fisherton tunnel into the new station. This was built adjacent to the Wilts Somerset & Weymouth terminus but, since the WS&WR was broad gauge, a transhipment shed and siding was provided for goods. On the same day Milford station was closed to passengers and the direct line at Laverstock, between Milford and Basingstoke, taken out of use. The single track line from Porton joined the double track line from Milford at Fisherton Junction, which later became Tunnel Junction. The Salisbury and Yeovil Railway will be covered in Volume Two.

From the start there were four tracks over Fisherton Street bridge; from the south, these were the Southampton bay platform siding, the Down main line, the middle line, and the Up main line. The 1859 'one-sided' Fisherton station comprised one through platform about 800 feet long, with a Southampton bay platform. After calling at

Passenger Train Service November 1859 Salisbury (Fisherton)			
Time at Salisbury	Train	From	To
7.15am	7.15am	Salisbury	Gillingham
7.50am	7.0am	Gillingham	Salisbury
8.0am	8.0am	Salisbury	Southampton
8.15am	8.15am	Salisbury	Waterloo
8.15am	7.0am	Southampton	Salisbury
10.15am	9.0am	Southampton	Salisbury
10.35am	10.35am	Salisbury	Southampton
10.50am	8.0am	Waterloo	Salisbury
11.0am	9.45am	Southampton	Salisbury
11.15am	11.15am	Salisbury	Gillingham
11.15am	10.25am	Gillingham	Salisbury
11.20am	11.20am	Salisbury	Waterloo
12.47pm	11.35am	Southampton	Salisbury
1.43pm	10.15am	Waterloo	Salisbury
1.55pm	1.55pm	Salisbury	Gillingham
2.5pm	12.45pm	Southampton	Salisbury
2.10pm	1.20pm	Gillingham	Salisbury
2.20pm	2.20pm	Salisbury	Southampton
2.45pm	2.45pm	Salisbury	Waterloo
4.0pm	4.0pm	Salisbury	Southampton
4.40pm	3.30pm	Southampton	Salisbury
5.40pm	3.0pm	Waterloo	Salisbury
5.55pm	4.50pm	Southampton	Salisbury
6.15pm	6.15pm	Salisbury	Gillingham
6.10pm	5.20pm	Gillingham	Salisbury
6.20pm	6.20pm	Salisbury	Southampton
6.40pm	6.40pm	Salisbury	Waterloo
7.58pm	5.0pm	Waterloo	Salisbury
8.5pm	8.5pm	Salisbury	Gillingham
8.20pm	7.20pm	Southampton	Salisbury
9.20pm	9.20pm	Salisbury	Southampton

passengers. The South Western also worked the Salisbury & Yeovil Railway, which will be considered in Volume Two.

Board of Trade Inspections 1859
Col. Yolland made his inspection and reported on 16th April 1859:

'I yesterday inspected portions of the London and South Western Railway at Salisbury, between the Junction at Milford and the Junction with the Salisbury and Yeovil Railway at Fisherton, altogether making up a length of 1 mile 72 chains of which the portion lying between the Milford and Fisherton stations is throughout laid double, with three lines of railways over some portion of the way and a portion at Fisherton has even five lines of railway – but the piece of new road from the Basingstoke and Salisbury line to the branch between the aforesaid two stations is only laid single, and I have the honour to report ...that a portion of these lines have been laid with double-headed rails weighing 80lbs per linear yard in lengths of 16 feet and the remainder with rails of the same pattern only weighing 75lbs to the yard in lengths of 21 feet. Part is laid with ordinary joint chairs and the remainder with bracket chairs.

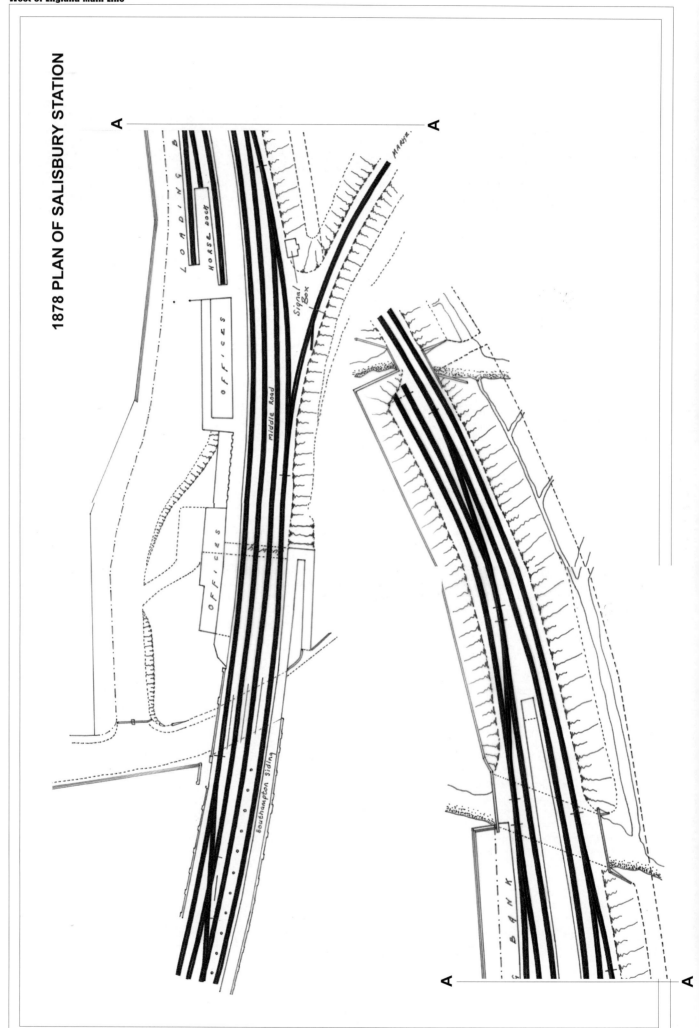

1878 PLAN OF SALISBURY STATION

the ticket platform on the embankment Down trains proceeded into the main platform, but Up trains had to run past the platform on the Up main line to call at the ticket platform and then reverse back into the platform through a trailing crossover.

The delays caused by calls at the ticket platforms for ticket inspection were unpopular with passengers but the procedure was necessary because Salisbury was an 'open' station until 1893. The original two-storey building was similar to those at Whitchurch and Andover but was larger and had a different design of ground floor windows. Surviving photographs show a long glazed roof supported by the station house on one side and iron columns on the railway side covering both the platform and the Down line. This appears to be akin to others of the same period, at Yeovil Town and Exeter Queen Street. The station remained in this form until 1878. On 7th May 1859 the *Salisbury and Winchester Journal* reported:

'REMOVAL OF THE SOUTH WESTERN RAILWAY'
On Monday last the passenger traffic of the South Western Railway was transferred from the old station at Milford to the new station lately erected by this company at Fisherton. It is a most commodious building, with a glass roof over the platform, which is one of the longest in England, and is nearly 800 feet in length. The station at Milford has been closed, except for goods traffic, and all passengers for London, Portsmouth, Southampton or the West will now start at Fisherton. The only alteration is that trains will now start a few minutes earlier than before.

An LSWR advertisement in the *Salisbury and Winchester Journal* on 7th May 1859 showed the train services from the new Salisbury station. They comprised six weekday departures to Southampton, Portsmouth and Waterloo via Bishopstoke at 8.7am, 10.35, 2.25pm, 4.0, 6.22, 9.20 (although the 9.20pm had no Waterloo connection) and four to Waterloo via Andover, at 8.25am, 11.20, 2.45pm and 7.5. Since arrival times at Waterloo for both the Andover and Bishopstoke routes were the same it would appear that passengers changed into Southampton to Waterloo trains at Bishopstoke and Basingstoke respectively. There were also three weekday trains to Gillingham, at 11.5am, 1.43pm, 6.8, timed to connect with Waterloo arrivals. The public timetable gave arrival and departure times at Salisbury on all routes, including Gillingham to Southampton for which no doubt a change of train was required. Coach advertisements stated that the 10.25am from Gillingham was a fast train to London via Salisbury and Basingstoke. It would appear that to honour the undertaking given to Col. Yolland trains ran through between Waterloo or Basingstoke and Gillingham.

The timetable also included coach services from Salisbury station, to Marlborough at 1.0pm on Tuesdays and Saturdays, to Ringwood daily at 11.15am from the Red Lion, and to Amesbury on Mondays, Wednesdays and Fridays at 3.30pm.

THE SALISBURY RAILWAY AND MARKET HOUSE

In the mid-1850s concern was expressed in Salisbury that the traditional trade in the Market Place, particularly in corn, cattle and cheese, would be lost to the new railways then under construction unless the market had its own railway. Following meetings of interested parties the Salisbury Railway and Market House Company was established in 1855. On 14th July 1856 the company gained its Act for a short line to be constructed by the LSWR from its Basingstoke and Salisbury branch and for the construction of a Market House at the Market Place. The plan was prepared in 1855 by the engineer John Strapp, who was also the South Western's engineer. The level of the main line was raised by the 1857 South Western Bill, to which the Market House company objected on the grounds of the increased cost of its railway, so amending clauses were inserted in the 1857 Act. Thomas Brassey constructed the standard gauge line at the price originally agreed, £1,501 8s 8d, although there was now a steep gradient down from the station end. The line was built for goods traffic only so no Board of Trade inspection was required. It opened for traffic in May 1859. In accordance with the 1857 Act the railway was worked, maintained, repaired and regulated by the South Western and its successors.

The Market House itself was a splendid structure completed in 1858, some 77 feet by 174 feet with a Bath Stone façade to its frontage in Castle Street, at the end of the Market Square. The railway ran over the River Avon and through a back door into the Market House – both market and railway subsequently prospered.

ACCIDENT BETWEEN GRATELEY & ANDOVER 1861

On 5th June 1861 there was a collision between two portions of a goods train on the single track line between Grateley and Andover near Sarson Wood. The Grateley stationmaster, Mr Tulk, was killed and the 'breaksman' of the train, Charles Stiling, was severely injured. Col. Yolland investigated the accident on behalf of the Board of Trade and reported on 3rd July 1861 in lengthy terms; the following is a shortened account.

From Grateley the 6½ miles of single track to Andover was mainly on a falling gradient, with just one mile uphill. Traffic was worked by time bills with the aid of the electric telegraph. The 8.30pm Up goods train from Salisbury, comprising twenty-one vehicles with manned guards brake vans in the front and the rear, departed on time. Three wagons were detached at Porton and, on arrival at Grateley at 9.20pm, the engine stopped opposite the platform on the south side of the line. The train was uncoupled between the fourth and fifth wagons and the engine drew forward with a guards van, box wagon, a coal wagon destined for Overton, a permanent way wagon loaded with sleepers and a wagon loaded with slates, both for Andover. The next three wagons for Grateley were run by gravity into a siding south of the line and east of the platform, and the ninth wagon of the train (loaded with lime for Andover) run by gravity down to the front part of the train, followed by five wagons from sidings to the north of the line at Grateley. Then a horse box at the rear of the train was run into a siding. On receipt of the 'all right' from guard and brakesman the driver, Thomas Wilson, set off about 9.33pm but on arrival at Andover at about 9.40pm a porter pointed out that he had only five vehicles on, so Thomas Wilson immediately reversed to retrieve the rest of his train.

Meanwhile at Grateley, after the engine and front portion of the train departed, the stationmaster Mr Tulk decided to remedy the situation by letting the second half of the train run by gravity downhill to Andover. Mr Tulk and the brakesman of the train rode in the second vehicle, a long open wagon. and a porter rode in the guards van at the rear. About 10.7pm the front and rear portions of the train met in a cutting on a curve where those in charge of each portion had a very limited view of the line ahead, near milepost 70 at Sarson Wood. Six wagons were thrown off the line, Mr Tulk was killed and Charles Stiling severely injured, but the porter in the brake van at the rear escaped unhurt.

Having examined the couplings of the wagons where the train was divided Col. Yolland concluded that probably the two portions of the train had not been coupled up. He said there was absolute proof of gross negligence by the driver and guard of the train, and to a lesser extent the fireman. Driver and guard should have looked back to see the state of the train after leaving Grateley and that they should have followed the suggestion of the guard and the porter at Andover. This was to shunt the train there, to consult the Andover stationmaster and to contact the Grateley stationmaster by electric telegraph. He went on to state that Mr Tulk, the Grateley stationmaster, lost his life from an 'excess in zeal' in the performance of his duties and an 'absence of discretion'. Mr Tulk was anxious to clear the line so that the next goods train from Exeter would not be delayed on the single line. The South Western regulations did not cover this eventuality on a single line so Col. Yolland made appropriate recommendations to rectify the matter.

PROPOSED REMOVAL OF WHITCHURCH STATION

In November 1861 a group of locals, led by the Rev. Temple, requested that the South Western remove Whitchurch station to another, more convenient, site but the Board rejected this as too expensive. However on 17th July 1862 a Directors' committee, including Mr Portal who was a local resident and Mr Mortimer, received a deputation again led by the Rev. Temple and including Mr W. Bailey and five others with a memorial. The deputation proposed to give land for a new station to the west of the existing station and to construct new approach roads at their expense from

A unique photograph of Andover Junction station looking east about 1875, before the widening of the station for the new Swindon line. The Up side waiting shed was moved here from Walton in 1858. The original station house with five upstairs windows has been extended. The Redbridge line bay platform is behind the small ground level wooden signal box in the background. The track ballasting, point rodding and foot crossing over the line were destined to change soon. Compare this with the 1880 station plan. David Howard collection.

Whitchurch and New Barn. This new station, nearer to the town centre and the road to St Mary Bourne, would accommodate both passenger and goods traffic and Lord Portsmouth had offered land. The proposal was to be recommended to the Board but in September 1862 the South Western received a petition signed by 61 residents opposing the re-siting of the station! No more mention of this proposal has come to light.

ACCIDENT AT ANDOVER 1863

On 28th December 1863 there was a collision between two passenger trains at Andover station, when five passengers were shaken but none seriously injured. On behalf of the Board of Trade Capt. Rich conducted an enquiry and reported on 16th January 1864 in lengthy terms. The following is an abridged account.

The Down express train departed from London at 10.50am and arrived at Whitchurch on time. It was made up of an engine and tender, five first and second class carriages, with a guard's brake van at the rear. At Whitchurch the express was scheduled to pass the Up parliamentary train, which was normally shunted into a siding clear of the single platform to allow the express to pass. This section was a single line with sidings and passing places.

The 'parliamentary' train was timed to leave Salisbury at 11.20am, but was 36 minutes late in leaving Salisbury, so orders were given over the electric telegraph that the trains should pass at Andover instead of Whitchurch. The Up parliamentary train consisted of two tender engines, fifteen passenger carriages, with one guards van in the middle, and two horse boxes at the rear, one of which was taken off at Grateley. The 'parly' was the first to arrive at Andover, her engine whistle was sounded three times

and the auxiliary and station signals taken off to let her into the station.

As the parliamentary train passed under the bridge 250 yards to the west of the station the express train was observed at about the same distance to the east at such a speed that the signalman and others saw that a collision might occur. The station signal stood against the express but the signalman, fearing a collision, seized the rope to pull the signal against both trains. The rope promptly 'unshipped and the signal fell over, so as to admit the express and keep out the parliamentary train'.

The express came to a halt with the locomotive foul of the crossover line and the Up parliamentary was unable to pull up. A buffer of the leading engine struck the buffer of the express, 'from which the latter recoiled with her train, about six carriage lengths, shaking some of the passengers'.

The two engines of the parliamentary train were thrown off the rails. The buffers of the pilot engine were broken, and the framing and driving axle bent. The buffer beam of the second engine was also broken, and several carriages of the parliamentary train 'had their sides injured', but none of the passengers suffered harm.

Following evidence from the stationmaster, signalman, pointsman, porter and a platelayer and train crews Capt.Rich concluded that the driver of the express had approached the station too quickly and so was unable to stop at the danger signal. He regarded the signal, worked by a rope over two pulleys, as awkward and liable to fail in an emergency. The South Western was gradually altering them. The loop at Andover was also too short at the western end but this defect had already been remedied.

As at Basingstoke in 1858 a major factor was the difficulty in stopping; the only

brakes were on the engine tender and in the brake van and had to be screwed down.

SOUTH WESTERN DISTRICT MANAGEMENT 1864

As the LSWR expanded a new system of management was required. In 1864 the General Manager, Archibald Scott, organised the line into seven districts, No.5 District covering the Basingstoke, Salisbury and Yeovil lines. The District Superintendent was Mr Davis assisted by Inspector Deverill and they were based in the District office, believed to have been located at Grosvenor House, just across Churchfield Road from Salisbury station. However, this arrangement was due to be changed after the doubling of the Salisbury & Yeovil line in 1867, when apparently No.5 District was combined with No.6 District based at Exeter.

In 1884 the number of Districts (the railway was divided into administrative districts) was reduced to five and the line came under a new Central District to Portsmouth, Salisbury and branches, while the Western District had all the lines west of Salisbury. By 1898 the Central District Superintendent was Mr A.H.Wadden, based at offices at Eastleigh.

From 1853 to 1870 the LSW Civil Engineer was John Strapp, often referred to in Inspecting Officers reports. During his tenure of office there was a Maintenance of Way Department responsible for the civil engineering while the erection of signals was the responsibility, oddly, of the Carriage Department. These departments feature in the Accounts Journals of the period and later the responsibilities passed to the Civil Engineer's and Signalling and Telegraph Departments, apparently in 1870. Following his appointment the South Western's Civil Engineer, between 1870 and 1887 Mr William Jacomb, organised his new

ANDOVER JUNCTION TIMETABLE October 1867

Time	Train	From	To
5.5am	3.30am Goods	Basingstoke	Exeter
6.0	1.30am Goods	Nine Elms	Yeovil Junction
6.50	6.0 Goods	Basingstoke	Andover Junction
7.10	7.10 Pass & Goods	Andover Junction	Waterloo
8.38	6.35 Pass & Goods	Southampton	Andover Junction
8.50	8.20 Passenger	Salisbury	Waterloo
9.26	7.0 Passenger	Waterloo	Exeter
9.30	9.30 Pass & Goods	Andover Junction	Southampton
10.42	9.50 Goods & Pass	Basingstoke	Andover Junction
10.47	10.47 Gds & Pass	Andover Junction	Basingstoke
11.59	7.30 Passenger	Exeter	Waterloo
12.36pm	10.50 Express	Waterloo	Exeter
1.22	12.0 Passenger	Southampton	Andover Junction
1.41	11.40 Passenger	Waterloo	Exeter
1.50	1.50 Passenger	Andover Junction	Southampton
2.12	10.10 Passenger	Exeter	Waterloo
4.50	3.30 Passenger	Southampton	Andover Junction
4.59	1.30 Express	Exeter	Waterloo
5.53	3.50 Passenger	Waterloo	Exeter
6.0	6.0 Passenger	Andover Junction	Southampton
7.30	5.10 Passenger	Waterloo	Salisbury
8.31	4.30 Passenger	Exeter	Waterloo
9.45	4.0 Goods	Yeovil	Nine Elms
10.55 – 11.20	2.30 Goods	Exeter	Nine Elms
11.10	5.30 Goods & Pass	Exeter	Nine Elms
1.0 – 1.20am	8.30 Goods	Yeovil Junction	Basingstoke
2.0 – 2.2am	10.50 Goods	Nine Elms	Exeter
2.55	1.30am Goods	Basingstoke	Yeovil Junction

SALISBURY TIMETABLE October 1867

Time	Train	From	To
1.0am	10.0pm Goods	Southampton	Salisbury
1.25am	1.25am Goods	Salisbury	Bishopstoke
2.52 – 3.25	10.50pm Goods	Nine Elms	Exeter
3.42 – 4.0	1.30am Goods	Basingstoke	Yeovil Junction
6.0 – 7.20	3.30 Goods & Pass	Basingstoke	Yeovil
6.45	6.45 Goods & Pass	Salisbury	Wimborne
7.10 – 7.35	1.30 Goods	Nine Elms	Yeovil Junction
7.30 – 8.0	7.15 Goods	Milford	Yeovil
7.55	7.55 Passenger	Salisbury	Southampton
8.0	8.0 Goods	Salisbury	Milford
8.15	5.40 Goods & Pass	Dorchester	Salisbury
8.20	8.20 Passenger	Salisbury	Waterloo
8.35	7.5 Goods & Pass	Southampton	Salisbury
10.0	8.50 Passenger	Southampton	Salisbury
10.7 – 10.15	7.0 Passenger	Waterloo	Exeter
10.12	10.12 Passenger	Salisbury	Weymouth
10.20	10.15 Goods	Milford	Yeovil
10.40	10.40 Passenger	Salisbury	Southampton
11.0	11.0 Goods	Salisbury	Milford
11.4	9.50 Passenger	Southampton	Salisbury
11.15	10.5 Passenger	Wimborne	Salisbury
11.18 – 11.20	7.30 Passenger	Exeter	Waterloo
11.40	11.40 Passenger	Salisbury	Southampton
12.45pm	11.20 Passenger	Southampton	Salisbury
1.3 – 1.13	10.50 Express	Waterloo	Exeter
1.26 – 1.36	10.10 Passenger	Exeter	Waterloo
1.30	1.30 Passenger	Salisbury	Wimborne
2.11	12.45 Passenger	Southampton	Salisbury
2.15	2.15 Passenger	Salisbury	Southampton
2.20 – 2.30	11.40 Passenger	Waterloo	Exeter
4.11	1.40 Passenger	Weymouth	Salisbury
4.18 – 4.28	1.30 Express	Exeter	Waterloo
4.23	4.23 Passenger	Salisbury	Southampton
4.25	3.10 Passenger	Southampton	Salisbury
5.0	5.0 Goods	Salisbury	Milford
5.12 – 5.17	1.25 Goods & Pass	Yeovil	Southampton
5.35	5.30 Goods	Milford	Salisbury
6.10	4.50 Passenger	Southampton	Salisbury
6.23 – 6.34	3.50 Passenger	Waterloo	Exeter
6.35	6.35 Passenger	Salisbury	Southampton
6.40	6.40 Passenger	Salisbury	Dorchester
7.10 – 8.20	4.0 Goods	Yeovil	Nine Elms
7.26	6.0 Passenger	Wimborne	Salisbury
7.44 – 7.54	4.30 Passenger	Exeter	Waterloo
8.18	5.10 Passenger	Waterloo	Salisbury
8.25	7.0 Passenger	Southampton	Salisbury
8.25	8.25 Passenger	Salisbury	Southampton
9.45 – 10.0	2.30 Goods	Exeter	Nine Elms
10.15 – 10.30	5.30 Goods & Pass	Exeter	Nine Elms
11.40 – 12.10	8.30 Goods	Yeovil Junction	Basingstoke

for the Central District building cottages at Grateley.

THE ANDOVER AND REDBRIDGE RAILWAY 1865

On 12th July 1858 the independent Andover and Redbridge Railway gained its Act for a line along the bed of the 1796 Andover & Redbridge canal, purchased and closed to navigation in 1859. It was subsequently filled in with chalk excavated from quarries in the adjacent hillsides as this length was required for the railway. The promoters had hoped for Great Western involvement but, by another Act of 12th December 1862, the company amalgamated with the South Western. Between Romsey and Kimbridge Junction it shared the route of the 1847 Bishopstoke to Salisbury line which was double track, the rest of the line being single. Emphasising its inconvenient location, the 1854 Andover station thus became Andover Junction, while the canal basin near the town centre was also filled in, to form the site of Andover Town station.

On behalf of the Board of Trade Col. Yolland made his inspection, reporting on 2nd February 1865. The line, 20 miles and 12½ chains in length, was single with passing places at the stations, and land had been purchased for a double track between Andover Town and Andover Junction. Where the line occupied the course of the old canal there was sufficient space only for a single line and some bridges were constructed accordingly for a single line only. Yolland noted 'additional platforms at Andover Town, Fullerton and Horsebridge stations' and that the platform at Andover Junction was unfinished. The line between Andover Junction and Andover Town was unfinished and 'not in good order'; gravel ballast was required, while the double junction with the main line 'should be opened at the eastern side'. 'Should trains be run to Stockbridge races' he recorded, a turntable would be required there.

Col. Yolland returned for a re-inspection on 27th February when he noted a weak embankment near Andover Junction, commented on the unnecessary number of sharp curves, and also said that if the line became part of a through route to the north the permanent way must be strengthened. Given assurances by the South Western to restrict speeds to less than 30mph, worked by light (20-25 ton) locomotives and that if trains terminated at Stockbridge a turntable would be provided, he approved the line.

It opened on 6th March 1865 with stations south of Andover Town at Clatford, Fullerton Bridge, Stockbridge, Horsebridge and Mottisfont, together with Tasker's Siding at Clatford for the Waterloo Ironworks. At Andover Town there was a level crossing on Bridge Street which in later years proved a troublesome hold-up to heavy road traffic. The original line closely followed the alignment of the canal, including some very sharp curves. A gradient as steep as 1 in 62 was required up from the former canal basin at Andover Town to Andover Junction, which in later years required a banking loco for heavy goods trains.

Civil Engineer's Department into London, Central and Western Districts, each supervised by a District Engineer. The Basingstoke to Salisbury line came under the Central District Engineer, based in offices at Eastleigh. Later on, in 1884, the South Western appointed contractors for long term general building work and the Central District contract went to Mowlement & Co. who carried out construction of station buildings, staff cottages and other general work. However, by 1902 Perry & Co., who had the London District contract, had also taken over that

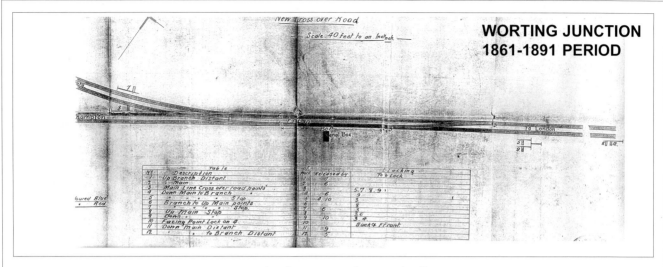

The first train to arrive at Andover Junction from Southampton carried only five passengers and the locomotive slipped to a halt twice on greasy rails while climbing up from Andover Town. The *Salisbury and Winchester Journal* reported that 'About 100 people were present on the arrival here (Andover) of the first train, but beyond this no interest was apparent'.

Initially there were four passenger and one mixed train each way daily between Southampton and Andover Junction but traffic was disappointing and from October 1866 the service consisted of one train making three trips each way daily. Initially it originated from Southampton giving the first arrival there, from Andover, at a most inconvenient 11.39am but from 1868 the branch train was based at Andover Junction with the first of the three daily departures at 7.30am. An interesting development came in 1869 when the South Western purchased three acres of land at Nursling from Lady Hill for £300. This land was excavated as a gravel pit, served by a siding, and the gravel used for ballasting sections of the Basingstoke and Salisbury line from 1869, although gravel from other sources had been used before then. The opening of the Swindon Marlborough & Andover and the Hurstbourne to Fullerton lines in the 1880s increased the volume of traffic and resulted in the rebuilding of the line with double track, as Col. Yolland had predicted would be required. We shall return to the Andover & Redbridge line in Chapter Three.

THE SALISBURY & DORSET RAILWAY 1866

The independent Salisbury & Dorset Railway between Alderbury Junction on the Bishopstoke line and West Moors on the Southampton & Dorchester opened on 20th December 1866 and was worked by the LSWR. There were connections at Salisbury station between Waterloo trains and those to Wimborne, Dorchester, and Weymouth and the new line saved 36 miles in comparison with the previous indirect route from Salisbury via Bishopstoke. Salisbury station became even busier with passengers changing trains between the four LSWR lines and the GWR one. The single platform was

convenient for passengers but operationally congested.

THE OCTOBER 1867 TIMETABLE

The October 1867 Working Timetable gives a full picture of the Basingstoke to Salisbury line together with connecting lines. Between them the Salisbury & Yeovil and the South Western had completed the double track between Salisbury and Exeter, the last section between Gillingham and Templecombe opening on 1st October 1867. However, as we will see, on our section of line only Worting Junction, Oakley and Whitchurch was double track although work on doubling thence to Andover was well advanced. The section from Whitchurch to Salisbury was thus single with passing loops at Andover, Grateley and Porton.

There were eleven Down trains west of Worting Junction but two of these terminated at Andover Junction so only nine ran between Andover and Salisbury. The four principal West of England passenger trains from Waterloo to Exeter were all booked to stop at Basingstoke and Salisbury and, if necessary, had to wait at Whitchurch for an Up train to clear the single line. There were five Down goods trains, of which one terminated at Andover.

The Up service of eleven trains was similar with five passenger trains from Salisbury to Waterloo, two passenger and goods trains from Andover, to Waterloo and to Basingstoke, three goods Salisbury to London and one to Basingstoke. On the Yeovil line there were nine Down trains from Salisbury comprising five passenger (four through from Waterloo) and four goods, including three from Nine Elms and the 7.15am from Milford to Yeovil.

Joining the Basingstoke to Salisbury line at Tunnel Junction were also eight passenger trains from Southampton to Salisbury via Bishopstoke and four from Wimborne to Salisbury of which one had originated from Dorchester and one from Weymouth. There were also three goods trains from Southampton of which two terminated at Milford and three goods from Milford to Salisbury, including the 7.15am to Yeovil.

Between Andover Junction and Southampton there were three trains in each direction running via Fullerton Bridge, Romsey, Redbridge and Bletchynden, one of these being designated a passenger and

goods. These three trains were worked by one engine and set of coaches, the daily schedule starting and ending at Southampton.

The provision of train services suggests that a significant proportion of both passenger and goods traffic arriving at Salisbury from the Yeovil and Exeter line, and passengers from the Great Western line, went forward on the Southampton line, with some transferring at Bishopstoke for Portsmouth. Indeed it would appear that leaving Salisbury for the east there was more traffic for Southampton than London. However, at this time the South Western might have been routing some of its goods traffic for London via Bishopstoke.

In the New Year of 1867 there was heavy snowfall in the area, followed by a sudden thaw which brought down snow accumulated on the sides of the steep cuttings of the single track line between Grateley and Porton. The 5.10pm train from London on Saturday 7th January ran into a snow drift some seven feet deep and the 7.55pm Up train from Salisbury had been stopped at Porton station. Notified of the problems by electric telegraph the Salisbury District Superintendent, Mr Davis, took a heavy goods locomotive and a gang of men out to assist but they became stuck in another drift two and a half miles before Porton. Eventually the trains were dug out and the 5.10pm eventually arrived at Salisbury at 11am on Sunday, some 15 hours late.

DOUBLING THE LINE

In 1860 the line from Basingstoke was completed to Exeter Queen Street and, together with subsequent extensions, brought an increasing volume of traffic east of Salisbury. As we have seen the short section between Fisherton Junction and Fisherton station had been opened in 1859 as a double line. Along the original line from Worting Junction to Fisherton Junction land had been purchased for a double track. All bridges over the line had been constructed for a double line but as an economy measure earthworks and bridges under the line had been constructed only for a single track. There were passing loops, with the exception of some works completed for a double formation in 1846-48. The mile and a half from Worting Junction to Oakley involved just one bridge under the line and some modest earthworks. Doubling this section eliminated a potential bottleneck on the South Western system since a late-running Up train from Andover blocked the line and prevented a Down train from entering the section, holding up following trains. On 24th December 1861 the double track was opened from Worting to Oakley.

Board of Trade Inspection Worting to Oakley 1861

Col. Yolland visited the works and reported on 24th December 1861: *'I have inspected the second line of rails on the Basingstoke and Salisbury section of the London and South Western Railway, between the junction with the main line at Worting near Basingstoke, and Oakley station, a length of about one mile.*

'The permanent way consists of double headed rails weighing 80lbs to the yard in lengths of 21 feet, fixed in cast iron chairs, each weighing 26lbs, by means of wooden keys; the chairs being fastened down to transverse sleepers 9ft long 10in x 5in half round, of Scotch Fir creosoted, by means of 3/4inch wrought iron spikes. The sleepers are placed at 3 feet apart on the average. The joints of the rails are secured by means of fishplates. The ballast is of gravel and is stated to be 1 foot deep under the bottom of the sleepers. The over bridges were originally constructed for a double line of railway and there is only one under bridge on this length which has required to be doubled. The abutments of this bridge are of brick and it is spanned by cast iron girders which are sufficiently strong by calculation and exhibited moderate deflections. [This is Bridge No.145 at Oakley village].

'This second line of rails is in fair order, but when I made the inspection the levers for working the distant signals at Oakley station required to be moved to the Up platform. The station signal to be set further back from the edge of the platform. The clock to be placed so as to be seen from the platform and an indicator to be put up at the facing points at the commencement of the single line. I have this day heard from the

Resident Engineer, Mr Strapp, that the first of these requirements have already been completed – and an indicator was ordered for the facing points.

'I am therefore of opinion that their Lordships sanction for the opening of this short portion of the second line of rails between Worting Junction and Oakley station, may now be given.'

At this stage doubling between Basingstoke and Salisbury came to a halt; the South Western completed the double track on their Yeovil to Exeter line in 1866 and the Salisbury & Yeovil completed their double track in 1867. It would appear that at this time traffic west of Salisbury exceeded that to the east, possibly some of the freight traffic being routed via Bishopstoke.

Board of Trade Inspection Oakley to Whitchurch 1866

On 23rd May 1866 Col.Yolland reported as follows:
'I have inspected the second line of rails on two portions of the London &South Western Railway, on situated between Oakley and Whitchurch stations on the branch line between Basingstoke and Salisbury 6 ¾ miles in length, the other between Sutton Bingham and Crewkerne…

'The permanent way is the same on both portions. It consists of a double headed rail that weighs 80lbs per lineal yard, in lengths of 21 feet, fixed in cast iron chairs that each weigh 30lbs, by means of wooden keys placed outside the rail. The chairs being fastened to transverse sleepers by hollow trenails with spikes driven through them, those on each side of the joint being secured on the inside by a fang bolt and nut. The joints of the rails are fished with 2 plates together weighing 2lbs and 4 bolts. The sleepers are 9ft long by 10 in. x 5 in. and half round. Scotch fir and Baltic timber creosoted being used between Oakley and Whitchurch. They are placed at an average distance of 3 feet apart from centre to centre.

'The ballast is of gravel, chalk and flints (stated) *to be 1 ft deep below the under side of the sleepers* (a few of) *the under bridges*

which are all arched and built in brick have been widened. All are standing well and are sufficiently strong.

'In making my inspection I noticed the following. At Oakley station there are 2 sidings east of the station, off the Up line, that require a signal to prevent a train from coming on to the Up main line except when the Up signal is at danger. These signals should lock each other so that both cannot be off at the same time, and it would probably be desirable to connect the two sidings together and only connect one with the Up main line.

'At Whitchurch the Down distant signal is to be made a repeating signal to another to be placed at a greater distance from the station. The posts and signal on the Down platform require to be set back to 6 feet from the edge of the platform. Facing points have to be taken out, and the road made good at Overton and Whitchurch stations, when authority to open the line for traffic is given. Gradient boards are also required.

'On these conditions I recommend that their Lordships sanction for the opening of these two portions of the 2nd lines of rails may now be given.'

On 1st June 1866 the second line of rails between Oakley and Whitchurch was brought into use.

Board of Trade Inspection Whitchurch to Andover 1867

Capt. Tyler made his inspection of the new works and reported on 30th November 1867.

'I have inspected the second line of rails which has been laid upon the London and South Western Railway between Whitchurch and Andover. This portion of railway is about 7 miles long. The permanent way of the new line has been laid with double headed rails weighing 80lbs to the yard, and in lengths of 24 feet. The chairs weigh 30lbs each, and are fastened to the sleepers by oak treenails with 5/8in iron spikes driven into them, except on either side of the points where fang bolts are used on the inside of the rails. The joints of the rails are secured by suspended wrought iron fish-plates, weighing 22½lbs per pair, and 4 screw-bolts and nuts.

'Two girder bridges under the railway have been widened, and the brick arches of two others have been extended in a similar form to the original structures. These works have been substantially done.

'Good gravel ballast has been brought from a considerable distance for the new line, and is in course of being laid also in place of chalk ballast upon the first line.

'The fences require some improvements, as I have pointed out on the spot – by way of maintenance.

'I am of the opinion that the second line of rails may be safely opened for traffic.'

Capt. Tyler did not mention Hurstbourne viaduct so it would appear that it had been originally constructed for a double track. On 2nd December 1867 the double track between Whitchurch and Andover was

Iron girder bridge (No.145) was doubled in 1861 for the second line of rails between Worting Junction and Oakley station.

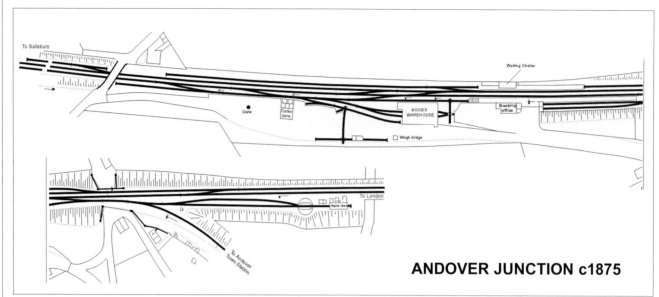

ANDOVER JUNCTION c1875

opened. As we shall see, Andover had become Andover Junction after the Redbridge line had opened on 6th March 1865.

Board of Trade Inspection Porton to Fisherton Junction 1868

Col. Yolland made his inspection and reported on 26th May 1868: *'I have inspected the second line of rails between Porton station and Fisherton Junction, Salisbury, on the Basingstoke and Salisbury section of the London & South Western Railway.*

'The permanent way laid down on this second line of rails is somewhat better than the line first opened for traffic in 1857. It consists of a double headed rail that weighs 80lbs per lineal yard in lengths of 24 feet, fished at the joints with two plates, together weighing 22½lbs, and fastened with four bolts and fixed in cast iron chairs that each weigh 30lbs.

'The chairs are secured to transverse sleepers, placed on the average 3 feet apart, by means of wooden trenails with a plug and 5/8 inch spike driven through them, except those next the joints, where on the inside of the rails the chairs are fastened down by fang bolts.

'The sleepers are of Scotch Fir and Baltic Timber creosoted, 9 feet long by 10 inches by 5 inches scantling rectangular next the joints, and half round for the intermediates. The rails are secured in the chairs by wooden keys placed outside the rails.

'The under-bridges and culverts have been widened in brickwork, and the work appears to have been substantially done – and the line is in good order, with about one foot of gravel ballast under the sleepers.

'At Porton station there is a small turntable on a short siding east of the station, which is too near the Up line. It is to be taken away, and the facing points at the end of the single line east of the station, are to be locked in their proper position by the Down distant signal when it is taken off to admit a Down train into the station. The Up siding west of the station buildings is to terminate in a blind siding, leaving its points closed and locked against the Up line, by the Up distant signal when it is taken off to admit an Up train.

'A crossover road has to be taken out here, as well as one at Fisherton Junction, but they cannot be dispensed with until authority is given to open the line. The railway company are desirous of opening the second line on rails on 1st June, and the company Engineer, Mr Strapp, has informed me that he will execute the aforesaid requirements with as little delay as possible. If Porton station is intended to be a passing place for Up and Down trains, it is desirable that some shelter should be provided on the Down platform.

'I am of the opinion that the sanction of the Board of Trade for the opening of the second line of rails between Porton station and Fisherton Junction, Salisbury may now be given.'

As mentioned by Col. Yolland the double track opened between Porton and Fisherton Junction, Salisbury on 1st June 1868. This now left Andover to Porton as the only single track section between Waterloo and Exeter and this was tackled in two stages.

Board of Trade Inspection Andover to Grateley 1870

Col. Yolland on 29th January 1870: *'I have inspected the second line of rails on the main line of the London and South Western Railway to Exeter, between Andover and Grateley, a length of about 6 ½ miles. The land was purchased, and the over bridges and the only viaduct on this length were constructed for a double line, when the railway was first made – and the embankments, cuttings and 6 under bridges have now been widened for this second line of rails.*

'The permanent way consists of a double-headed rail that weighs 80lbs per lineal yard, in lengths of 24 feet, fixed in cast iron chairs that each weigh 32lbs, by means of wooden keys placed outside the rails. The chairs are mostly fastened to transverse sleepers by hollow trenails with a 5/8 inch iron spike driven through them. In a few cases fang bolts have been used. The joints of the rails are secured by two fish-plates with 4 bolts and nuts to each joint – the pair of fish-plates weighing 22lbs.

'The sleepers of Baltic timber creosoted, are 9feet long by 10in x 5in rectangular, placed on the average 3 feet apart. The ballast is of gravel, chalk and flints and is stated to be 6 inches under the sleepers.

'This second line is in good order throughout, but when the line was first opened it was not usual to take the precautions which are now adopted as regards signals with respect to crossover roads and sidings joining main lines.

'Thus at Andover station it will be necessary that the crossover road should be worked by levers from the frame in which the signals are worked, and interlocked with them, and the facing points leading out of the siding should be worked by the distant signal, so that no engine or train shall be enabled to come out of the siding without the permission of the signalman.

'Again at Grateley the points leading out of the two sidings should be secured by bolts worked with the distant signals – so that nothing should quit these sidings when the distant signals are taken off for a train to pass – and the facing points at the end of the double line must be locked right for the proper road by the distant signal when it is taken off for a train to arrive from the west.

'There are two short sidings one at Andover and the other at Grateley which are to have catch points introduced.

'Mr Strapp the company's Engineer, has promised that these things shall be attended to and completed during the month of February – and I therefore recommend that the sanction of the Board of Trade may now be given for opening the second line of rails between Andover and Grateley.'

On 1st February 1870 the double track from Andover Junction to Grateley was opened.

Board of Trade Inspection Grateley to Porton 1870

Col. Yolland reported on 25th June 1870: *'I have inspected the second line of rails on the main line of the London & South Western Railway to Salisbury, between Grateley and Porton, a length of about 5 miles and 46 chains. The permanent way consists of a double headed rail, returned as weighing 80lbs per yard, in lengths of 24 feet secured* in cast iron chairs, weighing 32lbs each, by means of wooden keys placed outside the rails. These cast iron chairs are fastened to transverse sleepers placed on the average about 3 feet apart, centre, by hollow trenails with 5/8 inch spikes driven through them, two trenails being used to each chair, except in a few cases where fang bolts have been used.

'The sleepers are 9 feet long by 10 inches by 5 inches rectangular of Baltic Timber creosoted. The joints of the rails are fished in the usual manner, with 2 plates, together weighing 22lbs, and 4 nuts and bolts. The ballast is of gravel, chalk and flint, stated to be 6 inches deep, under the bottom of the sleepers.

'There are only 2 under-bridges, built in brick which have had to be widened, and the whole line is in good order, but the connection with the existing double line at the Porton station will not be made until authority is given to open.

'This is the last portion of single line on the whole length between London and Exeter, and although there are a few things to be done, which I shall enumerate, at Grateley and Porton stations, I recommend that the sanction of the Board of Trade may be given for the opening of this second line of rails, as the company's Engineer Mr Strapp has agreed to do what I pointed out as necessary to provide for the public safety.

'At Grateley, the points leading out from the Up siding on the eastern side of the station, to be locked open to the blind siding when the Up distant signal is taken off. The points of the crossover road should be interlocked with the station and distant, Up and Down signals and the points leading out of the Down siding, west of the station, should be interlocked with the Down station signal.

'At Porton, the Up siding east of the platform should terminate in a blind siding, and the points leading out of the sidings should be interlocked with the Up station signal.

'A crossover road is about to be put in and the points should be interlocked with the station and distant, Up and Down signals.'

The Grateley to Porton double track section finally opened to traffic on 1st July 1870, completing the doubling of the whole main line from Waterloo to Exeter. A number of ballast engines were employed in the doubling and a temporary wooden engine shed was provided for them at Overton. No doubt there was also a locomotive water supply here, probably pumped from the nearby River Test. At each station a new Up platform was provided with waiting shelter at Overton, Whitchurch and Grateley and the Down side at Oakley and Porton. They were reached by a foot crossing from the station house. During 1869-1870 the gravel ballast had been supplied from a gravel pit at Nursling on the Andover & Redbridge line.

HURSTBOURNE SIDING
The seven miles of line between Whitchurch and Andover traversed productive agricultural country, much of which formed part of the estate of Hurstbourne Park, owned by Earl Portsmouth. He also had estates in North Devon and was at one stage chairman of the Devon and Cornwall Railway which constructed the line to Okehampton, operated by the LSWR. His agent first approached the South Western in 1869 for provision of a siding; this was unsuccessful but the following year terms for a new siding to the east of Hurstbourne viaduct were agreed. This was opened on 1st August 1871 on the Up side and was shunted by Up goods trains, becoming the responsibility of the Whitchurch station agent. The 1871 Working Timetable stated: 'Hurstbourne Siding will be opened on 1st August, the only train to call there will be the 8.55pm Andover to Basingstoke goods'. Soon Earl Portsmouth built a grain store here, but as we shall see in Chapter Three, a passenger station was opened here in 1882.

SIGNALLING THE LINE
Over the 1854 to 1878 period of this chapter the signalling of the Basingstoke to Salisbury line evolved gradually from the primitive poorly understood arrangements of the first years. By the end of the period an essentially modern system of conventional signal boxes with interlocking points and signals were in use, with block instruments regulating the sections to adjacent boxes.

When the line opened to Andover in 1854 Capt. Tyler recommended that the levers for points and signals at Worting Junction should all be on one side of the line and that distant signals were required at Whitchurch and Andover. At this stage levers were located near the points and signals which they operated with accompanying electric telegraph connecting station offices. At junctions a wooden hut was provided for the men on duty. The signals were of the early cross bar and disc type.

Early mishaps illustrate the shortcomings of these arrangements. On 22nd September 1857 the locomotive of the 4.20pm Down train was diverted into a siding at Whitchurch damaging two buffers. Facing points had been left open resulting in the pointsman being dismissed. On 8th October 1862 the 1.25pm Up train from Exeter was derailed at Andover due to the porter not being at the points in time to turn the train into the loop sidings, the train being delayed for 1¾ hours. The interlocking of point and signal levers grouped in a single frame, which would eliminate such accidents, was still more than a decade away.

The first recorded steps toward conventional signalling were taken as follows:

16th February 1860. The South Western decided to erect semaphore signals from Messrs. Stevens on the Exeter line then under construction.

24th December 1861. Col. Yolland required that the levers for working the distant signals at Oakley station should be moved to the new Up platform.

11th May 1865. The South Western decided to install semaphore signals at the Junctions at Worting, Woking and Weybridge.

26th October 1865. The South Western decided to install a brick house to replace the wooden hut for the protection of switchmen at Tunnel Junction. This is the first record of Tunnel Junction signal box.

26th May 1868. Col. Yolland required the locking of specified points and signals at Porton.

7th September 1868. Salisbury Fisherton Tunnel. Henry Wake paid to build pointsmen's box.

8th October 1868. The South Western decided to fit Milford Junction with interlocking points and signals. This is the first record of Milford signal box.

8th April 1869. Instructions issued for new signals at Milford Junction, standard signal is now a semaphore signal.

30th June 1869. Stevens & Son were paid for the installation of new signalling apparatus at Salisbury Tunnel Junction.

21st September 1869. Saxby and Farmer were paid for the enlargement and extension of Milford Junction signal box, including discs, semaphores, point connections and laying on gas to box and signals. The Down distant is now a semaphore.

29th January 1870. Col. Yolland required the interlocking of specified points and signals at both Andover and Grateley.

25th June 1870. Col. Yolland required the interlocking of more specified points and signals at both Grateley and Porton.

August 1870. New semaphore station signals replaced discs at Andover Junction, Porton and Grateley for Up and Down trains.

22nd September 1870. The South Western decided to provide a small signal cabin to cover the levers on the Up platform at Porton, and that the levers at Grateley and Andover should be covered cheaply.

12th July 1875. The South Western decided to replace the old cross bar and disc signals at Grateley, but no new signal box.

As we can see, the Board of Trade, as represented by Col. Yolland from 1868, required the South Western to concentrate levers together in one frame and to interlock specified points and signals on the line. This implies that lever frames with this facility were being installed. Apparently these lever frames were open to the elements until cabins were provided from 1870 onwards. An 1870s period photograph at Andover Junction shows the weather-boarded cabin at platform level with no room for a full locking room. It was not until the 1871 Regulation of Railways Act that the Board of Trade powers of inspection were extended from inspection of new lines, including the laying down of a second line of rails as carried out by Col. Yolland, to alterations at existing locations.

It was not until 1873 that another Act required certain minimum signalling standards and Stevens & Son produced an improved lever frame with tappet locking. An interesting feature at both Whitchurch and Salisbury Milford in the late 1860s was gas piped to the signals for illumination purposes. When the signal gas lamps were replaced by oil lamps is not clear.

Salisbury Tunnel Junction. The double line from Porton was opened in 1868 and the following year Stevens & Co. were paid for the installation of signalling apparatus in the recently-built brick signal box. In the later South Western period a train emerges from Fisherton tunnel and takes the Southampton line.

The regulation of trains on the early single line was straightforward with the South Western undertaking to work the Andover line with one engine in steam in 1854 and with one engine in steam in each single line section in 1857. Even by 1859 there were only four passenger trains each way, the timetable specifying where trains should pass and changes could be made by use of the telegraph. In 1870 the whole line was double track and block instruments were introduced to regulate trains.

END OF AN ERA

By 1876 the line, originally a single track branch from Basingstoke, had become an established part of the LSWR West of England double track main line with through services from Waterloo and Nine Elms to Exeter, Torrington, Ilfracombe and Devonport. The South Western eventually purchased the independent Salisbury & Yeovil Railway from its shareholders in 1878 but the one-sided station at Salisbury had become a traffic bottleneck and new works were required here, as we shall see in Chapter Three. In contrast to its Basingstoke branch, where the Great Western had mixed the gauge in 1856, almost all the Wilts Somerset & Weymouth lines remained broad gauge. In 1874 they were converted to standard gauge, the Warminster to Salisbury line being converted between 18th and 22nd June. Now the time was ripe for a connection between the South Western and Great Western to enable wagons to be transferred between the two rather than the loads to be transferred in the transhipment shed.

APPENDIX TO CHAPTER TWO
SOUTH WESTERN ACCOUNTS
JOURNALS 1854 - 1870

Research by Mick Hutson at the Public Record Office has unearthed much information from the South Western Accounts Journals, here presented in summary form.

1854
14.6.54 Whitchurch and Andover. William Gue paid £540 on account for contract for both stations.

30.6.54 Whitchurch and Andover. William Gue paid another £585 on account for both stations.
30.6.54 Whitchurch and Andover. John Walker & Co. paid £10 for two 8-day clocks, one for each station.
30.6.54 Overton, Whitchurch and Andover. Carriage Department credited £262 2s 3d for signals. *(At this time there was no Signalling Department and the Carriage Department put Up signals)*
7.8.54 Whitchurch and Andover. F.R.Bill paid £256 10s for switches and crossings.
21.8.54 Andover. J.Maple & Co. supply 7 oak chairs @ £1 6s 9d.
14.9.54 Andover. Thomas Clarkson paid £10 1s 6d for carpeting and £20 8s 10d for
blinds.
14.11.54 Overton. D.Nicholson & Son paid £330 on account for station (certificate from J.Strapp, Engineer).
30.11.54 Worting. Joseph Bull paid £150 for building a pair of labourers' cottages
30.11.54 Oakley. R,Awberry & Co. paid £97 2s 6d for land for a station at Clerkengreen. *(Clerkengreen was the location of Oakley station)*
21.12.54 Andover. W.Gue paid £164 4s 11d for two coal pens on slopes of bank, £101 4s 1d for engine house, £36 18s 10d for sheep pens.
21.12.54 Andover. Locomotive Department credited £53 1s 7d for tank.
21.12.54 Overton. H.Pooley & Son paid £5 10s for patent weighing machine.

1855
7.3.55 Whitchurch and Andover. Dunn & Hattersley Co. paid £220 for two 5 ton cranes.
21.3.55 Overton. D.Nicholson & Son paid further £660 for station.
21.3.55. Andover. W.Gue labour and materials to erect large goods warehouse, recovered from Andover Road station, and luggage stores.
7.4.55 Overton. D Nicholson & Son paid £532 11s 10d for additional works.
14.4.55 Andover. Dunn & Hattersley Co. paid £56 for two cranes.
30.6.55 Overton. Carriage Department credited £49 19s 1d for signals.

31.7.55 Overton. John Walker & Co. paid £4 10s for 8 day clock, and £4 4s for clock in signalman's box.
21.9.55 Overton. A.Hallaman (clerk) rent paid before the station was completed £7 4s
14.10.55 Chief Constable Samuel Meredith paid £5 14s 3d for police attendance to men on the Basingstoke & Salisbury line – paid every month up to 1857

1856
29.2.56 Overton. Mr Budden paid £54 15s for parcels office.
31.3.56 Paid Thomas Brassey £46 7s for tools for the Andover line.*(At this stage the South Western took over maintenance of the line)*
14.5.56 Purchase cottage from Brassey at viaduct on Basingstoke & Salisbury line for £20. *(Authors' note - possibly the cottage under Monxton Viaduct)*
31.5.56 Oakley. Land from Awberry formally purchased.
30.6.56 Oakley. Payments for minor works. W.Glover £20 9s 10d, W.Barham £28 14s 9d, J.Bartlett £1 8s 1d, J.Bartlett £98 16s 4d for rail and chairs.
30.6.56 Oakley. Carriage Department credited £64 10s 8d for two signals at Clerkengreen.

1857
26.2.57 Whitchurch and Andover. William Tite paid commission of £150 18s 8d for erection of stations November 53 to October 56
14.4.57 Porton and Grateley. Joseph Bull paid on account for building stations, £400 each.
7.6.57 Porton and Grateley. John Walker paid £24 for clocks for stations.
21.6.57 Porton and Grateley. H.Pooley & Son paid for two weighing machines £5 18s each.
30.6.57 Porton and Grateley. Hazeldine & Co.paid for one hand truck at each station at £1 16s each.
30.6.57 Porton and Grateley. J Maple & Co. to provide 4 oak chairs @ £1 6s 9d each, and 4 timber chairs @3s 9d each for each station.
30.6.57. Carriage Department credited for 2 auxilliary, 1 safety and 2 night signals each at Porton and Grateley (£76 5s each station) and 1 of each at Andover (£47 12s 6d).
7.11.57 Oakley. Thomas Clarkson paid £1 15s 8d for carpets.
31.12.57 Oakley. Thomas Budden paid £78 8s 1d for building waiting room, shed, clock, drains, cesspool.

1858
14.3.58 Oakley. E.B.Gammon put up wagon gauge £4 9s 3d.
31.3.58 W.Gue & Son – contract to erect cottages at Broken Cross (1), Newton Toney (1) and Porton (2) @ £190 each.*(Broken Cross is between Porton and Salisbury where the A338 road crosses the line at Ford)*
14.4.58 Oakley. Thomas Budden work to closets £28 10s 8d.
30.4.58 Oakley. John Walker 8 day dial £3 3s.
30.6.58. Grateley. Joseph Bull paid £1274 for contract for stations.
21.10.58 Andover. H.Pooley & Son weighing machine moved to Eling. New machine supplied by H.Pooley & Son £58.

21.10.58 Salisbury Fisherton. Thomas Brassey paid £1283 18s 6d towards total contract price of £9349 for station, also £1620 12s 10d towards total contract price for line to Fisherton. Total contract price fully paid 14.8.59.

21.11.58 Grateley. W Gue & Son erect two pairs of cottages £380.

21.11.58 Grateley. F.Churton points, crossings and ironwork for new siding £9 10s 6d

30.11.58 Whitchurch and Andover. E.B.Gammon lightning conductors, Andover 19s 10d, Whitchurch £1 1s 9d.

21.12.58 Overton. W.Gue paid £19 9s 2d for repairing roof, doors and fireplace in porters room.

21.12.58. Andover. W.Gue for taking down engine shed at Andover and re-erecting same at Basingstoke with new engine pits £90 7s, putting up shed over Andover platform £105 10s.

21.12.58 Grateley and Porton. W.Gue paid £1 15s 9d each for staying chimneys.

31.12.58 Oakley. Maintenance of Way Department credited £4 4s for 24 sleepers for new siding, and £5 1s 2d to extend siding. *(At this time there was no Engineers Department, and track was the responsibility of Maintenance of Way.)*

31.12.58 Andover. Maintenance of Way credited £5 5s for 30 sleepers for new siding.

31.12.58 Porton and Grateley. Joseph Bull paid £229 16s 7d for platforms, fencing, wells, pumphouses and painting at Grateley, and £229 16s 6d at Porton.

1859

14.2.59 Grateley. John Cutting paid £2 4s for cartage of water from village to station previous September *(before the well and pumphouse were in use)*.

7.5.59 William Smart paid to asphalt platforms at Andover £19 6s, and Whitchurch, Grateley and Porton £14 - £15 each.

7.6.59 Andover. Thomas Budden to fix weighbridge from H.Pooley &Son £68 5s 9d

30.6.59 Grateley. Joseph Bull paid £17 3s 5d for new platform wall.

30.6.59 Salisbury Fisherton. Joseph Bull paid £67 5s 2d for pointsmans boxes.

7.11.59 Salisbury Fisherton. Joseph Bull paid £1330 for new engine house. Also £14 14s 5d for 'watch box' and £4 5s 5d for noticeboards at the ends of the tunnel.

7.11.59 Salisbury. Joseph Hodgkinson paid for points and crossings for transfer between the two gauges £40 17s 6d.

31.12.59 Overton. T.Budden paid £131 12s for alterations to porters room, parcels office, store room and closets.

31.12.59 Salisbury Fisherton. J.Maple & Co. paid £21 for 16 chairs.

31.12.59 Salisbury Fisherton. Maintenance of Way credited for new sidings for transfer of traffic £242 10d.

1860

29.2.60 Salisbury Fisherton. Joseph Bull paid £62 13s 6d for new engine pits.

14.6.60. Thomas Brassey paid £89,000 for building the line from Andover to Salisbury Junction; Fisherton to Milford, and forming 'fork Lines' from main line to Salisbury Milford £41,290 11s. Extra works Monxton viaduct £1315 5s 3d with total extras £5,628 16s 11d including £145 7s 9d for works in connection with Salisbury cattle show.

21.9.60. Salisbury Fisherton. Thomas Brassey paid £8,100 12s 10d for line to Fisherton and £7,743 18s 6d for erecting station, plus £2,650 for sidings to engine shed, locomotive turntable, tank house and water columns.

7.11.60 Salisbury Milford. Joseph Bull paid £323 5s 1d for new dwelling house for station agent.

1861

14.6.61 Salisbury Milford. F.R.Fisher paid £393 17s 1d for temporary station following fire. *(Authors' note. This appears to be the replacement of the original Milford station destroyed by fire on 27th March 1858, but payment was made three years later.)*

30.6.61. Oakley. M.J.Shaw paid £28 19s for girders to widen bridges between Worting and Oakley. Maintence of Way Department credited with £431 for line widening.

21.9.61. Salisbury Fisherton. Horne & Co. paid £140 for horse shunting of trains. (Also at Yeovil and Exeter)

7.10.61. Salisbury Fisherton. J.Errington paid 5% commission on £22,345 19s 6d paid to Thomas Brassey for line and station.

21.10.61 Oakley. Henry Wake paid £446 5s 4d for widening bridges.

21.1.62. Salisbury Fisherton. Thomas Budden paid £978 for new waiting room.

21.2.62 Oakley. Thomas Budden paid £161 4s 10d for building work in connection with doubling the line.

7.3.62 Salisbury Fisherton. Thomas Budden paid £402 for additional works to new refreshment room.

21.3.62 Overton and Whitchurch. Thomas Budden paid for foundations for sheds on Up side, Overton £1 15s, Whitchurch £1 17s 6d.

21.11.62. Oakley. Joseph Bull paid £580 as contract for building new station, and a further £434 10s 10d on 31.12.62. T.Clarkson paid £3 2s 6d for carpet and oil cloth for station.

14.12.62 Overton and Grateley. Henry Wake paid £63 19s 6d for building platform wall at Overton, and £85 19s at Grateley.

31.12.62 Salisbury Fisherton. Thomas Budden paid £278 17s 8d for building new boundary wall, stores and workshops for enginemen.

31.12.62 Salisbury Fisherton. Musselwhite & Son paid £43 9s 1d for new ticket platform, Salisbury being an 'open' station.

7.3.63 John Walker paid £42 for four double sided clocks for Overton, Oakley, Whitchurch and Andover.

7.6.63 Andover. W.Gue paid £301 18s 4d for builders work.

21.8.64 Salisbury Fisherton. J.Hodgkinson paid £176 for extending and fixing roof.

7.9.64. Whitchurch. J. Soper paid £1 12s 6d for pipes and fittings for signal box.

7.10.64 Overton. Musselwhite & Son paid £129 10s 1d for building new engine shed on the doubling account.

31.10.64. Andover. G.Wood paid £111 18s 3d for laying on gas.

14.11.64 Whitchurch. R.A.Davis paid for timber for new platform in connection with doubling.

21.12.64. Salisbury Fisherton. T.Fisher paid £135 13s 2d for building new room for guards, and £199 9s 11d for new 'exit enclosure'.

31.12.64 Overton. Maintenance of Way Department credited for wages and materials for new siding.

31.12.64 Whitchurch. Maintenance of Way Department credited for wages and materials for new cattle pens.

21.1.65 Rhymney Iron Co. paid £2,599 16s 5d for double headed rails and fishplates for doubling of Basingstoke and Salisbury line.

21.3.65 Salisbury Fisherton Tunnel. W.H.Preece & Co. paid £9 9s 4d for 'two bells with tappers' at Salisbury Tunnel.

14.5.65 Salisbury Fisherton. J.Hodgkinson paid for work in connection with new iron footbridge at Salisbury.

30.6.66. Oakley and Whitchurch. Carriage Department credited £22 for low auxiliary signals.

31.12.66 Oakley. Maintenance of Way Department credited for wages and materials for new siding.

21.2.66 Worting. Stevens & Son - two wrought iron signals and fittings £257 5s 3d.

7.9.68 Salisbury Fisherton Tunnel. Henry Wake paid £44 7s 10d to build pointsman's box.

7.9.68 Gravel Pit Bridge, between Grateley and Andover. G.Batten paid £291 16s 8d for widening bridge.

30.9.68 Salisbury Fisherton Tunnel. Henry Wake paid £1 18s 8d for whitewashing bridge *(Possibly to improve visibility of signals)*

21.11.68 Whitchurch. G.Batten paid £215 4s 8d for building a bridge at station, called Lord Portsmouth's.

30.6.69 Salisbury Milford. H.Wake paid for works to footbridge and creosoting signal box.

31.8.69 Grateley to Porton and Boscombe to Idmiston. H.Wake & Co. paid £658 10s for widening bridges.

21.9.69 Salisbury Milford. Saxby & Farmer 'amount paid to J.Bull & Sons for enlarging and erecting a signal box at Milford Junction £93 11s 1d. Fitting up telegraphic machinery in above signal box and adjacent thereto, laying on gas to box and signals, providing discs, semaphores, point connections, wires etc. £697 13s 2d', apparently completed 4.69.

7.11.69 Boscombe and Idmiston. H.Wake & Co. paid £688 13s 7d for widening and strengthening two underbridges.

30.6.70 Andover to Salisbury line. Paid W.Glover £1 16s 11d for painting and writing gradient posts.

30.6.70 Grateley to Porton. Reported that the cost of doubling had been £7,504 10s 4d for rails, chairs, sleepers. etc.

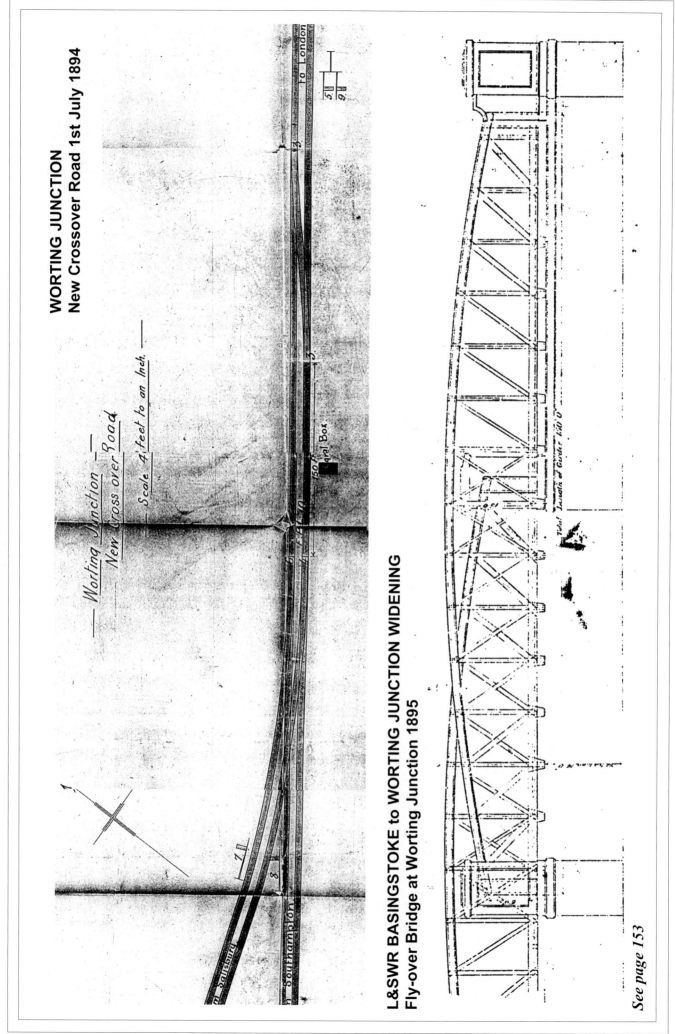

WORTING JUNCTION
New Crossover Road 1st July 1894

Worting Junction
New Cross over Road

Scale 4 feet to an Inch.

to London

to Southampton

to Salisbury

Signal Box.

L&SWR BASINGSTOKE to WORTING JUNCTION WIDENING
Fly-over Bridge at Worting Junction 1895

See page 153

CHAPTER THREE
THE LONDON SOUTH WESTERN PERIOD 1878-1899

EXTENSION OF SALISBURY STATION 1878

By the 1870s the original single through platform at Salisbury station had become inadequate for the rapidly growing traffic. The obvious solution was to build an Up platform opposite but much of the land here was owned by the Great Western and occupied by their engine shed. Relationships between the London and South Western and the broad gauge companies, which had been taken over by the Great Western, were less than cordial, particularly after the South Western's illegal take-over of the Exeter & Crediton in 1847. At Salisbury, co-operation between the two was fairly normal. They were not in competition and increased traffic benefited both. But as we shall see in Volume Two the 1875 take-over of the Somerset & Dorset Railway, jointly by the South Western and the Midland Railways, was seen as a betrayal of trust by the Great Western and relations between the companies again reached rock bottom. The arrival of the South Western at Devonport in 1876 also deprived the Great Western of its monopoly of the Plymouth traffic. So this was not the time for delicate negotiations with the aggrieved rival company.

Board of Trade Inspections 1878-79

Conversion of the Great Western's Salisbury branch to standard gauge in 1874 provided an opportunity to transfer wagons directly and in February 1878 a connection was opened opposite the South Western's one sided station near the now redundant transfer shed. This was just the first of a number of changes made in 1878-79. On behalf of the Board of Trade Col.Yolland made his inspection and reported on 24th July 1878: *'I have inspected the new station which has been constructed by the London & South Western Railway on the Up side, and at the eastern end of the original one sided station at Salisbury.*

'The points and signals connected with this new Up station are worked from a new signal box which has a locking frame containing 29 levers of which 6 are at the present time spare ones.

'The facing point lock moved by lever No.22 wants adjustment and a pair of facing points on the Down main line should be done away with by connecting the middle road with the Up instead of the Down main line at its eastern end, and making the points trailing instead of facing points. In other respects the interlocking is correct, and the requirements of the Board of Trade complied with.

'There is an abundant length of platform accommodation provided for this Up side station. Where there are station buildings the width of the platforms for a length of about 320 feet is 15 feet, and where there are no station buildings, but only shelter overhead, the width is 18 feet 9 inches for a length of about 220 feet.

'But the platform accommodation has practically been spoilt by the introduction of single posts midway on it for the support of the shelter overhead opposite to the part where there are station buildings, instead of supporting this shelter by brackets from the side walls of the station buildings, and removing these posts altogether from the platform and leaving it clear with its full width of 15 feet; and on the remaining part where there are no station buildings by supporting the shelter overhead by two instead of one post placed in the centre of the 18¼ feet wide platform, as it must be remembered that a bay has been provided at the eastern end , and on the north side of this long Up platform for passenger traffic and the northernmost of the two posts will be inconveniently near the north edge of the platform.

'With the exceptions which I have stated the station is a good station, but it will be found I am afraid very inconvenient and not so good as might have been provided if Parliament instead of allowing these stations had compelled the Great Western and London & South Western companies to have one joint station at Salisbury.

'With reservations I have made I can now recommend the Board of Trade to sanction the use of this new station at Salisbury for working the traffic and thus of doing away with another one-sided station.'

On 26th July 1878 the Board of Trade notified the South Western of Col. Yolland's approval, and on 19th August 1878 the new Up side station was opened. Col.Rich made his inspection and reported on 3rd April 1879 *'I have inspected the new connection at the west end of Salisbury station on the London & South Western Railway.*

The junction points of the new siding are worked from a ground frame, which is situated close to an accommodation level crossing about 330ft from the siding junction. The points are interlocked with the signals but the work cannot be completed until the signal and locking arrangements in No.3 cabin are completed as the latter cabin is to work in connection with the No.2 signal box. The ground frame requires covering with a cabin. It will then be called the Gate Cabin Salisbury West End and will take the place of the old Gate Cabin , which is close alongside the accommodation level crossing. The old cabin is to be done away with. The repeater to the Up distant signal should be moved from the old cabin to the new cabin.

'Subject to these remarks the works may be temporarily approved but cannot be finally approved until No.3 cabin in Salisbury station yard is completed as the signals at No.3 are to be slotted to act as home signals for the gate Cabin Salisbury West End.'

The original 1859 station at Salisbury. From 1878 to 1902 it formed the Down side buildings, with the Up side located at the other side of Fisherton Street.

In 1898 the original Castle Street Bridge at Salisbury, illustrated on page 128 was replaced with this plate girder structure seen from the south. John Nicholas.

On 6th June 1879 Col. Rich of the Board of Trade wrote privately to Mr E.W. Verrinder, the South Western's Assistant Superintendent of the Line:

'My dear Mr Verrinder,

As the station roads at Salisbury have not been altered I do not think I can require the company to alter the signal arrangements for the crossover road, by which the engines go from the sheds to the Up line but I am satisfied that there ought to be a second arm on the post next the goods shed. The present signal to be for trains on the Up line and a lower arm for trains or engines crossing from Down to Up line.

'You must recollect that this crossover road becomes really a running line for the engines. Now one of our commonest accidents is a shunting engine running out, while a main line train is passing and I feel confident that some time or other a passenger train will be stopped inside No.2 signal, that it will start again when the signal near the goods shed is lowered and that an engine will be very apt to start over the crossover road at the same time and collide with the passenger train.

'I see that this crossover road cannot be locked with the present signals at the goods shed unless you have a 2nd arm for the crossover road, in which case it can and ought to be locked with the present signal'.

Col. Yolland again reported on 10th May 1879 that he had recently passed through Salisbury and had noticed that no attention had yet been paid to that part of his 1878 report requiring replacement of the posts supporting the awning.

Salisbury Up Side Station 1878

An LSWR drawing dated 26th June 1878 covers the station from Fisherton Street eastwards. Essentially the South Western had acquired a strip of land up to 35 yards wide in the water meadows on the north side of the line and had brought in material to widen the embankment for about 350 yards, stopping just short of a stream spanned by Bridge 234. Bridge No.235 over another stream was widened. The new platform, about 640 feet long, had been built alongside the Up main line, together with an Up bay platform about 300 feet long. Beyond the bay road were two more tracks serving a horse dock, carriage dock and loading bank.

A new Salisbury No.1 signal box was provided close to the site of the later East signal box and the drawing gave full details of the function of each of the 29 levers. For example at the end of the Up platform there was a bracket signal with three dolls, No.4 loading bank to Up main, No.5 (bay) platform road to Up main, No.6 Up main starting signal.

North of the line a new station approach road ran up from gates on Fisherton Street to give pedestrian and vehicular access to the new station offices and loading docks. A spacious cab yard was also provided outside. The single storey station buildings were of mainly timber construction, painted and sanded to look like stone, and incorporated booking office, waiting rooms and refreshment rooms. The timber construction may have had insufficient strength to carry the weight of the awning, which may account for the roof supports so disliked by Col. Yolland. There was a second, pedestrian, entrance to the Up station from Fisherton Street. Passing through gates immediately to the south of the line there was a footpath almost underneath the Southampton bay as far as the platform end, there turning into a subway under the line, and up a ramp into the new Up station.

Until the 1902 re-building this was the Salisbury station which was the cause of much complaint, not from Salisbury residents, but from passengers changing trains here, particularly in bad weather. For example, passengers arriving from the Southampton or Wimborne direction and requiring to take a train to Andover or Waterloo had to leave the station completely, walk down South Western Road, cross Fisherton Street and then by either route reach the Up station. The time taken was responsible for missed connections and passengers with luggage found it particularly difficult. No doubt better off passengers

could afford the services of a porter, or even a short cab ride for station to station. There was recognition of the problem in the 1880s when certain trains from Wimborne were examined at Downton and a telegram sent to Salisbury to warn if there were or not any passengers for stations east of Salisbury.

MORE EXPANSION AT SALISBURY

In the 1880s and 1890s traffic continued to increase, requiring more accommodation at Salisbury for both locomotives and freight. The growth in traffic reflected the expansion of the South Western system west of Exeter in the 1870s, particularly in the Plymouth area and the winning of more business from existing stations. In 1890 traffic from the Plymouth area was boosted by the opening of the double track route through Bere Alston, eliminating the bottleneck of the single track Great Western route through Yelverton which the South Western had used. Freight traffic in particular had increased and South Western traffic arriving at Salisbury from the west diverged into the two routes for both London and the South Coast, requiring re-marshalling of trains. Additionally, as soon as standard gauge freight working started on the Great Western's Salisbury branch some of it was transferred to the South Western, particularly coal from the late 1880s onwards.

The original 1859 three road engine shed on the Down side of the line to the west of the station could not cope with the demand so in early 1885 locomotive capacity was doubled when a second three road engine shed was opened alongside. A detailed account of the development of the engine sheds at Salisbury is given in Chapter One.

To the west of the extended engine shed on the Down side more land had been acquired and a seven road West Yard was laid out, although the date of connection has yet to come to light. Most Down goods trains called and many started or ended their journeys here. Additionally, East of Fisherton Street bridge, more land had been acquired to the north of the line. Bridges Nos.234 and 235 were extended and large volumes of fill brought in to widen the embankment, about fifteen feet high. Just where this fill came from is not known but in 1880-82 the long cutting west of Andover Junction was being widened for the construction of the Swindon Marlborough and Andover Railway, so this is a possible source. The East Yard comprised seven sidings terminating at or behind the 1878 Up station. It was brought into use, with a new ground frame and altered connections, in 1898 although if there was an inspection of the original main line connection it has not been found.

The original 1859 Castle Street bridge, No.231, had elegant curved girders and lattice sides and in 1898 was replaced by a more substantial plate girder bridge on brick abutments. This still only carried the two main line tracks but in 1910 a third girder was added when the headshunt of the East Yard was extended as we shall see in Chapter Five. However, the original 1859 Castle

Street bridge was removed by T.Scamell and re-erected nearby for Nelson Street to cross the River Avon, just upstream of bridge No.232.

It would appear, initially, that the few wagons exchanged at Salisbury were shunted to the transfer siding by one company to be collected by the other. Either horses or locomotives were used; an 1898 accident report for instance, mentions 'the employment of horses for shunting one or two vehicles at a time'. Eventually an arrangement was reached whereby Great Western locomotives worked their trains into the East Yard, whilst South Western locomotives worked theirs into a reception siding outside the Great Western terminus.

Following the changes of 1878-79 there was a No.2 signal box on the Up side opposite the 1859 station building, close to the new connection with the Great Western. To the west of the platform, near the engine shed, was the No.3 signal box. Following the gauge conversion and connection to the South Western, the little-used Great Western single track branch from Warminster saw an increase in traffic. Coal from Bullo Pill in the Forest of Dean came initially, followed by more Welsh coal after the opening of the Severn Tunnel in 1886.

In 1888 there was one coal train, a daily 9.20am working from Salisbury to Bishopstoke, running on Mondays Only as the 4.20am from Salisbury to Southampton. In summer 1895 there were four trains. Coal trains left Salisbury at 8.10am for Eastleigh and 11.0am or 2.30pm for Southampton; loco coal trains left Salisbury at 11.15am 'when required' and 1.50pm for Nine Elms. With an increasing volume of coal the Great Western completed the doubling of its Salisbury branch in 1902.

Inspection of New Works 1896-1898

Maj.Marindin inspected a new crossover road between the Up main line and the middle line and approved its use subject to changes in interlocking in his report of 3rd July 1896. The points and additional disc signals were worked from No.2 cabin which then contained 19 levers of which two were push-pull. Lt.Col.Addison inspected new works and gave his approval in his report of 28th April 1898: '*I have inspected alterations at the north end of Salisbury station on the London & South Western Railway. These comprise a new through road from the Down main line to the Up sidings, and a trailing connection with the sidings on the Up main line and other alterations inside the sidings. There are also additional shunting signals.*

'*The points on the through road are worked from Salisbury 'A' signal box, containing 29 levers, all in use, 6 being push and pull levers. The Up line connection is worked from a ground frame, containing 4 levers (1 push and pull), which is controlled in the usual manner from the signal box. I noted the following requirements:-*

1. No.7 lever to lock 23 in both positions.

2. Levers 4 pull and 11 push in "A" box to be interlocked with 2 push in the ground frame.

'*The station is to be built and the lines will, I understand, shortly be remodelled. In the meantime it should be very clearly understood that in working points and signals for the yard, on the Up side, the signalman must act entirely under instructions he receives from the shunters and not on his own initiative, his view of the yard being very limited indeed. Gongs have been provided to enable the shunters to communicate with the signalman.*

On 1st July 1896 two through passenger services each way between Cardiff and Portsmouth began. These may have been through trains but it seems more likely that a though carriage shunted across the Salisbury connection sufficed. Indeed there is evidence that there were through carriages between Portsmouth and Bristol before 1896. A temporary double junction was brought into use in October 1899 before the permanent connection was provided in 1903.

THE SALISBURY ACCIDENT 1898

On 23rd September 1898 there was a collision at Salisbury station. Col. Marindin investigated the accident on behalf of the Board of Trade and reported on 8th October in lengthy terms; what follows is a shortened version.

A loaded Great Western third class carriage coupled to a loaded South Western carriage truck was standing on the Down main line alongside the Down platform, waiting to be attached to the 3.8pm Down train, when Adams T3 class 4-4-0 No.568 running tender first from the east end of the station to the engine shed hit the carriage truck. There was no derailment but the carriage truck and carriage were damaged and 12 of the passengers injured.

The Down platform at Salisbury was on the south side of the line, not opposite the Up platform to the east of it. In addition to the Up and Down main lines there was a long carriage siding between the two, connected to the Down main line, from east to west, near the No.1, 2 and 3 signal cabins. No.2, or B cabin, was on the north side of the line. The Down main line was covered by a veranda supported by posts between the Down main line and carriage siding, on an easy curve to the right, but when there were vehicles on the middle siding the view from an approaching engine was bad. The only signal involved was the No.2 cabin Down home.

Witnesses included Edward Knight, station master, who reported that the Great Western four wheeled third class carriage had brought a party up from Teignmouth the previous day, and was due to return with the party attached to the 11.45am Down train from Waterloo which left Salisbury at 3.8pm. It was standing in the

Our first view of the re-built Andover Junction station, in 1899 with Beyer Peacock 0-6-0 No.372 on the Down Through line with a heavy evening goods train. Visible under the awning is a Southampton line train in the bay platform and behind the goods train the East signal box and signal posts. To the bottom left is the shadow of a train waiting on the Up local line adjacent to the island platform. Compare this with the 1875 plan on page 136. Dennis Cullum Collection.

middle road. When the 11.45am from Waterloo arrived the last vehicle was a loaded carriage truck destined for Tisbury, but since the third class carriage had to come off at Sherborne it had to be in front of the carriage truck. The carriage truck was taken off the train by a horse on to the middle road, and the Great Western carriage pulled up to it. The 11.45am train had been shunted on to the middle road at the west end of the station out of the way of the 1.0pm Waterloo Down train due at 2.55pm, and due to depart at 3.2pm, before the 11.45am train. While the 1.0pm was standing at the platform the Great Western carriage and carriage truck had been brought out by horse to the rear of the 1.0pm train and left standing there, shunter Cooper being in charge of the operation. The 11.45 train would, after the 1.0pm train had left, have been backed into the platform and coupled to them. Here about half the passengers got into the Great Western carriage. The 1.0pm train left at 3.5pm and then there was nothing standing on the Down main line except the two vehicles in question, although the middle road was full of vehicles. Two minutes later there was a collision.

Edwin Ottaway had served 25 years on the line, the previous 10 as signalman, and was on duty at B, or No.2, cabin. He agreed with Mr Knight's evidence, that the two vehicles stood on the Down line opposite the booking office, some 26 yards from the boarded crossing at the platform end, but out of his view due to vehicles standing on the middle road. He accepted the light engine from A cabin, stopped it at the Down home signal, offered it to C cabin who accepted it and, completely forgetting the two vehicles standing on the Down line pulled his home signal off for the locomotive, which shortly after collided with them.

Driver Francis Lancashire and fireman Alfred Tozer of Exmouth Junction shed, with 29½ and 15 years railway service respectively, had come on duty at 11.30am,

worked the second division of the 12.45am train from Exeter, due at Salisbury at 2.49, and after turning at the shed were to return to Exeter with the 4.54pm from Salisbury. Visibility was difficult with coal piled high on the tender, the sun in their faces, vehicles in the middle road and the pillars of the station veranda; the fireman saw the two vehicles too late for the driver to stop.

Maj.Marindin could find no fault in the mode of working through Salisbury station, and concluded that the collision was due to the forgetfulness of signalman Ottaway, who himself admitted that he alone was to blame.

THE SWINDON MARLBOROUGH & ANDOVER RAILWAY 1882

The Swindon Marlborough and Andover Railway gained its Act on 21st July 1873 for a line to join the South Western main line at Abbotts Ann, a mile and a half west of Andover Junction station. Prior to the Act there had been an agreement on 7th July between the two companies. The SM&AR was to pay the South Western for the construction of a third line from Abbotts Ann to Andover Junction together with the necessary extension of the station for the SM&AR paying 6% annually of the costs incurred. A significant clause in the agreement was an undertaking by the South Western to double the Andover and Redbridge line and ease its worst curves.

To assist with the SM&AR construction a new siding was connected at Andover Junction, inspected by Maj. Marindin who reported on 9th March 1881: *'I have inspected the new siding connection at Andover Junction on the London & South Western Railway. This connection, together with others at the south east of the station yard situated at a long distance from the cabin, is worked from the ground, but is bolted by rod from the station cabin, which contains 25 levers correctly interlocked.*

'The arrangements are not so satisfactory as would be the case if there were a second

cabin to work all the points and signals at the south end of the yard but, as the whole of this arrangement will be revised upon the opening of the Swindon Marlborough & Andover Railway probably within a year, I do not think that the case of this new siding need be objected to.'

The report was accompanied by plan dated February 1881, covering (from the east) most of the station platforms to just beyond the bridge over the line to the west and just beyond the new siding with trailing connection from the Up main line, together with the signal box lever function diagram. No.4 lever controlled the Up siding to Up main point bolts, referred to by Maj. Marindin. The contractors were able to use this siding to remove material excavated from the long cutting, west of Andover Junction station, when it was widened to accommodate the SM&AR sidings and the single line to Red Post Junction. Two bridges over the line, constructed in brick to accommodate a double track, were demolished and replaced by the longer girder bridges on brick abutments which remain to this day.

Inspection of the Swindon Marlborough & Andover Railway 1882

The first section of the SM&AR between Swindon and Marlborough opened in July 1881 but elsewhere progress was slow. Eventually, on 21st March 1882, Maj.Marindin inspected the section from Grafton to Andover Junction which was opened to traffic on 1st May 1882. The *Salisbury & Winchester Journal* of 6th May 1882 reported: 'On Monday a portion of the line between Andover and Grafton was opened', and there was the usual lunch, at the Star & Garter Hotel. Disputes, which had arisen with the Great Western over the use of its Savernake and Marlborough branch, were resolved and on 3rd February 1883 there was a ceremonial opening. A

Andover Junction station building as extended for the opening of the Swindon Marlborough & Andover Railway in 1882.

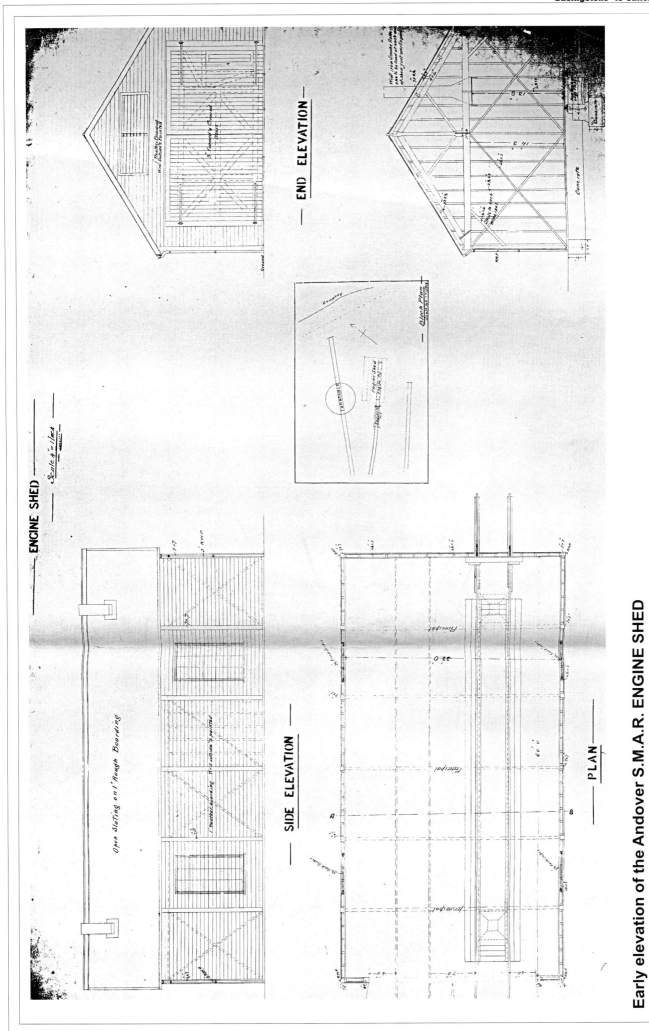

Early elevation of the Andover S.M.A.R. ENGINE SHED

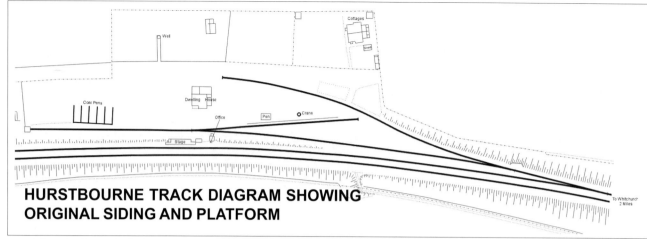

HURSTBOURNE TRACK DIAGRAM SHOWING ORIGINAL SIDING AND PLATFORM

special train from Swindon Town to Andover Junction ran the full length of the line and a sumptuous lunch was taken in Andover Town Hall.

At Andover Junction the station was extensively enlarged at the expense of the Swindon Marlborough and Swindon line. The improvements included extension of the station house, the Andover and Redbridge bay and the adjacent Down main line platform gained an arc-roofed platform canopy. The SM&AR was an independent company with its own staff and rolling stock but it had friendly relations with the South Western who often hired rolling stock to the small company when required. The agreement of 15th August 1882 between the two companies included SM&AR running powers over the South Western between Andover Junction and Southampton, and for the doubling and realigning of the Andover & Redbridge line, completed in 1885.

On 5th February 1883 the complete line from Swindon Town to Andover Junction was opened with seven weekday trains each way. South Western and SM&AR through carriages ran between Southampton and Swindon. The new line was constructed to the north of the South Western main line, the new Up platform being an island with the SM&AR trains using the outer face. The SM&AR had sidings and an engine shed. The land had been purchased by the SM&AR, the South Western constructing

all the new works which were maintained by the SM&AR.

Thus in 1882 the South Western gained a modern Andover Junction station with Up and Down through roads and platform loops, a new Up platform and subway, and new signalling from two new signal boxes. With few subsequent alterations the station was well able to cope with traffic over the next century.

THE MIDLAND & SOUTH WESTERN JUNCTION RAILWAY from 1884

In its 1884 Act the SM&AR merged with the Cheltenham extension company and changed its name to the Midland & South Western Junction Railway. The MSWJR extended its line to Andoversford and on 30th June 1891, extended its services using running powers to Cheltenham (Lansdown) on the Midland Railway. Using the 1882 agreement for running powers the MSWJR extended its own goods train service to Southampton on 1st November 1892, followed by passenger train services on 1st June 1893. These trains, consisting of MSWJR locomotives and rolling stock and operated by MSWJR train crews, normally ran between Andover Junction and Southampton Town. Much of the goods traffic was to and from Southampton Docks, owned by the South Western, who were keen to increase such traffic. From 1893 MSWJR trains included through carriages between Southampton,

Cheltenham and Bradford, Leeds, Sheffield, Derby, Liverpool and Birmingham, providing a very useful cross-country service from Andover.

It was claimed that the quickest route between Cheltenham and London was via Andover rather than Gloucester but timetable analysis has not yet provided evidence for this. In the summer of 1895, at Andover Junction, a through coach leaving Cheltenham at 10.25am was attached to the 10.25am express from Exeter to arrive at Waterloo at 2.33pm. In the Down direction the 1.0pm express, from Waterloo to Exeter, detached a through coach to Cheltenham arriving at 5.10pm, after waiting 20 and 45 minutes respectively at Andover Junction.

The friendly relationship between the two companies included senior appointments such as the South Western's Sam Fay who became the MSWJR General Manager between 1892 and 1899 before returning to the South Western as Superintendent of the Line. His successor on the MSWJR was James Purkess, another South Western man. The South Western also hired out locomotives and carriages to the MSWJR when required.

The MSWJR found that its worst bottleneck was the single track Savernake to Marlborough section, which carried GW branch trains in addition its own services. Thus the MSWJR assisted in the promotion of the Marlborough and Grafton Railway to provide a new independent route. The company gained its Act in 1896 and work began immediately on the double track line almost seven miles long. This opened to traffic on 26th June 1898 and an improved timetable began on 1st July 1898. This was just in time for the army manoeuvres on Salisbury Plain in August 1898 which brought unprecedented numbers of trains carrying troops and their equipment from the north and Midlands to Ludgershall. As we shall see in Chapter Four the MSWJR continued to improve its route in the early 1900s.

HURSTBOURNE STATION 1882

As we have seen in Chapter Three a siding had been opened at Hurstbourne in 1871. On 5th January 1882 the South Western board agreed to build a new station at Hurstbourne at a cost of £2,158, including the purchase of the siding from Earl Portsmouth. The works were completed

Hurstbourne station opened in 1882. The wooden platforms and buildings reflected the location, partially at the top of the high embankment.

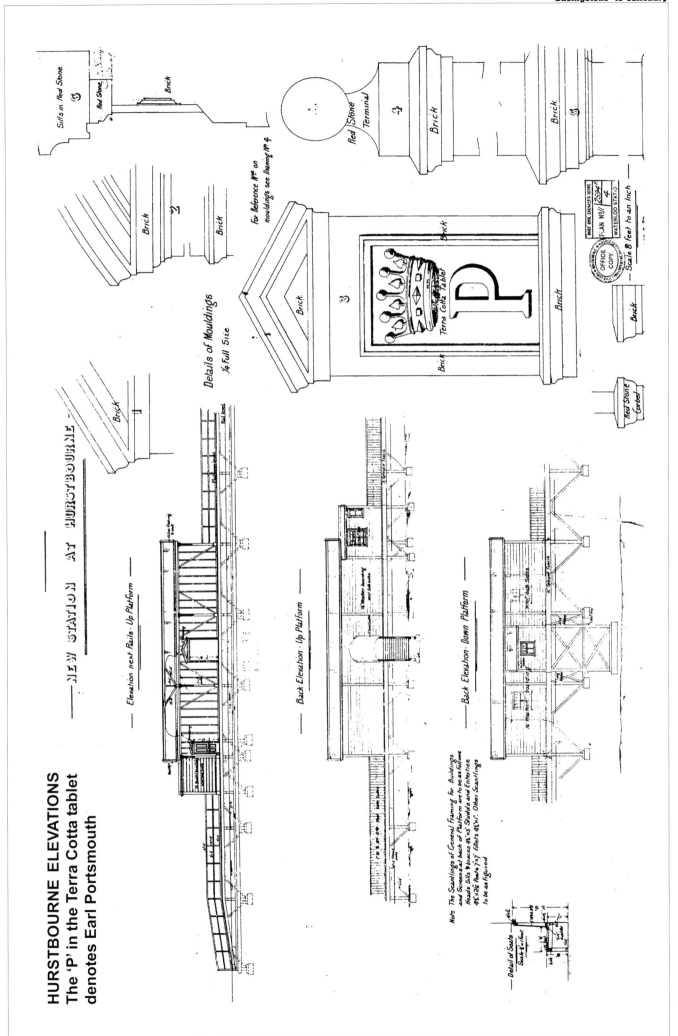

HURSTBOURNE ELEVATIONS
The 'P' in the Terra Cotta tablet
denotes Earl Portsmouth

NEW STATION AT HURSTBOURNE

Elevation next Rails - Up Platform

Back Elevation - Up Platform

Back Elevation - Down Platform

Details of Mouldings
¼ Full Size

Sills in Red Stone

Red Stone Terminal

Terra Cotta Tablet

For Reference Nos on
mouldings see Drawing No 4

Red Stone Corbel

Scale 8 feet to an Inch

Note. The Scantlings of General Framing for Buildings
and Screens at back of Platform are to be as follows
Heads, Sills & braces 4½x3 Studs and Entertres
4½x2½ Posts 7x5 Fillets 4½x4. Other Scantlings
to be as figured

Detail of Scale

HURSTBOURNE ELEVATIONS

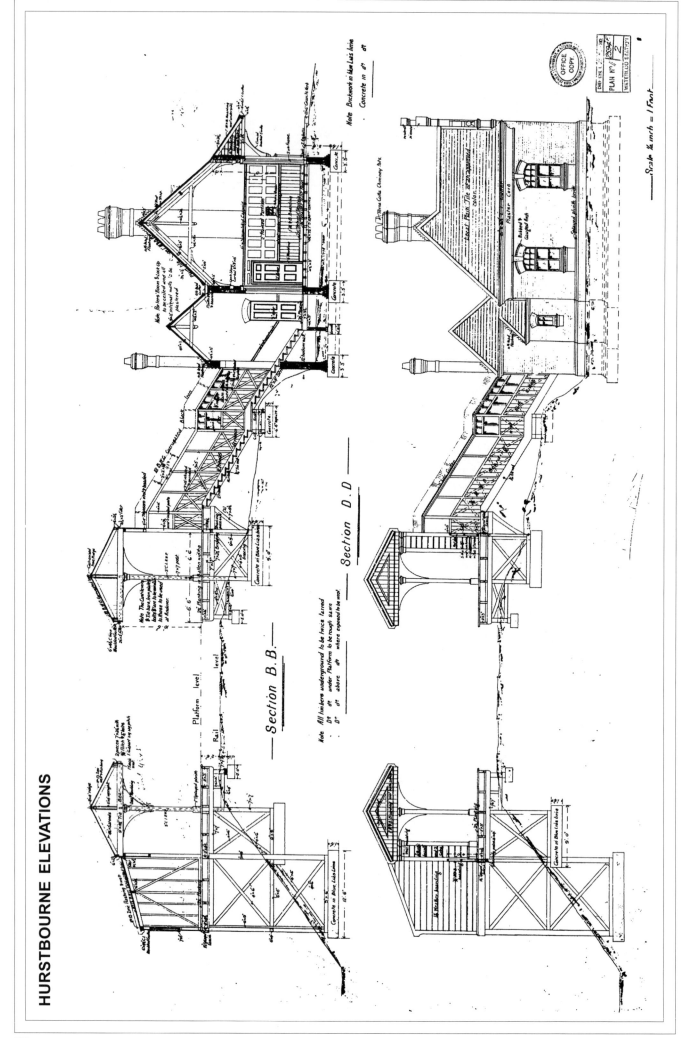

— Section B.B. —

— Section D.D. —

HURSTBOURNE ELEVATIONS

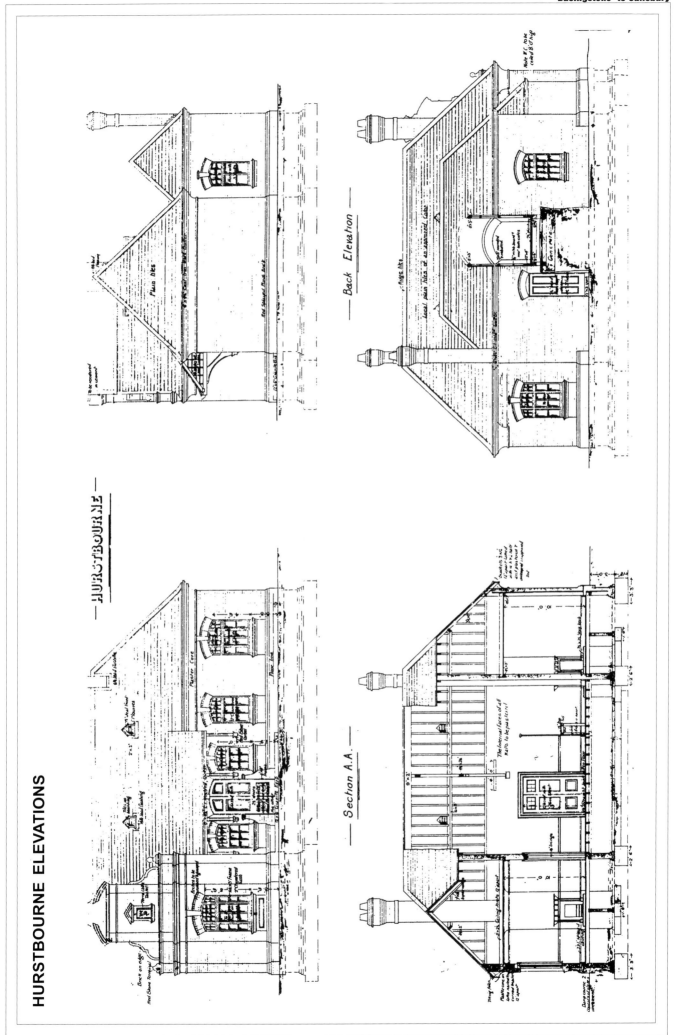

— HURSTBOURNE —

— Back Elevation —

— Section A.A. —

Whitchurch station, following the new works of 1885, looking west from the Newbury Road Bridge. The 'Hurstbourne Loop' has been built to the rear of the Up platform, signalled for the departure of Down trains but not the arrival of Up trains. This loop platform was constructed for trains running over a connection which was never built so it turned out to be a 'white elephant'. The Didcot Newbury & Southampton crosses under our line just behind the approaching train. The footbridge was installed in 1897 and the splendid goods shed was served by wagon turntables and spur lines.

and Col. Yolland reported on 8th December 1882: '*I have inspected the new station which has been constructed by the London & South Western company at Hurstbourne between Whitchurch and Andover Junction stations. It is situated about 2 miles from Whitchurch and 5¼ miles from Andover Junction stations. The signal box contains 11 levers; the interlocking is correct.*

'*Name boards are required at the station and public conveniences should be provided on each platform. At the present time a urinal only has been provided on the Up platform.*

'*On the understanding that these requirements are complied with I can recommend the Board of Trade sanction to the use of this station.*'

The station and signal box opened to traffic on 1st December 1882 initially being served by main line stopping trains. From 1885, however, these were augmented by the new service between Whitchurch and Fullerton.

Middle. Fullerton Junction station, as re-built in 1885, with an approaching train destined for Andover Junction. To the left are the two platforms provided for the new double track line from Hurstbourne Junction.

Bottom left. Oakley station showing the layout as inspected by Maj. Marindin in 1882. Considering its isolated rural situation there are a good number of wagons in the sidings. Colin Chivers Collection.

The new works underway at Worting Junction in 1897, showing the original double junction between the Southampton and Salisbury lines, signals and signal box. The original Saxby & Stevens signalling was authorised by the South Western in 1865.

THE NORTHERN & SOUTHERN JUNCTION RAILWAY 1885

The LSWR faced a threat to its monopoly of the Southampton traffic when on 5th August 1873 the Didcot Newbury & Southampton Railway Act was passed. Unlike the MSWJR, which it saw bringing more traffic to its system, the South Western anticipated that the DNSR would provide the Great Western with a competing route between London and Southampton and therefore opposed it. The southern section of the line passed under the main line near Whitchurch station and was opened to Winchester (Cheesehill) on 1st May 1885. One proposed route to Southampton involved a connection between the two lines at Whitchurch; it would then follow a new course to near Chilbolton, on the Andover and Redbridge line, and thence by running powers into Southampton.

By an Act of 10th August 1882 the Northern and Southern Junction Railway was empowered to build a line some seven miles long from Hurstbourne Junction to a new Fullerton Junction station on the Andover & Redbridge line. This was promoted by the South Western to block the advance of the Didcot company and an Act of 20th August 1883 authorised deviations. The contract was awarded to J.Firbank and involved heavy earthworks including a two mile cutting and gradients

as steep as 1 in 105 climbing up the valley. The double track line was opened on 1st June 1885 with intermediate stations at the picturesque villages of Wherwell and Longparish. At the same time a third platform was provided on the Up side at Whitchurch.

Board of Trade Inspections 1885

Maj. Marindin made his inspection and made two reports on 22nd May 1885: *'I have inspected the Northern and Southern Junction Railway, a new double line 7 miles 9.5 chains in length extending from Hurstbourne Junction on the main line of the L&SW Railway to Fullerton Junction on the line between Andover and Stockbridge.*

'The service of trains on this branch will for the present be between Whitchurch and Fullerton but this is a temporary arrangement only; it is probable that these two stations will not long continue to be terminal stations for the traffic.

'The width of the line at formation level is in cuttings 30ft and on embankments 32ft, the gauge is 4ft 8½ in and the width between the lines is 6ft. The permanent way is laid with the standard L&SWR pattern, and is in good order, the ballast being gravel of excellent quality. The fencing is of post and rail. 'The steepest gradient has an inclination of 1 in 105 and, while sharpest curve has a radius of 20 chains, there is only one with a

less radius than 40 chains. There are some long embankments and chalk cuttings, but the slopes are in all cases standing well. The highest embankment is 58ft in height, and one cutting through hard chalk is 143 chains in length, with a depth at the peak of 47 ft. There are 13 overbridges all of which have brick abutments. Of these 11 have brick arches, largest span 52ft on the skew, and the other 2 have wrought iron girders with spans of 59½ ft and 50½ ft. There are 12 underbridges all with brick abutments, of these 10 have brick arches, largest span 26ft, and 2 have wrought iron girders with spans of 15ft and 12ft. The girders have sufficient theoretical strength, and those under the line were stiff under test. There are only 2 culverts of any size. The whole of the works are well constructed, the brickwork being of first class character, and there is not a sign of settlement in any of the bridges. There are no tunnels and no level crossings of public roads.

'There are new stations at Longparish and Wherwell, and at both places every siding accommodation and convenience are provided. The signalling is carried out in the following new cabins;-

Hurstbourne Junction containing 17 levers of which 4 are spare.

Longparish station containing 15 levers of which 3 are spare.

Wherwell station containing 15 levers of which 2 are spare.

The station at Fullerton and the signalling arrangements there have been already inspected.

'The line is thoroughly well finished throughout, and the only requirements that I noted were;-

1st The repeater of the Down starting signal for the branch at Hurstbourne Junction, as this signal is round a curve and in a cutting, out of sight from the cabin.

2nd The provision of railings on the parapets of bridges at 3m 18c and 3m 36c, at each end of Longparish station.

3rd The removal of a few chipped chairs where pointed out, and the completion of the positioning of the keys by rails on a short length of line.

'Subject to the satisfaction of these requirements, and upon receipt of an

Looking east from the Salisbury line under the flyover with some masonry yet to be completed.

Looking west at work in progress on the Battledown flyover with the Up Southampton home signal to the left.

understanding from the company that all trains shall be stopped at all the intermediate stations between Whitchurch and Fullerton, so long as these stations remain unprovided with turntables and that footbridges for passengers shall be provided at Fullerton and Whitchurch if the traffics continues to be run backwards and forwards between these stations for a longer period than one year from the present date, I can recommend that the opening of this new line for passenger traffic may be sanctioned.'

'...when on my way to inspect the Northern and Southern Junction Railway, a new branch of the LSWR, I inspected at the request of the officers of the company some alterations which have been made at Whitchurch station for the accommodation of the trains running off the new branch, which will, as temporary measure, pending completion of a junction with the Didcot & Newbury Railway, run backwards and forwards between Fullerton station and Whitchurch station.

'The Up platform at Whitchurch has been lengthened and widened, and a new platform line has been laid in at the back of the platform, the trains which will on their arrival stop at the Up main line at the Up platform, and will be started on the return journey from the back platform line.

'The points and signals are worked from the station cabin which contains 18 working levers correctly interlocked.

'As a temporary arrangement only I can recommend that the use of the alterations at Whitchurch may be sanctioned but if the present plan of building a joint station upon a larger scale be not carried out until the next year it may be necessary to require that an overbridge for foot passengers shall be erected for the accommodation of the exchange traffic for the new branch and the Engineer of the company stated that this requirement would be attended to.'

[The connection to the Didcot line was never built and it was not until 1897 that the recommendation for a footbridge was implemented.]

In March 1888, shortly after the line opened, there were five passenger trains each way between Whitchurch and Fullerton, also serving Hurstbourne on the

main line, the first Down and last Up being designated passenger and goods. The first Up train started at Stockbridge and the midday train went to and from Basingstoke. The line was used for a few South Western diversions away from the Eastleigh route; there was little local traffic to be carried, but there were some cheap excursion trains along the line. During the 1898 army manoeuvres on Salisbury Plain one line was used for storing empty troop trains. In addition some trains from Salisbury (Milford) to Nine Elms and Kensington used the line after reversal at Kimbridge Junction, where a turnover engine was supplied.

THE ANDOVER & REDBRIDGE LINE
As we have just seen the Andover & Redbridge line gained traffic as a result of the opening of the MSWJR and the Hurstbourne to Fullerton line and a number of improvements were made. First to be doubled was the short section between Andover Junction and Andover Town, the new works being inspected by Col.Yolland on 11th December 1882. He approved the opening, which occurred on 1st January 1883 but required changes at Andover Town. He re-inspected and approved these in his report of 11th May 1883. On 2nd February 1885 Fullerton Bridge station was closed, to be replaced by Fullerton Junction station a few hundred yards away. During 1884 and 1885 the remainder of the line was doubled, and the sharp curves inherited from the canal's alignment eased.

Traffic on the Andover and Redbridge line built up steadily, particularly after the inauguration of through MSWJR goods and passenger trains in 1892 and 1893. While these called only at Romsey, the South Western services called at all stations. Much of the traffic on the Andover and Redbridge line above Kimbridge Junction passed on to the main line at Andover Junction and some at Hurstbourne Junction. Although there were but a few daily timetabled trains between Fullerton Junction and Whitchurch, traffic notices record a number of special trains on the line. There were sheep specials from Salisbury Milford and Stockbridge to London, excursions between Basingstoke and the South Coast and military specials from Salisbury Milford to London,

particularly in connection with the 1898 manoeuvres. In 1899 some troops from new camps on Salisbury Plain were conveyed by train along the line to Southampton Docks for embarkation on ships conveying them to fight in the South African war.

CROSSING THE LINE
When the line was constructed in the 1850s all the stations had a single platform, including Salisbury with two platform faces. As the line was doubled, stations acquired Up and Down platforms and sleeper crossings were provided for both barrows and passengers. With increasing traffic and higher train speeds the South Western provided alternative crossings, starting at busy junctions. From 1860 a footbridge connected the LSW and GW stations at Salisbury. Subways were provided at Basingstoke in 1871, Salisbury Up side station in 1878 and Andover Junction in 1882. Footbridges were installed at Grateley in 1893, Whitchurch in 1897, Porton in 1902 and Overton in 1919. Wooden footbridges were cheaper than steel ones but lasted for some thirty or forty years before they had to be replaced. However, foot crossings remained at Oakley and Hurstbourne until the stations closed, there being a distinct dip in the Up platform at Oakley for the crossing.

INSPECTIONS OF NEW WORKS
Oakley 1882
On 26th April 1882 Maj.Marindin reported: *'I have inspected the new crossover road at Oakley station. The points of this crossover road and all the signals at the station are worked from the signal cabin, but the points of another crossover road and those of Up siding connections are worked from the ground, and bolted by wire from the cabin, all the levers being correctly interlocked. Orders have been given to have these wire-bolted points worked from the cabin, and to provide some necessary disc signals at the safety points. The company should report when this has been done, the use of the connections may then be finally approved.'*

Worting Junction 1884
On 31st July 1884 Colonel Rich reported on his inspection of a new trailing crossover at Worting Junction, that the points and signals had been correctly interlocked. Accompanying his report was a 40ft to an inch plan showing the conventional double junction with the signal box on the Down side. It contained a 12 lever frame controlling distant and home signals from all three directions; the two Down distant signals were mounted on a single post, with the Down home signals mounted on separate dolls.

Overton 1898
On 6th October 1898 Maj. Marindin reported: *'I have inspected the new crossover road at Overton. The signal cabin contains 18 levers, of which 5 are push-pull levers, and the interlocking is correct. I can recommend that the use of the new crossover road may be sanctioned.'*

Left. . Looking west through the completed flyover with the Down Southampton line in the foreground and the second signal box constructed. Next the Up Southampton line connections will be removed when it is diverted over the flyover. The second signal box lasted only between 1897 and 1904.

'The signal cabin contains 20 working levers, of which 5 are push and pull levers, and the outlying ground frame contains 7 working levers of which 2 are push and pull levers.

'In the cabin Nos.8 and 11 levers should be interlocked, but, in other respects everything is satisfactory and subject to this interlocking being done within a fortnight, I can recommend that the use of the new connections at Grateley may be sanctioned.'

It would appear that these works were brought into use on or about the date of the Minute, 20th August 1898, as they were to prove essential for the very heavy military traffic over the next few weeks.

Porton 1899

On 28th April 1899 Maj.Addison reported:
'I have inspected a new trailing connection with the Down line, for a siding, at the east end of Porton station.

'The points and signals are worked from the station signal box, which contains 17 levers, all in use, 4 being push and pull levers, and the locking appears to have been correctly added to and altered where necessary.

'The Up advance starting signal is to be moved a little, to improve the view of the signal from the footplate.

'I can recommend the Board of Trade to approve the use of the new siding.'

BATTLEDOWN FLYOVER 1897

The South Western was carrying an ever-increasing volume of traffic, to the extent that the main line from Waterloo to Basingstoke and beyond was widened to four tracks during the 1890s and 1900s. Furthermore many of the junctions were rebuilt with flyovers to eliminate conflicting.

The quadruple main line from Basingstoke to Battledown was opened on 30th May 1897, when the junction was moved 53 chains to the east to of Worting signal box. Between Basingstoke and Worting there were Up slow, Up fast, Down fast, Down slow tracks. By means of facing crossovers these became Up Southampton, Up Salisbury, Down Salisbury and Down Southampton tracks. At Battledown there was a new flyover carrying the Up

Southampton line over the Up and Down Salisbury lines and some new connections, including a new signal box, were provided at Battledown.

Inspection 1898

On 6th October 1898 Col. Marindin reported as follows: 'I have inspected the new connections at Battledown, near Basingstoke where there is a new fly-over junction between the lines from Southampton and Exeter.

'A new loop siding on the Down Southampton line has been connected up, with facing points leading into it from both the Down lines, and the necessary signals have been provided.

'The signal cabin contains 22 levers of which 1 is a push and pull lever.

'I can recommend that the use of the new connections may be sanctioned.'

GRATELEY EXTENSIONS 1898

On 6th October 1898 Col. Marindin reported to the Board of Trade: 'In compliance with the instructions contained in your Minute of 20th August I have inspected the new connections at Grateley on the London & South Western Railway.

'Both platforms have been lengthened, a set of slip points connected with the Up siding has been put in on a main line crossover road, and a new main line crossover road, worked from an outlying ground frame controlled from the signal cabin, has been provided.

ARMY MANOEUVRES & GRAND REVIEW 1898

In August and September 1898 the army organised extensive manoeuvres for the southern army on heath land at Trigon Camp on the Isle of Purbeck in Dorset. They used Wareham station while the northern army, based at Perham Down Camp, used the MSWJR stations at Luggershall and Weyhill, as well as Grateley, Porton and Salisbury stations. Soldiers and their equipment came from all over England, Wales, Scotland and Ireland. Preparations for the manoeuvres took months and hundreds of pages of Special Traffic Notices went out jointly over the names of General C.J.Burnett, Quartermaster General at the War Office and G.T. White South Western Superintendent of the Line.

A full treatment of the train services provided for the manoeuvres is given in Chapter Ten.

Below. Looking east through the completed flyover from the Salisbury line.

Looking across the new Salisbury station from platform 1 to platform 4, where the refreshment rooms were managed by Spiers and Pond as part of their general catering contract with the South Western.

CHAPTER FOUR
THE LSWR IN THE TWENTIETH CENTURY

SOUTH WESTERN DISTRICT MANAGEMENT

Just before the turn of the century, on May 31st 1899, the new Superintendent of the South Western Railway, Sam Fay, re-organised the railway into four districts each headed by a District Superintendent. Our line came under the No. 3 Central District comprising Oakley to Yeovil Junction and Town, Hurstbourne and Fullerton, Andover to Redbridge, Chandlers Ford to Salisbury, Salisbury and Dorset line, Tunnel Junction to Bournemouth, and Weymouth and Branches. The District Superintendent was Mr A.H.Wadden, with offices at Eastleigh, where the Central District Civil Engineer was also based. In 1912 the new General Manager, Herbert Walker, reorganised the District structure again reducing the number to three by amalgamation of the two London Districts comprising now, London, Central and Western Districts. The Central District Superintendent, by 1914, was Mr S.W.Milford who moved to new offices at Southampton West station.

PNEUMATIC SIGNALLING AT GRATELEY STATION 1901

Sam Fay, Superintendent of the Line from 1899, had twice visited the USA to study signalling equipment and methods with a view to their incorporation in the planned re-building of Waterloo. Both Sam Fay and J.W.Jacomb-Hood were very impressed with the pneumatic signalling systems being adopted in the USA and opted to install the U.S. pneumatic system over the alternative electric system, on the grounds of cost and reliability.

The first two such installations on the South Western, or indeed in Great Britain, were at Grateley, where a new signal box was required to control the new layout for the enlarged station and the junction with the new branch to Amesbury. The installation was by the British Pneumatic Railway Signal Co. of Westminster who tendered £5,974 for the work at Grateley station, about twice the cost of conventional signalling. All the components for the installation were manufactured at their Chippenham works by Evans, O'Donnell & Co., who jointly owned the British Pneumatic company with an American partner.

The new cabin at Grateley had an interlocking frame with 72 levers, of which nineteen were spare initially, the 'levers' pitched at 3in. centres, with a length of twenty-four feet. The conventional alternative was a mechanical frame of 87 levers at 5in. centres some 36 feet long. There was also a Ground Frame of eight levers controlling two crossovers at the Andover end of the station. The 'levers' consisted of a series of handles mounted vertically on horizontal slides, which were pulled out horizontally about two inches towards the signalman. Thus valves opened releasing low pressure air, which in turn opened a relay at the signals and points which allowed higher pressure air to cylinders of 5in. diameter to operate the signals and 10 inch diameter for the points. At Grateley station there was a petrol engine connected to a compressor which supplied air at a pressure of normally fifteen pounds per square inch. This operated the points and signals and a lower pressure of about four to seven pounds per square inch connected the levers in the signal. The low pressure air was carried in half inch pipes and the higher pressure in two inch pipes. At fifteen pounds per square inch the 10in. diameter operating cylinders for the points were large, but the system was less susceptible to trouble from leakages than a system with a higher operational pressure.

Board of Trade Inspection 1901

An indication of the pioneering nature of the new works was that most unusually the Board of Trade sent not one but two inspecting officers, Colonel Yorke and Major Pringle, to make their inspection of Grateley

Work in progress at Grateley about 1900, as pipes are installed for the pneumatic control of points and signals. The station has been widened and in the background the two track brick arch road bridge is being replaced. New signals carrying 'not in use' Xs are in place.

The 1901 Grateley signal box in 1966, by this stage converted to conventional lever frame operation. John Scrace.

signal box on 30th July 1901. Their report was lengthy but important.

'We have the honour to report for the information of the Board of Trade that at the request of the company we have inspected the signalling and interlocking at Grateley station on the London & South Western Railway where the company have erected a complete installation of the low pressure pneumatic system of operating points and signals.

'The inspection was of unusual interest as the system though well known and well spoken of in America has not been previously tried in the United Kingdom.

'It is not necessary to describe at length all the mechanical detail of the system but it may be briefly stated that it combines three salient features viz:-

(i) The protection afforded by mechanical interlocking.

(ii) The movement of the points and signals by pneumatic power.

(iii) Interdependence between the levers or handles in the frame in the signal box and the position of the points and signals.

As to (i) the mechanical interlocking of the levers or handles in the frame is on the 'tappet' principle and is carried out in strict accordance with modern requirements.

The only matters requiring attention are levers Nos.14 and 15 should lock No.41 and 43 lever No.12 should lock 41 and 43 when 30 and 31 are pulled No.42 and 44 to be free of each other.

As to (ii) the pulling of the lever or handle in the signal box opens a valve which permits air at a pressure of 7lbs per square inch to pass to the mechanism alongside of the switches or signal whereby a second valve is opened which admits air at 15lbs pressure into the cylinder and causes the switches or signals to be moved in the required direction.

As to (iii) as soon as the movement of the switches or signal is completed a third valve is opened which permits the air at 15lbs pressure to flow to the signal box and there to complete automatically the movement of the lever or handle in the frame which up to this time could not be placed in its final position. As soon as the movement of the lever has in this manner been completed (and not till then) is it possible to pull any other lever which depends for its release on the pulling of the first e.g. a signal lever which is released by a point lever.

'This method of causing the air after completing its work at the switches or signal to flow back to the signal box and there complete the stroke of the lever provides a valuable means of 'detecting' the position of the switches or signal which seems to render it impossible for any mistake to be made should the air pipes or any portion of the mechanism fail.

'All points where facing or trailing are also 'detected' and locked in each position by means of plungers on the suction plates and the arrangement is such that the locking must take place before the valve is opened which permits the air pressure to return to the signal box. In this manner it is rendered certain that the switches or the signals as the case may be must be placed and in the case of switches must be locked in the correct position before any subsequent movement of the lever in use or of other levers can be made.

'Putting aside the question of cost as to which no reliable data for the purpose of comparison are at present available it may be said that the pneumatic system of operating switches and signals possesses some advantages over usual manual system at present adopted in this country.

'Among those advantages and in addition to the safety afforded by the method of locking and detection already described the following may be mentioned viz:-

Economy of space in the signal box, ease with which the levers or handles can be moved and the absence of point rods and signal wires. But the installation must be regarded as experimental and it is not possible for us at present to express any final opinion as to its suitability to the conditions of working which exist in this country.

'In accordance with the permission given by the Board of Trade in their letter of 19th July the facing points on the Amesbury single line branch have been placed at a distance of 300 yards from the signal box. In all other respects the arrangement of the station and signals is in accordance with the usual practice.

'Some alterations to the platforms, permanent way and station at Grateley are in progress but were not sufficiently completed for us to inspect and report upon them. These works should therefore be submitted for inspection hereafter in due course.

'In the meanwhile we can subject to compliance within a month with the slight alteration in the interlocking which is mentioned in this report recommend the Board of Trade to sanction the use of the pneumatic system of signalling and interlocking at Grateley station.'

Pneumatic operation of the station area started on 21st July.

AUTOMATIC BLOCK SIGNALLING ANDOVER TO GRATELEY 1901

The second new pioneering feature was a completely new concept, the installation of automatic signalling on the 6 miles 40 chains of double track main line between Andover Junction West and Grateley signal boxes. There were six block sections, each protected by a home signal arm, with its distant signal mounted on the previous post, the pneumatic signals being operated by an electro-pneumatic valve controlled by a track circuit for the block section. Each pair of signals was mounted on a hollow post, the air pistons and valves being encased in the base and the signal arm operating rods running up inside the post. As soon as a train cleared the block section the signals automatically cleared, in contrast to being pulled 'off' by the signalman when he accepted a train. The intermediate Monxton signal box was closed only three years after installation in 1898 and the tender for the intermediate signalling was £3,500.

Board of Trade Inspection 1901

Trials of the automatic signalling had commenced on 1st September 1901 and Major Pringle returned on 20th October for its inspection. He reported as follows on 24th October:

'I made an inspection on the 20th of the electro pneumatic (low pressure) block signalling between Andover Junction and Grateley on the London & South western Railway.

'The method of block signalling is new in the United Kingdom. The Board of Trade assented to the experimental installation on condition that ordinary block working was maintained between the given points.

'Before describing the system adopted it may be pointed out that the company have departed from two of the principles laid down in their original description of the proposed installation. There is not a clear block section maintained between following trains; and the signals are actuated at a point alongside, and not 100 yards in advance.

'The distance of about six miles of double track between Andover and Grateley is divided into six block sections. There are no points or connections on either of the lines. These block sections vary in length from 1,385 to 1,932 yards. Each section has been provided with a signal post carrying two arms. The upper arm is the home or block signal for the section immediately in advance of the post, while the lower arm (forked) is the distant or caution signal for the section next in advance. The signal arms or lamps are used to indicate whether the block section in advance, or next in advance, respectively, is clear or occupied by a train.

'The actual work of lowering the signal arm from the 'danger' to the 'clear' position is accomplished by air pressure acting in two cylinders attached to the base of each signal post. The arms are taken back to the 'danger' position when the air pressure in the cylinder is released. The air pressure is maintained in the cylinders so long as the circuit of a track battery, in which the rails

are used as conductors, is maintained. The rails at the commencement of each of these block sections are insulated, so that for each block section there is a separate track circuit.

'In the normal position, when no trains are running, the track circuits are completed and all the signals stand at the 'safety' or 'clear' position.

'The wheels and axles of a train entering a block section short circuit the track battery current of that section with the result that valves are operated which allow the air in the cylinders to escape and the signals arms are taken to danger.

'On arrival of the train at the second block section both the signals on the second post similarly go to 'danger'. As soon as the remainder of the train has cleared the first block section the track battery circuit of the first section again becomes operative, and the upper or home signal on the first post is taken to the 'clear' or safety position. The lower arm on the first post, however, remains at danger until the train has passed out of the second section.

'It will be apparent that this system of block signalling is at variance with one universally adopted principle on English railways, namely:- the normal position of fixed signals, which as laid down in Railway Rules and Regulations section 29 is 'danger'.

'Further, the system does not appear to provide 'adequate interval of space between following trains', which is laid down in Board of Trade Requirement No.1 as being necessary for the Block Telegraph system. In the Railway Clearing House Regulations for Train Signalling by Block Telegraph, Rule 4, a quarter of a mile has been laid down as the adequate interval of space necessary between following trains. But on

The Up starting signal for the loop at Grateley mounted on a traditional wooden post. The pneumatic pipes run up to the cylinder and piston which operates the signal arm.

The interior of Grateley signal box in 1902 showing the slides and interlocking below, together with the more traditional Tyers electric train tablet apparatus for regulation of the single track section to Newton Tony.

Diagram of selected signal

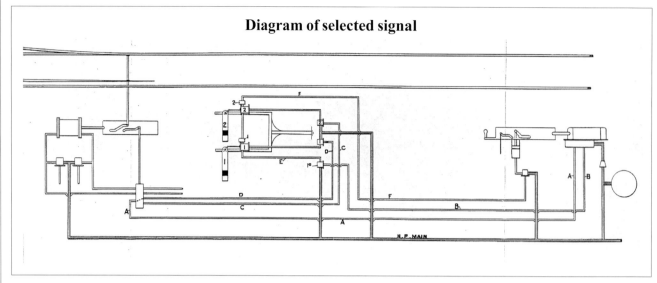

the experimental system under report a following train is accepted under the caution given by the lower arm, as soon as the following train has passed out of a section, so that the hard and fast interval prescribed between trains resolves itself into the distance between any signal post and the insulated rail joint ahead, which may be taken as a few feet only.

'I do not think that the first objection i.e. the normal position of the signals gives adequate grounds for rejecting the automatic system under experiment so long as trains have the power to hold signals in rear of them at danger, and the means employed are reliable. But in the absence of human agency definite regulations regarding failures, and the method of dealing with them will be necessary. The second point raised is of more importance and, if the system under report is accepted, will require greater consideration, more especially in connection with the distance between the signal posts and the position of the insulated rail joint.

'Since writing the above, the company's letter dated 25th October has been received, in which they ask definitely for permission to bring the installation permanently into use. They state that in a period of eight weeks the experiment has been under careful observation, and three failures of signals remaining at danger have been noted. Certain regulations for dealing with failures of block working are proposed.

'But one point, which calls for consideration appears to have been overlooked. A large proportion of the passenger and brake van stock in use on the London & South Western Railway have Mansell wheels in which there is no metallic connection between the tyres and the axles. It will I think be necessary if this system of signalling is to be adopted to provide for this metallic connection in some way, otherwise on passenger trains the wheels and axles of the engines alone will be able to short circuit the track battery current. In the case of a break down, it would then be possible for the signals to authorise the

entrance of a second train into a block section already occupied by a portion of another train.

'Before the system therefore is authorised for permanent use, it would be necessary to provide at least for metallic connection between the tyres and axles of brake vans. I believe moreover, that an experiment involving so many radical changes from existing procedures demands a longer period of observation than 8 weeks, before being finally accepted as meeting adequately a satisfactory standard. I therefore advise the Board to reserve their decision upon the question of permanently authorising the installation until a full 3 months shall have lapsed from 5th December, the date on which the experiment came into operation. In the meantime the company should be called upon to report the number and causes of all failures which may occur in the installation during the next five weeks.'

Following the period of trial working, Maj. Pringle eventually gave his approval on 20th February 1902 with the automatic signals being brought into use on 20th April 1902. However, at the South Western's Traffic Committee meeting on 30th April 1902 the Superintendent of the Line, responding to Maj. Pringle's concern, recommended that all main line passenger vehicles with Mansell wheels have a metallic connection fitted between the axle and wheel to ensure continuity of electric current. Subsequently the automatic block signalling between Andover and Grateley remained in use until 1919 and during these seventeen years there is no record of any accident.

It is interesting to note that these reports expressing valid concerns were written by senior professional staff of the Railway Department of the Board of Trade. During this period it was one of the most important arms of government. Ten years later the Maritime Department of the same Board of Trade allowed a new large ocean liner to go to sea with lifeboats sufficient only for a small fraction of those aboard, resulting in

heavy loss of life after the *Titanic* hit an iceberg in 1912.

Automatic Signalling - Irregularities of Working

The South Western was required to send the Board of Trade regular summaries of any irregularities and the following copies survive (left)

In a letter of 14th August 1902, enclosing the above report to the Board of Trade, the South Western Secretary Godfrey Knight stated that during the ninety-one days under review 5,980 trains had passed through the section of line protected, inducing automatic movements of 35,880 signals. 'With the exception of the fourteen cases listed' he continued, 'all the movements have been correct and regular and this proportion of irregularities would probably compare favourably with that under ordinary mechanical signalling. In each of the irregularities the signals remained at danger although the section ahead was clear, resulting in delays to traffic but with no possibility of accident. There had been no single failure of a signal to return to danger after a train has passed into the section it controlled'.

The company considered that the principle of working sections of railway under this principle had been 'perfectly established. Enough had been seen of its advantage in favour of quick and convenient handling of traffic quite apparent, while the carrying capacity had been largely increased at a minimum of expense.'

These new installations attracted much interest from railway managers, signalling engineers and the national press to the extent that on 31st July 1901 the South Western put on a special train from Waterloo to convey a large party to inspect the new installation at Grateley. The party included many well-known railwaymen from Britain, the Continent and America, invited by the British Railway Pneumatic Signal Co. On 1st August 1901 the London *Times* published

20th April to 20th July 1902

No.	Date	Particulars	Cause
1.	21.4.02	No.4 Up Signal	Broken track battery wire
2.	22.4.02	No.2 Up Distant	While testing relay in No.3 Up
3.	24.4.02	Distant arm under Andover Down Advance	Contact springs on Down Advance out of adjustment
4.	27.4.02	No.5 Up Signal	Andover outer Home signal controlling
5.	8.5.02	Do	Do
6.	23.5.02	Do	Do
7.	23.5.02	No.4 Down Signal	Intermediate battery too strong
8.	3.6.02	No.5 Up Signal	Andover outer Home signal controlling
9.	4.6.02	Do	Do
10.	13.6.02	Do	Do
11.	23.6.02	No.1 Up Home	Spring follower too tight on piston
12.	24.6.02	No.2 Up Distant	Overheated pistons
13.	5.7.02	No.4 Up Signal	Faulty relay valve
14.	13.7.02	Do	Leak in track circuit due to broken bond wire

21st January 1903 to 20th April 1903

No.	Date	Particulars	Cause
1.	28.1.03	Nos.4 & 5 Up Distants	Reported by Traffic Department as being at danger but on examination found to be in good working order.
2.	29.1.03	Nos.2 & 3 Down Distants	Air pressure through the reducing valve to low to operate signal
3.	14.2.03	No.4 Down Home	Armature failed to lift owing to weak battery
4.	11.3.03	No.4 Up Home	Reported by Traffic Department as being at danger but on examination was found to be in good working order
5.	6.4.03	No.3 Up Distant	Arm spindle being insufficiently lubricated
6.	8.4.03	No.5 Down Home	Reducing valve not passing sufficient air to actuate signal
7.	13.4.03	No.1 Down Home	Compressor not started soon enough to maintain pressure for working the signals
8.	18.4.03	No.3 Up Distant	Armature of magnet out of adjustment

a substantial report headed *Pneumatic Railway Signalling* following the press visit to Grateley. A very full account of the Grateley station visit and installation was published in the *Engineer* on 2nd August 1901, and of the automatic block signalling between Andover and Grateley on 30th May 1902.

The South Western was sufficiently confident of the new pneumatic system to employ it in the new ground frame and two new signal boxes brought into use at Salisbury in November 1902, employing a slightly higher air pressure. In the light of experience gained and Board of Trade recommendations on the Andover to Grateley automatic block signalling, the South Western further developed the systems. In the following years pneumatic signal boxes and automatic signalling were installed by the South Western from Woking (exclusive) to Basingstoke as the line was quadrupled in 1903/4, and signal boxes at several other locations.

An indication of the maintenance required is given in a Special Traffic Notice which stated that cleaning of the pneumatic cylinders at Grateley would take place from 4.0am to 4.0pm on Sunday 12th July 1914,

during which time various levers would be disconnected. Mr Lovelock, the stationmaster, was to provide a flagman, as required, with a similar operation being carried out at Salisbury.

During the 1914-1918 war increasing traffic on the Midland & South Western Junction line required the installation of a new junction and signal box at Red Post Junction, west of Andover. The automatic signalling between Andover and Grateley was taken out of use in 1919, apparently saving £1,000 annually on maintenance. Signalmen who worked at Salisbury reported that one maintenance problem with the pneumatic system there was the ingress of water, either by leakage or by condensation and this had to be drained off. All pneumatic equipment at Grateley signal box was taken out of use and was replaced by a conventional mechanical lever frame. However, the pipes used for the pneumatic operation were left in place both in the signal box and in the trackbed and in 1992 some of these were discovered in the ground when the platforms at Grateley were lengthened. The automatic signalling between Woking and Basingstoke remained in use until 1966

and the pneumatic equipment at Salisbury East and West boxes until 1981.

THE AMESBURY & MILITARY CAMP LIGHT RAILWAY

As far back as 1872 there had been military manoeuvres at Beacon Hill and Bulford, and as we have seen in the late 1890s the army purchased some 60 square miles of Salisbury Plain for camps and training areas. As Chapter Three recounted, there were manoeuvres and a grand parade at Boscombe Down involving 50,000 troops in September 1898. Porton was the station closest to Boscombe Down but it had short platforms and just one short siding in the small goods yard. The South Western conveyed many of the troops and their equipment, most departing from Salisbury Milford goods and Porton stations, but the limitations of the existing stations became obvious. The army needed one or more stations where a succession of full length trains each conveying 500 men, their horses, guns and limbers, ammunition and other equipment could arrive to be unloaded on wide platforms. Almost immediately in April 1899, just months after the manoeuvres, the platforms and goods yard at Porton station were significantly extended.

Before the manoeuvres, in 1897, the army was already aware of these limitations and approached the South Western for the provision of a branch to Amesbury and Bulford where camps were to be built. The Great Western also saw the possibilities of military traffic and promoted a line down the Avon valley between its lines at Pewsey and Salisbury. A significant factor here was the passing of the 1896 Light Railway Act which facilitated the cheaper promotion of rural railways by use of a Light Railway Order rather than Act of Parliament. The LRO allowed cheaper construction including steeper gradients, sharper curves and lighter track. Although superficially attractive, cheaply constructed railways were hardly likely to fulfil the needs of the army, although a Light Railway Order did cut some costs.

Under the provisions of the 1896 Light Railway Act the Great Western obtained an Order on 6th August 1898 for a line between Pewsey and Salisbury, subject to War Department agreement, to cross 4½ miles of its land. This, in the event, was not forthcoming. With the support of the War Department the South Western gained a Light Railway Order on 24th September 1898 for a branch to Amesbury and Shrewton leaving the main line near the Newton Tony intermediate signal box opened the previous month. The cost of the branch, 10 miles 62 chains long, was estimated at £62,517 and in January 1899 a contract was let to J. T. Firbank. After a life measured in just months in 1899 Newton Tony intermediate signal box, 75 miles 42 chains from Waterloo, was

Steam navvy in use during construction of the Amesbury & Military Camp Light Railway. Due to photo damage part of the arm and jaws of the navvy have at some time been sketched in. Peter Yarlett Collection.

replaced by another Newton Tony box, 75 miles 1 chain from Waterloo, to control the points and signals required for Firbank's contractors siding.

Newton Tony Junction Inspection 1899
On 28th April 1899 Maj.Addison made his report: *'I have inspected alterations between Grateley and Porton stations. At the west end of Grateley station there is a new trailing connection with the Up line, worked from a ground frame containing 4 levers all in use including 1 push and pull lever. The frame is controlled from the station signal box, which now contains 21 levers (5 push and pull), all in use.*

'At Newton Toney, the old block signal box has been abandoned and a new temporary box provided about ½ mile nearer to Grateley, which contains 12 levers (3 push and pull) all in use. Here there is a main line crossover road and a new Up siding with trailing connections on both main lines. The signalling is also new.

'The alterations referred to above have been carried out to facilitate the construction of the Amesbury & Military Camp Light Railway and the present arrangements are only of a temporary character. The advance starting signals at Newton Toney are a considerable distance from the box which is really a ground box at present, the view of the signalman being consequently somewhat limited, but treadles will, I understand, be placed ahead of the signals and no objection need therefore be raised.

'Subject to everything being correctly coupled up and the permanent way being made good where necessary I can recommend the Board of Trade to approve the temporary alterations.'

The report was supported by a signalling diagram, showing distant, home and starting signals in both directions, three pairs of trailing crossovers and the box itself on the Down side.

The War Department changed its mind about the line between Amesbury and Shrewton in November 1899, although Firbank had already started on the earthworks. The South Western gained an Abandonment Order in 1901, reducing the line to 4 miles 78 chains. The South Western Act of 9th August 1899 authorised the extension of Grateley station and the construction of a third independent line to the north of the main line thence to Newton Tony. Apart from earthworks this involved the demolition of three brick bridges spanning the double track and their replacement with plate girder bridges spanning three tracks, with room for a fourth if required. As we have seen the new works at Grateley station included replacement of the signalling, of which more in the next section.

Firbank's men worked fast, cutting through the chalk with steam-powered excavators. The temporary second Newton Tony signal box, 75 miles 1 chain from Waterloo, was replaced in September 1901

by a third signal box, Newton Tony Junction 75 miles 10 chains from Waterloo, which controlled the points and signals here. On 4th December 1901 a minute of the South Western Traffic Committee read: *'The War Office want to occupy quarters at Bulford Camp during the winter months and ask if the new line to Amesbury will be opened at an early date. The line may be used at any time for military purposes.'* Maj. Pringle made his inspection on 28th February 1902. The single track branch between Newton Toney Junction and Amesbury was opened to public goods services on 29th April 1902 and passenger services on 2nd June. It would appear however, that there had been military traffic previously and the third track from Grateley to Newton Tony Junction was opened on 24th May 1902. The initial train service comprised six weekday passenger trains from Amesbury to Grateley, two of which ran through to Andover Junction.

Board of Trade Inspections 1902
Maj. Pringle made his inspection and on 28th February 1902: *'I made an inspection today of the new works in connection with the Grateley widening on the London and South Western Railway.*

'This widening commences at Newton Tony Junction west of Grateley station and terminates at that station. It has been constructed for use in connection with the Amesbury and Military Camp Light Railway which commences at the same point.

'The works extend over a total length of 2 miles, 40 chains. The formation is for a double line and a single line of rails only has been laid. A space of 9ft 6in separates the two main lines from the new line which is to be used for Up and Down traffic.

'The steepest gradient has an inclination of 1 in 115 and the sharpest curve outside station limits has a radius of 86 chains.

'The earthwork is embankment and cutting nowhere exceeds 27 feet in height or depth.

'The Company's standard four post and rail fencing is used. No difficulty has been experienced in the way of drainage.

'The permanent way consists of Bessemer steel rails weighing 87lbs per yard in 32 feet lengths. These are carried in cast iron chairs (46¾lbs each) supported by the usual creosoted sleepers, 12 to the rail length. Gravel and rock ballast is laid below the sleepers to a stated depth of 12 inches.

'Bridging. There are three overbridges on the length each of a single span of from 53 to 82 feet. The type of construction used is wrought iron girders carried on brick abutments. These bridges and the permanent way are in satisfactory condition. There are no other works of any importance.

'Grateley is the only station on the line and the connections and signalling at the end of the widening were inspected on 26th July 1901, and has been reported in R 11301/01.

'Newton Tony Junction and the arrangements at the western termination form the subject of my report of this date in R3438. The single line has been equipped for working by the electric tablet system, and subject to the receipt of an undertaking on the part of the company that this or one of the other modes of working single lines will be adopted, I can recommend the Board of Trade to authorise the new works.'

Maj. Pringle also reported on 28th February:
'I made an inspection today of the new works at Newton Tony Junction on the London and South western Railway.

'This junction is situated at the 75th milepost on the company's main line between Basingstoke and Salisbury. The single line widening to Grateley (see R.3429) and the Amesbury and Military Camp Light Railway from a junction with the Up and Down main lines at this spot.

'In addition to these new connections which includes four new facing points a new signal cabin has been erected to control the junction. This has been constructed on the Up side of the main lines in the place of a former block post. In addition to the usual block instruments for the Up and Down main lines electric tablet instruments have been provided for single line working on the new widened line to Grateley and on the Amesbury and Military Camp Light Railway. The frame in the signal cabin contains 37 levers of which 4 are spare. There is also in the cabin a gate wheel by which the gates of an adjoining public road crossing the light railway on the level are worked. These gates are interlocked with the signals and points. The interlocking in the frame is correct.

'On the Down main line on the single line from Grateley in the Down direction and on the light railway in the Up direction one distant signal has been provided and these distant signals are applicable to one only of the two home signals in advance of them. I do not think the junction is sufficiently important to call for the provision of additional distant signals, more especially as all trains now have to slow down to exchange or hand over tablets. But the Up distant signal on the light railway should (as in the other cases) be made to refer to the line which will be in ordinary use. This I understand will be the single line to Grateley. The company agreed to make this alteration i.e. Nos.33 and 34 to lead No.32. Subject to this alteration being effected I can recommend the Board to authorise the use of the new works at this Junction.'

The branch was originally constructed with a single track and built to main line standards, with a passing loop at Newton Tony station,

although land had been purchased and over-bridges built for a double line. Although built under a Light Railway Order the only light railway features were the steep gradients of 1 in 55 and 1 in 60 as the line climbed up from the valley of the River Bourne at Newton Tony to a summit on Boscombe Down before descending towards the River Avon at Amesbury. For a country branch line this would have been no problem but trains exceeding eight bogies, as most military specials did, required double-heading on this section. The Amesbury terminus was purpose-built for military traffic, with full length Up and Down platforms military platform and three loading docks, turntable, and locomotive water supply. The latter was important because locomotives, including some from other railways, ran long distances direct with military trains to Amesbury and were required to return within an hour or so. There was no engine shed at Amesbury; locomotives were initially supplied by Andover shed but after the direct route via Amesbury Junction was opened they were supplied by the much larger Salisbury shed. This included extra assisting locomotives.

Part of the abandoned section to Shrewton beyond the terminus was used for a nest of four sidings, each long enough to berth a military special train. Similar branches and military platforms were built by the South Western at this time, including the Bordon branch and Military Sidings at Okehampton.

Amesbury did not remain the terminus for long as in 1906 public services were extended to Bulford station, and military trains to Bulford Camp. There were other extensions of military railways to Sling, Larkhill and Rollestone during the 1914-18 war, but these are beyond our remit.

The civilians of Amesbury travelled to nearby Salisbury by road even after the railway opened, the Grateley line requiring an inconvenient change of train. To overcome the problem the South Western gained another Light Railway Order on 28th April 1903 for a short double track spur from near Newton Tony station to curve round to join the main line in the Salisbury direction and, following the Board of Trade inspection, the new works opened to public traffic on 8th August 1904. Disappointingly, despite extensive research, a Board of Trade Inspection has not yet come to light.

On the main line all the points and signals installed in 1901 at Newton Tony Junction and the signal box, 75 miles 10 chains from Waterloo, were abolished. All that now remained was the double track main line together with the single track from Grateley which here diverged towards Amesbury. A new signal box was provided at the new Amesbury Junction, 75 miles 53 chains from Waterloo, from where a double track curved away to the north to join the original branch

Newton Tony station shortly after the opening of the Amesbury branch.

The new Salisbury station buildings of 1901.

alignment at a new Newton Tony Junction, 75 miles 47 chains from Waterloo. Here the double track from Salisbury to Newton Tony station joined the original single track from Grateley. At Amesbury Junction the 32 chain new line from Amesbury ran under the main lines and then climbed up to join the Down main line, the new line to Amesbury being only 22 chains from the Up main line.

The gradient up from the branch under the main line bridge to the Down main line was 1 in 45, which was difficult for starting a heavy troop train from the home signal. The reason for the expensive burrowing junction here for just four trains from Amesbury to Salisbury is not clear as there were other locations such as Woking with far greater need. Public passenger services commenced on 8th August 1904 with four trains daily from Amesbury to Salisbury and five retained from Amesbury to Grateley or Andover Junction.

The army planned extensive manoeuvres in the summer of 1909 and, in anticipation of the extra traffic, the line between Newton Tony and Amesbury stations was doubled. An intermediate signal box and crossover was provided at the summit of the line at Allington, 78 miles 15 chains from Waterloo, and opened to traffic on 23rd May 1909. All the new works were on the branch and not on the main line. Maj. Pringle made his inspection and recommended approval of the new works on 24th June 1909.

There was a need for double track and extra block sections when the line was at its busiest. The heavy military trains had to

stop at Newton Tony station for the attachment or detachment of assisting engines, which often had to return light engine to assist the following train. A better-known example of such working was between Braunton and Ilfracombe on summer Saturdays with heavy holiday trains.

Apart from the military there was local traffic between Bulford, Amesbury and Salisbury. The public train service to and from Grateley and Andover declined until the last weekday train ran in 1919, and the last Sunday train in 1920. However, the line remained in use for goods and military traffic. Traffic between the branch and Waterloo was by connections at Porton, or sometimes Salisbury. From 1914 a milk van service between Bulford and Waterloo was provided for local farmers sending their milk to the London market. Freight carried on the Bulford branch included coal and many other supplies for both local people and the army bases.

Manoeuvres were held in 1909 for the newly-formed territorial army requiring forty-two special trains to run to Amesbury along the newly-opened double track but no details have yet come to light. However, special traffic for the summer 1914 manoeuvres has been well documented and details are given later in this chapter.

THE MIDLAND & SOUTH WESTERN JUNCTION RAILWAY

Early in the century the MSWJR also developed its system to cope with increasing traffic, not only the through

traffic steadily building up between the north, midlands, Cheltenham, Andover and Southampton, but also the rapidly increasing traffic generated by the army camps being constructed on Salisbury Plain. On the MSWJR main line sections of single track were doubled in stages, so that on 28th September 1902 the line from Cirencester to Cheltenham had been completed. On 2nd November 1902 almost eighteen miles of double track had been opened between Weyhill and Marlborough, although the four miles between Andover Junction and Weyhill remained single.

The War Department built its own line between Ludgershall station on the MSWJR and the new camp at Tidworth, and this opened to military traffic worked by the MSWJR on 8th July 1901, to War Department goods traffic on 21st May 1902, public goods traffic on 1st July and public passenger traffic on 1st October. In connection with this the MSWJR built a bay line and platform, engine shed and turntable at Ludgershall. Receipts at Tidworth station soon became the greatest on the MSWJR, much of this traffic joining our line at Andover Junction.

DRUMMOND'S SIDING, SALISBURY 1901

To the east of Salisbury Tunnel Junction the track on the third side of the Laverstock triangle, opened in 1857, had been closed since 1859 and subsequently lifted. However, the embankment and bridges were still in situ and in 1901 a long refuge siding, sometimes known as Drummond's Siding,

A Basingstoke line train passes Salisbury Tunnel Junction signal box in the South Western era. Drummonds Siding is behind the photographer. R.K.Blencowe Collection.

connected to the Up Eastleigh line was laid along this alignment.

Maj. Pringle made his inspection and reported on 1st March 1901. *'I made an inspection on the 27th ult. Of the new works near Salisbury on the London & South Western Railway.*

'A new siding, which forms a trailing connection with the Up line, has been laid down between Salisbury Tunnel and Milford Junction. The points for this siding are worked from a ground frame which is bolted by a release lever in Salisbury Tunnel signal cabin. A key for the door of the ground frame is also kept in the signal cabin except when in use. The ground frame contains 4 working levers, one of which is a 'push & pull' disc signal lever.

'Salisbury Tunnel signal box is old and the frame now contains 20 working levers of which two are 'push & pull' levers, and one lever works a set of catch points which have been laid in the Up line in case of a runaway from a goods train using the new siding.

'But as the gradient on this Up line is only 1 in 627 rising towards Eastleigh and as, moreover, the company have issued instructions that no vehicles are to be left standing on the Up line while the siding is in use, I consider that the No.20 catch points should be removed and the lever that actuates them made spare. The frame in the signal cabin will then contain 19 working levers and one spare.

'The company have agreed to do this and presumably will report the completion of the work.

'The catch points on the new siding are not so close to the fouling point with the main line as is desirable, but having in view the fact that the siding is for temporary use and also the instructions issued by the company regarding the working of the

siding I do not think it necessary to ask for these catch points to be brought further forward.

'I can therefore recommend the Board to confirm their provisional sanction for this siding subject to the removal of No.20 catch points.

'I suggest that the diagram of locking tables submitted to be returned to the company for necessary correction and resubmission.'

According to the 1932 *Southern Railway Magazine* Drummond's Siding was used for the storage of wagons.

REBUILDING SALISBURY STATION 1902

Towards the end of the nineteenth century the difficult relationship between the LSWR and the Great Western was improving, not least because of the existing through traffic, as exemplified by the Cardiff to Portsmouth passenger service started in 1896 and the growing volume of South Wales steam coal. Moreover, there were opportunities for the Great Western for through excursions to the South Coast resorts such as Bournemouth, and through trains to the army bases under construction on Salisbury Plain.

Both the South Western, and its passengers, were well aware of the shortcomings of Salisbury station, split into two across Fisherton Street. Prolonged negotiations lead to an complicated agreement of 28th January 1898 between the companies for exchange of land and more transfer sidings. The South Western was to contribute towards a new Great Western engine shed, and a new double track running line connection. The South Western was able to retain and extend the existing 1859 station and platforms and also to widen its station layout to the four through platforms which

remain to this day. In addition the Great Western completed its double track between Warminster and Salisbury and built a new engine shed. The South Western too built a new engine shed and extended its East and West yards and carriage sidings.

Plans were approved in October 1899 and J. T. Firbank was appointed the main contractor. As mentioned earlier, Firbank had also been awarded the contract for construction of the Amesbury & Military Camp Light Railway. It seems likely therefore that he may well have used spoil from his excavations on this line to be used for the embankments etc here at Salisbury.

Salisbury Inspections 1901-1903

Building a new station while traffic was still running required the work to be done in stages thus the Board of Trade Inspecting Officer Maj. Pringle made a series of inspections. The first report came on 8th January 1901: *'I today inspected more temporary works at Salisbury station on the London & South Western Railway. At the east end of the station a new siding has been laid on the Down line side which forms a connection with the Down main line. The signalling arrangements have been carried out in the existing Salisbury "A" signal cabin. The frame contains 30 levers all in use, of which 9 are push and 7 pull levers working disc signals. The necessary additional interlocking has been introduced, and the arrangements are satisfactory. I can therefore recommend the Board to authorise the use of the new works.*

Maj. Pringle made his next inspection on 7th and reported on 8th August 1902. *'I made an inspection yesterday of certain new works at Salisbury station on the London & South Western Railway. Extensive alterations are still in hand at Salisbury station connection with accommodation for passenger working arrangements and signalling.*

'In place of the four old signal cabins the company have erected two new cabins one at either end of the station and the points and the signals will shortly be worked on the low pressure pneumatic system.

'At present connections have been made and a compressor which will be worked by electric power (obtained from the Corporation of Salisbury) and are not in position. My inspection was therefore limited to testing the mechanical interlocking in the new cabins. A further inspection of the new works will be necessary when the works have been completed and are in working order.

'I. Salisbury East Signal Cabin. The frame contains 47 working levers and 17 spaces. The following alterations in the locking should be made.

(a) No.23 to lock No.26 both ways.

(b) No. 35 disc signal to be removed and the position of No.49 disc signal to be altered

Salisbury shed not long after opening.

to the west of No.41 points and to be led by either No.47 or No.50.

(c) With No.29 points normal No.28 to be led by either 26 and 25 or by 49 and 25.

(d) No.23 to be made free of Nos.26, 47, 55 and 50 provided that the signal (No.23) is used only for setting back engines to trains standing at the Down local or Down through platforms.

This the company have agreed to.

II. Salisbury West Signal Cabin. The frame contains 49 working levers and 15 spaces. The following alterations in working should be made.

(a) No.5 to be free of No.42.

(b) No.45 to interlock No.40.

(c) No.43 to be free of Nos.30, 25, 17 and 8, provided that this signal (No.43) is used solely to set back engines on trains

standing on the Up local and Up through platforms.

(d) The interlocking of points and signals on the adjoining Great Western Railway lines which are controlled to a certain extent from the South Western Railway West (the report stated East) cabin requires examination at the next inspection. This is a question which so far has not been dealt with by either Lt Col. Yorke or myself.

III. At both ends of Salisbury station several cases occur where the company operate two signals selected by the position of points by a single lever.

Where the two signals are splitting signals referring to one and the same road the Board of Trade may I think accept the arrangement. On the other hand I feel that the objection in cases where the two signals

refer to two different lines is greater and I am not now prepared to advise the Board to finally accept such an arrangement in the case of a new installation.

'I propose that the question be left open at the present moment so that the company may have an opportunity of expressing an opinion on the subject.

'Subject to the completion of the alterations in locking and to a further inspection of the arrangements when they are complete I can recommend the Board of Trade to authorise the company to make use of the new works at Salisbury station.

'P.S. Some alterations have been made since the company submitted the diagrams to the Board and the officers of the company informed me that new diagrams would be forwarded showing the final arrangements.'

For his third inspection Maj. Pringle returned the following year and reported on 20th February 1903: 'I made a re-inspection on the 19th instant, of the new works at Salisbury on the London & South Western Railway.

'The works in connection with the new station at Salisbury are completed with the exception of the bay line platform at the East end. These comprise a new island and a new Up platform, together with a lengthening of the Down platform. The station buildings are also practically all new, and afford adequate accommodation for passengers.

'A new means of communication between the three platforms has been provided by the addition of a covered subway, while the old over footbridge has been improved.

'Salisbury West Signal Cabin.
The alterations in locking called for in my report dated 8th August 1902, have been

The light interior of Salisbury shed with a selection of Adams and Drummond locomotives.

Salisbury shed with several Drummond and Urie 4-6-0s.

effected, I inspected the arrangements for intercommunication between the Great Western Railway and the London & South Western Railway companies lines, and although these are in some particulars open to objection, I think they made be accepted. The frame in the West Cabin now contains 48 working levers and 17 spaces.

'Salisbury East Signal Cabin.
The frame in this cabin now contains 46 working levers and 18 spaces. The alterations in signalling and interlocking required in my above mentioned report have been carried out. The air pressure for this pneumatic installation is maintained by one of two motors, one being held in reserve. One of the motors is driven by steam and the other by electric power. I understand the former is proving the more economical method.

'I attach two diagrams showing the completed arrangements at these two signal cabins. These differ slightly from those first supplied by the company. The arrangements being satisfactory, I can, subject to the completion of certain unfinished platform work, recommend the Board of Trade to authorise the new works at Salisbury station.'

The New Salisbury Station 1902
By the time the South Western had finished, very little remained of the previous Salisbury station. Surviving were the Fisherton Street girder bridge carrying four tracks, the original Down and Southampton bay platforms lengthened and raised, the 1859 station building converted to offices and the footbridge over to the Great Western. The four through platforms were designated from north to south, No.1 Up Local, the island Nos.2 Up Through and 3 Down Local, and 4 Down Through, with Down bays 5 and 6. Nos.1 and 3 were directly connected to the Great Western,

facilitating through passenger train services. Adjacent to the 1859 station a new two storey building incorporated a spacious light and airy booking hall, booking and enquiry offices, refreshment and waiting rooms and the access ramp to the subway connecting the platforms. On 9th July 1902 the Engineering Committee was instructed to order an electric motor and gearing for £84 from the General Electric Supply Co. for assisting loaded luggage trolleys up one of the subway inclines but there is no evidence of its installation. According to a 1906 plan there were also waiting and refreshment rooms on the other platforms, all of which were sheltered by wide long awnings.

East of Fisherton Street bridge part of the former Up platform had been removed to provide a siding for the horse and carriage dock. The Post Office had previously built its sorting office here adjacent to the railway. Beyond the East Yard had again been widened to some 13 sidings and lengthened as far as Fisherton Viaduct, bridge No.233. Opposite, on the Down side, were five carriage sidings. West of the station an extensive new locomotive shed, described in detail in Chapter One, was constructed south of the line adjacent to Cherry Orchard Lane Bridge No.241. The new Salisbury shed had one of the largest locomotive allocations on the South Western, reflecting not only motive power requirements on the four existing South Western routes but also new traffic transferred from the Great Western and the rapidly increasing War Office traffic on Salisbury Plain. Between the new shed and the station to the south of the line the West Yard of six sidings was provided.

As we have seen, a major constraint in the rebuilding of the station was Fisherton Street bridge, and in the short distance thence to the 1859 station the Up through track curved sharply at about eight chains radius. Since all trains normally stopped at

A pair of Adams express 4-4-0s on an up train in platform 2, with the Great Western station behind.

The interior of Salisbury East signal box in 1979, little changed from the 1902 original. Peter Swift.

Top right. On the ground floor were the pneumatic cylinders.

The west end of Salisbury station in 1911. There are no signal wires or point rodding, instead the pneumatic point motors are housed in wooden boxes and the signal pneumatic cylinders are mounted up the signal posts.

Salisbury station looking along platforms 3 and 4 in 1911.

Salisbury such a sharp curve was not seen as a problem for trains starting from the platform. But in 1906 this was the site of a tragic accident.

THE SALISBURY ACCIDENT 1906

The South Western Railway provided a fast and efficient service of trains between Southampton Docks and Waterloo in close co-operation with the principal steamship companies serving the seaports of the world. Many of these shipping lines, including the American Line, had changed their English home port from Liverpool to Southampton, but then began to transfer mails and some passengers at Plymouth, disembarking to tenders in Cawsand Bay. Fast rail services from Plymouth allowed an earlier arrival in London than staying on the ship until Southampton, often after calling at Cherbourg.

The American Line, whose four steamships maintained a weekly trans-Atlantic service, was a valuable customer

The east end of Salisbury station in 1911 showing the four through platforms and the Bournemouth bay, and the long footbridge extending right over to the Great Western station to the right. At the end of the straight Up Through line serving platform 2 is the sharp curve where the boat train came off the rails in the 1906 accident.

The remains of Eagle Saloon carriage No.84, re-railed after the crash.

to the South Western. When the line announced in 1904 that it was going to start calling at Plymouth on the eastbound sailings the South Western put on a special boat train service to Waterloo for the passengers from a newly-built 'Ocean Quay' terminal at Stonehouse Pool, with engine changes at Devonport and Templecombe. These fast trains ran to a schedule, but at almost any time of day or night depending on the liner's arrival at Plymouth, once a week but usually Saturday. Tragedy struck in the early hours of Sunday 1st July 1906 when the train sped through Salisbury and came off the line on the sharp curve at the east of the station,

with the loss of twenty-eight lives, and much material damage. The crash awoke the whole city. The direct cause of the accident, speed well in excess of the 30mph limit through the station, was immediately obvious but the official enquiries were unable to cast any light on why an experienced crew, who both died in the tragedy, had made such an error.

This was the greatest loss of life in any accident on the South Western and after several investigations, by the South Western itself, a Coroner's Inquest returned a verdict of 'Accidenta! Death' although the jury felt the company carried part of the blame. The

following information comes from the report by Maj.Pringle following his enquiry.

The train from Stonehouse Pool consisted of bogie luggage van No.17, three bogie first class corridor coaches, Nos.47, 38 and 84, and bogie kitchen brake van No.492, which conveyed 43 passengers who had disembarked from the *S.S. New York*, the guard, a ticket collector and two waiters. The locomotive from Templecombe was L12 class 4-4-0 No.421 with Driver Robins and Fireman Gadd. As the train approached Salisbury at an estimated 60mph the whistle was sounded but the train did not slow for the 30mph speed restriction round the sharp curve of ten chains radius just to the east of the Up through platform. As the train came off the track, just before 2.0am, it first destroyed or damaged the last ten vehicles of the 10.12pm Waterloo to Yeovil milk empties. As it passed on the Down through line it then hit the old Beyer Peacock 0-6-0 No.0351 which was standing in the Down bay platform. The boat train locomotive was badly damaged, the first three coaches completely smashed and the last two coaches badly damaged. The locomotive and first twelve vehicles of the milk train were undamaged. Debris was scattered over a wide area at the east of the station. Of the forty-three passengers, twenty-four were killed or fatally injured and seven more injured. Driver Robins and Fireman Gadd on the express, Guard Chinnor on the milk train and Fireman Chick on the footplate of the 0-6-0 were killed. Subsequently a memorial to the dead was provided in Salisbury cathedral.

Wreckage strewn across Fisherton Street Bridge. To the left is the front end of the ill-fated L12 class 4-4-0 No.421; to the right the underframe of one of the carriages. The Great Western station is behind.

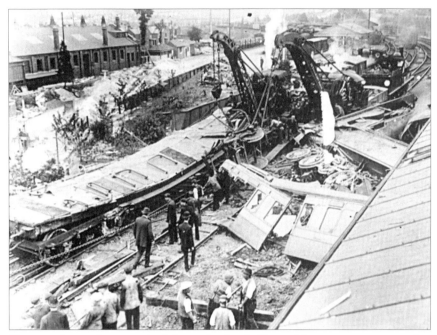

The wreckage photographed from the footbridge with two cranes removing the remains of a carriage, and the tender of No.421 on its side. Just above the cranes can be seen the horse and carriage dock built on the site of the 1879 Up station.

After the rescue of the injured and the recovery of the dead the task of clearing the wreckage began, with the use of three steam cranes, which arrived from Nine Elms, Eastleigh and Exmouth Junction. Only thirteen hours after the accident, by 3.0pm on the Sunday afternoon, one track had been cleared but it took many days to complete the job including repairs to the Fisherton Street Bridge.

So what caused the accident? During his three inspections in 1901-3 of the new Salisbury station Maj.Pringle had not raised any concern about the sharp curve. Driver Robins was competent, experienced and a teetotaller and was aware of the speed restrictions on the line. But in the thirty-three hours or so immediately preceding the

accident Driver Robins had had at most eight hours sleep, working varying shift patterns, although this was not unusual at the time. It is possible that he 'nodded off' for a fatal few seconds after sounding the whistle just west of Salisbury. Certainly the shift patterns acceptable in 1906 would be unacceptable today for drivers of trains, lorries or coaches. The Foreman of the Coroner' jury said: *'We consider a certain amount of blame must attach to the Company as well as the driver, and we have tried to give expression to it.'*

Subsequently the speed limit through Salisbury was reduced from 30 to 15mph and the Stonehouse Pool boat trains were re-scheduled to stop at Exeter and Salisbury, instead of Templecombe.

A very full account of the accident, the background, and the official enquiries conducted has been written by Norman Pattenden, an experienced professional railwayman, and published by the South Western Circle in 2001.

NEW WORKS AT SALISBURY 1908-1910

In 1908 there was correspondence between the South Western and the Board of Trade concerning problems arising from the interlocking between the advanced starting and distant signals on both the Up and Down main lines. The problems arose frequently during the operation of changing engines, when a special key had to be used to release the electrical locking. The Board of Trade agreed 'on the distinct understanding that all trains stop at the station,' hardly surprising in view of the accident two years previously.

With increasing numbers of goods trains using Salisbury East Yard, particularly from the Great Western, there was a need for a longer headshunt, also providing an exit on to the Up main line for some of the longest of trains. The alignment was widened for three tracks and at Castle Street bridge No.231 in 1910 a long girder on the north side spanned both the road and footpath, contrasting with the shorter girders and brick arch of 1898 for the main lines. Maj. Pringle made his inspection and reported on 22nd June 1910: *'I made an inspection today of the new works at Salisbury Tunnel Junction on the London & South Western Railway. A new trailing connection has been laid with the Up main line at the west end of Salisbury Tunnel, to provide means of exit from a shunting siding, which has been extended eastward.*

'The connection is out of sight of both the adjacent signal boxes – Salisbury Tunnel Junction and Salisbury East. Special arrangements for working have therefore been made.

'The points are worked from a new ground frame "B" which contains 4 levers all in use. The frame is electrically controlled from both the above mentioned signal boxes, and the release is only obtained by the mutual and simultaneous co-operation of both signalmen. Telephonic and bell communication has been arranged between the ground frame and the two signal boxes.

'Two outgoing goods semaphore signals control the exit from the siding, and are worked from the ground frame and mechanically slotted by Salisbury Tunnel Junction signal box. Certain of the running signals have been moved backwards in position, and corresponding alterations have been made in the track circuit work and "train waiting" indicators.

'Salisbury Tunnel Junction signal box contains an old mechanical frame with 21 levers all in use.

The Nine Elms and Northam steam cranes prepare to remove the wrecked L12 No.421, with Beyer Peacock 0-6-0 No.0351 in the bay platform.

On 18th April 1914 Drummond F13 class 4-6-0 No.334 leaves Salisbury East Yard with the 11.15am freight to Eastleigh, passing over the new section inspected by Maj. Pringle in 1910.

'*Salisbury East signal box contains an old power worked (low pressure pneumatic) frame with 64 levers of which 17 are now spare. The interlocking is correct, and the general arrangements are satisfactory. I can therefore recommend the Board of Trade to approve these new works.*'

CHANGES IN BASINGSTOKE AREA 1904-1914
Battledown Junction 1904 - 1914
On 16th December 1904 Maj. Pringle reported thus: '*I made an inspection yesterday of the new works at Battledown. The Down through line from Basingstoke at this junction has been extended towards Micheldever, and the following new connections laid.*

a) New facing points on the Down through main.

b) New trailing points on the Micheldever Down branch line.

The necessary additional signals have been added

The new points and signals are worked from a new signal box (Battledown) which replaces the former junction box. The frame contains 22 levers of which 5 are spare. The interlocking is correct. The general arrangements are satisfactory and I advise the Board of Trade to approve the new works.'

On 1st October 1914 the South Western General Manager, H.A.Walker, reported to the Board of Trade: '*Certain crossover roads in existence at Battledown Section Box situated west of Basingstoke station were found to be unnecessary and have been removed. The connections giver by these crossover roads were:- 1st between the Up and Down Exeter lines, and 2nd, between the Down Exeter, or through line and the Down Southampton line. In consequence of these removals various alterations were necessary in he signalling arrangements, and these are detailed on the accompanying diagram for the information of the Board of Trade.*'

New works at Basingstoke 1906-1907
On 26th January 1906 Maj. Pringle reported: '*I made an inspection today of the new signalling arrangements at Basingstoke station. The system now adopted is the low-pressure pneumatic system, similar to what is in use elsewhere on the company's system, whereby both signals and points are operated by compressed air.*

'*Two new signal boxes have been erected which control the whole of the station and yard working, and these have been equipped*

In the early 1900s when the main line through Basingstoke was widened from two tracks to four, more land was taken to the south of the line. The old London & Southampton station of 1839 illustrated on page 119 was demolished and new buildings constructed on the Down side. The platforms were reached by steps from street level.

The substantial new South Western station buildings at Basingstoke.

with power frames. All the lines have been provided with track circuiting.

a) *Basingstoke East Box - has a frame with 60 levers of which 15 are now spare.*

b) *Basingstoke West Box – a frame with 68 levers of which 13 are spare. A ground frame with 4 levers, of which 1 is spare is controlled from the West Box.*

1. The interlocking is correct with the following exceptions

a) *East Box – No.21 signal to be made to apply to No.1 siding road only and to lock with No.19 points.*

b) *West Box – No.54 release lever to lock No.44 points both ways.*

2. The new signalling arrangements have not yet been brought into use, and the necessary track section indicators have not yet been provided in the signal boxes. I was unable therefore to see the working of the points and signals.

I noticed that in both signal boxes the view of the signalman is somewhat unnecessarily obscured by boarding over the lever frame arranged for carrying the block instruments and indicators, and I suggested that an improvement in this respect might be effected. This the company promised to give effect to.

3. The extensive alterations in the station yard as regards passenger accommodation and working have been completed, but I did not make an inspection of these new works.

4. Subject therefore to the completion of the two interlocking requirements named in para 1. and to a re-inspection of the whole of the works when they have been brought into use I recommend the Board to approve these new signalling arrangements.'

Maj. Pringle returned for his re-inspection and reported on 6th May 1907: *'I made a re-inspection yesterday of the new works at Basingstoke station. The works in connection with the rebuilding of the station have now been completed.*

'There are now four through roads through the station. The old Down platform has been converted into an island platform, and a new Down local platform has been built. There are general and ladies waiting rooms on each of the three platforms, together with refreshment rooms and conveniences for both sexes. A subway has been constructed for the use of passengers connecting the platforms. Electric luggage lifts have been provided for the transport of luggage, milk etc. The waiting rooms are electrically lighted and heated by steam.

'Basingstoke East & West Signal Boxes. The interlocking requirements made in my

report dated 26.1.06 have been completed. Track circuit indicators for the main lines have been fixed in the signal boxes, and all points are now equipped with electrical detectors.

'I tested the ironwork in two underbridges which have been extended to carry passenger roads. The spans vary from 60 feet to 20 feet in length, and the ironwork showed moderate deflections under engine load, and has apparently sufficient theoretical strength.

'The arrangements are generally satisfactory and I can recommend the Board to finally approve these new works.'

As from 1897 the section from between Basingstoke station and Worting Junction and Battledown flyover had been quadruple track. In fact the quadruple track through the traffic bottleneck at Basingstoke station had been brought into use before Maj. Pringle's inspection on 18th December 1904. This was the last section required to complete the 50 miles of quadruple track from Waterloo to Worting Junction which facilitated the passage of all trains to both the West of England and Bournemouth main lines.

Although outside the remit of this volume it may be added here that the South Western 1900 Act authorised new sections of quadruple track. The work took place between Worting Junction and Southampton, subsequently opened at Micheldever station, between Weston and Wallers Ash, between Allbrook and Eastleigh and between St Denys and Northam, all works completed by 1907. The long-term ambition of the South Western was for a four track railway all the way from Waterloo to Southampton but this was not realised.

Park Prewett Asylum Railway 1917

Following its authorisation on 31st October 1912, on 10th December the Clerk of the Hampshire Asylum Committee wrote to the Board of Trade about their proposal to build a new asylum at Park Prewett Farm about a mile and a half west of Basingstoke station. They had agreed with the South Western that they provide a siding to convey construction materials to the site.

The purpose of the letter was to advise that after the opening of the asylum it might be desired to convey visitors to the asylum from Basingstoke station over the railway.

By the time of its delayed opening in August 1917 the asylum had been taken over by the Canadian army. The branch was steep and curved and wagons were propelled up the branch by a shunting engine.

THE 1908 BLIZZARD

On Saturday 25th April 1908, just as people were looking forward to summer, a blizzard

An imperfect, but nevertheless interesting, view of Andover Junction station looking east after the great blizzard of 25th April 1908. Peter Swift Collection.

hit the Andover area, blocking many local roads. At Andover Junction the snow drifted on to the Down platform making passage very difficult. Main line trains were delayed by up to an hour, and on the branches by even more. The level crossing gates at Andover Town could not be closed using the wheel in the signal box and could only be closed by hand with great difficulty, staff were kept busy clearing points and the branch service ran as and when possible. The blizzard hit hard on Salisbury Plain with Tidworth, Bulford, Larkhill and Hurstbourne suffering drifts of up to six feet. With remarkable speed the thaw started the next day and there was some local flooding but a week later flowers and fruit trees were in full bloom.

ZENITH

By about 1909 the West of England main line from Basingstoke to Exeter had reached its zenith. For the half century, following its completion in 1857, the South Western had invested in the line steadily, culminating in the quadrupling of the main line from Basingstoke to the Battledown flyover in 1897. There had been the Andover and Grateley resignalling of 1901, the rebuilding of Salisbury station in 1902, and of Yeovil Junction station in 1909.

The capacity of the line to handle heavy traffic had been enhanced by the provision of automatic block signalling between Andover and Grateley, and intermediate signal boxes at St Mary Bourne, Enham and Laverstock. This capacity was demonstrated daily in the summer months by the 10.45am Plymouth, 11.0am North Cornwall and 11.10am North Devon expresses from Waterloo. These followed each other for 184 miles before passing Coleford Junction at 2.22pm, 2.42pm and 2.49pm respectively, with five minutes allowed for locomotive changes at Salisbury and Exeter Queen Street. This required skilful work by the enginemen on the hilly route, quick locomotive changes in the five minutes scheduled at both Salisbury and Exeter, and also concentration by the signalmen to facilitate a clear road with no signal checks. During the small hours the line was busy with freight, with overnight fast goods trains from London's largest goods station, Nine Elms, to Yeovil, Plymouth, Templecombe and Torrington. One of these was important enough to warrant its own, unofficial name, 'The Tavy' the 10.35pm fast goods from Nine Elms which arrived at Plymouth Friary at 6.53am calling only at Salisbury, Exeter and Devonport. In the opposite direction much traffic was carried, including cattle, meat and milk, ships' cargoes from the docks at Plymouth and the fruit and flowers despatched from Bere Alston.

With the exception of a few small additions the South Western system was practically complete and competed with the Great Western at many locations including Basingstoke, Whitchurch, Salisbury, Yeovil,

Oakley station looking east in 1919.

Oakley station looking west in 1919.

Whitchurch station circa 1919.

Whitchurch station looking west in 1919. The Fullerton branch train comprising a small tank engine, a two coach local set and van, is berthed in the down siding whilst a number of passengers wait on the Up platform for a train already signalled.

Chard, Exeter and points west, particularly Plymouth. The LSWR competed keenly with the Great Western for all traffic on offer including, as we have seen, the prestigious boat train passengers from Plymouth.

THE TRAFFIC POOLING AGREEMENT 1910

In competition with the South Western at Yeovil, Exeter and beyond, the Great Western had the disadvantage of longer routes via Trowbridge and Bristol respectively and for some the GWR really did mean the Great Way Round. To overcome this it doubled twenty-three miles of single track line and built thirty-three miles of new double track, opening via Lavington to Westbury in 1900, and from Castle Cary to Taunton in 1906. This new route shortened their Yeovil line by fourteen miles and to Exeter and beyond by twenty miles. As we have seen, the South Western had also been investing steadily in the line and more was planned, including the doubling of the remaining twenty miles of single track of the North Devon line, authorised by parliament in 1906.

However, by 1909 it became clear that the extra investments made by the two companies in the west country were not yielding the growth in income necessary to justify any more. Accordingly negotiations were initiated between Viscount Churchill and Sir Charles Scotter, the chairmen of the GW and LSWR. The outcome was an agreement to pool all competitive traffic in the west country, signed on 13th May 1910. Receipts were to be shared between the two companies in proportion to traffic carried in 1908, less 25% working expenses on the distances saved. The first immediate result was that the South Western withdrew its Ocean Liner express services between Stonehouse Pool and Waterloo which had seldom if ever covered their costs. Work on doubling the North Devon line costing £75,640 was abandoned.

Economies were made gradually. On 1st January 1917 the operation of the Chard branch was taken over by the Great Western, who extended their service between Taunton and Chard Joint to Chard Junction, and joint East and West signal boxes at Yeovil Town replaced separate South Western and Great Western boxes.

Between 1913 and 1918 there were closures of intermediate signal boxes at St Mary Bourne and Abbey Ford (between Gillingham and Templecombe) on the main line and west of Exeter at Cowley Bridge, Crediton East, and Neopardy, with joint signal boxes at Launceston and Lydford each replacing two. The result of the signal box closures was to lengthen the block sections involved and to limit the number of trains at busy times, but achieving significant savings for the two companies. In 1917 the railmotor

Taken shortly after the previous photograph the up passenger train of non-corridor stock, hauled by a Drummond 4-4-0, has arrived.

Andover Junction station in later South Western days looking east from Millway Road Bridge with West signal box on the left.

Porton station looking east in Edwardian days with shunting in progress in the goods yard. The permanent way gang poses for the photograph.

services from Exeter Queen Street to Topsham and Honiton were withdrawn and the halts at Roundball and Whipton Bridge closed in 1921 and 1923. Further economies were made after the grouping.

SPECIAL TRAFFIC ARRANGEMENTS 1914

The Special Traffic Notices of 1914 give a full picture of the traffic handled by the South Western over and above that on scheduled services and details of many of these special trains appear in Chapter Nine.

However, many of the features form part of our story here and show the South Western well able to cope with a wide variety of special traffic. There were now sufficient sidings, station platforms and signal boxes. The new Salisbury shed could supply sufficient locomotives, and pilotmen for 'foreign' locomotives and there was a sufficient water supply. Amesbury was well-provided for with water whereas at nearby Weyhill it was drawn from a well eighty feet deep by a horse plodding a circular track while harnessed to a pole connected to the pump. There was also the expertise of the railway management who were able to organise the complete operation efficiently, for our line the Central District Superintendent's Office staff at Southampton West.

The South Western operated a number of special passenger trains along our line, in connection with horse races at Salisbury, Ascot, Sandown Park and others. There were also a number of cheap excursions run both by the South Western on its own account and for others such as Mr Hunt, whose excursions picked up at many stations along the Test Valley from Oakley to Nursling, including Longparish and Wherwell.

Other companies also operated excursion trains using their own locomotives and carriages over parts of the line. An example was the Great Western excursions from Bristol to both Bournemouth West and Portsmouth via Salisbury, South Western pilotmen and guards being provided from and to Salisbury. There were also a large number of military special trains run for territorials on exercises on Salisbury Plain, and also to the Bordon and Wareham. Many specials of course worked to Amesbury, the station built to deal with military traffic. Those from the Great Western, at both Salisbury and Basingstoke, were worked by Great Western locomotives with South Western pilotmen. Another special brought an LBSCR locomotive to Grateley. The peak day was Sunday 2nd August when four specials arrived at Grateley and twelve at Amesbury. Two days later war was declared and manoeuvres on Salisbury Plain ended as the British Expeditionary Force prepared for embarkation to France and the Western Front.

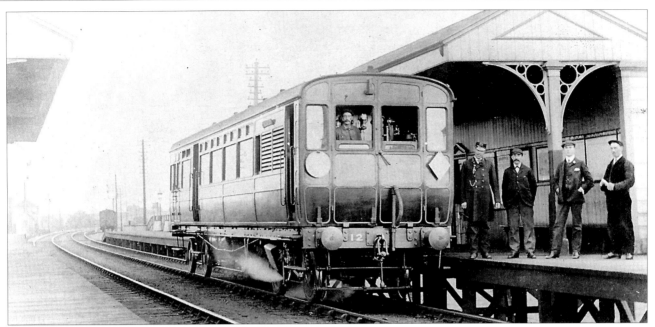

Drummond steam railcar No.12 at Hurstbourne station on a Whitchurch to Fullerton service. This railmotor service was introduced in 1906 in an attempt to reduce costs but lasted only a few years.

A very important special traffic was livestock conveyed from sheep fairs at various places such as Overton, Andover and Salisbury itself, and on adjacent lines such as, Stockbridge, Wilton and Weyhill. Large numbers of cattle wagons were required, often in excess of a hundred but they first had to be cleansed and sanded, often at Salisbury Milford, and then berthed strategically, often some miles from the sheep fair where siding space was often limited. Sheep specials of up to 50 wagons then ran usually to Nine Elms, but sometimes to Portsmouth, along the South Western network often via little used routes such as Fullerton Junction to Hurstbourne Junction.

THE HURSTBOURNE TO FULLERTON BRANCH UP TO 1914

The double track branch line saw little local traffic and, in an effort to reduce costs, the South Western allocated a couple of steam railcars to Andover shed in 1906. However, the venture lasted only until 1910 when they were replaced by a conventional locomotive and carriages. In another attempt to reduce costs further the South Western reduced the line to a single track on 17th July 1913. A Tyers No.6 instrument was used for the section between Hurstbourne Junction and Fullerton Junction and points for the sidings at Longparish and Wherwell operated from ground frames unlocked by the train tablet. The existing double track junction at Hurstbourne Junction was retained, the double track branch converging to single track after a couple of hundred yards just beyond branch Bridge No.1, so that Up or Down branch trains could be held here if required. In the absence of loops at these two stations the sidings could be shunted only by Up trains, Down direction wagons for Wherwell and Longparish circulating via Fullerton Junction.

Six months later Maj. Pringle inspected the new works and reported on 21st January 1914: *'I made an inspection today of the new works between Hurstbourne Junction and Fullerton Junction on the London & South Western Railway.*

'This branch, formerly a double road, has been converted into a single line by the removal of a pair of rails. The total length of the branch is about 7 miles, and it now forms on tablet section. In addition to the removal of one road throughout and the provision of facing points at the two terminal junctions, the following alterations have been affected:-

1. Hurstbourne Junction. A new Up outer home signal has been provided on the branch, and the Down facing points have been reversed in position so as to normally lie from the main line. Tablet catching and delivering apparatus have been fitted, and a tablet instrument provided. The old signal box contains a frame with 17 levers, of which 3 are spare, and the general arrangements are satisfactory and the interlocking is correct.

2. Longparish station. The Down line platform on which the station buildings stand serves for both Up and Down traffic. Only one connection, facing trains from Hurstbourne Junction, and providing access to loading dock, etc., remains. This is now worked from a ground frame with 2 levers in use, which is controlled by the electric tablet for the section. There are no signals, and the signal box is no longer in use.

3. Wherwell station. Here also the old Down platform only is utilised. The signals have been removed, and the signal box is disused. The single remaining connection is worked as at Longparish from a ground frame with 2 working levers, controlled by the tablet. The interlocking at these two places is correct.

4. Fullerton station. The Up main distant signal applicable to the branch has been removed, and the new facing points (and siding connection formerly worked from a ground frame) situated 243 yards from the signal box, is worked direct from the box – the bolt of the facing points being detected as required. The frame in the junction signal box contains 28 levers, of which 1 is spare. The following additional interlocking is necessary:-

Nos. 12 and 22 levers to interlock.

'I understand that the goods train service upon this branch is very small, and that the number of wagons upon trains does not exceed 5 or 6. In the circumstances the risk of vehicles breaking away and running back to the junction may I think be disregarded.

'Subject to the completion of the named requirement I recommend the Board of Trade to approve the alterations and new method of working upon this single branch line, on the understanding that an undertaking to work the traffic upon the electric tablet method is furnished by the company.'

Similar economies could have been made by 'switching out' the two intermediate signal boxes, but possibly the timing was dictated by the need for track or signalling renewals, the Up line being lifted north of Wherwell and the Down line beyond. It now took about twenty minutes for a train to run through the single line section but this did not cause difficulty.

As we have seen in the 1898 and 1914 special traffic arrangements, the South Western carried a wide variety of extra traffic over and above scheduled trains and it made full use of its network, including the Hurstbourne to Fullerton branch. Through an accident of history trains between the extensive Salisbury Milford goods station

Following the 1914 collision between two Up goods trains just to the west of Andover Junction West signal box H15 class 4-6-0 No.488 is surrounded by wrecked wagons. Fortunately nobody was killed or injured. **John Alsop Collection**

and the London area could run up the main line through Porton only after inconvenient reversals at both Milford Junction and the busy Salisbury station. Therefore special trains for both the army and following sheep fairs ran east from Milford, with the engine running tender first, through Dean and Dunbridge to Kimbridge Junction. Here a turnover engine was attached to the rear of the train which now ran through Stockbridge and Fullerton Junction to reach the main line at Hurstbourne Junction. The first locomotive waited at Kimbridge Junction to become the turnover engine for the next special, there often being three or four running in succession. There was also a number of cheap excursion trains from stations between Oakley and Hurstbourne to the South Coast.

WORLD WAR ONE 1914 to 1918

At the outbreak of hostilities on 4th August 1914 the government took control of the railways through the Railway Executive Committee, with Chairman Mr Herbert Walker, the South Western General Manager, who was knighted for his services in 1915. Government control of the railways continued until 15th August 1921.

The first task at the outbreak of war was the mobilisation of reservists and the return of Territorial Army units from their exercises on Salisbury Plain and elsewhere to their bases. Embarkation of the first five divisions of the British Expeditionary Force commenced on 10th August, with troop trains booked to enter Southampton Docks at 12 minute intervals. Between 10th and 31st August 670 troop trains arrived and one

day alone in September 100 troop trains arrived. As we have seen with the manoeuvres, these troops came from all over the country, travelling to Southampton via Basingstoke, Andover or Salisbury and it seems likely that some were routed via Whitchurch and Fullerton Junction.

The docks at Southampton in 1914 were the old docks near the terminus station, the new docks being constructed in the 1930s. During the 1914-18 war many of the great liners transferred back to Liverpool, both to avoid congestion at Southampton and German submarines in the English Channel. With its good railway connections Southampton docks played a major role in the embarkation of troops for the Western Front and their supplies of equipment, ammunition, food, horses, and even mail from home. Much of the coal required for both the merchant and royal navy ships was supplied from South Wales, with sixty wagon coal trains running from Salisbury to Eastleigh.

On Salisbury Plain the army had extensive facilities in 1914 and throughout the war these were enhanced and developed. Beyond Bulford station several extra sidings were laid in, including a forage siding and another to a butchery and bakery. Between Amesbury and Bulford Ratfyn signal box was opened to the Rollestone Military Railway which served numerous barracks, coal sidings, an electricity station, a balloon school flying shed and a hospital. The Rollestone Military Railway was operated by the War Department, exchanging traffic with the South Western. The descriptions

of the sidings and depots indicate the wide variety of supplies brought in for the army.

On the Bulford branch itself the Boscombe Down aerodrome construction site required railway access. A temporary Boscombe Down signal box, 78 miles 62 chains from Waterloo, was opened in 1917 to control connections to the new siding which was shunted by Up goods trains. Wagons of materials arrived as required, until the signal box and siding closed about December 1918. In 1916 the War Department acquired a large area of Idmiston Down to the south of the main line at Porton for what became the Royal Engineers Experimental Station and also for the Trench Mortar Experimental Station near Winterbourne Gunner. To convey materials and men to the camp the army built a 60cm gauge line, with various branches, from the goods yard at Porton station (it had been extended in 1901). Many of those working at the camp were civilians who travelled from Salisbury and elsewhere to Porton station and thence by the narrow gauge line to the camp. In June 1918 traffic had reached such a level that plans were drawn up for a standard gauge branch as well, but it was never built. Details are given in Chapter One in the section under Porton. Just after the war in 1919 there appears to have been a workmen's train service between Salisbury and Porton for civilian workers at the Experimental Stations.

Southampton docks were very busy with traffic for the British Expeditionary Force. Other ports, particularly Plymouth, therefore had to be used when more troops arrived in Britain from the Empire. For

By daybreak there was still some steam in the boiler of No.488. Both this and the previous photograph have been taken from the embankment to the north of the line. John Alsop Collection.

the factory's weekly output was about 1,000 tons of products including charcoal and wood oil, which went out by rail. Incidentally at the same time Messrs. Kynock Ltd. also established a similar plant at Bideford, North Devon, again with a new private siding. The Kynock factory was taken over by the government in 1917 until production ceased in 1919.

Traffic at Longparish increased to up to fifty loaded wagons a day forwarded from Taylor's and Knynock's works. Kynock was also a important employer in the area having more than 100 employees, many coming from the nearest town, Whitchurch. The South Western laid on special workmen's trains, morning and evening, between Whitchurch and Longparish, the train running empty between Longparish and Fullerton

This was not advertised to the public and was probably provided by extra trips run by the Fullerton to Whitchurch branch train which, by 1917, provided only three public services. Although no records have come to light it would appear that a number of special train services between South Coast ports and London for the army, and from Milford and Stockbridge to London for sheep, ran between Fullerton Junction and Hurstbourne Junction. Indeed, it was reported that the line was used extensively for troop movements. However, the capacity of the line for extra traffic had been considerably reduced by its singling in 1913.

On the West of England main line there were many special trains conveying men, munitions and other supplies to the large naval base at Devonport, the new or enlarged army bases at Okehampton and Fovant and many more too numerous to mention. Passenger train services were reduced but much more goods traffic was carried, a

example, Canadian troops arrived in Britain in October 1914 and the South Western provided 92 special trains to bring them to camps in the Amesbury area. An indication of the number of soldiers based in the area is given by the train service provided for Christmas leave in 1914 when the South Western laid on 237 special trains carrying about 180,000 men home from the Amesbury line, with similar arrangements for subsequent Christmases. When the USA entered the war in 1917 many more troop specials were provided.

The war produced millions of casualties, many of the wounded being landed at Southampton and conveyed to hospital in ambulance trains to numerous destinations, including on or by way of Andover Junction and the MSWJR.

There were also a number of developments on the now single-track branch from Hurstbourne Junction to Fullerton Junction, making use of timber felled in nearby Harewood Forest. In 1914 James Taylor Ltd. set up a sawmill near Longparish station and built a narrow gauge railway to link the sawmills with the goods sidings, and for some years forwarded considerable timber traffic. A more short-lived venture opened in 1915 adjacent to Taylor's sawmill, Messrs. Knynock's wood distillation factory. Traffic from the two ventures was now such that a new ground frame and siding were installed at Longparish for Messrs. Kynoch in 1915 and approved by the Board of Trade in 1916. Unlike other sidings on the branch this could only be shunted by Down goods trains, but

Above the locomotive cab are the remains of the loaded cattle truck which the fireman recalled sliding over the boiler. The South Western coaches occupy the sidings between the LSWR and MSWJR running lines, and three steam cranes are working to clear the line. John Alsop Collection.

Some of the wreckage has now been cleared enabling two steam cranes to move close to No.488. John Alsop Collection.

considerable amount such as timber, horses, hay, straw, construction materials, meat and grain being required for the war effort. Heavy freight trains of sixty-five wagons between Nine Elms and Salisbury were worked by the new Urie H15 class 4-6-0s, two being involved in wartime accidents at Andover Junction.

After Armistice Day millions of soldiers returned to their bases, many on Salisbury Plain, for demobilisation or return to their own country, the wartime transport arrangements running in reverse. In June 1919 traffic was very heavy on the Bulford line with seven locomotives diagrammed to work over it, several all day. A number of trains, due to their weight, required a pilot engine. Although the Headquarters Southern Command were at Tidworth the army established its demobilisation centre at Chiseldon, just south of Swindon on the MSWJR, and the new Red Post Junction opened in time for some of this demobilisation traffic.

THE ANDOVER JUNCTION ACCIDENT 1914

About 1.0am on Tuesday 13th October 1914, at Andover Junction, new H15 class 4-6-0 No.488 was in charge of the 8.10pm goods train from Exeter, comprising forty wagons, scheduled non-stop from Salisbury to Nine Elms, approaching at about 50mph. The train passed stop signals protecting a Yeovil Junction to Nine Elms goods hauled by F13 class No.334 which had stopped to pick up some wagons at the station. Hearing the rapidly approaching Exeter train all the railwaymen in the vicinity ran for their lives before the train hit and destroyed some

seventy wagons. Many cattle were killed but some survived to walk away from the wreckage. It would appear that since no passengers were involved the Board of Trade did not hold an inquiry, for no report appeared in the 1914 volume of Accident Reports. However, the South Western dismissed the driver of No.488 rather than imposing a lesser penalty.

Many years later the fireman of No.488 told Don Bradley, the distinguished locomotive historian, that his most vivid memory was *'the sight of a fully loaded cattle wagon sliding along the boiler and being flung through the air to land on the rear van of the train standing in the Swindon bay.'*

The wreckage was extensive but by 5.30am on Wednesday 14th one track had been opened for traffic and clearance was completed by the afternoon of Thursday 15th. Many trains were cancelled or curtailed and long distance services were diverted via Dunbridge. When the morning train from Whitchurch arrived with boys for Andover Grammar School they were delayed looking at the accident and arrived late for school, for which the miscreants received a caning. One of these was Tom Denning who later trained in the law and rose, as Lord Denning, to the top legal post of Master of the Rolls.

MINOR ACCIDENTS 1914

In the 1914 volume of Accident Reports several incidents, some minor some more serious, are recorded. On 18th September Mr J.Rutt, an assistant linesman at Basingstoke was oiling point connections between the Down through and Down local lines when he was struck by a shunting engine, somehow sustaining only bruises.

On 25th September John Rose, yard foreman at Andover Junction, suffered a crushed thumb when coupling wagons in a siding. On 20th November Albert Wareham, a labourer, was employed at Andover Junction removing a subway light in the face of the Down platform wall when he was caught by wagons being shunted along the line. His leg was run over and crushed rendering subsequent amputation necessary.

THE ANDOVER JUNCTION ACCIDENT 1916

At Andover Junction two years later, on 5th October 1916, some trucks ran away on the 1 in 220 gradient during shunting on the Up slow line and fouled the Up through line opposite Andover Junction East signal box. The same 8.10pm freight train of fifty-eight wagons from Exeter to Nine Elms, this time hauled by H15 class 4-6-0 No.490 running under clear signals, collided with the runaways and wrecked thirty-eight of them. The Board of Trade minute of 9th October read: *'I think this case can be dealt with by correspondence, and that an enquiry is hardly necessary. Please ask the company to furnish a plan showing the scene of the accident, together with the relative position of the signal boxes, points and signals concerned – at the time of the accident.'*

Again there was no enquiry since no passengers were involved, but changes were made to prevent such an accident happening again. Col. Pringle's reply of 28th October read: *'It is evident that the company have been utilising the Up slow line (passenger) by night for marshalling goods trains. This line is not trapped for the purpose. The result* on this occasion, due either to failure to apply brake on brake van, or to insufficiency of brake power, was that the vehicles (no doubt loose shunted) gradually crept foul of the Up fast line, and the collision and subsequent serious derailment ensued.

'The signalman in the East box should have noticed the position of the vehicles on the Up slow, but no doubt the time of the occurrence 1.5am and want of light rendered detection difficult.

'We should draw the attention of the company to the fact that the Up slow line is not fitted with trap points or fouling bars at the east end, and therefore is not equipped as it should be for shunting or marshalling purposes, especially by night, and ask them to provide the necessary trap adding that the necessity for similar protection at the west end will be also for consideration.'

CHANGES AT ANDOVER 1917

In January 1917 the layout controlled by Andover East signal box was changed. The middle No.2 Down main line was taken out of use, leaving the No.1 Down local as the only Down main line, through the platform.

The No.24 facing points were removed, the signalling simplified and the No.2 line reduced to a siding with trailing points only worked by the West box. From then on it could be used by goods trains which shunted back into the siding. Just why this connection was removed is not clear, however, there had been two recent accidents at Andover Junction but they both involved Up trains which made no use of this connection. The reason must have been good because there were occasions in the future when this facility was sorely missed.

Following the 1916 accident the South Western provided the catch siding recommended, and on 22nd October 1917 Col. Pringle reported: *'I made an inspection on the 21st instant of new works at Andover Junction on the London & South Western Railway. Consequent upon the collision which occurred on the 5th October, 1916, a new catch siding has been laid with facing points on the Up local line at the East end of the Junction station. The catch siding is covered with ballast. The new connection is worked from Andover Junction East signal box which contains an old frame with 42 working and 8 spare levers.*

'The additional interlocking is correct and the arrangements satisfactory. I recommend the Board of Trade to approve these new works.'

The report was accompanied by a track plan showing the new catch siding, which was covered in ballast and terminated just short of Charlton Road bridge.

RED POST JUNCTION 1917-1919

On 28th September 1916 the MSWJR secretary reported that: *'...in order to facilitate the working of military traffic between Weyhill and Andover Junction and avoid the heavy delays that are now taking place, it had been proposed to construct a loop and junction between the Midland & South Western Junction Railway and the main line of the London & South Western Railway at Red Post which would give the necessary accommodation to enable the increased traffic passing to and from our line at Andover Junction to be more expeditiously and economically dealt with.'*

The cost of the new works was to be £5,131 to be paid for by the War Office, who would sell it back at the end of government control of the railways, the MSWJR and LSWR paying half each. The new works were brought into use in two stages, first a loop siding then a passing loop and junction. On 22nd October 1917 Col. Pringle reported that: *'I made an inspection on the 21st instant of the new works at Red Post Junction, on the London & South Western Railway. A loop siding has been laid on the north of the single line (Midland & South Western Junction) from Weyhill at this junction. There is a new set of points on the single line facing trains from the direction of Andover. The points are worked from a new ground frame with two levers in use, which is controlled by the tablet for the single line section (Weyhill – Andover).*

'The interlocking is correct and the arrangements satisfactory. I therefore recommend the Board to approve these new works.'

Subsequently the South Western built Red Post Junction signal box to control the points and signals for the new double track junction between the main line and the double track loop section of the MSWJR. The works were brought into use on 5th January 1919. No inspection report for the new works has yet come to light. At this stage Red Post Junction was useful for trains of demobilised troops going up the MSWJR, but it would have been much more useful at the outbreak of war!

The 1916 Andover junction collision occurred when a goods train hauled by H15 class 4-6-0 No.490 running under clear signals on the Up Through line collided with wagons which had run away during shunting. No.490 finished up on its side to the east of the station near the Charlton Road Bridge, just beyond the MSWJR locomotive depot. Thirty eight wagons were destroyed in the accident. John Alsop Collection.

Andover Junction station on 30th April 1928 looking east. From left to right are the two-road LSWR corrugated iron engine shed with a couple of locomotives usually employed on the Hampshire lines, the joint turntable, the two-road MSWJR shed with a 4-4-0 employed on the Cheltenham services, and the Basingstoke main line. H.C.Casserley

Basingstoke station on 7th July 1926 looking east. Drummond S11 class 4-4-0 No.E.404 has a pigeon special train of mainly LMS vehicles, probably destined for the south coast. H.C.Casserley.

CHAPTER FIVE
THE SOUTHERN RAILWAY 1923 to 1947

THE GROUPING

The 1921 Railways Act organised the main line railways into four groups. The new Southern Railway comprised the London & South Western Railway, the London Brighton & South Coast Railway and the South Eastern & Chatham Railway, together with a number of smaller companies including the Sidmouth Railway. The Midland and South Western Junction Railway became part of the Great Western and the competition between the two came to an end.

SOUTHERN RAILWAY DIVISION MANAGEMENT

The General Manager of the new Southern Railway was Sir Herbert Walker; he continued with his South Western style of management but replaced Districts with Divisions. There were seven Divisions, our line remaining with the Central Division Superintendent at Southampton West, now Mr E.Hight with Assistant Mr E.Myles, but the boundary between the Central and Western Divisions was now just to the west of Salisbury. In 1930 it became the Southern Division.

SOUTHERN and GREAT WESTERN ECONOMIES

The 1920s and 1930s were difficult times and the Southern Railway had to manage its affairs carefully, in particular by cutting costs without affecting the service provided. In the 1920s one economy was the withdrawal of the post of stationmaster at lightly-used stations, which were then supervised by a stationmaster from an adjacent station who visited regularly to check the paperwork in the booking office and the train register in the signal box. Oakley and Hurstbourne lost their stationmasters and were afterwards supervised from Overton and Whitchurch respectively. Elsewhere, the Stockbridge stationmaster became responsible also for Fullerton Junction, Wherwell, Longparish and Horsebridge. In the 1930s the minimal passenger service between Whitchurch and Fullerton Junction was withdrawn and the line between Hurstbourne Junction and Longparish closed and lifted.

Further economies, made possible by developments in signalling engineering, was the replacement of two intermediate signal boxes by intermediate block signals, at Laverstock and Enham. Two junctions also closed with their signal boxes, Hurstbourne Junction and Red Post Junction, although the latter was soon rebuilt to cope with wartime traffic.

The Great Western was in a similar financial position and, following the end of 'hostilities' with the South Western in 1910, had made economies which benefited both companies. This included the South Western staffing the stations at Lydford and Launceston and the Great Western absorbing the Chard Joint to Chard Junction services into its Taunton to Chard branch. Indeed in 1927 there had been a Great Western 5.23pm passenger train from Reading to Salisbury, calling at all stations between Basingstoke and Salisbury but the balancing working appears to have run along the Great Western's own line.

In 1932 the Great Western closed its own passenger stations at Basingstoke (1st January) and Salisbury (12th September). Essentially the Great Western withdrew its own platform, booking and parcels office staff and these duties were then performed by the Southern Railway staff. At Basingstoke terminating passenger trains continued to use the same platform while at Salisbury they used the Southern platforms, although at both stations there were now many through trains. It would appear that a portion of the footbridge linking the Southern and Great Western stations at Salisbury was dismantled after this closure.

TRAFFIC OFFICERS CONFERENCE MINUTES 1927

Research by a colleague, Mick Hutson, has revealed a couple of interesting incidents in 1927. On 25th January the 8.45am Waterloo to Plymouth train overran the Laverstock

Basingstoke station on 17th August 1929. New Maunsell U class 2-6-0 No.A613 of Guildford shed waits with a Down stopping train from Waterloo or Woking to Salisbury. Milk churns and other parcels are unloaded, whilst Great Western vehicles appear in its station shortly before its closure. H.C.Casserley.

Adams A12 class "Jubilee" 0-4-2 No.E601 in immaculate condition on the Basingstoke turntable on 13ᵗʰ June 1931. It was hard work to turn locomotives on these manual turntables. H.C.Casserley.

Drummond S11 class 4-4-0 No.402 waits in the down bay platform No.5 at Salisbury with a train of non-corridor stock. After departure of the fast train in platform 4 it will follow, stopping at all stations as far as Templecombe or Yeovil. H.C.Casserley.

SOUTHERN RAILWAY WORKING TIMETABLE 1927
Weekday Trains at Whitchurch

Train	Whitchurch	To
10.5 Churns Waterloo	pass 12.24am	Yeovil Junction
7.6pm Goods Exeter	pass 12.35am	Nine Elms
8.45 Goods Exmouth Jcn	pass 1.0am	Nine Elms
10.45pm Goods Nine Elms	pass 1.57am	Exeter
5.10pm Goods Friary	pass 2.34am	Nine Elms
11.50pm Goods Feltham	pass 2.50am	Exeter
3.10am Churns Waterloo	5.27 – 5.29	Sidmouth Junction
2.50am Stone Surbiton	pass 5.47 **WFO**	Okehampton
5.20 Goods Basingstoke	5.56 – 6.5	Bulford
5.0am Goods Salisbury	6.36 – 6.46	Basingstoke
6.30 Loco & Van Basing	pass 6.50 **WOQ**	Horsebridge
4.15am Churns Victoria	6.58	Yeovil
7.8am Pass Horsebridge	arr. 7.52	
7.5 Pass & Milk Salisbury	8.4 – 8.10	Waterloo
7.45 Pass. Basingstoke	8.12 – 8.17	Exeter
8.10 Pass Salisbury	pass 8.47	Waterloo
9.5 Pass Whitchurch	dep. 9.5	Fullerton Junction
8.6 Pass Woking	9.27 – 9.30	Salisbury
6.55 Pass Yeovil	9.30 – 9.31	Waterloo
7.8 Goods Basingstoke	9.38 – 10.10	Andover Junction
8.0 Cattle Horsebridge	9.48 – 10.0 **WOQ**	Basingstoke
8.45 Pass Waterloo	10.4	Plymouth, Ilfracombe
7.25am Pass Exeter	pass 10.12	Waterloo
10.20am Pass Fullerton	arr.10.49	
11.0 Goods Whitchurch	dep 11.0 **MWFO**	Fullerton Junction
11.0 Engine Whitchurch	dep. 11.0 **TuThSO**	Overton
10.0 Pass Woking	11.17 – 11.18	Salisbury
6.30am Pass. Exeter	11.19 – 11.22	Waterloo
11.0 Pass Waterloo	pass 12.05	Ilfracombe, Plymouth
11.25 Pass Salisbury	12.15 – 12.16	Waterloo
12.35 Engine Overton	pass 12.44 **TuThSO**	Andover Junction
8.25 Pass Ilfracombe	pass 1.0	Waterloo
12.47 Pass Basingstoke	1.12 – 1.13	Salisbury
8.53 Goods Salisbury	1.14 – 1.40	Basingstoke
12.43 Pass Salisbury	1.36 – 1.47	Waterloo
12.39 Goods Fullerton	arr. 1.58 **MWFO**	
1.0 Pass Waterloo	pass 2.16	Plymouth, Ilfracombe
2.18 Engine Whitchurch	dep.2.18 **MWFO**	Andover Junction
11.45 Churns Clapham Jcn	pass 2.27	Yeovil
10.22 Pass Ilfracombe	pass 2.57	Waterloo
2.36 Pass Basingstoke	3.0 – 3.1	Salisbury
3.0 Pass Waterloo	pass 4.5	Plymouth, Ilfracombe
3.40 Pass Salisbury	4.33 – 4.34	Waterloo
4.20 Engine Andover Jcn	arr. 4.38	
2.24 Pass Waterloo	5.1 – 5.3	Salisbury
12.15 Pass Ilfracombe	pass 5.7	Waterloo
5.13 Pass Whitchurch	dep.5.13	Fullerton Junction
3.43 Loco Coal Salisbury	pass 5.34	Nine Elms
4.58 Pass Salisbury	6.3 – 6.7	Waterloo
5.0 Pass Waterloo	pass 6.24	Exeter
4.25 Goods Amesbury	6.29 – 6.54	Basingstoke
6.15 Pass Fullerton	arr. 6.41	
5.23 **GW** Pass Reading	6.36 – 6.38	Salisbury
6.50 Pass Whitchurch	dep. 6.50	Stockbridge
2.10 Pass Friary	pass 7.13	Waterloo
6.0 Pass Waterloo	pass 7.17	Plymouth
5.25 Goods Salisbury	pass 7.40	Basingstoke
6.8 Pass Waterloo	7.54 – 7.56	Salisbury
7.0 Pass Salisbury	7.55 – 7.57	Basingstoke
7.45 Goods Basingstoke	8.21 – 8.40	Exmouth Junction
3.50 Pass Friary	pass. 8.30	Waterloo
3.28am Stone Okehampton	pass. 9.0 **TuThSO**	Basingstoke
4.50pm Milk Sherborne	pass. 9.22	Victoria
8.47 Pass Salisbury	9.37 – 9.39	Woking
6.5pm Milk Sherborne	pass 10.1	Waterloo
9.48 Pass Basingstoke	10.12 – 10.13	Salisbury
8.18 Churns Waterloo	pass 10.36	Salisbury
4.47 Milk & Prcls Exeter	pass 10.43	Waterloo
8.33 Goods Nine Elms	pass 10.55	Exmouth Junction
9.15 Milk Templecombe	pass 11.5	Waterloo
11.5 Goods Basingstoke	pass 11.37	Salisbury

Note. The passing times at Whitchurch have been interpolated from times at Worting Box and Andover Junction
Other Trains of Interest
1. 7.54am passenger from Eastleigh to Salisbury ran via Andover Junction (9.0 – 9.20am)
2. 8.30am passenger from Salisbury to Southampton ran via Andover Junction (9.2 – 9.24am)

Down home signal at danger by 100 yards. The driver was suspended for one day but Guard Dart was not in his van, having walked through the train to the leading carriage to turn the lights on, prior to passing through Salisbury Tunnel. This was, apparently, a regular procedure when trains passed through Porton, the lights of the leading carriages not being connected to the switch in his van. A similar event occurred at Porton in August.

On Boxing Day 1927, the 12.43pm Waterloo to Salisbury train became stuck in a snowbound cutting between Overton and Oakley. The fifty passengers were rescued and accommodated overnight at Overton station, which must have been rather cramped but nevertheless welcome. Some 24 hours later, after the line had been cleared, the train left Overton for Waterloo at 3.5pm. A local service between Basingstoke and Salisbury resumed on the 28th, through trains running by way of Eastleigh until 30th, when the Longparish line also re-opened.

ACCIDENT AT ANDOVER JUNCTION 1929
On 18th November 1929 the 5.25pm Salisbury to Basingstoke goods, comprising fifty-six wagons and a heavy brake van hauled by King Arthur class 4-6-0 No.457 *Sir Bedivere*, overran signals at Andover Junction West and hit a shunting engine, driving it into cattle wagons laden with sheep from Weyhill Sheep Fair. The tender was derailed and the buffers locked, three cattle trucks and a private owner colliery wagon derailed, and one sheep killed.

LAVERSTOCK SIGNAL BOX CLOSURE 1930
On 28th April 1930 the Southern Railway Traffic Officers Committee decided to abolish Laverstock signal box, with signalling alterations. The cost was £117 but the annual savings in staff wages would be £282. The following minute records sets out the work:

'LAVERSTOCK BOX
(between Porton and Salisbury)
To be carried out on Tuesday, 16th December, commencing at 7.30am
This signal box will be abolished.
The existing up home signal, which will be operated from Tunnel Junction (Salisbury), will apply, in future, as the Laverstock up intermediate home signal.
The existing up distant signal, situate beneath the Tunnel Junction (Salisbury) up main starting signal, will apply as the distant signal for Laverstock up intermediate home signal, from which it will be situate 1,340 yards.
The existing down distant and down home signals will be abolished.'

'TUNNEL JUNCTION BOX (Salisbury)
To be carried out on Tuesday, 16th December, commencing at 7.30am.
A new down main distant signal, 25 feet high, will be provided 667 yards nearer Porton than the existing signal, which will be removed. The new distant signal will be 1,500 yards from the down main outer home signal referred to in the next paragraph.
A new down main outer home signal, 25 feet high, will be provided 450 yards in the rear of the down main home signal which will apply, in future, as the down main inner home signal.'
F.Bushrod Superintendent of Operation Southern Railway 9th December 1930

THE HURSTBOURNE AND FULLERTON LINE 1923-1934
After the grouping the Southern Railway found that passenger traffic between Hurstbourne and Fullerton continued to decline. There were just three trains daily with the first Up service running from Southampton to Whitchurch and the last

Down returning to Southampton. An A12 0-4-2 and single coach sufficed. At Longparish, although Kynock's factory had closed, Taylor's sawmills still forwarded up to thirty wagons a day. There were two coal merchants and an engineering works, together with some agricultural traffic. In April 1927 scenes for the film *The Ghost Train* were shot at and around Longparish station, with rain provided by Andover Fire Brigade.

As from 15th June 1929 some modifications were carried out to Hurstbourne Junction where the existing double track junction was replaced by a trailing crossover and a facing point from the Down main line on to the single branch. It is quite probable that the work was carried out as track renewals were required. However, on 6th July 1931 the three daily passenger trains were withdrawn and Wherwell and Longparish stations closed to passengers. These closures brought a saving to the Southern of a reported £1,389 per annum. Up and Down goods trains were still required to shunt the goods sidings and it seems likely that specials, both passenger and goods, continued to run. In 1934 Mr Gordon Howell of Andover saw the last Up goods train from the branch at Hurstbourne Junction which carried essentially a complete farm – livestock, equipment and employees of Mr Hamilton at Bransbury, between Longparish and Barton Stacey.

In June 1933 Engineer's Department drawings were produced for a new signal box at Hurstbourne station, on the Up side under the awning. If this had been implemented the old signal box could have

been closed and the station and signal box staffed only by a porter-signalman, thus saving on signalmen's wages. Such measures were implemented elsewhere, such as Newton St Cyres, but not at Hurstbourne, probably for reasons which now follow.

On 29th May 1934 Hurstbourne Junction was abolished and the track thence to just north of Longparish station taken out of use and subsequently lifted. However, at Longparish a new line was laid in to form a loop so that the locomotive of the surviving goods train from Fullerton Junction could run round its train before returning. On the main line both Hurstbourne Junction and Enham signal boxes were abolished. H.E.O. Wheeler (Superintendent of Operation) issued the following orders regarding the work to be carried out on the branch and to signalling in the area:

'HURSTBOURNE AND FULLERTON LINE

To be carried out on Tuesday 29th May (1934), commencing 9.0am.

The junction with the Hurstbourne and Fullerton line, together with the running signals to and from that line, at Hurstbourne Junction will be abolished.

The line between Fullerton and Longparish will, in future, be worked as a siding and be terminated with buffer stops at the Hurstbourne Junction side of Longparish ground frame "A".

The points at Wherwell and Longparish will continue to be released by the tablet, which will be normally kept in Fullerton box and must be carried by the Driver of a train running on this siding....

BETWEEN HURSTBOURNE AND ANDOVER JUNCTION

To be carried out on Sunday, 13th October, commencing at 6.0am.

Hurstbourne Junction and Enham signal boxes, together with the signals and points worked therefrom, will be abolished.

A new up home signal, 25 feet high, will be provided 2 miles 127 yards ahead of the existing Andover Junction East up main home advanced starting signal. The new signal will apply as Enham Intermediate up home signal and be worked from Andover Junction East box.

A new up distant signal, 19 ½ feet high, will be provided 1,052 yards in rear of the new signal referred to in the preceding paragraph and will apply as Enham Intermediate up distant signal.

A telephone will be provided at Enham Intermediate up home signal and in the event of a train being detained at this signal, Instruction No.12a, 1933, respecting the use of telephone at intermediate home signals must be observed. The telephone will also be available for use by Drivers and Guards in case of emergency, but it must e understood that in such circumstances Rule 178 must, in addition, be observed, whenever necessary.

Enham Intermediate up home signal will be specially fogsignalled.

The existing catch points in the up line, 550 yards the Andover Junction side of Enham signal box, will be moved forward 870 yards, and will be situated 700 yards in rear of Enham Intermediate up home signal.

The west end of Salisbury station on 15th September 1936. In the middle is Adams T1 class 0-4-4T No.10 on station pilot duties, to the left is the Southern shed with a Stephenson Clarke locomotive coal wagon, and to the right on the Great Western line a long rake of loaded private owner coal wagons including several of Read & Son, a Salisbury coal merchant. H.C.Casserley.

Hurstbourne viaduct on 21ˢᵗ April 1938. Urie H15 class 4-6-0 No.486 has a Down local, made up of a three coach non-corridor set, GWR van and SR van.

HURSTBOURNE STATION BOX

A new crossover road will be provided between the down and up lines, 225 yards the Andover Junction side of the signal box.

A new up distant signal, 13 feet high, will be provided 368 yards nearer Andover Junction than the existing signal, which will be removed. The new distant signal will be 1,000 yards from the up home signal referred to in the next paragraph.

A new up home signal, 25 feet high, will be provided 278 feet from the signal box.

The existing up home and up starting signals will, in future, apply as the up starting and up advanced starting signals respectively.

The structure of Hurstbourne Junction signal box was not removed, surviving into the 1950s.

ANDOVER JUNCTION EAST BOX

A new down main distant signal, 22 ½ feet high, will be provided 601 yards nearer Hurstbourne than the existing signal, which will be removed. The new distant signal will be 1,570 yards from the down main home signal referred to in the next paragraph.

A new post, 33 feet high, carrying the down main home and West box down main distant signals will be provided 347 yards farther from the signal box than the existing post, which will be removed.

The down main signal will, in future, be specially fogsignalled.

On completion of the above work down main line trains will be accepted by the Signalman at Andover Junction East box under Block Regulation 4 when the line is clear 440 yards ahead of the down main home signal.

F.Bushrod Superintendent of Operation Southern Railway 9ᵗʰ October 1934

CLOSURE OF RED POST JUNCTION 1936-7

RED POST JUNCTION BOX (ANDOVER JUNCTION)
To be carried out on Sunday, 27ᵗʰ September (1936), commencing at 12.5am

The existing up branch loop line, together with all branch line signals, will be abolished and all branch trains will, in future, work over the existing down branch loop line. Red Post Junction box will cease to be a block post for the branch line and the tablet section will, in future, be between Andover Junction West and Weyhill.

Southern Railway

RED POST JUNCTION BOX (ANDOVER JUNCTION)
To be carried out on Sunday, 4ᵗʰ April (1937), commencing at 8.0am

Red Post Junction box and all signals worked therefrom will be abolished.

New signals, which will be of the 2-aspect colour light type and 12 feet above rail level, will be provided as follows:-

Down home signal, to be known as Red Post Intermediate down home signal, situated on left hand side of down line, 2 miles 1436 yards ahead of Andover Junction West down advanced starting signal.

Down distant signal, situated on left hand side of down line, 1,180 yards in rear of Red Post Intermediate down home signal.

The new signals referred to in the preceding two paragraphs will be controlled from Andover Junction West signal box.

Up home signal, to be known as Red Post Intermediate up home signal, situated on left hand side of up line, 8 miles 114 yards ahead of Grateley up advanced starting signal.

Up distant signal, situated on left hand side of up line, 1,718 yards in rear of Red Post Intermediate up home signal.

The new signals referred to in the preceding two paragraphs will be controlled from Grateley box.
Southern Railway H.E.O.Wheeler Superintendent of Operation.

ANDOVER JUNCTION
To be carried out on Sunday, 8ᵗʰ August (1937), commencing at 12.5am.

The lines at Andover Junction Station will be renamed as follows:-

Existing	New
No.1 main road	Down main line
No.3 main road	Up through line
No.4 main road	Up local line
Swindon Branch No.1	No.1 branch line
Swindon Branch No.2	No.2 branch siding

The Signalling Instruction continued with details of changes to ground signals controlled by East Box and West Box.

It may be mentioned here that on 27ᵗʰ September 1936 the loop on the Great Western line at Red Post Junction was abolished. The junction between the Southern Railway and Great Western Railway at Red Post Junction was abolished and the signal box closed on 4ᵗʰ April 1937. These works had been opened in 1919 to

Urie H15 class 4-6-0 No.334 heads a Down local train between Andover Junction and Red Post Junction, with the MSWJR single track parallel to the double track main line. The three coach set comprises South Western wooden non-corridors re-built on longer Southern frames.

cope with the increased traffic handled during the 1914-18 war and, as we shall see, just six years later another junction had to be opened here.

MUNICH and WORLD WAR TWO 1938-1941

Just twenty years after the 1918 Armistice came the Munich Crisis of 1938. Following this, many preparations for impending war were made, including the construction of bomb-proof underground bunkers to provide railway control rooms. The Southern Divisional office controlling the main line was constructed near the entrance to Southampton tunnel and the London West office at Woking. The Southern Railway established its wartime headquarters at Deepdene near Dorking.

The Southampton Central Divisional Train and Traffic Control office played a major role both during and after the war. At the start of hostilities stations and yards where trains originated or terminated were required to telephone details of the load and times of all such trains, and certain Signalmen were required to phone in arrival, departure or passing times of all trains. On our line these apparently included Basingstoke West (for Down Salisbury line trains only), Oakley (for Up trains only), Andover Junction, Amesbury, Milford Yard, Salisbury East Yard (Up freight trains), Salisbury East and Salisbury Inspector (Up passenger trains). Grateley, Overton, Bulford and other stations, where trains terminated or originated, were also required to phone in details of load and time. Control office staff coped well with the burden of

'Operation Dynamo' (see next paragraph), and with keeping the system running despite heavy bombing damage. A full account of the work of the Exeter Central Divisional Train and Traffic Control office will appear in Volume 3.

In 1939 the pattern of the war was similar to that in 1914 with the British Army embarked to take up positions in France but in May 1940 the German Army broke through and trapped the British at Dunkirk. 335,000 soldiers were rescued by a flotilla of small ships from the Dunkirk beaches and brought to the south coast ports, particularly Dover, from where the Southern Railway conveyed them back to their bases inland in 'Operation Dynamo'. Many of these troop trains ran via Redhill (reverse), Guildford, and Woking (reverse) to run down the West of England main line to the camps at Amesbury and Bulford. Some trains ran further afield to Plymouth and from Andover Junction along the ex-MSWJR line to Ludgershall and Tidworth and from Salisbury to the GWR. From now until June 1944 all British and allied soldiers were based in camps and training grounds in Britain, in contrast to 1914-18 when most were in combat in Flanders.

In contrast with 1914-18, where most of the war was fought overseas, the Luftwaffe quickly established air bases just across the English Channel and the Battle of Britain took place in 1940, followed by a year or so of bombing of towns and cities, which included of course, the railways. The Southern in south-east England suffered to an almost unique extent. Many air bases were established in our area, particularly on

Salisbury Plain and also at Andover, Middle Wallop, Chilbolton and Boscombe Down. Construction materials for runways, hangers, control towers and airmen's quarters were brought by train to the nearest station and thence by lorry to the base, although a new siding off the Bulford branch was provided at Boscombe Down. Supplies of aviation fuel, ammunition, bombs, and all the food and equipment required also came by goods train and both civilian staff and servicemen used passenger trains.

In anticipation of the bombing of major cities such as London, Portsmouth and Southampton there was an evacuation of civilians, particularly children, to safer places. For example some Southampton schools were evacuated to Bournemouth, and other children to the north of Hampshire. Many trains carrying children evacuated from London ran down our line to the west country.

Following the Munich crisis the Bank of England built chalets on land adjacent to Portals Mill, including a 'shadow factory' for the printing of banknotes. On the outbreak of war the Bank of England transferred to Overton several of its departments employing 450 people who found accommodation locally during the week and travelled home for the weekend. However, the Southern Railway also laid on special trains between both Andover Town and Basingstoke to Overton for employees of both Portals and the Bank of England. Banknotes were printed both at London and Overton throughout the war, although the Overton Mill and works were bombed several times with some loss of life.

One bomb fell at Overton station and penetrated the ballast to a depth of eight feet, fortunately without exploding. A stick of bombs also fell in Andover, fortunately exploding in the back gardens, and missing a row of houses and the railway line.

There were significant changes to services, with a reduction of trains not essential to the war effort to provide paths and rolling stock for military trains. For example, several trains were combined into the 10.5am West of England express from Waterloo which was now made up to sixteen coaches for six destinations. Hauled by one of Bulleid's new Merchant Navy class, many of the passengers were now servicemen returning to their bases in Devon and Cornwall. From 1940 many ships were diverted away from Southampton Docks, including those bringing grain for the new Ranks Mill which were diverted to Avonmouth. New freight traffic therefore built up though Salisbury bringing grain not only to Ranks but also to the new grain silo opened at Andover.

Much of the peacetime freight traffic on our line was through traffic to and from the West of England, which became even more important in wartime. With submarines sinking merchant navy ships at an alarming rate the cattle, meat, milk, grain, vegetables and fruit conveyed was vital to feed the population. Construction materials conveyed including timber, slate, bricks, cement, sand, stone and gravel were required for essential construction and repair work. Munitions were conveyed by special train to and from many storage facilities, often with their own purpose-built sidings, such as Chilmark, Ernesettle, Whitstone further down the main line. Trains laden with bombs passed through Salisbury every day. On one occasion, with enemy planes overhead at

Salisbury, in the station was a train of forty-one ammunition wagons, a special train laden with bombs, a passenger train with almost 500 servicemen, and an ambulance train, with another thirty-five wagons of bombs in the West Yard!

WORLD WAR TWO 1942-1945
By the end of 1942 the United States had joined the war and planning for the invasion of mainland Europe began. Troops from America and the Empire began to arrive, often conveyed by fast ocean liners to distant ports on the Clyde, from where they dispersed to rapidly-built camps all over southern England. Instead of a long list of these establishments along the line, often short-lived, we note those in the Porton area which itself included Porton Down, Winterbourne Gunner, Cusse's Gorse, Winterbourne and Winterslow Road, the last three being for the American army with segregated barracks for black and white soldiers.

The railway system played a crucial role in the movement of troops, their equipment, the supply of materials and the civilian workers employed in the construction of the bases. Tanks and jeeps were loaded and unloaded regularly at many stations including Porton. Such was the number of civilian workers employed at the adjacent army base that the Southern Railway constructed Idmiston Halt. It opened on 4th January 1943, with the existing service bolstered with a special workmen's train between Salisbury and Grateley.

Various other works were carried out at this time on our line. For example. In 1942 there were extensions to Salisbury East Yard and to the ex-MSWJR sidings at Andover Junction. In 1943 a new Grain Silo Siding was installed at Andover and a new Junction

was constructed at Red Post Junction together with doubling of the ex-MSWJR line to Weyhill. In 1944 more work was done at Salisbury East Yard and after the war most of these works were inspected by the Board of Trade, the reports being given later in this chapter.

Much of the traffic on the Amesbury line was similar to that carried in the 1914-18 war, although the Larkhill Military Railway had been closed. Near the site of Allington signal box, closed in 1933, a new siding was laid in for the Air Ministry on the Down side in January 1944. This was used to bring in construction materials for new works at Boscombe Down Aerodrome.

On the Salisbury to Eastleigh line the Admiralty Sidings, serving munitions stores at Dean Hill, were opened in 1940 and Lockerley Sidings for the United States Supply Depot followed in 1943. Traffic for both this route, and the Andover & Redbridge line, converged at Kimbridge Junction where the two long Awbridge goods loops in each direction were opened, again in 1943.

In 1942 the RAF established an extensive ammunition depot in huts in Harewood Forest, where bombs and ammunition were brought for storage before use. In November 1942 a RAF siding, new run-round loop and overhead crane were constructed at Longparish station, although now it was connected only indirectly to our line via Andover Junction and Fullerton Junction, where an extra siding was also constructed. By the end of 1943 600 wagons of bombs were arriving here by train every month, in April 1944 1,200 wagons and by D-Day in June 1944 some 6,000 wagon loads were stored here. It would appear that most of these munitions came in trainloads either from Basingstoke or from the ex-MSWJR

H15 class 4-6-0 No.473 on Hurstbourne viaduct, 27th July 1938, heading a Down local train which comprises a three coach non-corridor set (similar to that on page 185), a gas tank wagon and an insulated van.

Hurstbourne viaduct on 27th July 1938 again. Adams A12 class 'Jubilee' No.598 leaves the station with a Down pick-up goods from Basingstoke to Andover or Bulford. The four opens in front of the brake van are all private owner wagons.

line to Andover Junction, and thence to Fullerton Junction and Longparish, with four trains a day on the branch. Munitions from the depot went by road to local RAF bases or was forwarded by train. Nearby was Barton Stacy Camp and just after the war this was used to accommodate American troops prior to demobilisation. The troops were conveyed by special trains from Southampton, and other ports, to Longparish station with as many as fourteen troop trains reported on one day. These were in addition to trains at the Great Western's Sutton Scotney station on the ex-DN&SR line.

Some of these works seem limited in comparison with those on the Great Western's Didcot, Newbury and Southampton line where passenger services were suspended for seven months while major improvements were made. Like the MSWJR this branch provided an important link from the Midlands to Southampton and served a number of army camps, including Barton Stacey near Sutton Scotney station.

After two years of planning *OVERLORD*, the D-Day invasion, began in June 1944 with troops and their equipment conveyed to the south coast, mainly by train. Railway traffic throughout 1944 was unprecedented during both the build-up to D-Day and the subsequent massive re-enforcement of the invading armies. During peacetime Salisbury East Yard handled about 560 wagons a day, as the war went on this rose to 1,000, and just before D-Day had risen to 1,200 wagons a day.

After the invasion there were ambulance trains from the south coast ports to inland field hospitals, many of them routed along the ex-MSWJR line. Soon, prisoners of war arrived to be accommodated in camps. After the American army had left Cusse's Gorse camp near Porton it was used for Italian POWs until the end of hostilities.

Following the end of the War in 1945 the whole operation went into reverse, with troops returning to their bases by train for demobilisation for the British and a ship home for those from the United States and the Empire. Col.Trench reported no less than 108 trains destined for Southampton Docks in 48 hours passing Red Post Junction, all carrying American troops on their way home, mainly from the Weyhill direction.

The extra traffic for the war was dealt with by railwaymen of all types who often worked far longer hours than normal. This was not without personal danger, with a number of railwaymen killed by enemy action while on duty, although no record has yet come to light on our section of line.

As mentioned earlier, the Board of Trade carried out inspections of wartime work after hostilities ended in 1945. Here is a brief resume of their work.

ANDOVER GRAIN SILO SIDING 1943

This siding was brought into use on 28th January 1943 the inspection being delayed until 11th October 1945, A.C.Trench reported to the Ministry of War Transport: *I made an inspection on 10th October, 1945, of the new works immediately west of Andover Junction on the Western Main Line of the Southern Railway. A siding has been constructed trailing in the Down Line, to serve a Silo belonging to the Ministry of Food.*

'The siding connection is in 95lb. material and is suitably trapped; it is operated by a new two-lever ground frame which is electrically released by lever No.2 in Andover Junction West Signal Box.

'There is a public footpath crossing in the immediate vicinity of this siding connection but the user is not affected in any way by the provision of the siding.

'I tested the additional and altered locking in Andover West Box and found it

correct. I was informed that the siding was used daily, occasionally more than once a day, for traffic of about 12 wagons a day, most of which came either from Avonmouth via the Great Western, or from Salisbury, and in either case it was worked by an ordinary goods train from Andover Junction, often the daily Basingstoke to Bulford goods train.

'The works are complete and in good order, and I recommend approval being given thereto.'

RED POST JUNCTION 1943

The level of wartime traffic passing over the Great Western ex-MSWJR single track from Weyhill to Andover Junction was such that only six years after Red Post Junction was abolished another was opened as of 5th September 1943. The Great Western line thence to Weyhill was doubled at the same time. The Instruction below details the work:

'SOUTHERN RAILWAY SIGNAL INSTRUCTION No.25 1943
RED POST JUNCTION
(between Andover Junction and Grateley)
To be carried out on Sunday 5th September, commencing at 8.0am
A new signal box, to be known as "Red Post Junction" communicating electrically with Andover Junction West, Grateley, and Weyhill (GWR) signal boxes, provided outside the new up branch line referred to in the next paragraph, will be brought into use. The new signal box will be 1 mile 383 yards from Andover Junction West, 5 miles 21 yards from Grateley and 2 miles 195 yards from Weyhill (GWR) signal boxes.

'A new up branch line will be provided alongside the existing branch single line between Weyhill (GWR) and Red Post Junction. The existing branch single line between these points will, in future, be known as the down branch line. The down and up branch lines will connect with the down and

up main lines respectively at Red Post Junction and be controlled from the new signal box. The existing single line between Red Post Junction and Andover Junction West will remain and connect with the down and up branch lines at Red Post Junction.

'The tablet instruments will be transferred from Weyhill (GWR) signal box to Red Post Junction signal box, the section for single line trains then being Red Post Junction – Andover Junction West. The tablets for branch trains will be delivered to and received from Drivers by the signalmen at Red Post Junction signal box.

'The following are particulars of the points and signals which will be operated from the new signal box:-

Facing points in up branch line leading to up main line, 181 yards Andover Junction side of signal box.

Facing points in down main line leading to down branch line, 277 yards Andover Junction side of signal box.

Points (trailing for up trains) in the branch single line leading from up branch line, 277 yards Andover Junction side of signal box.

Down main distant signal beneath Andover Junction West down main starting signal, 1,320 yards from down home signals referred to in next paragraph.

Down main home and down main to down branch home signals on bracket post, 22 ½ feet high, situated on left hand side of down main line, 296 yards from signal box.

Down main starting signal 12 feet high, on left hand side of down main line, 329 yards from signal box.

Existing Red Post intermediate down home and distant colour light signals, operated from Andover junction West signal box, will, in future, be operated from Red post Junction signal box and re-named Monxton Intermediate down home and distant signals; they will be 1 mile 1,246 yards and 1 mile 66 yards, respectively,

ahead of down main starting signal referred to in preceding paragraph.

Down branch distant, 15 feet high, on right hand side of branch single line 980 yards from down branch home signal mentioned in next paragraph.

Down branch home signal, 15 feet high, on right hand side of branch single line, 809 yards from signal box.

Down branch starting signal, 15 feet high, on left hand side of down branch line, 329 yards from signal box.

Up main distant signal, 15 feet high, on left hand side of up main line, 1,188 yards from up main home signal referred to in next paragraph.

Up main home signal, 20 feet high, on left hand side of up main line, 25 yards from signal box.

Up main starting signal, 30 feet high, above Andover Junction East and West up main distant signal, 685 yards from signal box.

Up branch distant signal, 12 feet high, on left hand side of up branch line, 1,000 yards from up branch home signals referred to in next paragraph.

Up branch home and up branch to up main home signals on bracket post, 25 feet high, situated on left hand side of up branch line, 10 yards from signal box.'

On 12th October 1945 A.C.Trench reported to the Ministry of War Transport: 'I made an inspection on 10th October, 1945, of the Southern Railway portion of the new works at Red Posts Junction, where the Great Western line from Cheltenham and Weyhill joins the Main Line of the Southern Railway between Salisbury and Andover.

'Prior to the war, the line from Weyhill was single, and was continued as a single line alongside the Southern Main Line from Red Posts Junction to Andover Junction Yard. In view of the heavy military traffic anticipated from Salisbury Plain and this

GW Line in general towards the Southampton direction, it was decided in 1942 that, among the preparations for "D" Day, the Line should be doubled from Weyhill as far as Red Posts Junction, and that this line should be continued, over a flat double line junction, on to Up and Down Lines of the Southern Railway at Red Posts, the existing single line to Andover Junction being retained.

'I was informed that not only had these additional connections and doubling proved to be of the greatest value in connection with the "D" Day invasion traffic, but also they were still being very heavily used for American troop trains from Salisbury Plain to Southampton Docks, two of which passed while I was on the spot. Recently they had 106 Troop specials into Southampton Docks in 48 hours, mostly from the Weyhill direction.

'The additional track from the point of junction of maintenance with the Great Western is on the north side of the former single line and consists of 95lb. American rails in 39ft lengths; vibrated concrete sleepers have been used for a considerable portion of the length, on Mendip ballast. The concrete sleepers appeared to be standing up well though speeds are of course low in view of the proximity of the junction. The Works generally are in accordance with the drawings submitted. A new Signal Box has been constructed with a frame of 22 levers of which three are spare; at present this Box is always open. Preece-3 wire block is in operation on the Southern main line with 3 position block to the G.W. branch and Tyers tablet over the Single Line to Andover. I tested the majority of the locking and found it correct. All necessary lights and arms are repeated, and the track circuits are indicated in the Box. The signalman expressed his satisfaction with the arrangements. This box now controls the colour light intermediate section signals on the down line between

On 21st July 1938 King Arthur class 4-6-0 No.773 *Sir Lavaine* of Nine Elms shed speeds non-stop towards Salisbury with the 10.35am from Waterloo *Atlantic Coast Express* through open countryside east of Andover Junction station, with the tower of St Mary's church Andover behind the train. Many of these fields have subsequently been built on.

At Bulford during the 1930s Adams T1 class 0-4-4T No.69, and two South Western coaches form a local train to Salisbury. They will join the main line at Amesbury Junction and then call at Porton.

Red Posts and Grateley, formerly controlled by Andover Junction West box.

'I was informed that the normal arrangements for traffic at present are that trains terminating at or originating from Andover use the single line between there and Red Posts Junction, whereas trains for destinations beyond, largely down the Test Valley Line to Southampton are passed over the new crossovers to the Southern Main Line at Red Posts Junction.

'The Works are complete and in good order and I recommend approval to them in so far as the Southern Railway portion of the work is concerned. I did not make an inspection of the Great Western portion of the work i.e. the doubling between Red Posts Junction and Weyhill.'

ACCIDENT AT ANDOVER JUNCTION 1943

At Andover Junction, about 2.30am on the morning of Saturday 27th November 1943, there was a collision between two trains on the up through line near the West signal box. Halted in the station was a passenger train used for conveying troops, fortunately empty. A fast West of England goods train ran into the back of the troop train, damaging two coaches and injuring its guard, Mr E.Wakeley of Basingstoke, who required hospital treatment.

Several of the wagons of the goods train were telescoped and thrown against the signal box blocking the stairs, so that entry and exit had to be by ladder. The smashed goods trucks were laden with empty boxes and other receptacles which were littered over the tracks. Both Up and Down lines were blocked. The station master, Mr

Hayward and his staff did their best to start the clear up, but steam cranes were sent to lift the heavy wreckage, the Down line being opened by 9.0am next day and the Up line by about 12.30pm.

This was the third such accident at Andover Junction involving the overnight Up West of England goods, as we have seen in Chapter Four the previous accidents being in 1914 and 1916.

NEW WORKS AT SALISBURY 1942-1944

A.C.Trench, on behalf of the Ministry of Transport, made an inspection and reported on 11th July 1947: *'...I made an inspection on July 8th, 1947, of the new works in Salisbury East Yard on the Southern Railway. In order to deal with additional wartime traffic, the existing sidings on the up side of the East yard were lengthened and 5 additional dead end sidings, together with a shunting neck were provided and brought into use in August, 1942, certain other facilities being added later in 1942 and in July, 1944, all as M.W.T.(Ministry of War Transport) works.*

'Exit from the sidings is via an existing trailing connection in the Up Main Line, the inner end of which has been slightly altered to suit the new layout. This connection is controlled by the existing ground frame, release of which is controlled by the Salisbury East box.

'The actual connection in the running line is unaltered as is substantially the ground frame control thereof.

'I was informed that the daily use of the East Yard rose to a peak of about 1100 wagons in 1944-5, and is now about 800,

and that the company are likely to wish to retain these wartime facilities permanently. The works are complete and in good order and I recommend that approval be given thereto.'

INSPECTION OF OTHER WARTIME WORKS

In 1945 A.C.Trench, on behalf of the Ministry of War Transport, made other inspections of wartime works on adjacent lines. These details are included here as some of this traffic ran on to our line.

On 11th October he reported on new works between Newton Tony and Amesbury on the Bulford branch: *'A new connection was provided for the Air Ministry for material trains for the construction of a large runway at Boscombe Down Aerodrome. When the runway was under construction as many as 12 trains a day had been working in the siding at this point.'*

On 12th October he reported on new works at Fullerton on the Andover to Southampton line: *'Siding accommodation had been provided for the Air Ministry in connection with traffic for an ammunition depot in the vicinity, and another connection to the Longparish goods branch. This had been used two or three times a day, and the siding used for the general working of munitions and other traffic.'*

On 15th October he reported on new works including extra sidings at Basingstoke in connection with additional traffic to be handled at Southampton Docks: *'The entrance to these up sidings from the Up Local line was controlled from Worting Box, the points being motor-operated by hand-generator.'*

CHAPTER SIX
THE EARLY BRITISH RAILWAYS PERIOD 1948-1964

NATIONALISATION 1948

Under the terms of the 1947 Transport Act British Railways came into existence on 1st January 1948 with high hopes for a new era for the railways which had served the nation so well during the war. On 2nd April 1950 there was an exchange of territory between the Southern and Western regions, with the Southern taking over the lines to the south of the Western Region, West of England main line and the Western taking over all the lines west of Exeter. Train services and rolling stock continued as before but civil engineering and signalling & telegraph staff came under new management with some changes in working methods and equipment. However, a complicated to-ing and fro-ing took place with boundaries yet again and from 1st February 1958 most of these earlier changes were reversed. The exception was that the Western Region retained control of

all lines in the Plymouth area, until 1963, when the Western Region acquired all the Southern routes west of Wilton!

During the 1940s and 1950s servicemen from the many army and air force bases in the area used the trains for their weekend leave, often outnumbering civilian passengers. Transport from the bases was rather Spartan and was usually in the back of an army truck, particularly to Andover and Salisbury stations however, sometimes Friday relief trains were provided from Salisbury to Waterloo. Royal Navy sailors travelling between Portsmouth and Devonport also often changed trains at Salisbury.

DIVISIONAL MANAGEMENT CHANGES

During the 1940s there had been several transfers of territory from the London West

Division, with offices at Woking, to the Southern Division. On 1st January 1948 there was a significant transfer of territory when the line from Worting Junction to the boundary with the Western Division, just west of Salisbury, was transferred from the Southern Division at Southampton to the London West Division at Woking. Also transferred were the lines from Salisbury to Milford, Andover Junction to Andover Town (all inclusive), and the Bulford branch. Thus the management of our line now came from the offices at Woking, not Southampton.

One aspect of the change was that Signalmen, Inspectors and others who had previously reported the arrival, departure or passing times of trains to the Southampton Central Control office now reported to London West Control at Woking. However, Andover Junction, Andover Town, Salisbury and Milford staff were still required to report to Southampton Central on trains to and from the Southern Division!

During the 1948-1964 period the Southern Region continued many of the policies of the Southern Railway so successfully implemented by Sir Herbert Walker. In particular the Southern saw its future with enhanced regular interval passenger services running on electrified main lines, continuing the investment interrupted by the war. Much of the first tranche of funding from the 1955 Modernisation Plan was invested in the infrastructure and rolling stock for the Kent Coast electrification together with the 'Hastings' and 'Hampshire' diesel electric multiple units. Electrification included full track renewal, which required several train loads daily of ballast from the Southern Region's Meldon Quarry. These ran 200

Top left. **Hurstbourne viaduct from the north in January 1951 during repair work, with an Up local freight train, possibly the afternoon service from Amesbury to Basingstoke. Contractors have tipped excavated materials down the embankment. In the foreground are the extensive watercress beds which provided much traffic for the railway, today conveyed by Vitacress's own lorries. Reg Randell Collection.**

Left. **Hurstbourne viaduct during repair work in January 1951 with an Up goods train hauled by a Drummond 4-4-0. All traffic uses the Up line whilst work is in progress on the Down side, with strengthening girders already in place. The narrow gauge contractors track and skip wagons can be seen. Reg Randell Collection.**

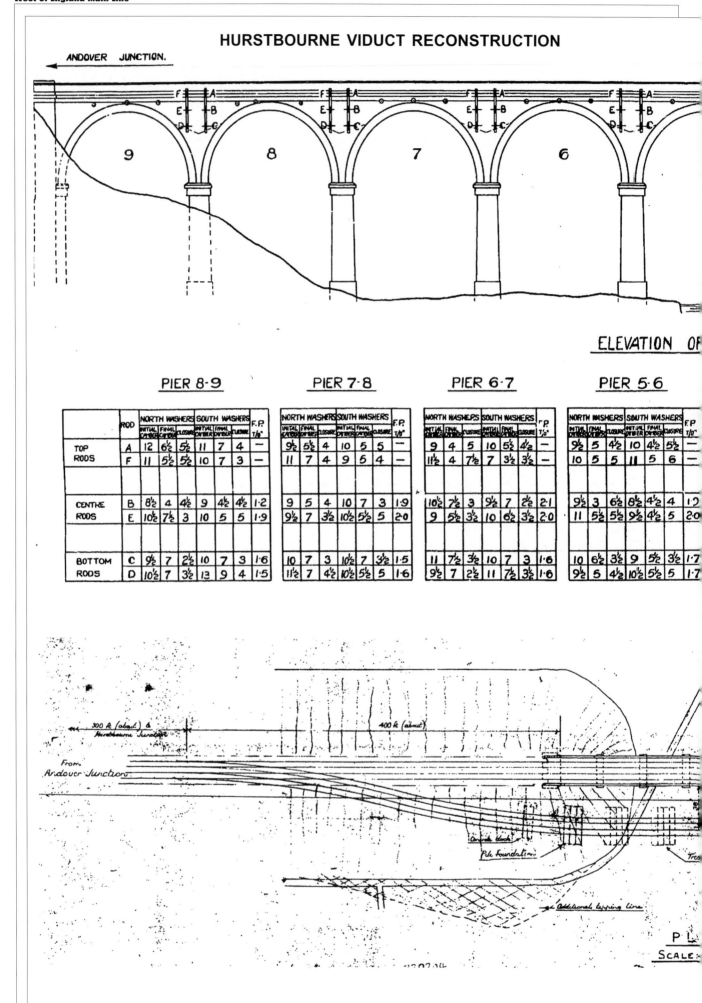

HURSTBOURNE VIADUCT RECONSTRUCTION

ANDOVER JUNCTION.

ELEVATION OF

PIER 8·9

	ROD	NORTH WASHERS			SOUTH WASHERS			F.P T/8"
		INITIAL CAMBER	FINAL CAMBER	CLOSURE	INITIAL CAMBER	FINAL CAMBER	CLOSURE	
TOP RODS	A	12	6½	5½	11	7	4	—
	F	11	5½	5½	10	7	3	—
CENTRE RODS	B	8½	4	4½	9	4½	4½	1·2
	E	10½	7½	3	10	5	5	1·9
BOTTOM RODS	C	9½	7	2½	10	7	3	1·6
	D	10½	7	3½	13	9	4	1·5

PIER 7·8

	ROD	NORTH WASHERS			SOUTH WASHERS			F.P T/8"
		INITIAL CAMBER	FINAL CAMBER	CLOSURE	INITIAL CAMBER	FINAL CAMBER	CLOSURE	
TOP RODS	A	9½	5½	4	10	5	5	—
	F	11	7	4	9	5	4	—
CENTRE RODS	B	9	5	4	10	7	3	1·9
	E	9½	7	3½	10½	5½	5	2·0
BOTTOM RODS	C	10	7	3	10½	7	3½	1·5
	D	11½	7	4½	10½	5½	5	1·6

PIER 6·7

	ROD	NORTH WASHERS			SOUTH WASHERS			F.P T/8"
		INITIAL CAMBER	FINAL CAMBER	CLOSURE	INITIAL CAMBER	FINAL CAMBER	CLOSURE	
TOP RODS	A	9	4	5	10	5½	4½	—
	F	11½	4	7½	7	3½	3½	—
CENTRE RODS	B	10½	7½	3	9½	7	2½	2·1
	E	9	5½	3½	10	6½	3½	2·0
BOTTOM RODS	C	11	7½	3½	10	7	3	1·6
	D	9½	7	2½	11	7½	3½	1·6

PIER 5·6

	ROD	NORTH WASHERS			SOUTH WASHERS			F.P T/8"
		INITIAL CAMBER	FINAL CAMBER	CLOSURE	INITIAL CAMBER	FINAL CAMBER	CLOSURE	
TOP RODS	A	9½	5	4½	10	4½	5½	—
	F	10	5	5	11	5	6	—
CENTRE RODS	B	9½	3	6½	8½	4½	4	1·2
	E	11	5½	5½	9½	4½	5	2·0
BOTTOM RODS	C	10	6½	3½	9	5½	3½	1·7
	D	9½	5	4½	10½	5½	5	1·7

300 ft (about) to Hurstbourne Junction

400 ft (about)

From Andover Junction

Concrete block

Pile Foundation

Trestle

Additional tipping line

PLAN

SCALE

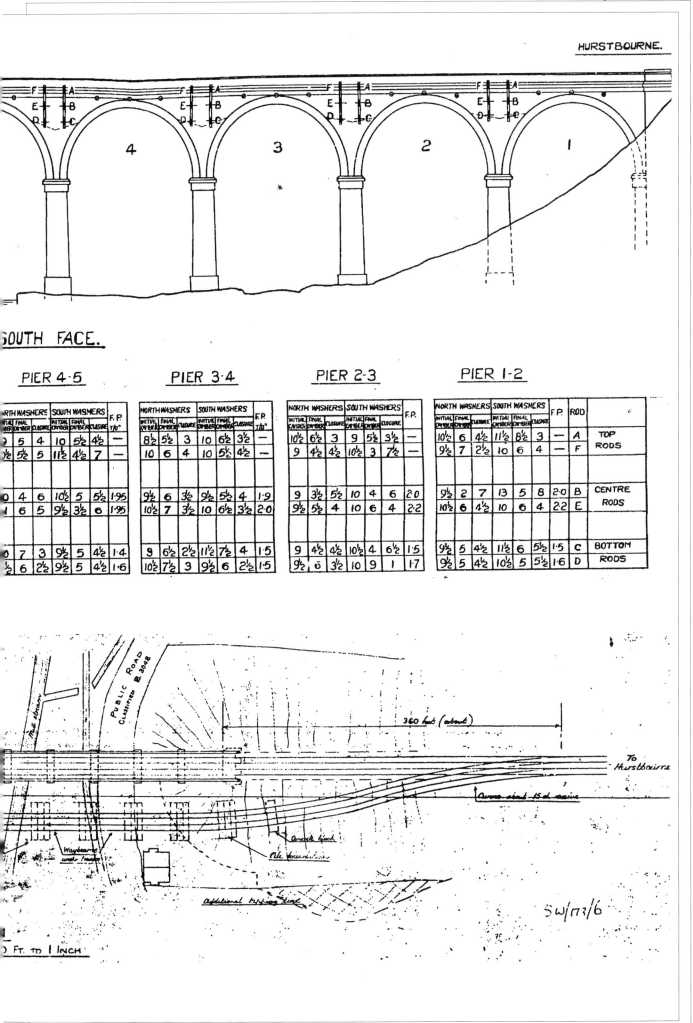

Left. Hurstbourne viaduct in January 1951. At this stage the Down line is used for all traffic, and concrete re-inforced with steel mesh has been laid on the Up side. Buildings in the station yard can be seen in the distance. Reg Randell Collection.

Middle left. For viaduct repairs in January 1951 there was single line working between Hurstbourne station and the site of Hurstbourne Junction. Here is a view from overbridge No.175 near Chapmansford Farm to the east at the temporary connection between the double and single tracks, crossed by the Up Atlantic Coast Express. Clearly visible is the old Hurstbourne Junction signal box, opened in 1885 for the Fullerton line to the right and closed in 1934 with the branch. Temporary points and signals here in 1951 would have been controlled from Hurstbourne station signal box, open 24 hours a day with relief men assisting the regular signalmen. Reg Randell Collection.

Bottom left. The last public passenger train on the branch was the 2.10pm from Bulford to Salisbury, two coaches hauled by 700 class 0-6-0 No.30317 seen here leaving the extensive Amesbury station. Peter Swift Collection.

miles up the West of England main line on 'Q', or 'when required' timetable paths.

On completion of the Kent Coast Phase Two in 1961 most of the Southern main lines had been electrified, the principal exceptions being the steam-worked Weymouth and West of England main lines west of Sturt Lane Junction near Farnborough. At its well organised publicity events, the Southern Region made it clear that they expected to electrify both these main lines as far as Weymouth and Exeter. For example in June 1960 there were celebrations of the centenary of Exeter Central station. But during the early 1960s the Waterloo to Weymouth and West of England main lines gained a reputation for excellent steam hauled services, particularly expresses such as the 'Atlantic Coast Express' hauled by Merchant Navy class Pacifics.

OTHER DEVELOPMENTS

One of the first trials of main line diesel locomotives took place on the line on 29th October 1951 when Bulleid-designed No.10202 started working two return trips between Waterloo and Exeter, 687 miles per day. After display at the South Bank exhibition, No.10201 joined it on more trials from February 1952. In March 1953 Ivatt-designed Nos.10000 and 10001 arrived from the LMR; the quartet worked four diagrams, three of which involved daily round trips between Waterloo and Weymouth, and Waterloo and Exeter. In 1954 they were joined by 10203 but in 1955 all were transferred to the West Coast main line and did not return.

After 100 years of use, by 1951 Hurstbourne viaduct was found to be in

Few photographs of Beattie locomotives on our line have yet come to light, and this is certainly unusual. On Saturday 14th May 1955 the Railway Enthusiasts Club ran a special three coach train to Bulford hauled by Beattie 2-4-0 well tank No.30587 brought up from Wadebridge. At Grateley station the special train waits in the up side sidings whilst early diesel electric No.10203 passes with the 1.0pm from Exeter to Waterloo. This and other early diesels were transferred away later that year. R.C.Riley courtesy the Transport Treasury.

need of heavy repairs. A number of surviving drawings illustrate possible remedial action including a replacement viaduct parallel to the original, and strengthening with steel girders underneath the nine arches. The method chosen was to excavate underneath the track down to the arches which were then strengthened with concrete, with single line working to enable work on one side at a time. A contractor laid a narrow gauge track to move materials.

On the afternoon of 6th January 1959 there was a serious slip near the railway cottages at Porton when several hundred tons of waterlogged chalk and soil suddenly slid down the embankment and blocked both lines. The 5.15pm Salisbury to Waterloo train was on its way but a serious accident was avoided by the chance presence of the

ganger Cecil Chandlers. Knowing the train was due, he managed to warn the signalman who was able to stop the train. The Down track was cleared fairly quickly but it took a train of ballast wagons to clear the line completely, the men working overnight with the aid of Tilley lamps, a task completed on 8th January at 6.45am.

THE HAMPSHIRE DIESEL MULTIPLE UNITS

One of the first manifestations of the British Railways 1955 Modernisation Plan to be seen in the Hampshire area was the introduction of new diesel multiple unit trains. In autumn 1957 they took over many of the passenger services previously hauled by older South Western locomotives including M7s and T9s, including services

from Portsmouth and Southampton to both Andover and Salisbury. Eighteen new two coach multiple units took over the duties of twenty steam locomotives and forty-two coaches, with train mileage doubled to provide more frequent services to an almost 'clock-face' timetable. With the 500hp diesel engines mounted in a compartment behind the driver's cab the distinctive throaty roar of the new trains could be heard sometimes a mile away. There were technical problems but the new services saw an overall 50% increase in passengers. A third coach was added and new 600hp engines installed, and four more units were acquired for extension of services from Southampton to Basingstoke and Reading.

By 1964 Hampshire units departed Andover Junction and Salisbury at 55 and 42 minutes past the hour respectively for Portsmouth via Southampton, and Basingstoke at 17 and about 23 minutes past the hour for Reading and Southampton respectively. Since no units were berthed overnight at Andover Junction the first Up train from Salisbury ran to Andover Junction and thence Portsmouth. There were some exceptions to this basically 'clock-face' pattern, which also resulted in better connections; at both Andover Junction and Salisbury a Hampshire unit was often berthed in the bay platforms awaiting departure.

CLOSURES UP TO 1964
The Contracting Railway

As we have already seen in Chapter Five the Southern Railway had decided that losses on the Whitchurch to Fullerton service were unacceptable and closed the line above Longparish in 1934. A number of other loss-making lines, including the Basingstoke & Alton and Lynton & Barnstaple, were also closed in the 1930s. From 1948 Southern

Red Post Junction signal box of 1943 was still in use in the early 1960s to control main line signals only, the MSWJR having been reduced to a single line only. The junction and its signals were abolished in 1960. Rod Hoyle.

Region managers continued to keep a careful eye on loss-making lines and stations. The main issue was that local road transport became more competitive for both passenger and freight traffic. Local bus services had the flexibility to serve the centres of towns and villages, while many stations were inconveniently sited. Buses ran at times convenient for local travel, while such flexibility was much more difficult for the railway. The workmen's train service between Salisbury and Idmiston had run to basically the same schedule since 1943. However, in the late 1950s, when their hours of work at the army base at Porton Down were changed, the train times did not. So, an alternative bus service was provided and the train service taken off. Sometimes railway routes were too indirect, such as that between Amesbury and Salisbury six miles by road compared with thirteen miles by rail. The abolition of wartime petrol rationing heralded an increase in the use of private cars for those who could afford them.

For ten years after the 1939-1945 war the railways carried large volumes of freight but the 1955 ASLEF strike and deregulation of road transport resulted in a transfer of freight from rail to road. The first casualties were the small goods yards at country stations where customers were served by lorry from the nearest large goods yard, although many customers continued to operate from the same premises.

Rationalisation at Salisbury
As we have seen in Chapter Five the rationalisation of railway facilities at Salisbury began as early as 1932 when the Great Western Railway closed its own passenger station and all its passenger trains used the Southern Railway station. Shortly after nationalisation the Western Region engine sheds at both Basingstoke and Salisbury were closed in November 1950 and all their locomotives and staff transferred to the Southern Region sheds close by. At Salisbury the WR turntable was

retained until 1958, when the whole site was redeveloped as a combined stationery store. As part of the regional boundary changes of 2nd April 1950, the Western Region line from Salisbury to Dilton Marsh Halt, just outside Westbury, was transferred to the Southern Region which from then on had complete responsibility for Salisbury.

The Longparish Branch
Although connected only indirectly to our line, after the war the RAF munitions depot in Harewood Forest, served by Longparish station, received ammunition from other similar depots as they were closed down. Eventually this ammunition was sold and transported by rail to ports for export and the long, painstaking, task of clearing the site began. RAF depot traffic eventually ended in 1955. The remaining public goods service, by then running three days a week for coal traffic, ended on 28th May 1956. In 1957 the line was used for testing the new 'Hampshire' diesel multiple units, and for driver training on them. Subsequently the line was used to store condemned rolling stock before scrapping, until it was taken out of use in 1960 and lifted, apart from a short siding section at Fullerton.

The Amesbury and Bulford Branch
As we have seen in Chapter Four the Amesbury and Bulford branch had been built in the early 1900s to serve the needs of the War Office, to transport men and equipment to and from the bases on Salisbury Plain. The branch was opened from Grateley, the direct curve from Salisbury being opened later as an afterthought, with Amesbury station being more than a mile from the town centre. The passenger train service from Bulford and Amesbury to Salisbury was indirect, via Newton Tony. This was almost twice the distance of the more convenient bus service which inevitably led to the demise of the rail passenger traffic, dwindling to such an extent that a 700 class 0-6-0, pulling a single coach, sufficed for the branch service. It was

withdrawn on 30th June 1952, which also reduced the service at Idmiston and Porton. On the 10th October 1954 the double track curve from Newton Tony Junction to Amesbury Junction was closed completely. Amesbury Junction signal box remained as a block post on the main line but was re-named Allington on 25th September 1955.

The branch from Grateley remained open for freight and military traffic. The double track section between Newton Tony and Amesbury was singled in 1953 and from 1954 two daily freight trains were ran, one direct from Basingstoke, the other from Salisbury, after reversal at Grateley. There was considerable activity on the branch when army reservists arrived by train during mobilisation for the Suez crisis in 1956. Before the Grateley to Bulford branch was completely closed, on 4th March 1963, it was traversed by several railtours, your co-author travelling in a push-pull set hauled by an M7 class 0-4-4T.

The Midland and South Western Junction Line
The changes in regional boundaries of 2nd April 1950 resulted in the transfer of the MSWJR line, between Red Post Junction and Grafton, from the Western Region to the Southern. At Andover Junction the Western Region engine shed and staff came under the Southern Region next door. Although there had been investment in the line to carry heavy wartime traffic, post-war traffic declined and its division between two regions did not help matters. Public passenger train services on the Tidworth branch were withdrawn on 19th September 1955 and the branch subsequently worked by the War Department.

As part of widespread economies in the late 1950s the passenger service was reduced to one train daily each way between Andover and Cheltenham and a handful between Andover and Swindon the Western Region having regained control at this very late stage. Red Post Junction was taken out of use on 28th August 1960, when the line to Weyhill was singled, thus taking out of use all the 1943 enhancements. The MSWJR line now reverted to a single track from Andover Junction to Weyhill, but Red Post Junction signal box remained open as a block post controlling signals on the main line only, all points having been taken out of use.

The MSWJR passenger service was completely withdrawn on 9th September 1961 and most of the line completely closed. However, the line from Andover Junction to Ludgershall was retained for freight and military traffic and essentially worked as a siding from Andover Junction.

The Test Valley Line
Between Andover Town and Romsey the Test Valley line served a number of pretty riverside villages. Local traffic was light, though it included children travelling to Andover Grammar school, for which the Town station was convenient. Much of the passenger and freight traffic up to the early-1950s was

A 'Hampshire' diesel multiple unit waits in the bay at Andover Junction, to make a connection with the down train approaching in the distance. R.M.Casserley.

CLOSURES

Signal Box or Junction	Goods Yard or siding	Passenger station or branch	Closure date
		Amesbury branch	30th June 1952
Amesbury Junction -signal box retained			10th October 1954
Red Post Junction -signal box retained			28th August 1960
		MSWJR line	9th September 1961
	Porton		10th September 1962
	Andover Grain Silo		17th September 1962
	Amesbury branch		4th March 1963
	Grateley		10th June 1963
		Oakley	17th June 1963
Red Post Junction			1st September 1963
	Oakley & Hurstbourne		25th November 1963
Allington, formerly Amesbury Junction			20th January 1964
		Hurstbourne	6th April 1964
Hurstbourne			15th June 1964
	Market House branch		27th July 1964
		Test Valley line	7th September 1964

conveyed on through trains between Southampton, the MSWJ line and beyond, together with some freight on the Longparish branch. By the winter of 1954-55, of eight Test Valley passenger trains arriving at Andover Junction, only two proceeded further to the MSWJR line. As we saw in Chapter Two traffic on the Andover and Redbridge line, from its opening in 1865, was very limited until the MSWJR line opened. Apart from Andover Town the intermediate goods yards were closed in the early 1960s, leaving only the hourly 'Hampshire' diesel multiple unit passenger service on the line. As with the Winchester to Alton line (currently home to the Mid Hants Railway) this was seen as insufficient to justify retention of the line. Thus the passenger service was withdrawn on 7th September 1964, the line closing completely between Kimbridge Junction and Andover Town. The goods station at Andover Town remained open with several traders having their premises here, served by a transfer goods from Andover Junction, until it was closed on 18th September 1967. Thereafter Andover goods facilities were provided at the Junction. The tracks to Kimbridge Junction lay out of use until 1967 when demolition began; it was completed by November 1969.

As a postscript it may be added that in 2001 Wessex Trains inaugurated a service of five daily trains between Swindon and Southampton, running indirectly via Melksham, Trowbridge and Salisbury. A more direct and faster service between the two could have begun in 1957 with the 'Hampshire' diesel multiple units running via the Test Valley and MSWJR lines serving not only the expanding modern towns of Swindon and Andover but also Marlborough and Ludgershall.

Main Line Signal Box, Goods Yard and Station Closures 1948-1964
As can be seen from the table the Southern Region's programme of closure of small goods yards, intermediate signal boxes and less busy stations started in the early 1960s, before the Beeching Report. By the end of 1964 passenger services had been withdrawn from three branches and two main line stations and goods services from two branches, one private siding and four main line station goods yards. But just three signal boxes had been closed.

It may be added here that Whitchurch North became the town's only station when the passenger service between Newbury and Southampton was withdrawn on 7th March 1960, Whitchurch South goods yard closing in 1963, with through goods services lasting until 9th August 1964. All services between Salisbury and Bournemouth via Fordingbridge were withdrawn on 4th May 1964.

THE BEECHING REPORT 1963
The British Railways 1955 Modernisation Plan had proved to be expensive but following a trade recession was only partly implemented. Furthermore many classes of diesel locomotives had been purchased but found to be unsatisfactory in traffic, and road transport was taking over much traffic from the railways. Politicians and civil service mandarins decided that the increasing financial losses of the railways were unacceptable, that the future lay in road transport, and that as many railways as possible should be shut. To carry out the task Dr Richard Beeching came from ICI to become the new Chairman of British Railways and in March 1963 he published his recommendations, *The Reshaping of British Railways*, popularly known as the Beeching Report. This recommended the development of freight and fast passenger services on the main lines, concentrating on the profitable bulk flows of traffic and the closure of many unprofitable stations and branch lines.

A supporting set of maps showed that from Basingstoke to Exeter there was a healthy level of both passenger and freight traffic on the West of England main line, but the same was not true of the branches. Annual passenger traffic receipts at Basingstoke, Andover Junction and Salisbury were in excess of £25,000, at Overton, Whitchurch and Andover Town between £5,000 and £25,000 and at Oakley, Hurstbourne, Grateley, Idmiston and Porton less than £5,000. Annual freight tonnage at Basingstoke and Salisbury was in excess of 25,000 tons, at Andover Junction, Andover Town, Amesbury and Bulford between 5,000 and 25,000 tons and all other station less than 5,000 tons.

From Basingstoke to Exeter there was a proposed but unspecified modification of passenger train services but between Basingstoke and Salisbury only Whitchurch and Andover were to survive. On our main

line Beeching proposed the closure of Grateley, Hurstbourne, Idmiston Halt, Oakley, Porton, and Overton stations. Recently released Ministry of Transport files at the Public Record Office show that local people at Hurstbourne conducted a long correspondence about its closure and the poor replacement bus service. Overton and Whitchurch were to be open at peak times only and in 1964 British Railways expected to close Whitchurch later on.

Both at the time and subsequently, the Beeching proposals have been carefully scrutinised. Much of what he reported was correct but there were many flaws in his methods, for example all the revenue paid by Londoners travelling to the west country resorts from Waterloo was attributed to Waterloo. When their stations were shut most of the passengers transferred to road and the revenue was lost altogether to the railway. On our line passengers travelling to work at Portals Mill bought their tickets at other stations but had Overton been closed as proposed this revenue would have been lost. Furthermore no value was attributed to diversionary routes, despite the regular use of all or part of the Southern Region Basingstoke to Exeter and Plymouth line by Western Region trains when their own main line was blocked. In his defence he was merely putting into effect the orders he had been given. Only in recent years has the Ministry of Transport policy of building more and more roads without considering the alternatives really come into question.

REGIONAL BOUNDARY CHANGES 1963
On 1st January 1963 the Western Region took over all the Southern lines west of Dorchester, Blandford Forum, Wilton and Dilton Marsh near Westbury. Although this happened two months before the Beeching Report was published, the British Railways Board already knew its contents, the government already having decided the outcome. Thus the boundary change was made so that the recommendations could be ruthlessly implemented by managers chosen by Beeching. Very quickly it became obvious that the Southern lines west of Salisbury faced a very bleak future.

THE END OF AN ERA
The last day of the summer 1964 timetable on Sunday 6th September marked the end of an era for our line. On Saturday 5th the very last two 'Atlantic Coast Expresses' from Waterloo had run down the West of England main line to Ilfracombe, Torrington, Bude and Padstow. On Sunday 6th the last regular steam trains from Waterloo to Exeter ran, there then being none from Waterloo beyond Exeter on a Sunday. On the same day the last rites were performed for the Test Valley trains from Andover Junction.

Porton station in 1967 looking east was run down before its closure. The goods yard had been closed and lifted, and the signal box retained only to control trains and the remaining crossover. The platforms were illuminated after dark by Tilley lamps hung from the lamp posts. After closure the site was re-developed as the Porton Garden and Aquatic Centre. John Scrace.

Grateley station in 1966, run down with derelict sidings. Within a few years the signal box and station house were demolished and the footbridge replaced. John Scrace.

CHAPTER SEVEN
THE LATER BRITISH RAILWAYS PERIOD 1964-1993

IMPLEMENTING THE BEECHING REPORT

The last *Atlantic Coast Expresses* from Waterloo to Ilfracombe, Torrington, Bude and Padstow ran on Saturday 5th September 1964, bringing to an end a century of expresses between Waterloo and beyond Exeter Central. In the new timetable, introduced on Monday 7th September 1964, the new Western Region service of diesel locomotive hauled semi-fast trains between Waterloo and Exeter St Davids began, augmented with a variety of diesel multiple unit stopping trains west of Salisbury. The semi-fast service was basically two-hourly but none went west of Exeter. Passengers from Southern stations west of Exeter now had a service to Exeter St Davids, far less convenient for local passengers than Exeter Central, and here they were expected to change into a Paddington train if going to London. Passengers wishing to travel to Waterloo faced a very long wait for trains, deliberately timetabled inconveniently.

To rub salt in the wound the traditional best train of the day, the *Atlantic Coast Express* departing Waterloo at 11.0am, terminated at Salisbury. On the first day the 11.0am train from Waterloo arrived at Salisbury where some 150 passengers had to get out and wait for the Brighton to Plymouth train. Initially a few through services remained, the overnight newspaper train from Waterloo to Plymouth and Ilfracombe, the popular cross-country train between Brighton and Plymouth and the evening Plymouth to Eastleigh train.

Not immediately obvious was that the Western Region had also closed almost all the former Southern Region goods yards west of Exeter at the same time and, for the few that remained, diverted the goods trains to their own route. Only the Meldon stone trains for the Southern Region civil engineer remained. So at a stroke almost all the through traffic, both passenger and goods, to and from stations west of Exeter disappeared. For a century this through traffic had been a major feature of the line but now, from Basingstoke to Exeter, the line now had to earn its living from local traffic only.

After 7th September 1964 the stopping train service between Waterloo and Salisbury, basically two-hourly with extra trains in the peak, continued steam hauled although now not calling at the recently closed stations at Oakley and Hurstbourne. Steam engines continued to haul the limited freight trains, still serving sidings at Overton for Portals traffic, Whitchurch, Andover Junction and its two freight branches to Andover Town, Ludgershall, and Salisbury. The Western Region made sure that little freight now came up the main line from Exeter; even the milk tanks from Chard Junction to London were sent to Exeter St David's and thence the Western Region main line.

Southern Region Re-organisation

Following the 1963 transfer of the Western Division and its Exeter office to the Western Region, the Southern Region management structure was changed. Now there were just three divisions, South Eastern, Central and South Western. The South Western Division with offices at Wimbledon took over the bulk of the work previously done at the Woking and Southampton offices, although a Control Office was retained at Southampton. From now on our line was managed from Wimbledon. Stationmasters were replaced by Area Managers, responsible for a wide area and much of our line came under the Salisbury Area Manager.

Transport Users Consultative Committee Report 1968
Grateley, Idmiston and Porton

Established under the 1962 Transport Act, the Transport Users Consultative Committee for the South Eastern Area reported on the British Railways proposals to withdraw passenger services from Grateley, Idmiston and Porton. The confidential report dated 12th February 1968 has recently been made available by the Public Record Office.

Twenty-two written objections to the closure of Grateley and nine in respect of Idmiston and Porton, were received. Subsequently the T.U.C.C. held a public hearing of objections at St.Ann's Hall on Tuesday 31st October 1967, attended by twenty people together with representatives of British Railways and bus operators. Grateley station served a population of about 500 in the village a mile away and about 250 in Palestine about ¼ to ½ mile away; Idmiston and Porton served

Idmiston Halt in the 1960s looking south-west towards Porton. Most of its passenger traffic had been civilian workmen from Salisbury coming to work at the adjacent Porton Down base. Douglas Thompson.

about 1,400 people in the two adjacent villages again about ¼ to ½ miles away.

The 1966-67 weekday train service for the three stations ran between Basingstoke and Salisbury at approximately two hourly intervals. The Monday to Friday daily average number of passengers joining and alighting from each station was:

	week ending 16.7.1966				week ending 28.1.1967			
	Down trains		Up trains		Down trains		Up trains	
	J	A	J	A	J	A	J	A
Grateley	17	19	21	12	16	16	17	13
Idmiston	18	8	6	15	1	1	1	1
Porton	16	13	11	18	7	5	4	7

The Saturday figures were greater, particularly at Grateley where thirty-five passengers joined Down trains in 7.1966. The financial information supplied was:

	Grateley	Idmiston	Porton
Originating receipts per annum	£1,333	£401	£534
Station costs per annum	£1,817	£1,185	£1,774
Expected expenditure for next five years if station remains open	£2,865	£454	£789

Bus services to Grateley and Palestine were provided at irregular intervals by Amport and District Motor Services Ltd. The service connected a number of villages with Andover but there was no bus service to Salisbury. Idmiston and Porton had frequent bus services to Salisbury provided by Wilts & Dorset service Nos.9 (½ hourly) and 709 (2 hourly) and also occasional journeys by H. J. Armstead's service between Newton Tony and Salisbury. Passengers from Porton and Idmiston could also reach Andover by changing at Tidworth. To cater for workers from Grateley, the Amport company was prepare to run a couple of extra services costing £600 per annum.

Some twenty rail passengers travelling eastwards would suffer hardship should the station close, the bus journey to Andover taking 25-50 minutes in comparison to ten minutes by train. Most of these twenty passengers took the 7.13am train, nine to Andover and five to Overton. The replacement bus would require a start 23 minutes earlier in the morning and an arrival 26 minutes later in the evening. A watercress grower in Nether Wallop who drove to Grateley to despatch his produce bemoaned the fact that driving to Andover would involve a longer journey. Approximately seventeen passengers travelled westwards from Grateley daily, more on Saturdays; these comprised eight regular travellers and one railway employee. The rest were schoolchildren. The replacement bus service, involving a change at Middle Wallop, would require a start 13 minutes earlier in the morning and arrival 37 minutes later in the evening. The replacement bus service would be of no use for those visiting Salisbury for less than a full day. Although bus services from Porton to Salisbury were good one worker living in Porton would have great difficulty with travel to work in Andover. A train journey of 19 minutes would be replaced by bus journeys involving a change at Tidworth, with journey times between 56 and 155 minutes. At both Andover and Salisbury the buses arrived at the bus stations, ½ and ¾ miles from their respective railway stations, making connections more difficult. The report stating:

'After examining the written evidence and considering the representations made to them at the public hearing, the committee came to the following conclusions:-

i)   That the closure of Grateley station would cause considerable hardship, particularly to those who travel to and from Salisbury. The number of originating passengers is approximately 37 daily, 17 of whom travel in the Salisbury direction.

ii)   That in the case of Idmiston Halt and Porton the alternative bus service is more convenient and only a few cases of hardship and inconvenience would result if the train service were to cease.

The Committee considered that hardship would best be alleviated by the retention of Grateley station, possibly as an unstaffed halt with a less frequent service than now.'

Six months after this report, on 9th September 1968, Idmiston Halt and Porton Station were closed but Grateley station survived and subsequently prospered. Further up the line passengers travelling to work at Portals Mill contributed the survival of Overton station. A major shortcoming of the Beeching methodology, illustrated in the TUCC report, was that stations were judged by their own receipts so that Portals workers fares were attributed to other stations, but that if Overton station had closed that income would have disappeared.

Had the Beeching proposals been fully implemented then the only intermediate stations to survive would have been Whitchurch and Andover; probably the Waterloo to Exeter semi-fast trains would also have called at Whitchurch, making a stopping train service unnecessary. In a nightmare scenario, had the Western Region

Western Region Warship class No.801 *Vanguard* under the Battledown flyover, probably in the later 1960s since the third rail on the Southampton line is in place. The Transport Treasury.

Signal Box, Goods Yard and Station Closures 1964-1981			
Signal Box	**Goods Yard or Siding**	**Passenger station**	**Closure date**
	Whitchurch		7th June 1965
	Overton Goods		14th September 1965
Worting Junction & Oakley			20th November 1966
Whitchurch & Overton	Portals Siding, Overton		5th February 1967
	Salisbury Milford		21st August 1967
	Andover T'n Goods br'nch		18th September 1967
Salisbury Milford			1st January 1968
Grateley & Porton			2nd May 1968
		Porton & Idmiston	9th September 1968
Andover A & B			2nd December 1973
Salisbury Tunnel Junction			17th August 1981
Salisbury East			19th August 1981
Salisbury West			21st August 1981

been in charge, no doubt Worting Junction to Salisbury would have been reduced to a single track just sufficient for the two-hourly service.

Goods yard closures, started in the early 1960s, continued with Overton and Whitchurch in 1965; Portals Siding at Overton, the Andover Town branch and Salisbury Milford succumbed in 1967. However, goods facilities were maintained at Andover and at Salisbury (Fisherton), at the former Great Western station. At Salisbury the remaining traffic handled at Milford was transferred to Fisherton and at Andover (as the Junction had become) the Down sidings remained in use. The goods shed was used as a distribution depot for general merchandise for customers over a wide area, with vans from a number of different depots around the country.

Considerable economies were made as country signal boxes were closed and their functions taken over by new control panels at Basingstoke and Salisbury. Each signal box, open 24 hours daily, required three men and these posts disappeared as the boxes closed. On 20th November 1966 the new Basingstoke panel signal box took over the roles of Basingstoke East, Basingstoke West,

Worting Junction and Oakley signal boxes. On 5th February 1967 Basingstoke panel box also took over Overton and Whitchurch so that track circuit block signalling was in use as far as the area of Andover Junction 'A' signal box. Along with the new panels fitted at Woking and Eastleigh boxes, Basingstoke panel box took over the role of those signal boxes closed on the Basingstoke - Salisbury line.

On 2nd May 1968 track circuit block, controlled by Salisbury Tunnel Junction signal box as far as Andover Junction 'B' signal box, replaced the signal boxes at Grateley and Porton. Several years later, on 2nd December 1973, Basingstoke took over the role of the two Andover signal boxes, where a new ground frame controlled connections to the Ludgershall freight branch and sidings remaining in the yard.

A new signal panel opened in the original 1859 Salisbury station building, which had been used as a parcels office, between 17th and 21st August 1981. It took over the roles of Tunnel Junction, East and West signal boxes, although Basingstoke panel took over the main line almost as far as Laverstock. The new panel also controlled the new single track curve opened on 21st August 1981

between Laverstock North and Laverstock South Junctions, along the original 1857 alignment taken out of use in 1859. This provided a very useful diversionary route between Southampton and Basingstoke when the main line was blocked and saw regular use by freight trains between Eastleigh, Andover and Ludgershall. The route was also used by container trains to and from the Millbrook depots during the re-building of Southampton tunnel. Subsequently the Salisbury panel took over the role of other boxes, including Wilton, which will be covered in Volume Two.

BOURNEMOUTH LINE ELECTRIFICATION 1967

Up to 1964, Waterloo to Exeter and beyond had been the Southern's main line but following the boundary changes the Southern's General Manager pronounced "Bournemouth is our Main Line now". In September 1964, well-timed to offset the criticism of the Western Region timetable changes west of Salisbury, the Southern Region eventually announced the long-awaited approval of the Bournemouth line electrification. To ensure approval of the project the Bournemouth to Weymouth and Basingstoke to Salisbury lines were excluded from the electrification, hopefully to be dealt with later.

The project included track relaying between Brookwood and Bournemouth, multiple aspect signalling, and the provision of new rolling stock, some of which was

On 26th March 1966 West Country class 4-6-2 No.34108 *Wincanton* approaches Grateley on a down freight train, the first wagon carries a military tracked vehicle. John Scrace.

Top. On 19th April 1989 class 47 No.47060 departs from Salisbury with the 14 40 freight to Gloucester, the leading vehicles being ECC tank wagons used for conveying calcium carbonate from Quidhampton sidings near Wilton. John Scrace.

Above. On 3rd May 1989 class 56 No.56035 Taff Merthyr leaves Salisbury with the daily 0955 stone train from Merehead Quarry to Woking. In the bay platform is a 'Hampshire' multiple unit, then still used on some local services. John Scrace.

BR Mark 1 coaching stock about ten years old re-built for the line in 3TC and 4TC non-powered formations. Many train loads of ballast were worked up the West of England main line from Meldon Quarry, augmented with ballast from the Mendip Quarries near Frome on the Western Region. On arrival at Salisbury these either ran straight through or were berthed in the East Yard, before proceeding via Basingstoke or Eastleigh to the site where ballast was required. New modern signal boxes at Woking, Eastleigh and Basingstoke controlled the multiple aspect signalling and subsequently the latter took over control of the line to Salisbury as older signal boxes closed.

Engineering work for the Bournemouth electrification between Waterloo and Worting Junction affected Salisbury line trains. Often the engineers were in possession of the Up and Down main lines so that all trains had to use the local lines with some effect on timekeeping. Some services were cut back, including some off-peak steam-hauled Waterloo to Salisbury trains. These were replaced with Western Region diesel multiple units running between Woking and Salisbury, in connection with Portsmouth line trains and occasionally they reached Waterloo. These replacement diesel services continued until engineering work between Waterloo and Basingstoke had been completed and electric train services between the two commenced on 2nd January 1967. Electric train services between Waterloo and Bournemouth commenced on Monday 10th July 1967.

Following the 1964 approval of the Bournemouth line electrification, heavy repairs to steam locomotives came to an end so that by 1967 the available steam locomotives were run down and sometimes unreliable despite the best efforts of shed staff, drivers and firemen. At Nine Elms, Basingstoke and Salisbury sheds the surviving Bulleid Pacifics were joined by BR standard class 4-6-0s to keep the Salisbury line passenger services going, with standard tanks on what remained of local freight and shunting. The last steam hauled trains ran on Saturday 8th July 1967 when Basingstoke Driver Bert Pating and Fireman Ron Grace on BR 4-6-0 No.73029 took the 4.51pm Basingstoke to Salisbury stopping train and after turning took the last train to Waterloo where they were relieved. Salisbury shed closed but was retained as a signing on point for train crew until 23rd February 1969 when it was replaced by an office in the station building. After the end of steam many Southern Region locomotives arrived at Salisbury shed where they were stored until scrap merchants in South Wales were ready to receive them. Many went to Woodhams scrap yard at Barry where they were not cut up but rusted away until purchased for preservation. A number now haul trains on preserved lines and also main line steam specials.

Often electrification was good news for passengers on the modernised line but bad news for those beyond. For example, when the Woking to Alton line was electrified in 1937, with an enhanced half-hourly service, passengers beyond on the Meon Valley and Mid Hants lines lost their through trains and had to change at Alton. The Southern Region carefully considered this problem and came up with a unique solution. A 4-REP unit at the Waterloo end powered two un-powered 4-TC units which, at Bournemouth, were coupled to a class 33 diesel locomotive which worked one or two of them to Weymouth in push-pull mode. Controls and connections were also standardised on electric multiple units and class 73 electro-diesel locomotives. This operational flexibility was demonstrated daily in the 1980s with the 17.00 train from Waterloo powered simultaneously by diesel and electric traction comprising a class 33 diesel and 4-TC unit for Salisbury and two 4-VEP electric multiple units for Eastleigh detached at Basingstoke.

A number of timetable changes were unpopular with the travelling public at this time – the withdrawal of the off-peak service from Waterloo calling at all stations between Basingstoke and Salisbury, for instance. The 'Hampshire' diesel multiple unit service between Reading and Southampton was withdrawn and replaced with a stopping train service between Reading and Salisbury which connected at Basingstoke with semi-fast services between Waterloo and Bournemouth. Through passengers were not impressed with the Reading and Salisbury branch services and the enforced change of train at Basingstoke. There was now just one London commuter service, the 6.10pm Waterloo to Salisbury. Although Andover and Salisbury were served by the semi-fast trains between Waterloo and

Exeter, passengers for Overton, Whitchurch and Grateley had to change at Basingstoke. In the 1980s this Salisbury branch service was discontinued when the Waterloo to Salisbury through service was reinstated, using class 33 diesels and 4-TC units. By 1983 most of the services from Waterloo to Salisbury and beyond departed at ten minutes past every hour, the Reading to Salisbury service had finished but there were still three Basingstoke to Salisbury local trains, one of which proceeded to Portsmouth.

WATERLOO TO EXETER FROM 1966

As we will see in Volumes Two and Three, on 7th March 1966 the Western Region closed nine stations on the Salisbury to Exeter line, together with connecting lines and branches. The sad list was: Pinhoe, Broad Clyst, Seaton Junction and the Seaton branch, Chard Junction, Milborne Port, Templecombe (together with the Somerset and Dorset line), Semley, Dinton and Wilton. A year later, on 6th March 1967, Sidmouth Junction and the Sidmouth and Exmouth branches were also closed.

With the closure of these stations and branches the basic two-hourly semi-fast train service between Waterloo and Exeter called at Woking, Basingstoke, Andover and Salisbury and all surviving stations thence to Exeter. The Western Region now reasoned that with this two-hourly service much of the former West of England main line between Salisbury and Exeter could be reduced to single track with a few passing places. This was carried out in 1967 and has subsequently been seen as one of the most misguided of the Beeching cuts. Due to the lack of timetable paths most of the stone trains from Meldon Quarry now took

a longer route via Exeter, Taunton, Westbury, and Salisbury before re-joining their traditional route to the Southern Region engineer's yards. The Western Region had now contrived a situation that there was very little freight to be carried west of Salisbury, the main survivor being Ministry of Defence traffic at Dinton and Chilmark.

Instead of being the first line to receive new rolling stock the Waterloo to Exeter route now had to make do with other lines' cast-offs. The Warship locomotives and rakes of Mark 1 carriages, surplus to requirements on the Western Region main line, were now serviced at Newton Abbot, resulting in forty miles of extra running for several empty trains to and from Exeter St Davids every day. Some time later Newton Abbot depot closed and Plymouth Laira took over the work, resulting now in a hundred miles of empty stock running! However, the Southern Region also closed Salisbury shed, requiring rolling stock to work empty from Eastleigh more than twenty miles away. With responsibility split between two regions the downgraded Waterloo to Exeter service drifted for the next twenty years until the establishment of Network Southeast breathed new life into the line.

After a very short career on the line the unreliable Warships were replaced in October 1971 by Southern Region class 33s, reliable enough engines but rather underpowered for the job in hand, so schedules were extended. When a second locomotive was available double heading helped but the platforms at Waterloo were too short to accommodate two class 33s at the buffer stops and two more to take the train out. The class 33s working push-pull with four coach 4-TC units, a successful

Southern design for the non-electrified Bournemouth to Weymouth line, also took over the Waterloo to Salisbury services. More class 33s appeared on some Sundays when Bournemouth to Waterloo trains were diverted between Southampton and Basingstoke by way of the new Laverstock curve and Andover. In 1980 Waterloo-Exeter services were taken over by more powerful class 50 locomotives and rakes of Mark 2 coaches displaced from the Western Region main line duties by new High Speed Trains. As with the Warships before them, reliability was a problem. On one day a class 50 failed at Chard Junction and its replacement did not arrive for several *hours*. The provision of a standby locomotive at Yeovil or even Exeter was regarded as an extravagance.

In 1973, just ten years after the Beeching Report, British Railways reported that the Waterloo to Exeter line was one of the top ten earners when measured on revenue per coach mile. Expansion of the towns of Basingstoke and Andover and new houses built at many other places along the line brought more people including a steadily increasing number who commuted by train to Waterloo. Slowly the train service east of Salisbury evolved to accommodate this. West of Salisbury too, travel was increasing and the route from Wilton South to Sherborne was transferred back to the Southern Region to develop it further. Sadly, due to the long single line sections west of Salisbury, it was difficult to increase their frequency. But the Southern Region was able to extend some trains between Waterloo and Salisbury as far as Gillingham, starting a trend which has continued over the years.

Further afield on the Southern Region electric train services, first on the

47711 at Whitchurch with the 7.50am Yeovil to Waterloo train on 11th May 1993. R.K. Blencowe.

Bournemouth to Weymouth line and subsequently on the Southampton and Eastleigh to Portsmouth lines, began in the late 1980s. New class 442 'Wessex Electrics' came into service and subsequently were able to use the fully electrified Southampton-Fareham-Guildford-Woking route for diversions rather than the Laverstock curve. Some redundant 4-TC units were stored in sidings at Andover before making their final journey to the breakers yard.

FREIGHT TRAFFIC
There was an upturn in freight traffic in the late 1960s when Shellstar opened a number of distribution depots in the south and west of England, including Andover the centre of a very productive arable farming area, Gillingham and Lapford. In May 1969 a large modern warehouse was opened on the site of the MSWJR Andover engine shed, with a concreted area adjacent to the adjacent sidings. Trainloads of air-braked curtain-sided wagons came from the factory at Ince and Elton on Merseyside to Andover where pallets of bagged fertiliser were unloaded by fork-lift and stacked in the warehouse ready for distribution by road to farmers. Subsequently the depot was operated by U.K.F. In contrast at Andover the van services for general merchandise continued to run into the 1980s.

Two types of block loads of stone ran along the line. The familiar trains of vacuum braked wagons conveying Meldon Quarry ballast required by Southern Region engineers continued to run as required to Woking or beyond, though between Exeter and Salisbury they were usually routed via Taunton and Westbury. A new traffic to develop in modern air-braked wagons was stone from the Frome area used for roads and other construction projects. At Salisbury Tunnel Junction some ran through to the south coast terminals and some proceeding up the main line to Woking or beyond. This stone traffic also varied depending on where the current road construction was taking place.

THE GROWTH OF COMMUTING
As we have seen, back in 1964 just one train, the 6.49am from Salisbury calling at all stations, gave a Waterloo arrival at 8.59am by changing at Basingstoke, a journey time

of 130 minutes. There were a few hardy commuters then.

From 1967 electric trains catered for stations east of Basingstoke, and together with the closure of four intermediate stations on our line the early morning services developed.

By 1983 two trains, the 5.43am from Gillingham and the 6.40am from Salisbury, called at all intermediate stations to Basingstoke then ran non-stop to arrive at Waterloo at 8.6am and 8.26am. These were closely followed by the 7.15am from Salisbury and the 5.50am from Exeter St Davids, calling only at Andover and Basingstoke, which arrived at Waterloo at 9.7am and 9.12am, the stopping trains taking between 106 and 112 minutes to Waterloo. During the morning rush hour all trains except the Exeter called at all intermediate stations. The development of new houses right along the line and the provision of more car parking spaces encouraged the trend.

When the new Network Southeast class 159 service started in 1993 morning trains called at all stations to Basingstoke. They departed from Salisbury at 5.30am, 5.50am for Basingstoke, 6.10am, 6.32am, 7.11am all arriving at Waterloo before 9.0am. The last three starting from Yeovil Junction and the 7.47am, 8.15am arriving at Waterloo shortly after 9.0am. Salisbury to Waterloo times were about 90 minutes.

Although we have concentrated here on the commuter services to Waterloo there was also some commuting to the rapidly expanding towns of Basingstoke and Andover and into Salisbury which had its road traffic problems. Indeed this may well account for the greatly increased use of Grateley station in its rural location. Indeed Grateley Parkway might be an appropriate new name.

PERMANENT WAY DEVELOPMENTS
Based at the Civil Engineer's Office at Eastleigh Mr Graham Hatton was the Permanent Way Engineer for the line for about 10 years spanning the late 1980s and 1990s, and has kindly supplied much information about this period. His duties included periodic walking the whole line to maintain his intimate knowledge of the route and its infrastructure.

At Worting Junction in the 1980s there was concern at the maintenance costs of Battledown flyover, with some of the wooden parts of the structure rotting and requiring replacement in addition to routine maintenance. The round bearings carrying the bowstring structure had become flattened and also required replacement. At this time the Salisbury line service had declined reducing the number of conflicting movements so there was a proposal to abolish the flyover and re-arrange the junction crossovers at Worting. Later in the early 1990s there was another proposal to move the junction crossovers at Worting nearer to Basingstoke, at Winklebury from where there was a fifth track, the Up Slow Line installed in 1943. Speed limits at the new junction would have been raised to 100mph and plain line laid through Worting. The crossovers at Worting not only form a junction for the Bournemouth and Salisbury lines but in association with this additional crossovers were proposed for reversible running on th Up side for the growing cross-country traffic between the Bournemouth and the Reading lines which diverges just east of Basingstoke station. This proposal would also have facilitated the extension of the reversible signalling on the double track between Eastleigh and Micheldever as far as the new junction. This second proposal was cancelled at a late stage when the Signal Engineer decided that Basingstoke signal box could be re-wired rather than renewed, thus saving much money at a time when money was particularly short.

Many years after their closure the down platform at Oakley survived but just mounds of earth remain at Idmiston, where a rail for a lamp and approach paths to the platforms survive. The work done on Hurstbourne viaduct in 1951 was then and still is standard engineering practice for railway structures of its type, to make it more secure with ties between the walls of the viaduct to prevent them being forced apart, and concrete saddles on top of the original arches which sometimes allowed heavier loading. In the deep cuttings through the chalk between Hurstbourne and Andover, and also between Idmiston and Porton, the chalk spall which regularly fell from the sides after wet or frosty weather has been a problem since the line opened. A ditch was provided at the foot of the cutting for the chalk spall to fall into and this was periodically cleaned out with the chalk loaded into engineers' wagons during a possession, for many years by manpower but in recent years using a road-rail machine. Incidentally this is a problem in all chalk cuttings even more so with third-rail electrification, where a piece of chalk on the conductor rail or in this area can damage collection shoes.

Walking through Fisherton Tunnel at Salisbury required a possession of the Up or Down line from the signalman, and although the tunnel was straight all the approaching lines were curved, particularly from Eastleigh. Although there were refuges set into the tunnel walls it was always an unforgettable experience to be in the tunnel as a train ran through on the other line. In the original 1859 Salisbury station building the upper floor was used until recently for the Permanent Way staff and Structure Examiners. When structural alterations were made some years ago in one of the small rooms an old bible was found; in Victorian days these rooms had been used for accommodation of staff working in the refreshment rooms downstairs, and they had been provided with bibles. The two storey brick building at the west end of platforms 2 &3 apparently was originally used as a foot-warmer store, and later as the office for the Carriage and Wagon Examiners, popularly known as the "wheeltappers".

SALISBURY, ANDOVER and BASINGSTOKE RAIL DAYS

In August 1985 the Salisbury Area Manager Mr Gerry Daniels organised a Salisbury Rail Event in connection with the GWR 150 celebrations and the exhibition train was a major feature. In the Rail Event Brochure it was reported that in 1984 256,023 tickets were sold at Salisbury, there were 230 staff here and 230 weekday trains.

On the weekend of 21st and 22nd March 1986 Gerry Daniels organised the Andover Rail Day. The principal attraction was a service between Andover and Ludgershall, comprising six coaches hauled by ex-GWR No.4930 *Hagley Hall*, the first steam-hauled train to be seen on British Railways in the area since the end of steam in 1967. At Ludgershall a 'Hampshire' diesel electric multiple unit provided a service to and from the end of the line at Perham Down. At Andover there was a display of diesel and

electric rolling stock in the goods yard together with other exhibits including traction engines and the army provided a demonstration train of its own rolling stock. The event was well attended and was in the best traditions of railway publicity days. This was followed in October 1986 by a Salisbury Steam Spectacular involving three steam locomotives.

The next year in 1987 Gerry Daniels organised a Basingstoke Rail Week, including diesel specials to Andover connecting with steam trips to Ludgershall, and conducted visits to the signalling centre which controlled our line as far down as the outskirts of Salisbury.

NETWORK SOUTHEAST

The restructuring of British Railways in 1986 into the Inter-City, Network Southeast and Regional Railways passenger sectors replaced the previous regions. Although the Southern Region had done its best to develop its part of the line, which by now extended as far as Sherborne, the same was not true of the Western. Fortunately it was decided that the whole line, curiously as far as Pinhoe, should come under Network Southeast, and became its longest route. The new Director of Network Southeast was Chris Green whose charismatic style of management made an immediate impact. Within days the entire network from Kings Lynn, Dover and Pinhoe gained a new corporate image with red-painted station seats. In a bold marketing move there was the first Network Day when unlimited travel across the network was available for a £5 ticket. Your co-author took advantage of this deal and travelled from Basingstoke on a packed train to Honiton. That morning the booking staff had sold almost a thousand Network Day tickets with some travellers coming by car from North Devon. 'The best thing that's happened to this line for years' was the reaction in the booking office. And this was just the start.

The benefits of unified management rather than responsibility shared between two regions soon became apparent. Network Southeast was extended to include Exeter Central and cheap day returns were available but not on Intercity and Network Cards, which gave a one third discount on

many fares. There was an infrastructure improvement when a new passing loop was brought into use at Tisbury on 24th March 1986. Costing £435,000 and located to the east of the station, and controlled from the Salisbury panel, it broke up the long single track section between Wilton and Gillingham. Subsequently delays on this section have been reduced and it has facilitated an improved service as far west as Yeovil. The locomotives of class 47 and 50, together with their rakes of Mark 2 coaches, were repainted in the bright and distinctive blue lined with red and white Network Southeast livery which reinforced the new management even if performance was unaffected.

Ever since the end of steam the line had managed with rolling stock 'cascaded' second-hand from other lines but that was to change with total route modernisation in 1993. The main features were a new fleet of twenty-two three-coach class 159 diesel multiple units, based at a new depot opened on 12th July 1993 on the site of the old GW station at Salisbury. To accommodate this new stock station platforms were raised and lengthened. The location of the diesel depot, halfway between Waterloo and Exeter, eliminated the inconvenience and expense of empty stock working to and from remote depots at Plymouth and Eastleigh and facilitated the local management of the rolling stock. Multiple unit working meant three, six or nine coach trains could be divided as required, rather than the previous inflexible nine coach formations. Train services were improved both initially and with subsequent timetables, with the number of trains east of Yeovil increasing. The total cost was £46.5 million, but unfortunately there was not enough money available to reinstate at least some of the double track torn up in the 1960s. Total route modernisation was also employed on other Network Southeast routes; perhaps the best comparison is with the Chiltern Line from Marylebone, where there was redoubling of the London to Birmingham main line also reduced to single track by the Western Region in the 1960s.

Salisbury Traincare Depot

Located on the site of the Great Western yard, Salisbury Traincare Depot was and is still approached by connections from the main line to a long headshunt which extends along the Westbury line to buffers a little beyond Orchard Road bridge No.241. At this end of the depot are three carriage washers and, from this direction, are connections to nine tracks. Behind No.1 platform are stabling sidings, Nos.1-6, the remaining three running into the modern shed, where maintenance using all the clean modern facilities is carried out. All the class 159 multiple units return to the depot overnight apart from a pair stabled overnight at Exeter ready to form the first Up train of the day and one set stabled at Penzance on Saturday nights. As the depot is adjacent to the station, fitters can be sent over to provide immediate attention to any train while it is waiting at the platform. Apart from the depot sidings the bay platforms are employed for berthing trains before service.

On 1st June 2002 the 09 33 train from Exeter St David's to Waterloo formed by a class 159 diesel multiple unit crosses Monxton viaduct, between Grateley and Andover. John Nicholas

Salisbury Traincare Depot on Sunday 2nd June 2002 with class 159 and 170 trains berthed ready for duty. John Nicholas.

On 1st June 2002 a two coach class 170 diesel multiple unit approaches Battledown flyover with the 15 03 Waterloo to Salisbury train. On weekdays the class 170s provide an hourly service between all stations on the line and Waterloo. John Nicholas

CHAPTER EIGHT
SOUTH WEST TRAINS

PRIVATISATION

Although short of investment funds in the 1980s British Railways had become a more efficient organisation and the business sectors, such as Network Southeast, had managed some modernisation on several routes, including our line. There were concerns about replacement of ageing rolling stock, with British Railways permitted to replace three existing carriages with two new ones. Leasing of rolling stock was considered but the Treasury ruled that the capital cost would have to be counted as part of the Public Sector Borrowing Requirement and therefore forbade it. However, there would be no objection to a private railway company leasing rolling stock.

John Major followed Margaret Thatcher as Prime Minister and included in the Conservative Party manifesto for the 1992 general election was a commitment to privatise the railways. After the election was won privatisation was duly implemented; essentially Railtrack owned the infrastructure, contractors maintained the track and signalling, leasing companies owned the rolling stock and train operating companies won franchises to operate the trains.

In the first few years passenger and freight traffic increased and new rolling stock was supplied. However, there were many shortcomings in the relationship between Railtrack and its contractors. The company was unable to properly manage its major infrastructure project of modernisation of the West Coast Main Line and in 2002 it was replaced by Network Rail. Of great concern for our line was the escalating costs of modest infrastructure improvements; in 2002 for instance, the re-doubling of a mere eight miles of the Bicester to Anyho line cost £50 million. Several books have already been written on the privatisation of British Railways, considering both its strengths and weaknesses, and no doubt every reader will have his or her own opinions.

SOUTH WEST TRAINS

The seven year franchise for South West Trains was awarded by the Franchising Director Roger Salmon to the bus operator Stagecoach in 1995, one of the first franchises to be let. The franchise covered all the surviving ex-London and South Western routes radiating out of Waterloo which had previously been operated by Network Southeast, including Waterloo to Exeter but the Bristol, Salisbury, Southampton and Portsmouth services were awarded to the Wales and West franchise operated by Prism. Freight services were

taken over by English Welsh and Scottish Railways and Freightliner.

One of the efficiency savings anticipated at privatisation was a reduction in over-manning. Soon after South West Trains took over they offered generous redundancy terms to drivers to retire early but more than anticipated applied and were accepted. After they went it was found that some depots had insufficient drivers with the appropriate route knowledge so for several months there were consequent train cancellations until the issue was resolved.

South West Trains gradually improved the frequency of selected train services, with the twice hourly Waterloo to Woking stopping service increased to four per hour and the same increase to the Waterloo to Southampton service. There was a gradual improvement to train services between Waterloo, Salisbury and Yeovil though the scope of these was constrained by the single tack sections west of Salisbury. The twenty-two class 159 trains, which were employed on our line, were also used for a Reading to Brighton service.

Up to 2001 the train service at Overton, Whitchurch and Grateley was two-hourly off-peak, augmented with extra commuter rush hour services. However, a fleet of eight two car class 170 diesel multiple units was leased to facilitate a number of service improvements, with a ninth class 170 in 2003. Off-peak there were now hourly trains from Waterloo terminating at stations west of Salisbury at Gillingham, Yeovil Junction, Exeter, Paignton and Plymouth, calling only at Woking, Basingstoke and Andover. There was also a two hourly service with the same stops to Basingstoke and thence all stations to Salisbury.

Class 170 units were usually employed for the Waterloo to Salisbury locals but sometimes they were coupled to 159 units on longer distance trains and uncoupled at Salisbury.

The Salisbury Traincare Depot maintains all the South West Trains diesel multiple units and in 2002 employed 124 staff including depot drivers, cleaners, fitters and storemen. Much of the work is done at night, for many units arrive late in the evening and others depart very early in the morning. All but a handful of units are berthed overnight at Salisbury.

A feature of the privatised railway has been the introduction of extra services, some short-lived, by train operators other than those awarded a franchise for the line. As a result South West Trains extended some of their Waterloo to Exeter services to Paignton, and in 2001 to Plymouth. Also for some years one daily train each way between

Waterloo and Salisbury has run via Southampton, which is also the diversionary route if the Andover line is blocked for emergency or engineering purposes. On the other hand a second operator, Prism's Wales and West (later replaced by Wessex) runs three trains along the line, from Waterloo non-stop to Warminster, thence all stations to Bristol and Cardiff. Although not stopping these trains pass through Salisbury station at reduced speed.

On 26th November 2003, following heavy rain, a bridge just east of Salisbury was damaged. This resulted in the diversion of some trains through the little used platform 1 and the east yard reception line, whilst other trains were cancelled until 1st December.

THE FUTURE

In the seven-year franchise for South West Trains expiring in 2003 there were several proposals advanced for the future of the Waterloo to Exeter line. During 2001 the Chairman of the Strategic Rail Authority, Sir Alistair Morton, advocated a new enlarged Wessex franchise to operate all services in the South West not operated by First Great Western or Virgin Cross Country. This included the Waterloo to Exeter route which was to be taken away from South West Trains. The obvious railway centre for such a new Wessex franchise would have been Salisbury.

South West Trains submitted proposals to not only retain its existing franchise but also to develop the Waterloo to Exeter line, re-instating the double track lifted in 1967 and running a half-hourly service all the way to Exeter, as indeed it already had done between Waterloo and Salisbury. Behind the proposal was a requirement that the Strategic Rail Authority would fund the infrastructure improvements which, as we have seen between Bicester and Aynho, were becoming very expensive.

In 2002 the New Chairman of the Strategic Rail Authority Mr Richard Bowker changed his predecessor's policy by advocating just one franchise for each London terminus, citing capacity problems caused by multiple franchises at Paddington and Liverpool Street. This favoured the South West Trains bid to retain the Waterloo to Exeter service, but the cost of the proposed re-doubling was a major stumbling block.

A new seven year franchise of South west Trains was awarded by the Strategic Rail Authority to Stagecoach in 2003. No new major investment in the route was then anticipated.

On 11th September 1948 Merchant Navy class 4-6-2 No.35017 *Belgian Marine* brings the 12 noon from Waterloo *Devon Belle* slowly through Salisbury platform 3, the first scheduled stop being at Wilton. Platform 3 was usually used for departures to the Western Region. A.E.West

On 18th May 1963 rebuilt Merchant Navy class 4-6-2 No.35001 *Channel Packet* of Nine Elms shed approaches Battledown flyover with the Down 11.0am from Waterloo, the *Atlantic Coast Express*. S.C.Nash.

CHAPTER NINE
TRAFFIC AND SERVICES

Passenger Traffic

From the opening of the line to Salisbury Fisherton in 1859 local passenger traffic has developed with changing patterns of travel right up to the present day. In the early days the railway enabled local people to travel from their village to the market town or beyond. Country landowners and wealthy merchants were always able to use the line for travel to London and elsewhere, sometimes with their own carriages and horses carried by train. For most people travel was limited to day trips on market day for shopping in Basingstoke, Andover and Salisbury followed later by cheap day excursions from local stations to Southampton, Bournemouth, Portsmouth or Waterloo. Examples of such excursions in 1914 appear later in this chapter.

As the railway age developed in this agricultural area, better paid employment in small factories, shops and offices lead to daily travel to work in the larger towns of Basingstoke, Andover and Salisbury and to some smaller towns such as Overton where many were employed at Portals Mill. During the 1914-18 war many travelled by train from Whitchurch to work at Kynocks munitions factory at Longparish. The establishment and subsequent enlargement of army facilities on Porton Down created much civilian employment, to the extent that

Idmiston Halt was opened in 1943 and daily workmen's trains ran from Salisbury to cater for this demand. Other local traffic developed was the transport of children to grammar schools at Basingstoke, Andover and Salisbury.

By the 1960s a few local young men began to expand their horizons, commuting to better paid employment in London using the 6.49am from Salisbury, which called at Andover Junction at 7.22, and changing at Basingstoke into a Southampton line train to arrive at Waterloo at 8.59am. Return was by the 6.0pm from Waterloo to Plymouth which arrived at Andover Junction at 7.21pm and Salisbury at 7.45pm (1964 times). From the 1970s long distance commuting, particularly to London, has increased with train services improved in both speed and frequency and large station car parks have been built, usually on land previously occupied by goods yards.

As the West of England main line opened in stages between 1854 and 1860 the passenger traffic was local but after the South Western reached Yeovil, Exeter and beyond, long distance passenger traffic grew. Two types of passenger train service evolved; for local passengers calling at all stations, and non-stop or limited stop trains for long distance travellers.

Passenger Train Services up to 1964

To cater for local traffic there were about eight daily trains each way. In the Down direction most started at Waterloo and called at Surbiton, Woking, and then all stations to Salisbury. Others started from Woking or Basingstoke with connections from Waterloo and some ran through as far as Yeovil Town. There was a similar Up service but passengers on the 6.49am and 7.49am Up stopping trains from Salisbury to Waterloo could arrive earlier by changing at Basingstoke into a fast train from the Southampton line (1964 timings). In addition there were Fullerton branch trains serving Whitchurch and Hurstbourne, Amesbury branch trains serving Porton and Idmiston, and workmen's trains to Idmiston and Overton. Details varied over the years and are illustrated by a number of timetables included in this volume. In addition to the local trains many expresses called at Andover Junction and all at Salisbury.

Long distance passengers on the West of England main line required fast trains between Waterloo and Salisbury but many stopped at Andover Junction where there were branch line connections available. By 1867 there were four trains from Waterloo to Exeter, at 7.0, 10.50 (express), 11.40am, 3.50pm calling at Andover and Salisbury, with Exeter departures at 7.30, 10.10am,

Salisbury station on 17th February 1958 and a BR standard class 2-6-0 departs from platform 1 at 12.37pm with the 10.55am from Bristol to Portsmouth, after replacing a Western Region locomotive. S15 class 4-6-0 No.30826 waits in platform 2 with the 12.58pm stopping train to Waterloo, while 'Hampshire' diesel set No.1102 waits in platform 6 with the 12.42 stopping train to Portsmouth. Peter Groom.

Just west of Basingstoke, near Winklebury, on 17ᵗʰ June 1959 Battle of Britain class 4-6-2 No.34060 *25 Squadron* of Exmouth Junction shed passes the Worting Junction Down distant signals with a special train from Plymouth conveying racegoers to Ascot. Royal Ascot was and still is an important event in the horse-racing calandar. The train runs up the main line to Sturt Lane Junction where it takes the Ascot line. S.C.Nash.

1.30 (express), 4.30pm, in addition to stopping train services. In the peak of summer 1909 there were eleven fast trains from Waterloo to Exeter or beyond, at 6.10, 8.50, 10.45, 11.0, 11.10, 11.15am, 12 noon, 1.0, 2.50, 3.30, and 5.50pm, many of which called at Basingstoke and Andover Junction before the obligatory Salisbury stop. However, the 10.45am Plymouth, 11.0am North Cornwall, 11.10am North Devon, 12 noon East and North Devon, and 3.30pm Plymouth expresses all ran non stop from Waterloo to Salisbury, and there was a similar pattern in the Up direction.

In 1926 the 11.0am to Devon and Cornwall from Waterloo gained the title 'Atlantic Coast Express' running non-stop from Waterloo to Salisbury. Such was the traffic on offer that one daily winter service expanded to two on summer weekdays and up to six on summer bank holidays. During the 1950s the 11.0am ACE was scheduled to arrive at Salisbury at 12.23pm, made a stop at Sidmouth Junction and arrived at Exeter Central at 2.5pm. However, between 1962 and its demise in 1964 it was accelerated to reach Salisbury at 12.20pm and Exeter Central at 1.58pm with the Nine Elms Merchant Navy working right through to Exeter Central. Salisbury men assisted in bringing coal forward on the tender whilst water was taken at the station. The engine worked back on the 6.48pm milk train from Exeter Central to Clapham Junction. Apart from the ill-fated Plymouth boat trains the only regular service to omit the Salisbury stop was the short-lived 12 noon 'Devon Belle' from Waterloo to Ilfracombe and Plymouth, which had an unadvertised stop

at Wilton to change engines, the first advertised stop being at Sidmouth Junction.

Passenger Train services after 1964

In the summer 1964 timetable there were fourteen up trains calling at Andover but following the 1964 cutbacks west of Salisbury there was a basic two-hourly Waterloo to Exeter service calling at Woking, Basingstoke and Andover. This was augmented by a two-hourly stopping service from Basingstoke or Waterloo to Salisbury, with the odd extra peak hour service. By 1984 there were trains from Waterloo to Exeter at 6.50, 9.10, 11.10, 13.10, 15.10, 16.38, 17.38 and 19.10, from Waterloo to Yeovil at 1.40, 18.10 and 20.38, from Waterloo to Salisbury at 10.10, 12.10, 14.10, 17.00 and 22.10, and (with a Waterloo connection) from Basingstoke to Salisbury at 6.35, 8.34 and 16.53 (to Portsmouth Harbour). Essentially this provided Andover and Salisbury with an hourly service and the other stations two-hourly, augmented at the peak, a total of twenty-one up trains calling at Andover, and 14 at Whitchurch.

As mentioned in a previous chapter, a significant improvement in train services came in 1993 following the modernisation of the Waterloo to Exeter line by Network Southeast. The provision of new class 159 three coach diesel multiple units which ran in three, six or nine coach formations, a new diesel depot for the 159 units at Salisbury, extended platforms and improved station facilities, much improved the services on the line. The new timetable commenced in summer 1993 with off-peak Waterloo

departures at 35 minutes past the hour. Even hours covered to Exeter and odd hours to Salisbury, Tisbury, Gillingham or Yeovil and16.05 and 19.05, together with 5 minutes past the hour, giving a half-hourly service to all stations between Basingstoke and Salisbury between. Andover now had twenty-four up trains and Whitchurch seventeen.

The most recent improvement in train services came in the summer 2001 timetable when South West Trains brought in a fleet of eight class 170 two coach diesel multiple units to augment the existing class 159s. Between 08.35 and 19.35 there were now two departures from Waterloo, the 35 minutes past the hour departure calling only at Andover and Salisbury before proceeding to Plymouth, Paignton, Exeter, Yeovil or Gillingham, whilst the three minutes past the hour usually called at all stations to Salisbury. Now Andover had thirty-one Up trains to Waterloo and Whitchurch twenty-one. A feature in recent years has been the 10.15 from Waterloo to Salisbury via Southampton, with an 11.20 return service (2001 times). Apart from augmenting the Southampton line service these two trains enable Salisbury drivers to maintain their route knowledge should the Andover route be closed.

An evolving feature of passenger services at Salisbury has been the cross-country services which began with just one in 1896 between Portsmouth and Cardiff; these started to multiply when the new Salisbury station opened in 1902. Almost throughout the age of steam, locomotives were changed at Salisbury station, where ten minutes or more were allowed for the purpose. There were also services between Portsmouth and Bristol, and Brighton and both Cardiff and Plymouth. In recent years first Regional Railways and more recently Wessex Trains have developed these services with frequent diesel multiple units. Another, apparently short-lived, passenger service was a MSWJR though carriage between Cheltenham and Waterloo via Andover Junction which ran in 1895.

Other Passenger Train rated Traffic

A less well known aspect of the line other than the 'Atlantic Coast Express' were the everyday services which played such a very important economic role. First was the overnight newspaper and passenger train, in 1958 departing Waterloo at 1.15am with through vehicles for Bideford, Ilfracombe, Plymouth Friary and Padstow, calling only at Andover Junction, Salisbury, Yeovil Junction, Axminster and Exeter Central. At Salisbury vans of newspapers for all stations to both Weymouth and Yeovil Town were promptly transferred.

Milk traffic was originally conveyed in churns which were loaded into luggage compartments or vans of stopping passenger trains. At one stage there was a through milk van running daily between the Amesbury branch and Waterloo via Salisbury. South Western and early Southern timetables included a number of milk churn trains from Yeovil and Sherborne to Waterloo or Victoria. Milk churn traffic from stations on the Somerset & Dorset was routed via Templecombe and from MSWJR stations via Andover Junction. However, in the 1930s, dairy companies began to establish rail connected depots where local farmers brought their milk for cooling, storage and loading into large tanker wagons for conveyance to a number of receiving depots

in London, including Vauxhall just outside Waterloo. In the early 1950s there was a 5.35pm Yeovil to Gravesend milk train running via Woking, Guildford, Redhill, Tonbridge and Maidstone West. By the 1950s much of the churn traffic had disappeared. Tankers were loaded with milk at Torrington, Lapford, Crediton, Seaton Junction, Chard Junction and Semley and no less than five milk tank trains ran daily to the London area.

An important seasonal traffic involved fruit and flowers grown on the slopes of the Tamar and loaded into vans at Bere Alston and stations on the Callington branch. In North Devon there was similar traffic loaded at Braunton. Another traffic was rabbits trapped in Devon and Cornwall and packed 48 a time into wicker hampers. Much of this traffic was conveyed up the main line on the 4.40pm from Plymouth Friary to Eastleigh.

The clear chalk streams and rivers, crossed by our line, were utilised by watercress growers. Watercress in 7lb boxes, known as 'chips', were loaded at several stations including Whitchurch, Hurstbourne, Andover and Grateley for the London market. In the 1950s the 4.48pm stopping train from Basingstoke to Yeovil included a van for watercress and other traffic which was detached at Templecombe, for onwards conveyance along the Somerset & Dorset line and Bath to the Midlands and the North.

As described already, a traffic unique to our line was banknote paper produced at Portals Mill at Overton and forwarded to the Bank of England in London. In South Western days this was loaded in the mill into special horse drawn road wagons which were run on to special flat wagons at Overton station, conveyed by rail to Waterloo, where they were run off and taken to the Bank of

England. All the raw materials used by Portals arrived by train.

By the time our line had been opened to Exeter the Post Office had already established its principal travelling post office and sorting services between Paddington and the west country and between Waterloo and Dorchester. Bags of mail were conveyed in the guards compartments of many trains and at Salisbury the Post Office built its sorting office adjacent to the station. Mailbags to and from London were transferred to and from overnight Dorchester line travelling post offices at Eastleigh.

Of the parcels carried in luggage compartments and vans were boxes of shirts manufactured at Crewkerne and elsewhere, and gloves made at Torrington, Yeovil and Milborne Port.

SUMMER SATURDAY PASSENGER TRAIN SERVICES

A feature of the passenger working on the line was the heavy summer traffic conveying holidaymakers from the London area to and from the seaside resorts of East and North Devon and North Cornwall. This increased under the Southern Railway. Prime example was the 'Atlantic Coast Express' which under the Southern Railway usually comprised one train in winter with through coaches to Exmouth, Sidmouth, Ilfracombe, Torrington, Bude, Padstow and Plymouth, two trains on summer weekdays and up to six trains on a peak summer weekend. This traffic reached a zenith in the 1945-1964 period. In summer 1958 there were nine through trains from Waterloo to East Devon or beyond, with twenty-five on summer Saturdays. After the 1964 season this traffic rapidly disappeared with the new Western Region timetable west of Wilton. However, up to the Ilfracombe line closure in 1971

On 10th September 1961 Schools class 4-4-0 No.30905 leaves Andover Junction with a special train of mixed rolling stock taking passengers to the Farnborough Air Show. S.C.Nash.

Passenger Train Services Salisbury Weekdays Summer 1958

Train	Salisbury arr.	Salisbury dep.	To
1.50am Eastleigh Passenger & Mail	2.27am	2.41am	Yeovil Town
2.55 Salisbury Passenger & Mail		2.55	Bristol Temple Meads
1.15 Waterloo Passenger & News	2.57	3.5	Ilfracombe, Bideford, Padstow, Plymouth
3.24 Salisbury Passenger & News		3.24	Weymouth
3.26 Salisbury Passenger, News & Mail		3.26	Yeovil Town
2.30 Basingstoke Milk	4.7	5.0	Yeovil Town
6.16 Salisbury Diesel		6.16	Andover Junction & Portsmouth
6.20 Salisbury Diesel		6.20	Portsmouth
6.45 Salisbury		6.45	Waterloo
7.15 Salisbury		7.15	Bournemouth West
7.20 Salisbury *		7.20	Grateley
6.3 Portsmouth Diesel	7.27		
7.42 Salisbury Diesel		7.42	Portsmouth
7.44 Salisbury		7.44	Bristol Temple Meads
7.49 Salisbury		7.49	Waterloo
5.25 Swindon	8.4		
6.43 Bournemouth West	8.6		
8.10 Salisbury		8.10	Ilfracombe
6.55 Yeovil Town	8.14		through coaches to Waterloo
6.30 Exeter Central	8.23	8.29	Waterloo
7.3 Portsmouth Diesel	8.27		
8.42 Salisbury Diesel		8.42	Portsmouth
8.46 Salisbury	8.46		Waterloo
6.33 Woking	8.46	9.21	Templecombe
8.20 Semley	8.49		
8.50 Salisbury		8.50	Swanage
9.5 Salisbury		9.5	Weymouth
7.42 Bournemouth Central	9.10		
9.23 Salisbury		9.23	Bournemouth West
8.3 Portsmouth Diesel	9.27		
7.30 Exeter Central	9.27	9.33	Waterloo
9.42 Salisbury Diesel		9.42	Portsmouth
9.50 Salisbury		9.50	Littlehampton
9.3 Templecombe	9.50	10.1	Waterloo
8.30 Portsmouth	9.58	10.10	Bristol Temple Meads
7.20 Waterloo	10.3		
8.10 Bristol Temple Meads	10.13	10.23	Portsmouth
9.3 Portsmouth Diesel	10.33		
10.40 Salisbury Diesel		10.40	Portsmouth
9.0 Waterloo	10.50	10.56	Plymouth & Ilfracombe
11.0 Salisbury Parcels		11.0	Portsmouth
11.4 Salisbury		11.4	Yeovil Town
9.33 Portsmouth	11.5	11.17	Cardiff General
10.3 Portsmouth Diesel	11.27		
10.4 Bournemouth West	11.37		
11.42 Salisbury Diesel		11.42	Portsmouth
10.45 Basingstoke	11.52		
6.15 Plymouth North Road	11.52		
10.34 Portsmouth	12.4	12.18	Temple Meads
11.0 Waterloo ACE	12.23	12.28	Padstow, etc.
8.15 Plymouth Friary	12.23	12.33	Waterloo
11.3 Portsmouth Diesel	12.27		
10.55 Bristol Temple Meads	12.27	12.37	
11.5 Waterloo ACE **Q**	12.32	12.38	Ilfracombe etc.
12.42 Salisbury Diesel		12.42	Portsmouth
12.46 Salisbury		12.46	Exeter Central
12.50 Salisbury		12.50	Bournemouth West
12.58 Salisbury		12.58	Waterloo
10.30 Cardiff General	1.21	1.28	Portsmouth
12.16 Fareham Diesel	1.22		
10.54 Waterloo	1.26		
11.0 Brighton	1.31	1.40	Cardiff General
12.48 Templecombe	1.38		
1.42 Salisbury Diesel		1.42	Portsmouth
8.55 Ilfracombe	1.50		
9.35 Padstow ACE	1.57	2.3	Waterloo
11.30 Brighton	1.58	2.3	Plymouth Friary
10.30 Ilfracombe ACE	2.9	2.15	Waterloo
11.54 Waterloo	2.22		
1.3 Portsmouth Diesel	2.27		
2.42 Salisbury Diesel		2.42	Portsmouth
1.0 Waterloo	2.39	2.45	Plymouth Friary, Ilfracombe, Torrington
11.0 Plymouth Friary	2.49	2.55	Brighton & Portsmouth
1.20 Bournemouth West	2.51		
3.5 Salisbury		3.5	Exeter Central
3.15 Salisbury		3.15	Waterloo
2.3 Portsmouth Diesel	3.27		
3.32 Salisbury Diesel		3.32	Portsmouth
1.0 Cardiff General	3.47	3.57	Portsmouth
2.48 Basingstoke	3.55		
4.5 Salisbury		4.5	Waterloo
2.45 Portsmouth	4.8	4.17	Bristol Temple Meads
1.10 Exeter Central	4.25		
3.3 Portsmouth Diesel	4.27		
3.0 Waterloo	4.41	4.47	Plymouth Friary, Ilfracombe, Torrington
12.20 Ilfracombe	4.45	4.51	Waterloo
4.54 Salisbury		4.54	Templecombe
5.8 Salisbury Diesel		5.8	Portsmouth
5.15 Salisbury		5.15	Waterloo

Passenger Train Services Salisbury Weekdays Summer 1958 (cont.)

	5.20 Salisbury		5.20	Bournemouth West
	4.3 Portsmouth Diesel	5.27		
	4.6 Yeovil Town	5.33		
	5.35 Salisbury		5.35	Cardiff General
	5.19 Grateley *	5.41		
	5.42 Salisbury Diesel		5.42	Portsmouth
	4.48 Basingstoke	5.57	6.10	Yeovil Town
	2.20 Ilfracombe	6.16	6.22	Waterloo
	4.52 Bournemouth West	6.19		
	5.3 Portsmouth Diesel	6.27		
	3.54 Milk Clapham Junction	6.31	6.40	Exeter Central
	4.55 Bristol Temple Meads	6.35	6.43	Portsmouth
	6.55 Salisbury Diesel		6.55	Portsmouth
	5.0 Waterloo	7.0	7.6	Yeovil Junction
	7.15 Salisbury Parcels		7.15	Eastleigh
	5.52 Portsmouth Diesel	7.17		
	5.45 Portsmouth	7.25	7.38	Cardiff General
	4.25 Cardiff General	7.31	7.40	Portsmouth
	6.0 Waterloo	7.44	7.50	Exeter Central
	7.45 Salisbury Diesel		7.45	Portsmouth
	6.5 Swanage	7.52		
	4.35 Exeter Central	7.54		
	3.50 Plymouth Friary	8.2	8.11	Waterloo
	6.38 Portsmouth Diesel	8.10		
	8.15 Salisbury Diesel		8.15	Portsmouth
	5.39 Waterloo	8.19		
	8.22 Salisbury		8.22	Bournemouth Central
	7.0 Waterloo	8.25	8.31	Plymouth North Road
	6.20 Weymouth	8.28		
	7.3 Portsmouth Diesel	8.32		
	through coaches of 7.0pm Waterloo		8.39	Yeovil Town
	8.40 Salisbury Diesel		8.40	Portsmouth
	8.44 Salisbury		8.44	Woking
	6.37 Littlehampton	9.0		
	5.35 Yeovil Town Milk	8.38	9.2	Clapham Junction
	7.43 Bournemouth West	9.10		
	7.25 Bristol Temple Meads	9.19	9.30	Portsmouth
	8.3 Portsmouth Diesel	9.27		
	6.54 Waterloo	9.41	9.55	Yeovil Town
	6.48 Exeter Central Milk	9.55	10.3	Clapham Junction
	10.11 Salisbury Diesel		10.11	Portsmouth
	6.7 Axminster Milk & Parcels	10.37	10.48	Waterloo
	6.15 Portsmouth via South'pton T. Diesel	10.48		
	9.0 Bristol Temple Meads	10.51		
	4.40 Plymouth Friary	10.52	11.10	Eastleigh
	8.53 Portsmouth via Andover Diesel	10.55		
	10.28 Southampton Terminus Diesel	11.9		
	8.54 Waterloo	11.36		

*Workmen's train
Q = 'if required'

On Saturday 14th August 1965 Battle of Britain class 4-6-2 No.34090 *Sir Eustace Missenden Southern Railway* passes Salisbury Tunnel Junction with the 2.13pm Exmouth to Waterloo holiday train, the last season of its operation. S.C.Nash.

On 14th May 1955 King Arthur class 4-6-0 No.30780 *Sir Persant* of Nine Elms shed departs from Andover Junction with an up stopping train comprising a Bulleid three coach set with added vans. R.C.Riley, The Transport Treasury.

there were summer Saturday expresses but served from Paddington.

Post-war, on arrival at or departure from Waterloo, most of these trains comprised the full twelve bogies which the terminus could take. Restricted platform lengths at the West Country resorts limited train lengths, however, and many expresses served several of them. Even the principal

holiday resort at Ilfracombe, as rebuilt by the Southern Railway, was restricted to a maximum eleven bogies. Seats could be reserved in advance on these trains, and many included buffet or restaurant cars at least as far as Exeter. Indeed in 1955 three expresses between Waterloo and Ilfracombe had these throughout the journey.

The number of Saturday trains calling at intermediate stations on our line, such as Andover Junction, was about the same as weekdays but their schedules were adjusted to fit in the holiday expresses. As can be seen from the table which follows, many of the West of England holiday trains called at Surbiton or Woking to pick up holidaymakers

On 24th June 1956 standard class 4-6-0 No.73110 with a Bulleid three coach set waits in Basingstoke East Sidings with a Salisbury line stopping train prior to drawing forward into the station. The guard completes his journal, whilst King Arthur class 4-6-0 No.30784 *Sir Nerovens* awaits his next duty. R.C.Riley, The Transport Treasury.

Down Passenger Trains to Devon and Cornwall Saturdays Summer 1958

Waterloo, or other station, dep.	Intermediate stops, if any	Salisbury arr. Dep.	To
12.15am		1.50am – 1.58am	Padstow, Bude
12.25		2.4 – 2.12	Ilfracombe, Torrington
1.15 Passenger & News	Andover Junction	2.57 – 3.5	Ilfracombe, Bideford
1.25 Passenger & News	Andover Junction	3.10 – 3.17	Plymouth Friary, Padstow
7.33	Surbiton, Woking	9.20 – 9.26	Padstow, Bude
7.38	Surbiton, Woking	9.31 – 9.37	Ilfracombe, Torrington
8.5	Surbiton, Woking	9.47 – 9.53	Exmouth, Sidmouth, Seaton, Lyme Regis
8.22		9.57 – 10.4	Ilfracombe, Seaton
8.35	Surbiton, Basingstoke	10.28 – 10.34	Ilfracombe, Torrington
9.3 Portsmouth		10.42 – 10.47	Plymouth Friary
8.57	Woking, Basingstoke, Andover Junction	10.50 -10.56	Ilfracombe, Plymouth Friary
9.0	Surbiton, Woking, Basingstoke, Andover Junction	11.0 – 11.6	Exmouth, Sidmouth
10.15		11.49 – 11.55	Ilfracombe, Torrington
10.35 **ACE**		12.5pm –12.11pm	Padstow, Bude
10.45		12.16 – 12.22	Seaton, Lyme Regis
11.0 **ACE**		12.31 –12.38	Ilfracombe, Torrington
11.15		12.42 – 12.48	Plymouth Friary, Padstow, Bude
11.45		1.22 – 1.28	Exmouth, Sidmouth
12.5pm		1.35 – 1.42	Ilfracombe, Torrington
12.15 Portsmouth		1.49 – 1.55	Ilfracombe
11.30 Brighton		1.58 –2.3	Plymouth Friary
1.0	Woking, Andover Junction	2.39 –2.45	Plymouth Friary, Ilfracombe, Torrington
1.5	Andover Junction	2.50 –2.59	Exeter Central
3.0	Basingstoke, Andover Junction	4.41 – 4.47	Plymouth Friary, Ilfracombe, Torrington
3.5	Basingstoke, Andover Junction	4.51 – 4.57	Exeter Central
5.0	Woking, all stations Basingstoke to Andover Junction inclusive	7.0 – 7.6	Yeovil Junction
6.0	Basingstoke, Andover Junction	7.44 – 7.50	Exeter Central
7.0		8.25 – 8.31	Plymouth North Road

Up Passenger Trains from Devon and Cornwall Saturdays Summer 1958

Train	Salisbury arr., dep.	Intermediate stops, if any	Waterloo, or other station, arr.
6.30am Exeter Central	8.23 – 8.29	Basingstoke	10.9
7.30 Exeter Central	9.27 – 9.33	Andover Junction	11.8
9.3 Templecombe	9.50 – 10.1	All stations to Basingstoke, Woking	12.19pm
8.30 Exeter Central & Seaton, Lyme Regis	10.45 – 10.51		12.36
9.25 Sidmouth	11.29 – 11.35		1.5
9.25 Exmouth	11.52 – 11.58	Woking	1.38
9.38 Litleham & Seaton	12.9 – 12.15		1.56
8.10 Ilfracombe	12.19 – 12.25		2.8
8.15 Plymouth Friary	12.29 – 12.35	Woking	2.15
9.10 Torrington	12.40 – 12.49		2.37
8.10 Wadebridge	1.17 – 1.25		3.4
10.0 Mortehoe & Wollacombe	1.30 – 1.36		3.10
8.30 Padstow & Bude	1.42 – 1.48	Andover Junction	3.23
9.50 Plymouth Friary	2.7 – 2.13		Portsmouth
10.30 Ilfracombe **ACE**	2.17 – 2.23		3.53
10.48 Torrington **ACE**	2.35 – 2.43		4.19
11.0 Plymouth Friary	2.49 – 2.55		Brighton
11.30 Ilfracombe	3.16 – 3.22		5.3
11.45 Bude	3.26 – 3.32		5.6
12 noon Ilfracombe	3.36 – 3.42		5.15
11.0 Padstow **ACE**	3.47 – 3.53		5.24
1.45 Exmouth & Seaton	4.26 – 4.32	Andover Junction	6.13
11.35 Plymouth Friary & Sidmouth	4.40 – 4.46		6.19
12.45 Torrington & Lyme Regis	4.53 – 4.59	Andover Junction, Woking	6.40
1.45 Ilfracombe	5.48 – 5.55		7.36
2.22 Plymouth Friary, Padstow, Ilfracombe, Torrington	6.16 – 6.22	Andover Junction, Basingstoke, Woking	8.14
3.50 Plymouth Friary & Ilfracombe	8.2 – 8.11	Andover Junction, Basingstoke, Woking, Surbiton	10.1
4.40 Plymouth Friary	10.52 – 11.10		Eastleigh

ACE = Atlantic Coast Express
There was also a 12.16pm Templecombe to Bournemouth West via Salisbury.

There was a natural tidal flow of holiday trains. The extra Down expresses left Waterloo in the morning and had passed Salisbury between about 9.0am and 2.0pm, while the Up expresses were more spread out, passing through between 11.0am and 6pm, so there was a peak of about three hours in the middle of the day.

Compared with weekdays their schedules were about 5 to 10 minutes easier between Waterloo and Salisbury to maintain timekeeping. There was also the heavy Bournemouth line holiday traffic east of Worting Junction and South Coast trains between Tunnel Junction and Salisbury station. The art of driving such trains was summarised by the Eastleigh shedmaster Steven Townroe: 'to keep up with the train in front, and keep ahead of the train behind'. Another consideration was that all Down expresses called at platform 4, and Up expresses at platform 2, at Salisbury where they were allowed about six minutes for a change of locomotive, or sometimes to take water and change crew if the locomotive was running through. Being busy with trains to or from the Western Region together with light engines passing between the east end of the station and the engine shed, platforms 1 and 3 were not usually used for West of England expresses.

GOODS TRAFFIC
Local Goods Traffic

We start by considering the freight traffic forwarded from stations on the line – the varied output of local farms and industries. Agricultural produce was forwarded seasonally, the rolling chalk downs between Basingstoke and Salisbury producing heavy crops of cereals and straw, loaded at all stations on the line. Some grain traffic was

On 4th July 1959 recently repainted S15 class 4-6-0 No.30500 of Feltham shed arrives at Salisbury from Waterloo with a stopping train of Bulleid coaches led by three coach set 785. S15s occasionally worked passenger services in addition to the many heavy freight trains. Peter Barnfield.

forwarded from the Andover Grain Silo siding. Wheat was milled at the Rank Hovis McDougall premises adjacent to Andover Junction station and several vans loaded with boxed bags of flour were forwarded daily. Some other crops were also loaded, together with locally grown timber. Sawn timber was forwarded from sawmills at Andover and Salisbury. Livestock was loaded on weekly market days at Andover and Salisbury, often in large numbers. Annual sheep fairs at Overton and Salisbury produced traffic by the train load, mainly for London but also for the south coast. Details of this traffic, and also that from other stations including Stockbridge and Wilton, appears later in this chapter. Small consignments of general merchandise were forwarded in the scheduled road box services returning to Salisbury Milford, Nine Elms and elsewhere.

As with most railways the greatest volume of traffic received at every station was coal, mainly from collieries on the

On 3rd April 1965 Battle of Britain class 4-6-2 No.34089 *602 Squadron* passes Salisbury Tunnel Junction signal box with the 12.54pm Waterloo to Salisbury passenger train with Bulleid 3-coach set No.777, an all stations service between Woking and Salisbury. S.C.Nash.

About 1936 Adams T1 class 0-4-4T No.17 passes Salisbury Tunnel Junction with a train of non-corridor stock forming a Bulford to Salisbury service. C.H.Eden courtesy Peter Swift.

Western Region via Salisbury but also from mines in the Midlands and north via Feltham yard or Basingstoke. Other traffic received at most stations included construction and building materials such as stone, gravel, cement, sand, plaster, timber, girders, bricks and tiles. Farmers and agricultural merchants received seed, fertiliser, animal feedstuffs, and agricultural machinery. Small consignments of general merchandise from Nine Elms, Salisbury Milford and elsewhere were received by scheduled road van services. These consignments included meat, fruit, vegetables, clothing and footwear, wine, beer, lemonade, china, kitchen utensils and much else were sold in local shops or required by local businesses.

The military bases on Salisbury Plain and elsewhere on the line required all manner of inward supplies. When the bases were built or enlarged construction materials arrived by the trainload, there was regular coal, petrol and other stores traffic and munitions during wartime. Many military vehicles arrived by train. Some of these commodities were subsequently forwarded to other bases.

Through Goods Traffic
Much of the long distance freight running along the line was similar to that handled at local stations as already described but in much greater volume. Down traffic included a wide variety of road boxes conveying general merchandise from Nine Elms to Dorset, Somerset, Devon and Cornwall and more from Feltham Yard. A wide variety of other merchandise including coal, fertilizers and animal feedstuffs also ran down the line.

Long distance traffic up the main line also included general merchandise in road vans returning to Nine Elms. Livestock

traffic from North Devon and North Cornwall was substantial, particularly during the 1940s and 1950s when several livestock specials ran up every evening. Meat also came up from various slaughterhouses. Clay from Cornwall and North Devon came up, some destined for paper mills in North Kent. Other Up traffic included slate and slate dust from Delabole and granite from Wenford Bridge.

Some traffic unloaded from ships at Millbay Docks in Plymouth, such as Spanish new potatoes, was conveyed up to Nine Elms by special trains. Regular traffic since the 1890s of course was railway ballast from Meldon Quarry.

GOODS TRAIN SERVICES
The Development of Goods Train Services
The tabulated 1958 goods trains for Salisbury which follow represent the final stage of the evolution of services over a century. By this stage there were three types of scheduled trains, classified according to braking. Express Fitted (XF) consisted of vacuum braked wagons only and Semi Fitted (SF) had a number of vacuum braked wagons coupled to the tender. The third type was the basic unfitted freight. The 10.15pm Express Fitted freight from Nine Elms Yard to Plymouth was scheduled to arrive at Salisbury station at 12.4am, 82 miles non-stop in 109 minutes at an average speed of 45mph, while the 10.30pm Semi Fitted arrived at 12.59pm, 149 minutes non-stop at an average 33mph. A typical unfitted freight, the 5.30am from Basingstoke to Amesbury, say, arrived at Andover Junction at 6.26am, 18 miles non-stop in 56 minutes averaging 19mph. By contrast the 1.15am

News and Mail from Waterloo arrived at Salisbury at 2.57am, 84 miles non stop in 102 minutes and the 11.0am 'Atlantic Coast Express' took just 83 minutes.

We start by considering the long-distance goods trains on the line. At the London end of the main line there were two main terminals. Nine Elms Goods Station, site of the original 1838 terminus of the London & Southampton Railway, was the largest goods station in London. A couple of miles outside Waterloo, it was very conveniently located for collection and delivery of goods both by road and by river for many thousands of London customers. Feltham Yard, the second main destination, was a very large hump marshalling yard in the west London suburbs opened in stages and completed in 1921-22, with connecting freight services to all the principal railways in the London area.

There were normally two trains daily each way non-stop between Salisbury and Nine Elms and two more between Salisbury and Feltham Yard, each conveying up to sixty wagons. Pride of place went to the two overnight Express Fitted freights, the 10.15pm Nine Elms to Plymouth, which called at Salisbury station between 12.4 and 12.15am to change engines and for wagon examination, and the 4.15pm from Bideford to Nine Elms, which called between 10.15 and 10.22pm. Essentially these two services were Express Fitted only between Nine Elms and Exeter, limited to forty-five vacuum braked wagons, including road box vans conveying general merchandise between Nine Elms and principal goods stations in Devon and Cornwall. Marshalling took place at Exeter Central station. In both directions goods loaded in late afternoon or

On 3rd April 1965 BR standard class 2-6-0 No.76067 and a parcels train for the Eastleigh line passes the exit from Salisbury East Yard with Dunn's Seed warehouse in the background. S.C.Nash.

early evening arrived in time for delivery to customers early next morning.

Traffic to and from other main line companies in the London area ran to and from Feltham Yard, for Kent and Sussex via Woking, for the Great Central line via Basingstoke and for the MSWJR line via Andover Junction. To the west a large volume of traffic was interchanged with the Somerset & Dorset at Templecombe. There were other main line services linking Salisbury with Basingstoke and Woking, together with shorter distance trains, including Basingstoke and Salisbury to Amesbury. At Salisbury there were also services to Milford Goods and to Wimborne and Bournemouth. But there were about six daily freight trains between Salisbury and south coast yards at Eastleigh, Bevois Park,

Chichester and Brighton, some of which ran to or from the Western Region. In addition there were 'Q' paths ('when required') for extra freight trains, including the regular stone trains from Meldon Quarry and returning empties from Woking or Three Bridges.

Ten Down freight trains arrived and eight departed from the five sidings of Salisbury West Yard. Nine Up freight trains arrived and nineteen departed from the thirteen sidings of Salisbury East Yard. In addition there were freight trains to and from the Western Region via Westbury, particularly coal from South Wales to the south coast. There was a greater volume of traffic at the East Yard and it included transfer freights both to Milford Goods and transfers from there, after reversal in the station. Many of

these vehicles ran on road box schedules with general merchandise for smaller stations transferred overnight at Milford Goods. Another feature of the East Yard was that freight trains arriving from the west included wagons to go forward on trains to goods stations and freight yards at Nine Elms, Feltham, Basingstoke, Woking, Eastleigh, Bevios Park, Chichester and intermediate stations at which these trains called. More details of freight train services west of Salisbury will be found in Volume Two. Down freight trains for the Western Region usually ran through to Fisherton Yard, part of the former Great Western station.

THE SALISBURY PLAIN MANOUEVRES 1898

Outline details of these exercises have been given in Chapters One and Three but here we concentrate on the traffic carried and the train services provided for the event. Through the good offices of Nick Pomfret no less than five sets of South Western special notices running into many pages have survived. Some details of the routes followed on the South Western are given but unless of particular interest details of light engine and empty stock workings are omitted. Other trains which ran on the GWR to its Salisbury station, and down the MSWJR to Ludgershall or Weyhill stations, were not included in the South Western notices. Since the War Office was involved with planning troop trains there were also details of the regiment, numbers of officers, men, horses and guns and a small sample of these are included.

Special Notice No.1,352 of Special Traffic Workings in connection with the Army manoeuvres in the neighbourhood of Wareham, Salisbury and Ludgershall for

In 1964 Battle of Britain class 4-6-2 No.34066 *Spitfire* passes under Battledown flyover into the evening sunshine with a down empty milk tank train, apparently the 3.54pm Clapham Junction to Exeter Central. R T Rendell, The Transport Treasury.

Down Freight Trains Salisbury Weekdays Summer 1958

Train	Salisbury Station	Salisbury West Yard	To
10.15 XF Nine Elms	12.4 – 12.15am		Plymouth
10.30 SF Nine Elms	12.59 – 1.0	1.14 – 1.28	Exmouth Junction
12.30 SF Salisbury		12.30 depart	Torrington
12.22am Eastleigh	1.34 – 1.37am	1.47 – 4.30	T'combe(front) & Fisherton (rear)
2.10 Bevios Park	3.38 – 3.39	3.53 arrive	
12.43 Q stone empties Woking	3.44 – 3.55		
11.58 SF Feltham Yard	4.45 – 5.25		Exmouth Junction
3.55 SF Bevois Park	5.30 – 5.32		Exmouth Junction
3.27 Basingstoke	5.40 – 5.42	5.50 arrive	Fisherton
6.30 Salisbury	depart 6.30		
4.40 Q XF Southampton Docks	6.15 – 6.25		Templecombe
2.45 Feltham Yard	6.45 – 6.46	7.0 – 8.21	Exeter Riverside
3.0 Brighton SF	11.33 – 11.40		Templecombe
1.5 Salisbury	depart 1.5pm		Fisherton
11.30 Q XF Southampton Docks	12.59 – 1.4 or 12.59 – 1.20		Templecombe
1.50 Q SF Southampton Docks	3.13 – 3.18		Western Region or Exmouth Junction
			Fisherton or Templecombe or Western Region
2.48 Q SFSouthampton Docks	4.50 – 5.0		Western Region
5.30 Q ballast Three Bridges	5.3 - 5.11		Wilton South
9.45 Q Stone empties Tonbridge	5.19 – 5.22	5.26 – 8.50	Exmouth Junction
5.24 Milford	5.34 – 5.35	5.40 arrive	
5.59 Milford	6.8 – 6.10		Sal'bury East Yard
6.40 Q TuO Milford	6.50 – 6.52	6.57 arrive	
5.40 Q XF Southampton Docks	6.50 – 6.52		Western Region or Exmouth Junction
6.10 Basingstoke West Yard	9.20 – 9.26	9.35 – 10.35	Plymouth Friary
6.35 Wimborne	9.35 – 9.43		Sal'bury East Yard
3.35 Wimborne	10.0 – 10.2	10.12 arrive	
9.5 Q Engineers Redbridge	10.14 – 10.22		Exmouth Junction
9.13 SF Eastleigh	10.25 – 10.34		Fisherton
10.35 Eastleigh	11.52 – 11.54		Codford or Fisherton Q

Up Freight Trains Salisbury Weekdays Summer 1958

Train	Salisbury station	Salisbury East Yard	To
12.45pm SF Torrington	11.43 – 11.52pm	11.56 – 12.13am	Feltham Yard
11.55pm SF Templecombe	1.0 – 1.1	1.5 arrive	
1.35am Salisbury East Yard		depart 1.35	Eastleigh
5.25pm SF Torrington	1.32 – 1.40		Nine Elms
2.15am Salisbury East Yard		depart 2.15	Chichester
1.55pm Q stone Meldon Quarry	2.8 – 2.29		Woking Up Yard
4.5am Salisbury East Yard		depart 4.5	Bo'nemouth C.
4.15am Salisbury East Yard		depart 4.15	Milford
4.25am Salisbury East Yard		depart 4.25	Bevois Park
5.21pm SF Plymouth	2.42 – 2.45	2.50 – 4.35	Feltham Yard
9.25pm stone Okehampton	4.33 – 4.55		Woking Down Yard or Three Bridges
5.15am Salisbury West Yard pass	5.19		Milford
5.45am Salisbury East Yard		depart 5.45	Amesbury
6.33am Q Salisbury East Yard		depart 6.33	Eastleigh
4.52pm Wadebridge	6.14 – 6.24	6.29 arrive	
11.27pm Q Stone Okehampton	6.40 – 6.50		Woking Up Yard
6.55am Q Salisbury			Redbridge
7.55am Salisbury East Yard		depart 7.55	Eastleigh
7.55am Salisbury West Yard pass	8.0	8.5 – 8.20	Wimborne
10.7am Salisbury East Yard		depart 10.7	Milford
8.10am Q Templecombe	10.18 – 10.28		B'stoke U/Y
10.45am Salisbury East Yard		depart 10.45	Basingstoke Up Yard
11.18am Salisbury East Yard		depart 11.18	Milford
11.47am Salisbury East Yard		depart 11.47	Chichester
10.10pm Plymouth	11.25 – 11.29	11.33 arrive	
1.12 SF Salisbury East Yard		depart 1.12	B'stoke Up Yard

Up Freight Trains Salisbury Weekdays Summer 1958 (cont).

12.15pm Templecombe	1.20 – 1.32	1.37 arrive	
1.50pm Salisbury East Yard	depart 1.50		
			Romsey
3.0pm SF Salisbury East Yard		depart 3.0	Eastleigh
4.21pm Salisbury East Yard	depart 4.21		Milford
10.16am Q Stone Meldon Quarry	6.55 – 7.3		Woking Up
			Yard
7.3pm Q SF Salisbury East Yard		depart 7.3	Basingstoke
Up			Yard
1.23pm SF Exmouth Junction	7.8 – 7.9	7.13 arrive	
4.40pm Semley	7.43 – 7.49	7.53 arrive	
12.50pm Q Severn Tunnel Junction		9.15 – 10.27	Chichester
4.15pm XF Bideford	10.15 – 10.22		Nine Elms
11.2pm SF Salisbury East Yard		depart 11.2	Basingstoke
Up Yard			

Q denotes when required

SF denotes a semi-fitted freight.

XF denotes an express fitted freight

Fisherton was the name of the ex-Great Western station at Salisbury.

Light engine movements omitted.

Western Region Freight Trains arriving at Salisbury 1952

Train	From	Salisbury East Yard arr.
9.50am	Bristol	12.23am
7.45pm	Bassaleg	5.44am
1.0am	Cardiff	8.10am
9.15pm	Aberdare	9.44am
2.35am	Radyr	10.57am
3.30am	Cheltenham	11.57am
6.45am	Severn Tunnel Junction	1.44pm
4.10pm	Severn Tunnel Junction	11.20pm (Fisherton)

the week ending Saturday 20th August and including Special Trains with troops to Andover Junction en route to Ludgershall

All these trains ran down the main line via Basingstoke and Whitchurch. The last of these trains, on 18th, conveyed the 1st Battalion Royal Marines with seventeen officers, 500 men and four Officers' horses from Chatham in 18 vehicles supplied by the LCDR, which handed the train over to the South Western at Clapham Junction.

On Friday 19th there was a special train carrying advance parties of about 25 officers and 500 men, leaving Aldershot at 10.5am, running via Frimley (reverse) and Farnborough to Salisbury and Wilton.

Only details of trains for the northern army assembled on Salisbury Plain are included here. Throughout this period there were similar special services working to Wareham for the southern army.

The special trains destined for Ludgershall, Grateley and Wilton all ran along the main line by way of Basingstoke and Andover Junction. With one exception those destined for Milford ran by way of Basingstoke, Winchester (where there was a stop for water if required), Redbridge and Kimbridge Junction so that they could enter Milford (Goods) without reversal. The exception was the 4.15am from Waterloo, which ran down the main line direct and reached Milford (Goods) after reversals at Salisbury station and Milford Junction. The horses were conveyed in cattle trucks. None of these services ran to Porton, which was the station nearest to the manoeuvres area, because it had just one siding on the Up side and could not cope with this traffic.

The vans, conveyed on flat wagons, were loaded with tents, cooking equipment, fuel, fodder, and food. The horses were conveyed in cattle trucks and the men carried in one or two added coaches. On arrival the vans were unloaded in the railway docks, the horses harnessed to the vans, and the men then drove them to the destinations required by the army.

Typically these trains conveyed 22 officers, 585 men and 4 officers' horses. The first, from Dumfries, conveyed the 3rd Battalion Kings Own Scottish Borderers.

For the first train only coffee was to be supplied to the men at Andover Junction between 4.15am and 4.35am. The first four to terminate at Salisbury were instructed to back to the Up platform for unloading, and the empty stock returned by the same route on the South Western.

All stock for these ten trains was LSWR, typically conveying 18 officers, 475 men, 8 horses and 1 gun. For trains from Aldershot (Government Siding) a turnover engine was provided at Frimley Junction where the trains reversed. One train managed two trips, both the 2.0am and the 6.0am from Farnborough. On Saturday 27th August another 10 trains ran, to an almost identical timetable, all to Salisbury.

It would appear that both armies were in position for their manoeuvres by the evening of Saturday 27th August. Manoeuvres now commenced and the southern army made its way to join the northern army on Salisbury Plain in time for the grand review of troops at Boscombe Down on Thursday 8th September. This was a public event and an estimated 60,000 spectators attended, many of them arriving by special train.

Some of these trains required reversal during both the outward and return journeys. The train from Woking to Salisbury via Alton reversed at Eastleigh, the trains from Portsmouth Town and Weymouth to Andover Junction reversed at Salisbury, whilst the train from Bournemouth West to Andover Junction reversed twice, at Redbridge and Salisbury. The train which provided five return trips between Salisbury and Andover Junction

August 1898			
Day	Sta of origin	Number of Veh.	Arr. Andover Junct.
Monday 15th	Colchester	18 GER	2.23pm
Tuesday 16th	Dover	SER	11.55am
	Dover	SER	12.55pm
Thursday 18th	Edinburgh	25 NBR or GNR	6.28am
	Strensall	25 NBR or GNR	6.53am
	Brookwood	18 LSWR	8.20am
	Brookwood	18 LSWR	9.17am
	Waterloo	18 LSWR	10.24am
	Chatham	18 LCDR 1	10.48am

Special Notices Nos.1442 & 1462 dealt with Hired Transport
from 25th to 27th August 1898
Loaded South Western Trains conveying Hired Transport

Date	Train from	Destination	Vans, horses, men
Thursday 25th	1.45am Nine Elms	Ludgershall	36
	2.0am Waterloo	Ludgershall	20, 99, 75
	3.15am Nine Elms	Ludgershall	35
	3.35am Nine Elms	Ludgershall	172, 75
	10.5am Eastleigh	Milford	10, 122, 76
	1.15pm Waterloo	Grateley	5, 21, 11
Friday 26th	1.45am Nine Elms	Grateley	45
	3.35am Nine Elms	Grateley	90, 57
	6.55am Waterloo	Wilton	7, 14, 8
	8.30pm Kensington	Milford	47
	10.0pm Kensington	Milford	47
	11.35p Kensington	Milford	46
Saturday 27th	1.15am Kensington	Milford	46
	3.15am Nine Elms	Milford	245, 130
	4.15am Waterloo	Milford	200, 100
	4.15am Nine Elms	Milford	36
	4.45am Nine Elms	Milford	143, 75
	6.55am Waterloo	Grateley	1, 34, 18

Special Notice No.1475 dealt with special traffic working arrangements on
26th, 27th August 1898
Special Trains with Troops to Salisbury and Wilton Friday 26th August

Station of origin	Nos of vehicles	Route to Andover	Andover Junc dep.	To
Dumfries	18 MR	MSWJR	4.35am	Salisbury
Irvine	18 MR	MSWJR	4.45am	Wilton
Fleetwood	18 LNWR	MSWJR	5.5am	Salisbury
Altcar	18 LNWR	MSWJR	5.35am	Salisbury
Altcar	18 LNWR	MSWJR	6.5am	Salisbury
Altcar	18 LNWR	MSWJR	6.35am	Salisbury
Barry	15 GNR	Clapham Jcn	9.36am pass	Wilton
Barry	15 GNR	Clapham Jcn	9.55am pass	Wilton
Barry	15 GNR	Clapham Jcn	10.22am pass	Salisbury
Barry	15 GNR	Clapham Jcn	11.9am	Salisbury
Hounslow	LSWR	Hounslow	12.54pm	Salisbury

Special Trains with Troops from Aldershot and Farnborough to Salisbury
and Wilton Friday 26th August 1898.

Train from	Andover pass	Salisbury arr. dep.	Empty stock to
2.0am Farnborough	2.56am	3.25 – 3.50am	Farnborough
2.5am Aldershot	3.26	3.55 – 4.20am	Aldershot
3.0am Farnborough	3.56am	4.25 – 4.50am	Aldershot
3.5am Aldershot	4.26am	4.55 – 5.5am	Yeovil Junction
4.0am Farnborough	4.56am	5.25 – 5.35am	Yeovil Junction
4.5am Aldershot	5.24am	5.50 – 6.0am	Gillingham
5.0am Farnborough	5.54am	6.20 – 6.30am	Yeovil Junction
5.5am Aldershot	6.24am	6.50 – 7.0am	Tisbury
6.0am Farnborough	6.56am	Wilton 7.30 – 7.50	Dinton
6.5am Aldershot	7.26am	7.55 – 8.10am	Dinton

during the day was later utilised as a troop train carrying some 550 men and their equipment. A train of this capacity, say 16 or 18 six wheeled carriages about 35ft long over buffers, would be about 600 feet long. Others of the excursion trains may well have been long too, longer than the short 400 feet platforms at Grateley and Porton. It may therefore have been necessary to draw up to the platforms twice exceeding the scheduled two or three minutes allowed.

The march past at the Grand Review began at about 11.20am and was over by about 2.0pm, thus giving plenty of time for spectators to reach the parade ground after arrival of their trains. Porton station was closest to the parade ground, about three miles, which could be walked in an hour, whereas both Grateley and Salisbury were about eight miles. After the departure of the spectators the troops started to leave.

It took three days to load the 50,000 troops and their equipment, twice the number that had previously arrived in the Salisbury area by train, the southern army having been conveyed to Wareham. On the

South Western both the very limited facilities at Porton and the extensive facilities at Salisbury's Milford goods stations were used intensively, as were the MSWJR stations at Weyhill and Ludgershall.

The South Western made full use its route network to ease pressure on the main line, with all trains from Milford running east past Alderbury Junction. On reaching Kimbridge Junction some trains were halted and a turnover engine attached to the rear to draw the train forward to Fullerton Junction, thence via the branch through Wherwell to join the Up main line through Whitchurch. Turnover engines were provided at Milford and Kimbridge Junction. The engines of trains running from Milford to Whitchurch were to travel tender first from Milford to Kimbridge Junction, and then chimney first from Kimbridge to Fullerton Junction, Whitchurch and Up the main line.

Many of the trains from Milford to Nine Elms ran through R o m s e y , Southampton, and Basingstoke. Other trains from Milford to Nine Elms ran via Eastleigh, Fareham, Havant, Guildford, and Cobham. Those to Kensington ran via this route and then via S t a i n e s and Richmond. The standard formation of these trains on arrival at Milford was engine running tender first, van, 3rd class coach, 10 cattle trucks, van, trucks, van, conveying 35 road vans, 70 horses and 50 men.

SPECIAL TRAFFIC ARRANGEMENTS 1914

Each notice covers one or two weeks, and often runs to 20 or 30 pages, with separate issues for the London, Central and Western Districts. In the interests of brevity we consider grouped extracts from the Central District notices, which cover our line and its branches, issued by the Superintendent of the Line, Henry Holmes, and the Central District Superintendent, Mr S.W.Milford.

Special Military Trains to Salisbury Plain

As we have seen in Chapter Four the railway facilities for military traffic available at the southern end of Salisbury Plain in 1914 were much more extensive than for the 1898 manoeuvres and now little if any use was made of Salisbury or Porton for military specials. The principal line, a double track branch from Amesbury Junction, had at Amesbury a major station purpose built for military traffic. For Down main line trains there was the independent single track from Grateley to Newton Tony Junction for

Special Notice No.1580 dealt with Special Traffic Working Arrangements in connection with the Return of Troops for the week ending 10th September 1898.

Advertised Excursion and Special Passenger trains to Grateley, Porton and Salisbury Thursday 8th September 1898.

Train	Route	Destination
7.35am Salisbury	Main Line	Andover Junction 8.8am
6.20am Waterloo	Main Line	Salisbury 9.11am
5.40am Woking	Alton, Romsey, Clatford	Salisbury 9.19am
9.0am Andover Junction	Main line	Salisbury 9.33am
6.30am Portsmouth	Redbridge, Salisbury	Andover Junction 9.25am
7.35am Southampton	Eastleigh, Clatford	Salisbury 9.48am
7.20am Yeovil	Main line	Andover Junction 9.40am
6.0am Bournemouth	Redbridge, Salisbury	Andover Junction 9.50am
6.15am Crediton	Main Line	Andover Junction 10.5am
7.5am Weymouth	Wimborne, Salisbury	Andover Junction 10.10am
10.35am Salisbury	Main line	Andover Junction 11.10am
11.40am Andover Junction	Main line	Salisbury 12.13pm
12.45pm Salisbury	Main line	Andover Junction 1.18pm
2.0pm Andover Junction	Main line	Salisbury 2.33pm
3.15pm Salisbury	Main line	Andover Junction 3.48pm
4.0pm Andover Junction	Main line	Salisbury 4.33pm
5.15pm Salisbury	Main line	Andover Junction 5.48pm
5.50pm Salisbury	Clatford, Eastleigh	Southampton 8.15pm
5.55pm Andover Junction	Main line	Salisbury 6.28pm
6.0pm Salisbury	Clatford, Romsey, Alton	Woking 10.0pm
6.5pm Andover Junction	Salisbury, Redbridge	Bournemouth 9.55pm
6.20pm Andover Junction	Salisbury, Wimborne	Weymouth 9.45pm
6.30pm Andover Junction	Salisbury, Redbridge	Portsmouth 9.49pm
6.35pm Salisbury	Main Line	Waterloo 9.24pm
6.40pm Andover Junction	Main line	Crediton 10.56pm
7.0pm Andover Junction	Main line	Yeovil 9.23pm

which about 7 minutes was scheduled obviating a bottleneck. At Amesbury there were the Up and Down platforms together with no less than seven tracks serving long loading docks where full length military special trains could be loaded or unloaded. There were plenty of berthing sidings, a locomotive turntable and water columns. Usually about an hour was scheduled at Amesbury between the arrival of a military special and the departure of empty stock.

Military special trains included those from the Great Western system both at Salisbury and Basingstoke. The Great Western locomotive worked right through to Amesbury with a South Western pilotman, although an assisting engine was often required over the 1 in 55 and 1 in 60 banks between Newton Tony and Amesbury. On one occasion a London Brighton and South Coast locomotive also worked through from Havant to Grateley where there were also

extended unloading facilities. For these military and other specials Salisbury shed supplied many locomotives and men to pilot Great Western locomotives.

However, there was a similar situation on the MSWJR where at Ludgershall there were two through and three bay platforms, extensive sidings, a locomotive shed and turntable. From here ran the Tidworth branch, double track as far as Perham Down, with its extensive terminus. Many military specials from the Midlands and the North terminated at Ludgershall or Tidworth and do not feature in our account, although some ran to Amesbury after reversal at Andover Junction.

On Sunday 21st June a train conveying 100 men and 100 horses of the Cambridge University Officer Training Corps passed Clapham Junction at 12.40pm to arrive at Grateley at 3.37pm where 3 minutes were allowed to attach an assisting engine. The double headed train worked Up the gradients as steep as 1 in 55 as far as Amesbury where the assisting engine was detached before the train went on to Bulford Camp, arriving at 4.10pm. The empty stock departed Bulford Camp at 5.20pm, requiring the assisting engine between Amesbury and Newton Tony, some of which was Up at 1

On 18th May 1963 S15 class 4-6-0 No.30506 passes Worting Junction with the 10.48am freight from Feltham Yard to Exmouth Junction. This was a semi-fitted freight train, the vacuum-braked vans at the front being connected to the locomotive to provide extra braking power. R.C.Riley, The Transport Treasury.

Special Trains with troops on Thursday 8th September 1898.

Empty stock depart	Troops depart	Route	Destination
	7.30pm Porton	Staines	Brentwood
7.35pm Salisbury	8.40pm Porton	Main line	Farnborough
6.45pm Fullerton	8.0pm Porton	Salisbury, GWR	Dublin
7.25pm Fullerton	9.10pm Porton	Salisbury, GWR	Dublin
	9.11 Ludgershall	Clapham Jn, GWR	Barry
	9.15 Ludgershall	Frimley	Aldershot
	9.21 Ludgershall	Main line	Farnborough
	9.24 Ludgershall	Frimley	Aldershot
	10.15 Ludgershall	Main line	Farnborough
	10.45 Ludgershall	Main line	Farnborough
9.30pm Fullerton	10.50pm Porton	Salisbury GWR	Cork
	10.51 Ludgershall	Main line	Aldershot
10.20pm Fullerton	12.15am Porton	Salisbury GWR	Waterford

The Down Line between Wherwell and Fullerton was used for standing empty troop trains from 7.0pm on Monday 5th until 11.0pm on Thursday 8th, and all traffic had to use the Up Line with a pilotman.

Special Trains with troops on Friday 9th September 1898.

Empty stock depart	Troops depart	Route	Destination
	10.54 Ludgershall	Frimley	Aldershot
	12.15 Ludgershall	Frimley	Aldershot
	12.18 Ludgershall	Frimley	Aldershot
	12.21 Ludgershall	Frimley	Aldershot
	12.24 Ludgershall	Main line	Farnborough
From GER	1.45am Grateley	Staines	Colchester
	1.43 Ludgershall	Frimley	Aldershot
1.35 Andover Jcn	2.45am Grateley	Staines	Colchester
2.15 Andover Jcn	3.30am Grateley	Staines	Colchester
2.25 Bevois Park	4.25am Milford	Wherwell, Woking	Canterbury
From GER	5.45am Weyhill	Staines	Ipswich
	6.0am Weyhill	Staines	Ipswich
3.25 Bevois Park	5.25am Milford	Wherwell, Woking	Canterbury
4.25 Bevois Park	6.15am Milford	Wherwell, Woking	Canterbury
	7.30am Porton	MSWJR	Dublin
5.45 Bevois Park	7.45am Milford	Wherwell, Woking	Canterbury
From LCDR	8.20 Ludgershall	Wimbledon	Chatham
	8.25am Porton	MSWJR	Dublin
6.50am Nursling	8.30am Milford	Wherwell, Staines	Colchester
4.45 Bournemouth	9.10am Porton	MSWJR	Dublin
	10.0 Ludgershall	Main line	Nine Elms
12.5am Aldershot	10.10am Milford	Eastleigh	Gosport
From LNWR	10.35am Porton	MSWJR	Dublin
	10.3 Ludgershall	Main line	Waterloo
	10.6 Ludgershall	Main line	Nine Elms
9.20am Redbridge	11.0am Milford	Wherwell, Staines	Colchester
10.6am Redbridge	11.45am Milford	Wherwell, Staines	Colchester
5.45am Woking	12.15pm Weyhill	Wherwell, Alton	Aldershot
1.20am Aldershot	12.20pm Milford	Wimborne	Portland
11.45am Wilton	1.15pm Porton	Woking, Staines	Brentwood
2.30am Aldershot	1.30pm Milford	Eastleigh	Portsmouth
1.40 Farnborough	2.0pm Porton	Main line	Devonport
5.15am Aldershot	2.25pm Milford	Eastleigh	Portsmouth
From GNR	3.0pm Weyhill	Clapham, GNR	Perth
From GNR	3.30pm Weyhill	Main line	Nine Elms
12.25pm Yeovil	3.35pm Porton	Main line	Kingston
	3.40pm Porton	Main line	Devonport
	4.0pm Weyhill	Clapham, GNR	Glasgow
11.20am Exeter	4.30pm Porton	Main line	Kingston
4.0pm Dinton	5.45pm Porton	Clapham, LCDR	Woolwich
12.5pm Gosport	6.0pm Milford	Southampton	Jersey
5.0pm Tisbury	6.45pm Porton	Main line	Woking
From LCDR	7.10pm Weyhill	Clapham, LCDR	Chatham
	7.18pm Weyhill	Staines	Hounslow
5.15 Gillingham	7.35pm Porton	MSWJR	Dublin
5.55pm Gillingham	7.35pm Porton	MSWJR	Dublin
5.55 Templecombe	8.0pm Porton	MSWJR	Dublin
7.0 Templecombe	10.15pm Porton	MSWJR	Warrington
8.20pm Sherborne	11.15pm Porton	MSWJR	Warrington

in 60. Salisbury shed provided the assisting engine.

On Monday 22nd June there was a review of troops on Perham Down, near Ludgershall on the MSWJR, and cheap day return tickets were available from stations on our line, and branches.

Troops to Amesbury

On Saturday 18th July four troop specials were worked to Amesbury. These were the 8.14am from Basingstoke, 9.50am from Southampton West, and 11.36am and 11.50am from Andover Junction from the MSWJR, two of these requiring assisting engines provided by Salisbury between Newton Tony and Amesbury. The trains conveyed officers, men, horses, guns and limbers, ammunition wagons, harness and baggage.

On Sunday 19th July no less than 8 special trains from West Lancashire ran Down the MSWJR to arrive at Andover Junction between 9.45am and 2.25pm. Here a South Western engine was coupled to the rear of the train and all but one also called at Newton Tony to couple an assisting engine for the last part of the journey to Amesbury. The specials, of mixed vehicles, were allowed about an hour for unloading before returning as empty stock, the last one leaving Andover Junction for the MSWJR at 4.50pm. Salisbury provided all the locomotives and guards required.

From 20th to 25th July a variety of advanced parties of army units travelled to Amesbury, Bulford, Tidworth and Salisbury from various stations travelling in reserved compartments of

Special Trains with Troops Saturday 10th September 1898.

Empty stock depart	Troops depart	Route	Destination
	12 midngt Milford	Wherwell, Woking	Shorncliffe
	12.40am Milford	Wherwell, Woking	Shorncliffe
	1.15am Milford	Wherwell, Woking	Shorncliffe
	2.0am Milford	Wherwell, Woking	Shorncliffe
11.50 Whitchurch	1.30am Porton	MSWJR	Preston
	2.30am Porton	Salisbury GWR	Bristol
11.5pm Chard Jcn	3.20am Porton	Staines	Colchester
4.30am Dean	7.0am Porton	Basingstoke GWR	High Wycombe
	8.20 Ludgershall	Staines	Hertford
5.30am Fareham	8.45am Porton	Ascot	Hounslow
7.25 Templecombe	10.35am Porton	Main line, LCDR	Dover
8.15am Fareham	11.30am Porton	Clatford, Botley	Brighton
11.15 Andover Jcn	12.10pm Porton	Main line	Waterloo
10.10 Southampton	1.30pm Porton	Clatford, Nursling	Parkhurst
6.45am Woking	3.30 Ludgershall	Frimley	Aldershot
7.30am Romsey	4.0 Ludgershall	Frimley	Aldershot
8.0am Romsey	5.23 Ludgershall	Frimley	Aldershot
From GNR	6.50pm Porton	Main line, GNR	York
From GNR	8.0pm Grateley	Main line, GNR	Newcastle
From GNR	8.45pm Grateley	Main line, GNR	Newcastle
From GNR	8.50pm Milford	Wherwell, GNR	York
From GNR	9.35pm Milford	Wherwell, GNR	York
7.30 Stockbridge	9.40pm Porton	Salisbury GWR	Cork
From GNR	10.45pm Milford	Wherwell, GNR	York

The lack of siding accommodation in the area is well illustrated here by the requirements to bring stock from other companies just in time for loading and the berthing points on the South Western many miles from here.

Special Notice No.1,585 dealt with Special Traffic Arrangements for the week ending 10th September 1898 including Hired Transport returning from the neighbourhood of Salisbury

Special Trains with Hired Transport (Vans and Horses)

Date	Train	Route	Destination
Thursday 8th	12 mid. Milford	Dean, Redbridge	Nine Elms
	1.30am Milford	Dean, Redbridge	Nine Elms
	3.0am Milford	Dean, Redbridge	Kensington
	4.30am Milford	Dean, Redbridge	Kensington
	6.0am Milford	Dean, Redbridge	Nine Elms
	7.30am Milford	Dean, Redbridge	Nine Elms
	9.15am Milford	Dean, Redbridge	Kensington
	10.30am Milford	Dean, Redbridge	Nine Elms
	12 noon Milford	Dean, Redbridge	Kensington
	1.30pm Milford	Dean, Redbridge	Nine Elms
	4.30pm Milford	Dean, Redbridge	Nine Elms
	7.40pm Milford	Botley, Havant	Nine Elms
	9.25pm Milford	Dean, Redbridge	Nine Elms
	10.15pm Milford'	Botley, Havant	Nine Elms
	11.45pm Milford	Botley, Havant	Nine Elms
Friday 9th	1.0am Milford	Botley, Havant	Nine Elms
	2.30am Milford	Dean, Redbridge	Nine Elms
	3.30am Milford	Dean, Redbridge	Nine Elms

scheduled trains, sometimes with an extra van or truck provided for equipment. Some of these were transferred from the Great Western at Salisbury.

Movement of Territorial Forces Wednesday 29th July to Saturday 8th August 1914
On Wednesday 29th July two special trains worked to Amesbury. One from Neath, transferred to the South Western at Salisbury at 12.30pm, where a South Western assisting engine was attached to the Great Western locomotive. They then proceeded to work the train together via Amesbury Junction. After the hour allowed for unloading the

Great Western locomotive, with South Western pilotman, returned to Salisbury and the Great Western with the empty stock. The second troop train arrived at Andover from the MSWJR at 12.46pm and after reversals, both here and at Salisbury, ran via Amesbury Junction to arrive at Amesbury at 3.2pm.

Further contingents arrived in reserved compartments in scheduled trains. On Saturday 1st August three extra reserved coaches were attached to the 1.26pm stopping train from Bournemouth Central, as far as Southampton West, and then on attached to the 3.44pm to Salisbury, and finally on the 4.50pm to Bulford. On Sunday

2nd August there were 16 territorial specials to Amesbury and Grateley.

The Essex R.F.A. of about 21 vehicles, from Colchester St Botophs, ran via the North London line and the Byfleet curve to Grateley, where an assisting engine was put on for the final run to arrive at Amesbury at 4.17am. The empty stock departed at 5.20am and returned by the same route.

Three trains for the 3rd North Midlands Brigade R.F.A. travelled Down the MSWJR to Andover Junction where a South Western engine was attached and, with an assisting engine from Newton Tony, arrived at Amesbury at 5.13am, 5.40am and 6.10am. After unloading the empty stock left Amesbury at 6.15am, 6.50am and 7.20am.

Two trains for the Welsh R.F.A. from Neath arrived by the Great Western at Salisbury, where South Western pilotmen joined the locomotives and, with the assisting locomotive from Newton Tony, arrived at Amesbury at 6.50am and 7.42am. The empty stock trains left Amesbury at 7.45am and 8.20am by the same route, the pilotmen coming off when the trains re-joined the Great Western at Salisbury.

Two trains carrying the 4th West Lancs. from Liverpool Edge Hill arrived at Andover Junction via the MSWJR, and were taken by South Western to arrive at Amesbury at 8.52am and 9.56am, with the required assisting engine, the empty stock returning from Amesbury at 10.0am and 10.30am

Two trains conveyed the Leicester R.H.A. to Amesbury. They arrived at Basingstoke hauled by Great Western locomotives, which took up a pilotman here and worked through, with the usual assisting locomotive on the branch, to arrive at

In 1964 BR standard class 2-6-0 No.76055 passes under Battledown flyover with an Up semi-fitted freight. J T Rendell, The Transport Treasury.

Amesbury at 12.28pm. The returning empty stock departed from Amesbury at 1.30pm to run by the same route, setting down the South Western pilotman at Basingstoke.

The Home Counties Division travelled by three trains to Andover Junction and Grateley, the 10.55am from Waterloo arriving at Grateley at 2.10pm and returning to Waterloo at 3.30pm. An SECR train via Guildford and Woking arrived at Grateley at 2.42pm turning round very quickly to depart at 2.55pm to Guildford. The 9.45am from Grateley to Waterloo formed the 3.4pm from Waterloo which arrived at

Grateley at 5.40pm. Many of the soldiers were destined for Andover Junction, with the remainder going to Grateley

The Home Counties brigade of 326 men travelled from the LBSCR at Havant and ran via Fareham, Eastleigh and Andover Junction to arrive at Grateley at 3.10pm. This was hauled throughout by a LBSCR locomotive and crew, with a South Western pilotman and guard. The returning train left Grateley at 4.30pm for Havant but was allowed sufficient time at Andover Junction to turn the engine if required.

Two trains conveyed the London Brigade R.G.A. from Maiden Lane via Gunnersbury and Chertsey to Amesbury, arriving at 4.20pm and 5.35pm after attaching an assistant engine at Newton Tony.

Races at Sandown Park, Ascot and Windsor 1914

On Saturday 27th June a special train of four coaches departed Salisbury at 10.15am, calling for both passengers and horseboxes at all stations on our line except Hurstbourne and destined for Sandown Park racecourse near Esher. At Porton there was a connection with the 9.55am from Bulford and at Andover Junction with the MSWJR and the Southampton line. Race horses, for Esher, were also conveyed by the 8.20am from Salisbury to Waterloo. The returning train left Esher at 5.35pm with the same stops and connections. The same service was provided for races at Sandown Park on Friday 17th and Saturday 18th July, and for races at Hurst Park on Friday 24th and Saturday 25th July.

Between Tuesday 16th and Friday 19th June there was a similar 10.15am train of seven coaches from Salisbury to Ascot station for Ascot Races, returning at 5.45pm. This time passengers from Hurstbourne were to change at Whitchurch. In addition there was a 7.55am special train with passengers, horses and carriages from Stockbridge to Ascot running via Andover Junction (reverse), scheduled to take on horse boxes at Stockbridge and Overton, the train originating at Eastleigh.

On Saturday 20th June the 10.15am special train from Salisbury ran to Windsor for Windsor Races, returning at 5.17pm. Horse boxes were to be conveyed on the 8.20am milk train from Salisbury to Waterloo, detached at Weybridge, and

In 1908 territorials of the 21st County of London Regiment alight from a double-headed special train at Amesbury station, for manoeuvres on Salisbury Plain. Double-heading was required to take trains exceeding 8 bogies over the 1 in 55 bank at Boscombe Down. There were four platforms and loading docks available for unloading military trains at Amesbury.

In 1964 S15 class 4-6-0 No.30837 passes Salisbury Tunnel Junction with an up unfitted freight, possibly the 10.45am from Salisbury East Yard to Basingstoke. R.K.Blencowe Collection.

proceed forward on the 10.5am special from Clapham Junction.

Bibury Club (Salisbury) Races 1914

On Tuesday 7th, Wednesday 8th and Thursday 9th July the Salisbury Race meeting attracted many spectators, the South Western issuing cheap tickets from many stations, together with the MSWJR and the S&DJR. Many scheduled trains were strengthened with extra coaches with no ballast trains ran in the area on race days. Special trains ran for horses from Andover Junction at 9.35am, for first class passengers from Waterloo at 10.55am, and for passengers at cheap fares from Waterloo at 9.32am, and 9.38am on Tuesday only. The special trains called at Salisbury and terminated at Wilton, both stations being about three miles from the race-course on the downs to the south-west of the city. The return trains to Waterloo comprised a 5.45pm from Wilton and Salisbury for first class passengers only with a dining car and a 6.10pm from Salisbury, both running earlier on the Thursday when the races finished earlier. Mr Lawrence, the Salisbury stationmaster, could also run special trains to and from Wilton, if required.

Excursion Trains 1914

On Wednesday 8th July Mr Hunt's Excursion ran empty from Basingstoke to become the 6.5am from Oakley calling at all stations to Whitchurch, Wherwell, and Redbridge (reverse) carrying 650 passengers to Southampton and Bournemouth. A 6.30am special from Andover Junction, Town and Clatford conveyed 100 passengers to Fullerton where they changed into the special. Passengers for Southampton changed at Romsey. The special returned from Bournemouth at 9.5pm, and a special 10.40pm from Fullerton Junction connection was provided for Clatford and Andover passengers.

On Wednesday 15th July Mr Hunt's Excursion departed from Basingstoke at 6.35am calling at all stations to Whitchurch, Fullerton and Romsey, carrying about 350 third class passengers to Portsmouth Town via Eastleigh. The excursion returned along the same route leaving Portsmouth at 8.8pm and again a special train from Andover and Clatford provided a connection at Fullerton Junction for about 100 passengers.

On Tuesday 20th October there was Salisbury Pleasure Fair which attracted extra passengers to the city on all routes, and two special trains from and to Fordingbridge.

On Wednesday 9th September Mr Hunt's Excursion started from Chandlers Ford at 8.39am to call at all stations from Romsey, Wherwell and Oakley for Waterloo. Clatford passengers travelled to Andover Junction by scheduled train and thence on the 9.37am special to Whitchurch where the coaches were attached to the 8.39am from Chandlers Ford. Departure from Waterloo was at 11.55pm and the Andover Junction coaches were detached at Whitchurch and also called at Hurstbourne.

Milk Traffic

From June 1914 a through passenger luggage van was scheduled to run next to the engine on the 7.3am train from Bulford to Salisbury to convey milk for Clapham Junction, Vauxhall and Waterloo. The van went forward from Salisbury on the 8.20am milk train to Waterloo with the empty churn van returning to the branch on the 7.0pm from Salisbury. Photographs in the 1934 Southern Railway Magazine illustrate milk traffic at Salisbury. Three road-rail glass lined milk tanks from Forest Hill in London are loaded on six wheel flat wagons in the West Yard and a rake of milk vans are being loaded with churns in the dock adjacent to the East Yard.

SHEEP FAIRS
Stockbridge Sheep Fair

This was held on Friday 10th July 1914. 50 cattle wagons were provided at Stockbridge and Fullerton Junction. Eastleigh provided a locomotive at Stockbridge by 11.0am for shunting purposes, and if required, to head a special train of sheep to Havant. A special train with sheep left Stockbridge about 5.0pm for Nine Elms, running via Fullerton, Wherwell, Whitchurch, the Byfleet curve and Brentford, and there was a published schedule for this and other special sheep trains. Some local passenger trains through

Stockbridge had extra carriages added for the accommodation of dealers and others.

Salisbury Butts Sheep Fair
On Wednesday 15th July four special trains with sheep were to leave Salisbury (Milford) at times uncertain, but to a schedule, to Nine Elms. They ran to Kimbridge Junction, where a turnover engine was provided, thence via Stockbridge, Wherwell, Whitchurch, and either East Putney or Brentford. Milford was required to telegraph Kimbridge Junction to advise the departure time of each special and after arrival of each special the engine working it from Milford remained at Kimbridge to work the next special. If required another special was to run to Portsmouth or Havant. For this traffic 250 cattle wagons were to be collected at Salisbury, Milford and Romsey.

Overton Sheep Fair
This was held on Saturday 18th July 1914. 100 cattle wagons were collected at Andover Junction and Whitchurch and when they were required a telegraph was sent. A shunting engine from Salisbury was sent to Overton by 9.0am, and Salisbury provided the locomotives for the sheep specials to run from Overton to Nine Elms at times uncertain but to a given schedule. Extra coaches were added to certain passenger trains for dealers and others travelling to Overton.

Wilton Sheep Fair
This was held on Saturday 12th September 1914. 10 brake vans and 260 cattle wagons, suitable for cattle and sheep traffic, were worked to Salisbury (Milford) to be cleaned and sanded. By the Friday night 60 cattle wagons were to be ready at Wilton, 80 at Dinton, 80 at Grateley, and 40 at Salisbury (Fisherton). Two special trains with sheep were to leave Wilton for Salisbury at about

12.30pm and 2.0pm, and about three more from Wilton to Nine Elms. Some of the livestock arrived at Wilton by train, the wagons being worked to Milford to be cleaned and disinfected, with 130 cattle wagons and 6 vans stabled at Milford and 30 more at Romsey. A number of scheduled passenger trains were strengthened with extra coaches for the dealers and others and also a 6.37am Andover Junction to Wilton special passenger train was put on.

A special train of empty cattle trucks left Milford at 2.25am, detaching trucks at Dean and Dunbridge, to Romsey, leaving there at 3.30am to collect loaded cattle trucks at Dunbridge and Dean, arriving at Wilton at 5.25am for the sheep to be unloaded for the sheep fair. Three special trains, with sheep, were scheduled to run from Milford at 3.10pm, 5.0pm and 7.0pm to Nine Elms by way of Kimbridge Junction, where a turnover engine was provided, Stockbridge, Wherwell and Whitchurch. The locomotives ran tender first from Milford to Kimbridge Junction, and thence on the next train chimney first to Nine Elms. Special trains, with sheep, ran from Wilton to Nine Elms to a schedule by way of the main line through Porton. One or two more cattle special ran from Wilton or Milford to Eastleigh.

Salisbury Autumn Sheep Sale
This was held on Friday 30th October 1914 and Mr Wort at Milford was to provide 90 cattle wagons. If required two cattle specials were scheduled, the first leaving Milford at 8.0pm for Nine Elms via Romsey (run round), Wherwell, Basingstoke , Byfleet curve and Brentford, the second leaving at 9.0pm for Portsmouth.

Appleshaw Fair (Andover)
A special train with sheep was scheduled to run on Wednesday 4th November from Andover Junction to Nine Elms via the

Byfleet curve and Brentford. 60 cattle wagons and brake vans were to be provided. Salisbury was to send an engine to Andover Junction for shunting purposes at 2.0pm and afterwards to work the special to Nine Elms. The village of Appleshaw is near Weyhill, so it would appear that this special train originated at Weyhill on the MSWJR. The standard instructions for all these special trains carrying sheep were *'The load of all special trains with sheep must be limited to fifty wagons. Drivers of special trains with sheep are instructed to start and stop with great caution, as claims have been made for injury to sheep caused by violent stopping and starting. The steam brake should only be used in case of emergency. Station masters and guards must take care that the up special sheep trains are shunted in sufficient time to avoid delay to passenger trains.'*

Weyhill Fair
Perhaps the largest fair in our area was held at Weyhill, the first station on the MSWJR from Andover Junction. On 10th October 1922 after Weyhill Fair the MSWJR forwarded 129 loaded cattle wagons, two shunting engines being employed there all day.

On 5th April 1957 S15 class 4-6-0 No.30843 of Exmouth Junction shed enters Salisbury station with an up freight destined for Salisbury East Yard. This is an unfitted freight picking up traffic from several goods yards, the merchandise carried including round timber, livestock and milk. This train appears to be the 10.10pm from Plymouth Friary arriving at Salisbury East Yard at 11.33am. J T Rendell, The Transport Treasury.

Joseph Beattie's Lion class 0-6-0 goods locomotive No.176 *Dragon* in the sidings behind Basingstoke West signal box in the 1880s. The Lion class, and other 0-6-0s of the period, were used not only on goods trains but local passenger trains on the Salisbury line. Built in 1870 *Dragon* was withdrawn in 1891, whilst the signal box was replaced when the line was quadrupled in the early 1900s. Peter Swift Collection.

Beyer Peacock double framed goods 0-6-0 No.221 *Scotia*, again in the sidings behind Basingstoke West signal box in the 1880s, possibly the same day as the *Dragon* photograph judging by the young signal lad. *Scotia* was built in 1866 and withdrawn in 1894, although other members of the class were re-built by Adams and lasted into the 1920s, including No.0351 (badly damaged in the 1906 Salisbury accident).

CHAPTER TEN
LOCOMOTIVES AND ROLLING STOCK

A General Survey

To a great extent a survey of locomotives working on the line is also a survey of LSWR and Southern Railway locomotives. The main line to Salisbury from Basingstoke was engineered to carry the heaviest locomotives of the time and there can be few types which did not pass along the line. That said, most of those employed on main line trains were tender locomotives in their prime, while some classes lasted up to forty years.

During the Beattie period most passenger trains were hauled by 2-4-0s, with 0-6-0s on goods. When William Adams arrived his 4-4-0s took over the passenger services, usually those with 7ft driving wheels east of Salisbury. Those with 6ft 7in drivers were employed on the more hilly route to the west. He also produced more 0-6-0s for goods work and also the 0-4-2 'Jubilee' class for mixed traffic work.

Indeed as we shall see later in the 1952 locomotive duties on our line there was an dominant traffic requirement throughout for a locomotive which could pull a fast passenger train in one direction and return with a milk or fast goods in the other.

Drummond produced more 4-4-0s for express passenger work, the most famous being the T9 class, and they worked many express passenger trains until the 1920s. Forty years later T9s and other classes of Drummond express and mixed traffic 4-4-0s continued to give a good account of themselves on local services between Andover, Salisbury and the South Coast,

Drummond's 4-6-0s were less successful, but some did some good work.

The H15 class Urie mixed traffic 4-6-0s did excellent work during the 1914-18 war and the class continued to give good service on goods and local passenger trains until about 1960. Urie's sister N15 class, particularly following modification by Maunsell who extended the type, which acquired their King Arthur names, were the principal express locomotive on the line from the 1920s until the Merchant Navies arrived in the 1940s.

However, they continued on other services until the early 1960s when Nos.30451 Sir Lamorak and 30457 Sir Bedivere regularly appeared on the 3.35pm Waterloo to Yeovil Town train, which spent five minutes at Andover Junction to load and unload parcels. The third type of 4-6-0, the S15 class, also spent forty years on front line freight duties as well as some passenger turns between the 1920s and the 1960s.

Then came the Bulleid Pacifics, Merchant Navy and West Country classes, which gave excellent service on principal main line trains from their introduction in the 1940s almost until the end of the steam age. In the 1960s they were assisted, particularly between Waterloo and Salisbury, by BR standard 4-6-0s of the 73000 and 75000 classes, all steam locomotives being in a very run down state by the end of steam in 1967.

During the 1947-1957 decade Basingstoke shed was the home of the seven

N15X Remembrance class 4-6-0s. Apparently they had no regular booked duties to Salisbury but occasionally ventured along our line, sometimes reaching Exeter on summer Saturdays. Until about 1945 Lord Nelson class 4-6-0s worked regularly between Waterloo and Salisbury, the odd one reaching Salisbury with banana trains from Southampton Docks, and occasionally reaching Exeter on excursions such as those for Strongs of Romsey. From about 1959 Schools class 4-4-0s started to appear and some went as far as Exeter on summer Saturdays.

LSWR Engine Working Diagrams June 1919

The following extracts are taken from the Locomotive Engineer's Running Office, Eastleigh Works Engine Working Diagrams commencing June 1919. They exclude diagrams from Eastleigh, Fratton, Bournemouth and Salisbury, which covered services joining our line at Andover Junction or Salisbury. Duties west of Salisbury will appear in Volume Two.

Unfortunately there is not the detail in these engine working that there are in 1952 but almost all locomotives working in and out of Waterloo, during the day, were on passenger trains while nocturnal visitors were on milk or parcels trains. Those using Nine Elms and Feltham were goods trains. Diagrams, which took a long time to cover a fairly short journey, were probably goods trains calling at each station yard. Many top link duties, involving a single round trip

William Adams' first express locomotive was the 135 class 4-4-0 with 6ft 7in driving wheels. This is No.145, built in 1881, duplicated in 1902 becoming No.0145, and withdrawn in 1913, departing from Salisbury with an Eastleigh line train shortly after the re-building of the station. Peter Swift Collection.

between Waterloo and Salisbury, were probably performed by one crew who had their own engine.

Although this was eight months after the 1918 Armistice there was heavy and frequent scheduled traffic on the Bulford branch with one Basingstoke and six Salisbury diagrams involved, several for the whole day. Eight heavy trains were scheduled for a pilot locomotive over the Boscombe Down hump between Newton Tony and Amesbury. Which were passenger and goods is not clear but almost all the traffic was military. Traffic, probably military, at Grateley also required a shunting engine for almost three hours.

It would appear that there was a workmen's train between Salisbury and Porton taking civilian staff to the army base, probably completing their journey from Porton station to the base on the Porton Military Railway. This train appears to have left Salisbury at 7.0am, the empty stock was then berthed at Porton while the locomotive (Diagram 981) returned light to Salisbury, and another (Diagram 973) arrived light , coupled up to the coaches and left Porton at 4.50pm. In the 1940s and 1950s there was a similar service to Idmiston Halt, appearing as 1952 Salisbury Duty No.447.

On a Down train in Edwardian days at   Basingstoke is one of Adams later 4-4-0s, T3 class No.574. Peter Swift Collection.

Engine Working Diagram June 1919

Nine Elms Duty 7

	Waterloo	8.0am
10.24	Salisbury	12.43pm
2.30pm	Waterloo	

Nine Elms Duty 8

	Waterloo	8.50am
11.58am	Salisbury	1.13pm
3.25pm	Waterloo	

Nine Elms Duty 11

	Waterloo	5.0pm
7.30pm	Salisbury	9.20pm
2.15am	Waterloo	

Nine Elms Duty 17

	Waterloo	5.55pm
7.46pm	Salisbury	10.15pm
3.15am	Waterloo	

Nine Elms Duty 41

	Waterloo	10.50am
12.33pm	Salisbury	2.28pm
4.15pm	Waterloo	

Nine Elms Duty 60

	Nine Elms Goods	10.45pm
2.58am	Salisbury	3.25am
6.59am	Exeter	9.10pm
12.8am	Salisbury	12.35am
4.30am	Nine Elms Goods	

Nine Elms Duty 61

	Nine Elms Goods	12.25am
4.58am	Salisbury	0.20pm
12.50am	Basingstoke	1.50am
2.40am	Woking	3.40am
5.45am	Wimbledon	

Nine Elms Duty 62

	Feltham	2.5am
4.27am	Basingstoke	5.30am
8.44am	Salisbury	7.20pm
1.10am	Nine Elms Goods	

Nine Elms Duty 97

	Waterloo	3.0pm
4.52pm	Salisbury	8.50pm
11.24pm	Waterloo	

Nine Elms Duty 105

	Waterloo	10.5pm
3.44am	Yeovil Junction	4.15pm
10.45pm	Wimbledon	

Nine Elms Duty 109

	Waterloo	7.0am
10.3am	Salisbury	11.30am
3.0pm	Waterloo	

Nine Elms Duty 177

	Waterloo	3.10am
6.3am	Salisbury	7.55am
12.54pm	Waterloo	

Nine Elms Duty 196

	Waterloo	4.0pm
5.55pm	Basingstoke	7.10pm
8.29pm	Salisbury	9.35pm
1.40am	Waterloo	

Nine Elms Duty 224

	Waterloo	3.0am
4.54am	Eastleigh	5.30am
6.22am	Salisbury	5.42pm
9.15pm	Waterloo	

Nine Elms Duty 227

	Waterloo	10.35am
1.59pm	Salisbury	6.54pm
8.41pm	Waterloo	

Basingstoke Duty 180

	Basingstoke	8.0am
10.10am	Andover Junction shunting	12.25pm
2.59pm	Basingstoke	

Basingstoke Duty 242

	Basingstoke	5.15am
7.21am	Bulford	7.35am
7.40am	Amesbury shunting	6.26pm
8.40pm	Basingstoke	

Basingstoke Duty 252

	Basingstoke	7.30am
7.46am	Overton	8.20am
8.36am	Basingstoke shunting	

Andover Junction Duty 600

	Andover Junction	7.5am
8.31am	Southampton pilot	8.55am
9.13am	Eastleigh	9.25am
10.29am	Andover Junction shunting	1.25pm
2.53pm	Southampton	3.45pm
5.4pm	Andover Junction	

Andover Junction Duty 602

	Andover Junction	9.35am
10.58am	Southampton	12.35pm
2.4pm	Andover Junction	4.15pm
5.37pm	Southampton	6.35pm
7.57pm	Andover Junction	

Andover Junction Duty 603

	Andover Junction	7.0am
7.19am	Stockbridge	7.30am
8.7am	Whitchurch	9.20am
9.43am	Fullerton	10.20am
10.41am	Whitchurch	11.15am
1.5pm	Fullerton	2.35pm
4.13pm	Whitchurch	4.55pm
5.18pm	Fullerton	5.35pm
6.1pm	Whitchurch	6.50pm
7.13pm	Fullerton	7.25pm
7.42pm	Andover Junction	8.0pm
8.45pm	Romsey	9.1pm
9.44pm	Andover Junction	

Andover Junction Duty 604

	Andover Junction	11.40am
4.33pm	Romsey	5.35pm
9.55pm	Andover Junction	

Salisbury Duty 950

	Salisbury	7.30am
10.10am	Waterloo	1.0pm
2.56pm	Salisbury	

Salisbury Duty 951

	Salisbury	2.55pm
6.23pm	Waterloo	8.0pm
10.57pm	Salisbury	

Salisbury Duty 952

	Salisbury	10.14am
12.10pm	Waterloo	
	Wimbledon	2.5pm
6.16pm	Salisbury	

Salisbury Duty 953

	Salisbury	4.56pm
7.0pm	Waterloo	8.40pm
11.54	Salisbury	

Salisbury Duty 955

	Salisbury	8.55am
11.5am	Waterloo	1.35pm
3.30pm	Basingstoke	4.20pm
5.44pm	Salisbury	

Salisbury Duty 971

	Salisbury	3.40pm
7.59pm	Basingstoke	11.40pm
2.4am	Salisbury	

Salisbury Duty 973

	Salisbury	10.43am
12.45pm	Grateley shunts	3.30pm
3.59pm	Salisbury	4.15pm
LE		
4.25pm	Porton	4.50pm
5.3pm	Salisbury	

Salisbury Duty 981

	Salisbury	7.0am
7.16am	Porton	7.20am LE
7.35am	Salisbury	7.45am
8.30am	Bulford	8.50am
9.29am	Salisbury	11.45am
12.27	Bulford	1.0pm
1.42pm	Salisbury	2.45pm
3.22pm	Bulford	3.45pm
4.24pm	Salisbury	7.15pm
7.58pm	Bulford	8.25pm
9.8pm	Salisbury	10.35pm
11.18pm	Bulford	11.35pm
12.10am	Salisbury	

Salisbury Duty 982

	Salisbury	6.0am
6.30am	Tisbury	7.10am
7.45am	Salisbury	9.0am
9.45am	Bulford	10.5am
10.44am	Salisbury	1.0pm
1.39pm	Bulford	1.58pm
2.37pm	Salisbury	4.40pm
5.26pm	Bulford	5.45pm
6.24pm	Salisbury	

Salisbury Duty 984

	Salisbury	4.30am
6.45am	Basingstoke	10.35am
11.23am	Woking	11.45am
2.40pm	Micheldever	
	Basingstoke	5.10pm
7.13pm	Salisbury	

Salisbury Duty 985

	Salisbury	8.20am
12.45pm	Woking	5.45pm
	Guildford	5.59pm
	Godalming	6.22pm
	Woking	9.0pm
1.7am	Salisbury	

Salisbury Duty 986

	Salisbury pilot	5.30am
6.40am	Amesbury LE	
	Newton Tony pilot	7.15am
7.30am	Amesbury shunting	8.40am LE
9.15am	Andover Junction	10.5am
10.48am	Romsey LE	
	Eastleigh	12.30pm
2.21pm	Andover Junction	5.40pm
6.9pm	Southampton	7.30pm
9.18pm	Andover Junction	9.45pm LE
10.18pm	Salisbury	

Salisbury Duty 988

	Salisbury	5.50am
6.51am	Bulford shunting	4.25pm
5.40pm	Salisbury	

Salisbury Duty 989

	Salisbury	6.40am
7.30am	Amesbury	
	shunting pilot	8.50am
9.29am	Salisbury	

Salisbury Duty 990

	Salisbury	6.0am LE
6.30am	Newton Tony pilot	6.51am
7.6am	Amesbury pilot	10.12am
10.33am	Porton	1.7pm
1.24pm	Salisbury pilot	2.45pm
3.19pm	Amesbury pilot	3.52pm
4.2pm	Newton Tony LE	
	Bulford	6.0pm
6.6pm	Amesbury pilot	6.26pm
6.49pm	Grateley	8.8pm LE
8.30pm	Amesbury	8.52pm
9.35pm	Salisbury	

Drummond C14 class 2-2-0T No.743 at Whitchurch station on 12th October 1908 with the two coach train to Fullerton. By 1919 this was Andover Junction duty No.603. Peter Swift collection.

MSWJR Locomotive Rosters weekdays February 1884 Andover Shed

0-6-0T No.1 or No.2

6.20am	Mixed	Andover Junction – Cirencester
10.15am	Mixed	Cirencester – Swindon Town
12.42pm	Passenger	Swindon Town – Swindon (GWR)
1.40pm	Passenger	Swindon (GWR) – Swindon Town
4.0pm	Goods	Swindon Town – Andover Junction

2-4-0T No.6

9.22am	Passenger	Andover Junction – Swindon (GWR)
11.10am	Goods	Swindon (GWR) – Swindon Town
1.52pm	Passenger	Swindon Town – Andover Junction
4.30pm	Passenger	Andover Junction – Cirencester
6.50pm	Mixed	Cirencester – Andover Junction

GWR Locomotive Rosters weekdays September 1923 Andover Shed

7.10am	Mixed	Andover Junction – Tidworth
8.10am	Passenger	Tidworth – Ludgershall
8.30am	Passenger	Ludgershall – Tidworth
8.45am	Passenger	Tidworth – Andover Junction
9.30am	Passenger	Andover Junction – Ludgershall
10.15am	Mixed	Ludgershall - Tidworth
11.10am	Passenger	Tidworth – Ludgershall
11.30am	Passenger	Ludgershall – Tidworth
12.20pm	Passenger	Tidworth – Ludgershall
1.35pm	Mixed	Ludgershall – Tidworth
2.40pm	Passenger	Tidworth – Ludgershall
3.2pm	Passenger	Ludgershall – Tidworth
3.20pm	Passenger	Tidworth – Ludgershall
3.40pm	Passenger	Ludgershall – Tidworth
5.30pm	Passenger	Tidworth – Ludgershall
6.5pm	Passenger	Ludgershall – Tidworth
7.50pm	Passenger	Tidworth – Ludgershall
8.12pm	Passenger	Ludgershall – Tidworth
8.30pm	Goods	Tidworth – Ludgershall
9.50pm	Pasenger	Ludgershall – Tidworth
	Empty Stock	Tidworth – Ludgershall
10.20pm	Goods	Ludgershall – Andover Junction
8.0am	Passenger	Andover Junction - Cheltenham Lansdown
3.0pm	Passenger	Cheltenham Lansdown – Andover Junction
2.40pm	Passenger	Andover Junction – Cheltenham Lansdown
6.42pm	Passenger	Cheltenham Lansdown – Andover Junction

Locomotive Allocation

4-4-0	No.6
4-4-4T	No.17
0-6-0T	No.14
0-4-4T	No.15

Southern Region Locomotive Diagrams London West and Southern Districts Weekdays 15ᵗʰ September 1952, 'until further notice'

The following extracts have been taken from the Locomotive Diagrams for engines working between Basingstoke and Salisbury and other engines which reached Andover Junction from either the MSWJR, the Romsey direction or Salisbury from the Romsey or Wimborne direction. It excludes, of course, parts of the diagrams not relevant to our line. Western Region locomotives arriving at Salisbury station or Salisbury East Yard have also been omitted. Some Southern Region locomotives worked both east and west of Salisbury and are here included, although they will be covered in more detail in Volumes Two and Three.

There are more than thirty locomotive diagrams for our main line of which Salisbury covered eleven and Nine Elms eight, others from Feltham, Basingstoke, and Eastleigh and five from Exmouth Junction. For one locomotive diagram there were a number of crew changes, for example Nine Elms duty No.2, which took an N15 King Arthur class to Yeovil and back with crews from Nine Elms, Yeovil, Salisbury and Basingstoke, and similar duty No.3 also involved Guildford men from Salisbury to Woking.

Up to 1950 almost all trains had changed locomotives at Salisbury but the tender capacity of the Merchant Navies made it possible to run right through between Waterloo and Exeter. One advantage was the reduction in light engine movements at Salisbury, particularly for Up trains when light engines had to run through the station between the shed and the east sidings. The short-lived Devon Belle, 12 noon Waterloo and 1.40pm Exeter, was a Merchant Navy turn, the Nine Elms, Salisbury and Exmouth Junction Merchant Navies involved changing over at Wilton in both directions to ease congestion at Salisbury station.

In 1952 Ten of the top link duties were all performed by Merchant Navy Pacifics: Nine Elms duties 4, 5, 7, Salisbury 431, 461 and Exmouth Junction 494, 495, 496, 497 and 498. All involved a round trip between Waterloo and Exeter, almost 400 miles including shed visits. Salisbury firemen were provided to assist in getting coal forward while train crew were filling the tender with water, the water pressure here being higher to speed this up. Nine Elms men worked to Salisbury and back, Exmouth Junction men to Salisbury and back, while Salisbury men worked in both directions. In 1957 the 7.0pm Waterloo to Plymouth express was also hauled by a Merchant Navy to Exeter.

The next longest daily duties seen at Salisbury were for the two West Country light Pacifics that worked the Up and Down Plymouth to Brighton trains as far as Salisbury, about 300 miles daily.

For some weeks in1957 the 65ft Salisbury turntable was replaced by a 70ft model. During this period some locomotives used the GWR turntable but many visited the SR shed for servicing in the normal way and then worked forward on another train. This led to some unusual workings, such as Brighton based engines reaching Yeovil or Exeter.

In 1952 the ten Merchant Navies between them hauled not only all the principal West of England expresses, including the 1.25am newspaper train, but also milk and fast overnight goods trains, including the 9.10pm and 10.0pm from Nine Elms. Nine Elms duty No.5 took the 11.0am Atlantic Coast Express to Exeter but returned with a milk train to Clapham Junction. The milk and goods duties may have lacked the glamour of the express work but arguably they brought at least as much, if not more, revenue to the railway.

Halfway between Basingstoke and Salisbury was Andover Junction shed but its locomotives and men were employed not on the main line but on MSWJR and Hampshire lines services. This brings us to the forty or so duties covering services between the South Coast to Salisbury, Andover and beyond. About half of these were covered by Eastleigh, Salisbury and Andover sheds but there were also Brighton, Guildford, Fratton, Bournemouth and Yeovil turns together with the Western Region sheds at Swindon and Cheltenham. Many Hampshire services to Andover Junction were worked by T9 class 4-4-0s, so were scheduled to terminate in the Down main platform, where the locomotive could run round and shunt the stock to the bay before crossing over to the engine shed to turn and take water before returning to the coaches in the bay for departure. One train comprised a fitted M7 and push-pull set which could use the bay directly.

At Salisbury locomotives arriving with passenger trains from Portsmouth or Bournemouth into the Southampton bay platform could shunt the coaches straight back into the carriage sidings. Many passenger and freight trains from both Basingstoke and Salisbury to Amesbury were worked by Drummond 700 class 0-6-0s which could cope with the steep gradients on the branch, although the passenger service had been withdrawn on 30th June 1952, just a few weeks previous to these locomotive duties.

Andover men worked as far as Southampton or Cheltenham but sometimes were scheduled to change over with Eastleigh crews at Fullerton or Horsebridge, and with Swindon crews at Savernake or Marlborough. Cheltenham and Swindon WR men often worked to Andover. Salisbury men worked through to Portsmouth and Bournemouth but on some trains changed over with Bournemouth men at Verwood or Wimborne.

Adams 445 class 4-4-0 No.445 outside Andover LSWR shed in Edwardian days. Built in 1883 with 7ft 1in driving wheels they were first employed on the best Waterloo to Salisbury express trains and then on less demanding main line duties. In 1911 it was duplicated, becoming No.0445, and was withdrawn in 1925.

Locomotive Diagrams 1952

Brighton Duty No.731
6 MT (W.C. Class)

	Brighton	11.0am **P**
1.31pm	Salisbury	
	Loco Yard	
	Salisbury	2.55pm **P**
	(11.0am ex Plymouth)	
5.22pm	Brighton	

Worked by Brighton men

Brighton Duty No.732
6 MT (W.C. Class)

	Brighton	11.30am **P**
1.58pm	Salisbury	
	Loco Yard	
	Salisbury	3.52pm **P**
	(1.0pm ex Cardiff)	
6.24pm	Brighton	

Worked by Brighton men

Western Region Swindon Duty No.74
4 MT TK (45XX class)

	Swindon Town	7.20am **P**
9.5am	Andover Junction	
	Loco Yard	
	Andover Junction	12.0 noon **F**
	(6.40am ex Cheltenham)	
1.23pm	Romsey	2.12pm **F**
3.5pm	Andover Junction	
	Stable for No.77	

Worked by WR Swindon and Andover Junction men.

Western Region Swindon Duty No.75
4 M.T. (43XX class)

	Swindon Town	2.2pm **F**
3.53pm	Ludgershall	4.25pm **P**
4.32pm	Tidworth	4.45pm **P**
4.52pm	Ludgershall	6.5pm **F**
6.38pm	Andover Junction	7.15pm **F**
9.40pm	Swindon	

Worked by WR Swindon men

Western Region Swindon Duty No.76
4MT (43XX class)

	Swindon Town	10.15am **F**
1.58pm	Cheltenham	5.21pm **P**
8.17pm	Andover Junction	
	Stable for No.78	

Worked by WR Cheltenham men,

Western Region Swindon Duty No.77
4MT (45XX class) stabled off No.74

	Andover Junction	7.0am **P**
8.35am	Marlborough	9.6am **P**
9.17am	Savernake	

from here on works between Marlborough and Savernake and returns to Swindon at 8.50pm

Worked by Andover and WR Swindon men.

Western Region Swindon Duty No.78
4MT (43XX class) stabled off No.76

	Andover Junction	8.15am **F**
1.37pm	Swindon	

Worked by Andover and WR Swindon men

Western Region Cheltenham Duty No.21
4MT (43XX class)

	Cheltenham	4.10am **F**
7.28am	Andover Junction	8.4am **F**
10.10am	Southampton Docks	11.0am **LE**
11.8am	Bevois Park	11.30am **F**
1.12pm	Andover Junction	1.30pm **F**
5.22pm	Cheltenham	

Worked by WR Cheltenham and Andover men

Western Region Cheltenham Duty No.22
5MT (78XX class)

	Cheltenham	10.10am **P**
12.57pm	Andover Junction	1.3pm **P**
2.6pm	Southampton Town	4.36pm **P**
5.38pm	Andover Junction	5.42pm **P**
8.6pm	Cheltenham	

Worked by WR Cheltenham and Andover men

Western Region Cheltenham Duty No.23
4 MT (43XX class)

	Cheltenham	6.40am **F**
11.37am	Andover Junction	2.35pm **P**
3.55pm	Swindon Town	4.49pm **P**
6.8pm	Andover Junction	8.55pm **F**
	(7.4pm ex Southampton)	
1.2am	Cheltenham	

worked by WR Cheltenham WR Swindon and Andover men

Western Region Cheltenham Duty

	Cheltenham	5.42am **F**
10.18am	Andover Junction	
	Cheltenham	

worked by WR Cheltenham men

Western Region Bristol Duty No.365 Tuesdays and Thursdays Only
4 MT (43XX class)

	Salisbury Loco	2.40pm
2.45pm	Salisbury East	3.7pm **F**
5.50pm	Southampton Old Docks	8.4pm
8.38pm	Eastleigh	9.44pm **P**
10.36pm	Salisbury	
	Salisbury loco	
	Fisherton	3.30am **F**
4.49am	Westbury	

worked by Salisbury and Western Region men

Nine Elms Duty No.1
5P (N 15 class)

	Nine Elms Goods	3.30am **F**
5.45am	Weybridge	6.15am **F**
6.49am	Chertsey	7.28am **LE**
7.47am	Woking	8.45am **P**
9.28am	Basingstoke	10.45am **P**
11.52am	Salisbury Loco yard	
	Salisbury	3.15pm **P**
5.35pm	Waterloo	

worked by Nine Elms, Guildford, Eastleigh and Salisbury men

Locomotive Diagrams 1952 (cont.)

Nine Elms Duty No.2
5P (N 15 class)

	Waterloo	4.45am P
5.50am	Woking	6.33am P
8.49am	Salisbury	9.24am P
10.18am	Templecombe	10.46am P
12.7pm	Yeovil Junction	12.40pm P
12.45pm	Yeovil Town	
	Yeovil loco	
	Yeovil Junction	3.0pm P
	(1.6pm ex Exeter)	
4.32pm	Salisbury	5.15pm P
8.0pm	Waterloo	

worked by Nine Elms, Salisbury, Basingstoke, Guildford and Western District men
In later years this duty was worked by a *Schools* class 4-4-0.

Nine Elms Duty No.3
5P (N 15 class)

	Waterloo	7.20am P
9.58am	Salisbury	12.36pm P
1.49pm	Yeovil Junction shunting	
	Yeovil Town	5.40pm M
8.27pm	Salisbury	8.37pm M
10.18pm	Woking	12.33am F
1.43am	Nine Elms Goods	

worked by Nine Elms, Salisbury, Guildford and Western District men

Nine Elms Duty No.4
8P (MN class)

	Waterloo	9.0am P
10.50am	Salisbury	10.56am P
1.8pm	Exeter	
	Exmouth Junction loco	
	Exeter	4.30pm P
	(2.20pm ex Ilfracombe)	
6.27pm	Salisbury	6.33pm P
8.25pm	Waterloo	

worked by Nine Elms and Western District men

Nine Elms Duty No.5
8P (MN class)

	Waterloo	11.0am P
12.23pm	Salisbury	12.28pm P
2.6pm	Exeter	
	Exmouth Junction loco	
	Exeter	6.48pm M
8.12pm	Templecombe	9.5pm M
9.50pm	Salisbury	10.5pm M
12.20am	Clapham Jcn	

East of Salisbury worked by Nine Elms men, and Salisbury and Exmouth Junction men to the west.

Nine Elms Duty No.10
5P (N 15 class)

	Waterloo	5.39pm P
8.18pm	Salisbury	
	Salisbury loco	
	Salisbury EastYard	12.13am F
	(12.45pm ex Torrington)	
3.0am	Nine Elms Goods	

worked by Nine Elms, Feltham and Salisbury men

Nine Elms Duty No.11
5P (N 15 class)

	Waterloo	12.54pm P
2.14pm	Basingstoke	2.48pm P
4.2pm	Salisbury	
	Salisbury loco	
	Salisbury	
		10.40pm M
2.32am	Waterloo	

worked by Nine Elms and Salisbury men

Nine Elms Duty No.72
4MT (H 15 class) stabled off No.71 duty

	Portsmouth	7.29am P
9.15am	Salisbury	
	Salisbury loco	
	Salisbury East	11.18am F
4.11pm	Eastleigh thence to Basingstoke and Waterloo	

worked by Fratton, Salisbury and Eastleigh men

Feltham Duty No.101
6F (S 15 class)

	Feltham Yard	10.48am F
3.39pm	Salisbury West Yard	
	Salisbury loco	
	Salisbury	8.16pm P
10.20pm	Portsmouth	
	Fratton loco thence Fratton to Eastleigh and Feltham	

worked by Feltham, Salisbury, Fratton and Eastleigh men

Feltham Duty No.106
6F (S 15 class) (833 series) stabled off No.105

	Hove	3.50am F
5.15am	Chichester	7.20am F
10.29am	Salisbury	
	Salisbury loco	
	Salisbury East	2.20pm F
4.0pm	Basingstoke	

thence Eastleigh, Southampton, Feltham worked by Fratton, Eastleigh, Salisbury, Basingstoke and Feltham men

Feltham Duty No.116
6F (S 15 class) stabled off No.115

	Salisbury East	11.27am F
12.48pm	Eastleigh	1.23pm F
3.27pm	Chichester thence Fratton Yard, Feltham	

worked by Salisbury, Eastleigh, Guildford men

Guildford Duty No.236
5F (Q 1 class)

	Woking	4.50am F
10.40am	Rowlands Castle	11.0am F
11.40am	Petersfield thence Havant, Eastleigh	
	Eastleigh	8.56pm F
10.25pm	Salisbury WR stable for 237 worked by Guildford, Fratton and Eastleigh men	

Guildford Duty No.237
5F (Q 1 class) off duty 236

	Salisbury East	3.30am F
6.28am	Chichester thence Havant, Petersfield and Guildford worked by Eastleigh, Fratton, Guildford men	

Basingstoke Duty No.253
5 P (N 15 class)

	Basingstoke	9.2am P
	(6.35am ex Bournemouth)	
10.20am	Waterloo	
	Nine Elms loco	
	Waterloo	1.54pm P
3.14pm	Basingstoke	4.48pm P
6.0pm	Salisbury	
	Salisbury loco	
	Salisbury	8.50pm P
10.52pm	Woking	1.25am M
4.7am	Salisbury	5.15am M
8.15am	Yeovil Jcn	9.0am M
9.5am	Yeovil Town stable for No.473 duty	

worked by Basingstoke, Nine Elms, Guildford, Salisbury and Western District men

Basingstoke Duty No.259
4 MT (U class)

	Basingstoke	7.45am F
10.50am	Andover Junction	
	Andover loco	1.8pm LE
1.28pm	Overton shunting	
	Overton	4.33pm F
5.8pm	Basingstoke	

worked by Basingstoke men

Basingstoke Duty No.262
4F (700 class)

	Basingstoke	5.30am F
8.51am	Bulford shunting	
	Amesbury	4.35pm F
6.53pm	Basingstoke worked by Basingstoke and Andover men	

Andover Junction Duty No.266
2P (T 9 class)

	Andover Junction	9.37am F
10.14am	Fullerton	10.40am F
11.5am	Longparish	11.45am F
12 noon	Fullerton	12.14pm F
2.16pm	Romsey	2.35pm F
2.55pm	Nursling	3.14pm F
3.24pm	Romsey shunting	
	Romsey	6.5pm F
6.39pm	Eastleigh	

worked by Andover and Eastleigh men

Andover Junction Duty No.267
BR class 2 (Mixed traffic tank) stabled off No.306

	Andover Junction	6.47am P
7.12am	Tidworth	7.50am P
8.14am	Andover Junction shunting	
	Andover Junction	10.35am P
10.48am	Ludgershall	11.0am
	Mixed	
11.7am	Tidworth	12.15pm
	Mixed	
12.22pm	Ludgershall	12.30pm
	Empty Train	
12.43pm	Andover Junction shunting	
	Andover Junction	4.12pm P
4.50pm	Romsey	5.3pm P

thence Southampton, Alton, Eastleigh worked by Andover and Eastleigh men

Andover Junction Duty No.268
2P (T 9 class) stabled off No.403

	Andover Junction	6.45am P
7.58am	Southampton Term.	8.33am P
9.52am	Andover Junction	11.25am P
12.18pm	Eastleigh thence Portsmouth, Romsey, Eastleigh worked by Andover, Eastleigh, and Fratton men	

Andover Junction Duty No.269
4 MT (43XX class) on loan

	Andover Junction	7.30am P
8.7am	Romsey	8.32am P
8.47am	Eastleigh	9.2am P
	(7.31 ex Woking)	
9.20am	Southampton Term.	10.10am P
11.6am	Andover Junction	11.9am P
1.30pm	Cheltenham	3.20pm F
7.42pm	Andover Junction worked by Andover men	

Andover Junction Duty No.270
4MT (43XX class) on loan

	Andover Junction	7.45am P
10.35am	Cheltenham	2.3pm P
4.37pm	Andover Junction	4.43pm P
5.50pm	Southampton Term.	shunt
	Southampton Docks	7.4pm F
8.41pm	Andover Junction worked by Cheltenham and Andover men.	

Eastleigh Duty No.271
7P (Lord Nelson class)

	Southampton Town	6.4am P
8.24am	Waterloo	
	Nine Elms loco	
	Waterloo	10.54am P
1.24pm	Salisbury loco yard	
	Salisbury	4.5pm P
5.31pm	Basingstoke	5.37pm P
7.7pm	Waterloo thence Nine Elms loco and Goods and F to Eastleigh worked by Eastleigh, Nine Elms, Basingstoke and Salisbury men	

Eastleigh Duty No.286
BR Standard (class 4 mixed traffic)

	Eastleigh, Southampton, Totton	

Locomotive Diagrams 1952 (cont.)

	Portsmouth	9.33am **P**
11.5am	Salisbury	12.44pm **P**
	(10.27am ex Bristol)	
2.6pm	Portsmouth, then Eastleigh, Fratton	

worked by Eastleigh men

Eastleigh Duty No.288
3P (D 15 class)

	Eastleigh, Southampton then	
	Portsmouth	10.34am **P**
12.18pm	Salisbury	1.28pm **P**
	(10.30am ex Cardiff)	
3.1pm	Portsmouth	5.45pm **P**
7.24pm	Salisbury	11.10pm **P**
	(4.40pm ex Plymouth)	
11.46pm	Eastleigh worked by Eastleigh men	

Eastleigh Duty No.290
2P (T 9 class)

	Eastleigh, Bournemouth,	
	then Eastleigh	6.30pm **P**
7.45pm	Andover Junction shunting, berth for	

No.266 worked by Eastleigh and Andover men

Eastleigh Duty No.292
2P (T 9 class)

	Eastleigh, Bournemouth, then	
	Eastleigh	5.42pm **P**
6.45pm	Andover Junction	7.35pm **P**
8.36pm	Eastleigh, then Southampton worked	

by Eastleigh men

Eastleigh Duty No.294
2P (T 9 class) stabled off 293

	Bournemouth Central	5.55am **LE**
6.18am	Broadstone	7.14am **P**
8.19am	Salisbury	9.25am **P**
10.57am	Bournemouth West	1.20pm **P**
2.59pm	Salisbury	5.7pm **P**
7.9pm	Portsmouth, thence Eastleigh worked	

by Bournemouth, Salisbury and Eastleigh men

Eastleigh Duty No.295
2 P (L 1 class)

	Eastleigh	6.40am **F**
10.45am	Andover Junction shunting	
	Andover Junction	3.11pm **LE**
3.16pm	Andover Town shunting	
	Andover Town	5.0pm **F**
5.5pm	Andover Junction	6.40pm **P**
7.50pm	Eastleigh	

worked by Eastleigh and Andover men

Eastleigh Duty No.298
2 PT (M7 class P&P)

	Eastleigh	7.56am **P**
8.54am	Andover Junction	9.30am **P**
10.24am	Eastleigh, thence Alton, Eastleigh	

worked by Eastleigh men

Eastleigh Duty No.306
BR class 2 (mixed traffic tank)

	Eastleigh, Fareham, thence	
	Portsmouth	11.19am **P**
1.27pm	Andover Junction, shunting stable for	

No.267

worked by Eastleigh and Andover men

Eastleigh Duty No.311
4 MT (H 15 class)

	Bevois Park	3.58am **F**
5.37am	Salisbury WR	
	Salisbury East	8.45am **F**
10.8am	Eastleigh, thence Nine Elms worked	

by Eastleigh men

Eastleigh Duty No.312
4 MT (H 15 class)

	Bevois Park	10.23am **F**
12.52pm	Salisbury	4.18pm **F**
5.52pm	Eastleigh worked by Eastleigh men	

Eastleigh Duty No.316
BR standard (4 MT)

	Eastleigh	9.30am **F**
12.5pm	Milford Goods shunting	
	Milford Goods	5.0pm **F**
5.35pm	Salisbury Fisherton	
	Salisbury loco	7.30pm **LE**
8.10pm	Andover Junction	8.50pm **F**
	(3.20pm ex Cheltenham)	
10.25pm	Eastleigh	

worked by Eastleigh and Salisbury men

Eastleigh Duty No.319
5F (Q 1 class)

	Eastleigh	12.20am **F**
1.45am	Salisbury West Yard shunting	
	Salisbury East Yard	4.25am **F**
5.54am	Northam Yard worked by Eastleigh and	

Salisbury men

Fratton Duty No.368
4MT (U class)

	Portsmouth	9.3am **P**
10.41	Salisbury	11.6am **P**
12.30pm	Yeovil Junction shunting	
	Yeovil Town	4.5pm **P**
5.42pm	Salisbury	6.57pm **P**
	(4.32pm ex Bristol)	
8.57pm	Portsmouth	

worked by Fratton, Salisbury and Western District men

Bournemouth Duty No.403
2P (T 9 class)

	Bournemouth, Southampton then	
	Portsmouth	7.45pm **P**
10.4pm	Andover Junction stable for No.268	

worked by Bournemouth, Eastleigh and Andover men

Salisbury Duty No.430
6MT (BOB class)

	Salisbury	6.45am **P**
9.20am	Waterloo	
	Nine Elms loco	
	Waterloo	11.54am **P**
2.20pm	Salisbury	3.5pm **P**
4.24pm	Yeovil Junction	
	Yeovil loco	
	Yeovil Junction	6.41pm **P**
	(4.35pm ex Exeter)	
7.54pm	Salisbury	
	Salisbury loco	
	Salisbury	12.5am **F**
4.33am	Exmouth Junction stable for No.472	

worked by Salisbury and Western District men

Salisbury Duty No.431
8P (MN class)

	Salisbury	8.15am **P**
10.8am	Waterloo	
	Nine Elms loco	
	Waterloo	1.0pm **P**
2.39pm	Salisbury	2.45pm **P**
4.42pm	Exeter	
	Exmouth Junction loco	
	Exeter	7.50pm **P**
	(4.40pm ex Plymouth)	
10.52pm	Salisbury worked by Salisbury and	

Western District men

Salisbury Duty No.432
5P (N 15 class)

	Salisbury	3.30am **P**
5.3am	Yeovil Junction	
	Yeovil Town	7.10am **P**
7.15am	Yeovil Junction	7.22am **P**
8.33am	Salisbury	8.42am **P**
11.16am	Waterloo	
	Nine Elms loco	
	Waterloo	5.9pm **P**

6.25pm	Basingstoke	7.4pm **F**
9.50pm	Salisbury	
	Salisbury loco	11.40pm **LE**
12.58am	Basingstoke loco stable for No.253	

worked by Salisbury and Basingstoke men

Salisbury Duty No.435
6F (S 15 class)

	Salisbury	1.0pm **P**
3.32pm	Waterloo	
	Nine Elms loco	
	Waterloo	6.54pm **P**
9.46pm	Salisbury	9.55pm **P**
11.11pm	Yeovil Junction	11.21pm **P**
11.26pm	Yeovil Town shunting	
	Yeovil Junction	3.55am **F**
	(4.30pm ex Wadebridge)	
6.25am	Salisbury East Yard shunting	

worked by Nine Elms, Salisbury and Western District men

Salisbury Duty No.436
5P (N 15 class)

	Salisbury	4.35am **F**
	(5.21 ex Plymouth)	
6.34am	Basingstoke	9.18am **F**
11.49am	Feltham Yard	
	Feltham loco	
	Feltham Yard	2.47pm **F**
3.42pm	Nine Elms Goods	
	Nine Elms loco	
	Waterloo	8.54pm **P**
11.20pm	Salisbury	

worked by Salisbury and Feltham men

Salisbury Duty No.438
6F (S 15 class)

	Salisbury	10.42am **F**
2.41pm	Basingstoke	
	Basingstoke loco	
	Basingstoke	7.4pm **F**
9.50pm	Salisbury worked by Salisbury and	

Basingstoke men

Salisbury Duty No.440
4MT (H 15 class)

	Salisbury	2.20am
		Stone Q
	(1.55pm ex Meldon Quarry)	
5.20am	Woking	
	Guildford loco	
	Woking	2.2pm **Stone Empties Q**
2.58pm	Basingstoke	3.5pm **Stone Empties Q**
5.25pm	Salisbury West Yard worked by	

Salisbury and Guildford men

Salisbury Duty No.441
4MT (H 15 class)

	Salisbury	4.55am
		Stone Q
	(9.20pm ex Meldon Quarry)	
8.15am	Woking	
	Guildford loco	
	Woking	12.23am **Stone Empties Q**
3.48am	Salisbury worked by Salisbury and	

Guildford men

Salisbury Duty No.443
2P (T 9 class)

	Salisbury	3.52am **P**
4.50am	Wimborne	
	Bournemouth loco	
	Bournemouth Centra	17.42am **P**
9.10am	Salisbury shunting	
	Salisbury	1.6pm **P**
	(via Eastleigh)	
2.22pm	Southampton T. then Woolston and	
	Eastleigh	8.22pm **P**
	(7.17pm ex Portsmouth)	
9.11pm	Salisbury worked by Salisbury and	

Eastleigh men

Locomotive Diagrams 1952 (cont.)

Salisbury Duty No.444
2P (T 9 class)

	Salisbury	7.15am **P**
8.50am	Bournemouth West	
	Bournemouth loco	
	Bournemouth West	4.52pm **P**
6.22pm	Salisbury worked by Salisbury and	

Bournemouth men

Salisbury Duty No.445
2P (T 9 class)

	Salisbury	7.47am **P**
9.36am	Portsmouth	
	Fratton loco	
	Portsmouth	1.3pm **P**
1.46pm	Eastleigh	1.49pm **P**
2.35pm	Salisbury	5.20pm **LE**
6.45pm	Bournemouth West	7.43pm **P**
9.17pm	Salisbury worked by Salisbury men	

Salisbury Duty No.447
2PT (M 7 class) shunting

	Salisbury	7.20am **P**
7.43am	Grateley	7.48am **LE**
8.12am	Salisbury shunting	
	Salisbury	4.35pm **LE**
4.55pm	Grateley	5.19pm **P**
5.41pm	Salisbury shunting worked by	

Salisbury men

Salisbury Duty No.450
4MT (U class)

	Salisbury	1.35am **F**
2.46am	Eastleigh, then	
	Southampton T.	7.27am **P**
	(5.58am Portsmouth)	
8.31am	Salisbury	
	Salisbury loco	
	Salisbury	10.37am **P**
	(8.10am ex Bristol)	
12.34pm	Portsmouth	
	Fratton loco	
	Portsmouth	4.45pm **P**
6.49pm	Salisbury	

worked by Salisbury and Fratton men

Salisbury Duty No.451
4F (700 class)

	Salisbury West Yard	7.37am **F**
3.15pm	Wimborne	3.25pm **LE**
3.37pm	Poole	3.39pm **LE**
3.44pm	Hamworthy Junction	4.25pm **F**
	(12.3pm ex Dorchester)	
4.43pm	Wimborne	6.50pm **F**
9.2pm	Salisbury WR worked by Salisbury	

and Bournemouth men

Salisbury Duty No.452
4F (700 class)

	Salisbury East Yard	4.5am **F**
7.11am	Bournemouth Central Goods	
		11.35am **F**
1.45pm	Poole	1.55pm **LE**
2.13pm	Wimborne	3.35pm **F**
8.45pm	Salisbury East Yard worked by	

Salisbury and Bournemouth men

Salisbury Duty No.454
4F (700 class)

	Salisbury West Yard	5.5am **F**
5.34am	Milford Goods	5.45am **LE**
5.53am	Salisbury East Yard	6.10am **F**
7.23am	Bulford	8.0am **LE**
8.5am	Amesbury	9.10am **LE**
9.44am	Salisbury worked by Salisbury and	

Basingstoke men

Salisbury Duty No.457
7FT (Z class) shunting Salisbury East Yard

Salisbury Duty No.458
2MT tank (E 4 class) shunting Fisherton Yard and Salisbury station

Salisbury Duty No.461
8P (MN class)

	Salisbury	8.5am **P**
11.19am	Exeter	
	Exmouth Junction loco	
	Exeter	2.30pm **P**
	(12.20pm ex Ilfracombe)	
4.45pm	Salisbury	4.51pm **P**
6.33pm	Waterloo	
	Nine Elms loco	
	Nine Elms Goods	10.0pm **F**
12.55am	Salisbury worked by Salisbury and	

Western District men

Salisbury Duty No.467
6F (S 15 class)

	Salisbury	10.0pm **P**
	(7.10pm ex Bristol)	
11.6pm	Eastleigh	1.15am **LE**
1.31am	Bevios Park	2.10am **F**
3.58am	Salisbury	4.55am **F**
	(11.58pm ex Feltham)	
7.25am	Yeovil Junction	11.50am **F**
	(4.30am ex Exmouth Junction)	
12.45pm	Templecombe	1.5pm **LE**
1.15pm	Gillingham	4.35pm **F**
7.52pm	Salisbury	

worked by Salisbury and Western District men

Salisbury Duty No.470
6F (S15 class)

	Salisbury	1.10am **F**
7.45am	Exmouth Junction	
	loco yard	
	Exmouth Junction	1.35pm **F**
8.0pm	Templecombe	8.20pm **P**
9.13pm	Salisbury	10.50pm **F**
12.41am	Basingstoke	3.30am **F**
5.50am	Salisbury worked by Salisbury and	

Western District men

Salisbury Duty No.471
6F (S 15 class)

	Salisbury West Yard	12.55pm **F**
2.0pm	Templecombe	2.55pm **F**
3.25pm	Yeovil Junction	4.31pm **P**
	(3.5pm ex Salisbury)	
6.5pm	Exeter	
	Exmouth Junction loco	
	Exmouth Junction	9.45pm **F**
	(5.21 ex Plymouth)	
2.35am	Salisbury East Yard	4.15am **F**
4.25am	Milford Goods	8.0am **LE**
8.7am	Salisbury loco worked by Salisbury	

and Western District men
By the early 1960s this had become a light pacific duty.

Western District Engines working over London West and Southern Districts

Yeovil Duty No.485
4MT (U class)

	Yeovil	5.15am **LE**
5.41am	Templecombe	6.15am **P**
7.8am	Semley	8.35am **P**
9.4am	Salisbury	9.47am **P**
11.50am	Portsmouth	
	Fratton loco	
	Portsmouth	2.33pm **P**
4.8pm	Salisbury	

	Salisbury loco	
	Salisbury	8.5pm **P**
9.25am	Yeovil Junction worked by Western	

District and Salisbury men

Exmouth Junction Duty No.494
8P (MN class)

	Exeter	6.30am **P**
9.53am	Salisbury	10.1am **P**
12.19pm	Waterloo	
	Nine Elms loco	
	Clapham Junction	3.54pm **M**
	(via East Putney)	
6.27pm	Salisbury	6.40pm **M**
11.53pm	Exeter worked by Western District,	

Salisbury and Nine Elms men

Exmouth Junction Duty No.495
8P (MN class)

	Exeter	7.30am **P**
9.27am	Salisbury	9.33am **P**
11.8am	Waterloo	
	Nine Elms loco	
	Waterloo	6.0pm **P**
7.44pm	Salisbury	7.50pm **P**
10.0pm	Exeter	

worked by Western District and Nine Elms men

Exmouth Junction Duty No.496
8P (MN class)

	Exeter	10.30am **P**
	(8.15 ex Plymouth)	
12.28pm	Salisbury	12.34pm **P**
2.15pm	Waterloo	
	Nine Elms loco	
	Waterloo	5.0pm **P**
7.0pm	Salisbury	7.6pm **P**
10.39pm	Exeter	

worked by Western District and Salisbury men

Exmouth Junction Duty No.497
8P (MN class)

	Exeter	12.30pm **P**
	(10.30 ex Ilfracombe)	
2.7pm	Salisbury	2.15pm **P**
3.40pm	Waterloo	
	Nine Elms loco	
	Nine Elms Goods	9.10pm **F**
11.37pm	Salisbury	11.45pm **F**
2.24am	Exmouth Junction	

worked by Western District and Nine Elms men

Exmouth Junction Duty No.498
8P (MN class)

	Exeter	5.55pm **P**
	(3.50pm ex Plymouth)	
8.3pm	Salisbury	8.9pm **P**
10.8pm	Waterloo	
	Nine Elms loco	
	Waterloo	1.25am **P &**
News		
3.11am	Salisbury	3.19am **P &**
News		
5.0am	Exeter worked by Western District	

and Salisbury men

Key
F Freight
LE Light engine
M Milk
P Passenger
Q When required

A number of light engine moves between station and locomotive depot, and shunting duties have been omitted due to lack of space.

PRESERVED STEAM LOCOMOTIVES
Following the appearance of GW 4-6-0 No.4930 Hagley Hall on steam specials on the Ludgershall branch on 22nd, 23rd March 1986 there have been a number of preserved steam special trains and light engines recorded by David Lindsell at Andover including:
20.9.87 S&DR 2-8-0 No.53809 on Ludgershall branch specials

19.9.87 GW 4-6-0 No.6998, failed, in down siding.
30.6.88 LM 2-8-0 No.48151 on Ludgershall clearance test train

The numerous Adams mixed traffic A12 'Jubilee' 0-4-2s worked on the line for half a century. No.534, built in 1887 and scrapped in 1928, is on a Down train for Templecombe at the west end of the old Salisbury station in September 1896. J.B.N.Ashford courtesy Peter Swift.

10.7.88 SR 4-6-2 No.34092 in branch sidings
18.10.92 SR 4-6-0 No.30777 on Down main line special
17.5.95 SR 4-6-2's Nos.35028, 34027 on Down main line special, "Waterloo Sunset"
12.2.00 SR 4-6-2 No.35005 on Down main line special
26.7.01 SR 4-6-2 No.34016 on Up *Cathedrals Express* from Bath 6th November 2002 No.4472 on VSOE Pullmans to Westbury.

These are examples only – a full list would be far too long.

DIESEL LOCOMOTIVES AND MULTIPLE UNITS

Diesel traction first appeared at an early stage on the line when from 29th October 1951 Southern Railway designed, No.10202, commenced work on a diagram covering the 1.25am and 1.0pm services from Waterloo. It returned from Exeter Central on the 7.30am and 5.55pm trains, covering some 687 miles per day. In 1952, No.10201 was also involved in 1953 Ivatt designed Nos10000 and 10001, and in 1954 No.10203, some Bournemouth line duties also being covered. In 1955 they were transferred to the London Midland Region and the experiment ended.

The new timetable in September 1964 saw the end of steam power on Waterloo – Salisbury – Exeter St David's trains. The new semi-fast service was provided by rakes of Mk1 carriages hauled by D800 'Warship' diesel hydraulic locomotives, based at Newton Abbot depot, and working empty to Exeter St David's. 'Hymeks' sometimes were provided when a 'Warship' was not available.

From 1964 the stopping train service from Waterloo, fast to Woking and then all stations to Salisbury, was initially steam hauled, often by 73000 BR standard 4-6-0s. But when the civil engineering work for the Bournemouth line electrification started many of these off peak services were provided by Western Region diesel multiple units calling at all stations between Woking and Salisbury, in connection with Waterloo to Portsmouth electric trains. When Waterloo to Basingstoke electric trains started on 2nd January 1967 these diesel services were restricted to Basingstoke to Salisbury. When the full Bournemouth line electric service began, on 10th July 1967, 'Hampshire' diesel multiple units provided a Reading to Salisbury stopping service in connection with electric trains at Basingstoke.

In October 1971 diesel hydraulic locomotives had gone out of favour and the class 42 'Warships' were replaced by

In January 1948 at platform 3 at Salisbury is Adams G6 class 0-6-0T No.237 employed in station pilot and yard shunting duties, for which several classes of tank engines were used over the years. J.T.Rendell, The Transport Treasury.

Waterloo Carriage Workings Summer 1913

The following extracts from train formations involve vans destined for stations or junctions on our line.

3.5am	includes	1 bogie van	Salisbury
		1 bogie van Wimborne via Salisbury	
		1 MSWJ van	Swindon
		2 MSWJ vans	Andover Junct
12.25pm		1 MSWJ van	Andover Junct
		1 PL van	Salisbury
		1 bogie van Bomo W. via Salisbury	
		1 MSWJ van	Swindon
		1 MSWJ van	Andover Junct
7.3pm		1 PL van	Salisbury
		1 6 wheel van	Semley
		2 MSWJ vans	Swindon
		2 MSWJ vans	Andover Junct

5.35am from Clapham Junction includes

| | | 1 MSWJ van | Andover Junct |

1944 Carriage Workings Weekdays

2-Set No.225

	arr.		dep.
	Eastleigh		7.54am
8.52am	Andover Junct.R.P.		9.39am
10.1am	Salisbury		

3-Set No.235

	Andover Junction	6.8am *
6.11am*	Andover Town	6.20am
6.24am	Andover Junction	6.34am
6.55am	Overton F.P.	7.20am*
7.40am*	Andover Junction	9.20am
10.23am	Eastleigh	

3-Set No.236

	Andover Junction	6.45am
7.58am	Southampton Term.	8.2am
9.9am	Portsmouth	11.45am
2.9pm	Andover Junction	3.20pm
3.59pm	Basingstoke R.P.	4.16pm
4.57pm	Woking	

3-Set No.238

	Basingstoke	6.40am
6.56am	Overton R.P.	7.20am*
7.40am*	Andover Junction	7.58am
8.38am	R'sey, thence Eastl'gh, South'pton	

3-Set No.241

	Basingstoke, Waterloo thence	
	Basingstoke R.P.	4.25pm *
4.38pm*	Overton R.P.	4.54pm
5.13pm	Andover Junction F.P.	6.55pm
7.50pm	Eastleigh	

3-Set No.242

	Basingstoke	10.45am
11.51am	Salisbury	12.55pm
3.45pm	Exeter	

3-Set No.243

	Bulford	8.0am
8.36am	Salisbury	8.55am
9.28am	Bulford	9.40am
10.13am	Salisbury	11.10am
11.45am	Bulford	11.52am
12.25pm	Salisbury	1.12pm
1.46pm	Bulford	1.53pm
2.27pm	Salisbury	2.58pm
3.32pm	Bulford	3.55pm
4.29pm	Salisbury	5.43pm
6.19pm	Bulford	6.26pm
6.58pm	Salisbury	7.55pm

8.30pm	Bulford	8.38pm
9.13pm	Salisbury	9.45pm
10.19pm	Bulford	

3-Set No.251

	Waterloo	7.20am
8.44am	Basingstoke	8.50am
9.27am	Andover Junction F.P.	9.30am
10.1am	Salisbury thence Yeovil	
	Salisbury	6.20pm
7.24pm	Basingstoke	7.40pm
9.7pm	Waterloo	

3-Set No.255

	Yeovil, thence Ilfracombe	
	Salisbury	8.55pm
10.11pm	Basingstoke	10.19pm
11.9pm	Woking	

3-Set No.260

	Winchester thence	
	Waterloo	10.54am
1.21pm	Salisbury thence Templecombe	

3-Set No.279

	Portsmouth thence	
	Basingstoke F.P.	4.25pm*
4.38pm*	Overton F.P.	4.54pm
5.13pm	Andover Junction R.P.	6.55pm
7.50pm	Eastleigh	

3-Set No.285

	Salisbury	8.28am
8.41am	Idmiston Halt	8.43am*
8.51am*	Grateley	6.5pm*
6.13pm*	Idmiston Halt	6.15pm
6.26pm	Salisbury thence Yeovil	

3-Set No.294

| | Woking | 6.30am |
| 8.48am | Salisbury thence Exeter | |

3-Coach Corridor Set "P" Type No.865

	Yeovil	7.12am
8.33am	Salisbury F.P.	8.42am
11.9am	Waterloo thence Clapham*	
	Waterloo R.P.	7.35pm
9.40pm	Salisbury	9.55pm
11.30pm	Yeovil	

3-Coach Corridor Set "P" Type No.872

	Salisbury	6.45am
9.20am	Waterloo, thence Clapham*	
	Waterloo	2.50pm
5.22pm	Templecombe thence Ilfracombe	

3-Coach Corridor Set "P" Type No.876

	Salisbury R.P.	8.42am
11.9am	Waterloo, thence Clapham*	
	Waterloo M.P.	7.35pm
9.40pm	Salisbury	

3-Coach Corridor Set "P" Type No.880

	Salisbury R.P.	6.45am
9.20am	Waterloo thence Clapham*	
	Waterloo F.P.	5.0pm
7.8pm	Salisbury	

3-Coach Corridor Set "T" Type No.903

	Waterloo F.P.	3.33pm
4.40pm	Basingstoke F.P.	4.48pm
6.2pm	Salisbury	

3-Coach Corridor Set "T" Type No.904

	Salisbury F.P.	11.50am
2.34pm	Waterloo, thence Clapham*	
	Waterloo F.P.	7.54pm
9.19pm	Basingstoke	

Southern Region diesel electric class 33s allocated to Eastleigh although the coaching stock was still allocated to Newton Abbot. However, the class 33's 1550 hp was much less than their predecessor's 2200 or 2300hp so loads were reduced and timings eased. The problem was occasionally overcome when a pair of class 33's were provided but the platform lengths at Waterloo precluded such working for every train. Class 33's were already in use on some Meldon to Woking ballast trains, sometimes double headed, usually routed via Westbury, and one stopping train, the 6.10pm Waterloo to Salisbury was provided by a class 33 with an 8TC unit.

Class 33's hauling 4TC coaching sets running in push-pull mode gradually took over stopping trains between Basingstoke and Salisbury, mostly running to and from Waterloo, replacing 'Hampshire' units working between Reading and Salisbury. In the 1980s the class 33 and 4TC sets began to work Waterloo trains beyond Salisbury

Top left. Adams T1 class 0-4-4T No.3 outside Basingstoke shed in Edwardian days.

Middle left. Inside the clean new Basingstoke locomotive shed shortly after opening. To the left is Drummond railcar No.1 which was here for six weeks from 1st July 1904 working on the Basingstoke and Alton line, assisted by car No.2. To the right are Adams A12 class 0-4-2 No.642 and a 4-4-0.

Bottom left. Drummond 700 class 0-6-0 goods engine No.689 about to depart from the original Salisbury station with a Down goods train. The locomotive was built in March 1897, and was two months old when the photograph was taken in May. The 700 class worked on the line until the early 1960s, particularly on the Amesbury branch trains. J.B.N.Ashford courtesy Peter Swift.

to Gillingham and other stations. However, in May 1980 more powerful class 50's, displaced by Western Region High Speed Trains, took over from class 33's on Waterloo – Salisbury – Exeter trains, until joined by class 47's starting in 1984. Following the closure of Newton Abbot depot these locomotives and rakes of coaches were maintained at Plymouth Laira depot, each requiring an unproductive daily 100 mile empty stock working.

The total route modernisation implemented by Network Southeast in 1993 saw the introduction of a fleet of 22 class 159 diesel multiple units, maintained at the new Traincare Depot at Salisbury. For many down services one class 159 unit is uncoupled at Salisbury reflecting the lighter loading of trains thence to Exeter, making use of the efficient coupling and uncoupling from the cab. Their availability was such that they could also cover a new service between Reading and Brighton. With increasing traffic however, in 2001, South West Trains augmented the Salisbury train fleet with 8 class 170 diesel multiple units, which were used to provide an off-peak hourly stopping train service between Waterloo and Salisbury in addition to the hourly semi-fast service. Some mixed class 159/170 formations also run east of Salisbury.

Several of the diesel locomotive classes already considered were also to be seen on freight trains, which after 1964 were soon reduced to only one or two a day. The main freight services comprised Mendip stone from Merehead and Whatley quarries to Woking and elsewhere which in more recent years have been hauled mainly by class 59 locomotives. Ministry of Defence services between Eastleigh and Ludgershall, and also Didcot and Ludgershall, over the years were handled by classes 31, 33, 37, 47, 50 and 73, but other classes were also seen, and since 2000 EWS class 66 have taken on much of the work.

David Lindsell has observed a variety of diesel locomotive workings at Andover including:

Top left. Two Drummond T9 class 4-4-0s, the leading one being No.718 built in 1899, on a down express in platform 4 at Salisbury in Edwardian days. T9s, known as Greyhounds due to their fast running, worked heavy express trains between Waterloo, Salisbury and Exeter for many years. They were still in use in the 1950s on Hampshire trains seen at Andover and Salisbury. Peter Swift Collection

Middle left. Drummond P14 class 4-6-0 No.449 in the Down sidings at Salisbury in 1911. All five of the class were allocated to Salisbury when they were built in 1910/11 and were used on the Exeter line. Like most Drummond 4-6-0s the design was unsuccessful, and No.449 was the last of the class to be scrapped in 1927. Peter Swift Collection.

1.8.84 33018, 33007 Down Freightliner to Southampton, diverted via Laverstock.
2.8.84 33006, 33012 Down stone empties
31.5.88 33102, 8TC, 33119 on 10.0am to Waterloo
7.2.89 73001 with MOD freight Woking to Ludgershall
24.1.95 D6508 (33008) on empty ballast hoppers Ludgershall branch to Eastleigh
1.4.95 47213 Down Freightliner to Southampton, diverted via Laverstock
4.5.95 20901 on Down weedkiller train
14.8.95 47703 running round 4TC unit going to Ludgershall for storage
26.2.97 37167 on 10.22 tanks train Quidhampton to Willesden
9.3.98 37294 shunting grain wagons during loading
16.3.98 37211 with up freight train of grain wagons from Andover and tanks from Quidhampton for Didcot.
19.4.98 37294, 37219 with MOD train of 26 loaded wagons Wales to Ludgershall
6.9.98 37715 on Up ballast wagon train
13.1.99 73134, 73141 with 6 loaded vans of fertilizer
4.9.99 37892 with Down train of 15 loaded MOD wagons for Ludgershall
10.9.99 37203 with loaded MOD train from Ludgershall
6.10.99 37719 with 6 wagons of fertilizer
10.7.01 58047 with 22 MOD wagons loaded with Land Rovers from Ludgershall

N15 King Arthur class 4-6-0 No.30456 *Sir Galahad* on an Up passenger train, probably a Salisbury to Waterloo stopping train, at Andover Junction in June 1949. For many years Salisbury shed had an allocation of at least ten of the class, including *King Arthur* himself, No.30453. R.K.Blencowe Collection.

CARRIAGE WORKING NOTICES
Weekdays commencing 8th June 1953 and until further notice

Train	Destination	Formation	Previous service Train From	Due
ANDOVER JUNCTION				
am				
6.45	Portsmouth & S.	3 lav. set	Berth	
6.47	Tidworth	2 W.R. set	Berth	
7.0	Marlborough	2 W.R. set	Berth	
7.30	Romsey	6-set (410 type)	Berth	
7.50	Cheltenham	3 W.R. set	Berth	
9.30	Eastleigh	3 lav. set	7.56 Eastleigh	8.54
10.8	Salisbury **FO***	6-set (410 type)	Berth	
10.35	Tidworth	2 W.R. set	7.50 Tidworth	8.14
11.9	Cheltenham	3 W.R. set	10.10 Southampton T.	11.6
11.25	Eastleigh	3 lav.set	8.33 Southampton T.	9.52
pm				
1.3	Southampton T.	1 W.R. van	10.11 Cheltenham	12.57
		3 W.R. set		
2.35	Swindon Town	2 W.R.set	7.4 Swindon Jcn	9.8
4.12	Romsey	3 lav.set	11.19 Portsmouth FP	1.27
4.43	Southampton T.	3 W.R. set	1.56 Cheltenham	4.37
5.42	Cheltenham	3 W.R. set	4.36 Southampton T.	5.38
		1 W.R.van		
6.10	Waterloo **FO**	2 thirds	Berth	
		8-set		
6.40	Eastleigh	3 lav.set	11.19 Portsmouth RP	1.27
7.35	Eastleigh	3 lav.set	2.20 Weymouth	6.45
	Berth	2 W.R.set	2.0 Ludgershall	2.13
	Berth	2 W.R.set	4.49 Swindon Town	6.8
	Berth	3 lav.set	5.16 Fawley	7.45
	Berth	3 W.R. set	5.35 Cheltenham	8.25
	Berth	6-set (410 type)	7.45 Portsmouth	10.4
BASINGSTOKE				
am				
8.50	Salisbury	1 corr.PMV	7.20 Waterloo F.P.	8.44
		3 set (770)		
		1 PMV (4)		
		5 set **FO**		
10.45	Salisbury	3 set	8.45 Woking	9.28
		Milk tanks	7.43 Clapham Jcn	9.51
pm				
2.48	Salisbury	3 set (770)	12.54 Waterloo	2.14
4.15	Waterloo	3-set (770)	3.15 Salisbury	4.8
		1 third		
		1 compo		
		5-set	Salisbury **FO**	
4.48	Salisbury	1 third	Berth	
		1 third	9.54 Waterloo	11.14
		3-set	2.54 Waterloo	4.14
5.37	Waterloo	1 PMV (4)	4.5 Salisbury	5.21
		3-set		
7.6	Salisbury	5-set	5.39 Waterloo F.P.	7.0
		1 first		
10.17	Salisbury	1 third	8.54 Waterloo	10.13
		3-set		
	Plymouth	1 corr.PMV	6.42 Waterloo	8.38
	Padstow	1 BY (4)		
	Exeter Central	1 PMV (4)		
		1 van B stove		
	Seaton Junction	1 PMV (4)		
GRATELEY				
pm				
5.19	Idmiston Halt*	1 third	7.35 Idmiston Halt*	7.43
		P & P set (363)		
IDMISTON HALT				
am				
7.35	Grateley*	P & P set (363)	7.20 Salisbury	7.33
		1 third		
pm				
5.30	Salisbury	1 third	5.19 Grateley*	5.27
		P & P set (363)		
SALISBURY				
am				
12.5 **F**	Plymouth	1 corr.PMV	8.54 Waterloo	11.20
	Padstow	1 PMV (4)	6.54 Waterloo	9.35
2.50	Yeovil Town	3-set	1.55 Eastleigh	2.36
		1 PMV (4)		
	Plymouth	1 PMV (4)		
	Exeter Central	2 PMV (4)		
3.19	Okehampton	1 PMV (4)	1.25 Waterloo	3.11
	Plymouth		1 bke compo (new)	
	Padstow		1 bke compo (new)	
			1 News van B	
	Torrington	1 News van B		
		1 bke compo (new)		
	Ilfracombe	1 cor. News Van		
		1 third		

Train	Destination	Formation	Previous service Train From	Due
		1 bke compo (new)		
	Yeovil Town	1 News van B		
3.30	Exeter Central	1 PMV (4)	8.54 Waterloo	11.20
	Seaton Junction	1 PMV (4)	6.54 Waterloo	9.35
	Yeovil Town	1 bke compo	1.25 Waterloo	3.11
	Templecombe	1 PMV (4)	8.54 Waterloo	11.20
3.52	Weymouth	1 News van B	1.25 Waterloo	3.11
		2 lav.set		Berth
5.15 **V**	Exeter Central	1 PMV (4)	1.25 Waterloo	3.11
		1 PMV (4)	8.54 Waterloo	11.20
		1 van B (stove)	6.54 Waterloo	9.35
	Yeovil Town	1 PMV (4)	2.58pm Gravesend	4.7
		Milk Tanks		
		1B.Y. (stove)		
6.10 **F**	Bulford	1 B.Y.	1.25 Waterloo	3.11
6.45	Waterloo	5-set	Berth	
		1 first		
		1 third		
		3-set		
7.20	Idmiston Halt	P & P set (363)	Berth	
		1 third		
8.15	Waterloo	5-set	Berth	
		1 first		
		1 third		
		3 PMV (4)		
8.42	Waterloo	3-set	7.10 Yeovil Town	8.33
		3-set (770)	Berth	
9.24	Templecombe	3-set	6.33 Woking	8.49
		Fish vans		
9.33	Waterloo	1 third	7.30 Exeter Central	9.27
		4-set (400)		
		1 open third		
		1 restaurant car		
		1 third		
		3-set	8.35 Semley	9.4
10.1	Waterloo	1 PMV (4)	6.30 Exeter Central	9.53
		3-set (770)		
pm				
12.46	Exeter Central	3-set (770)	7.20 Waterloo F.P.	9.58
		1 Cor. PMV		
	Seaton	1 bke compo	11.0 Waterloo	12.23
12.54	Waterloo	1 B.Y.	6.10 Plymouth	11.51
		1 Cor. PMV		
		3-set (770)		
		2 thirds	5.58 Portsmouth	8.31
	Neasden	Fish Vans	6.33 Woking	8.49
2.15	Waterloo	3 bke compos (new)	10.30 Ilfracombe	2.9
		2-set (63/75)		
		1 refreshment saloon	(12.30 Exeter Central)	
		1 kit. but. car (6/28)		
		1 third		
		1 2-set (63/75)		
		1 bke compo (new)		
		2 bke compos	8.55 Ilfracombe	1.49
2.55	Exeter Central	3-set	11.54 Waterloo	2.20
3.15	Waterloo	3-set (770)	8.55 Ilfracombe	1.49
		1 third	10.54 Waterloo F.P.	1.24
		1 compo		
		5-set **FO**	7.20 Waterloo	9.58
4.5	Waterloo	1 PMV (4)	7.20 Waterloo	9.58
		3-set	12.50 Templecombe	1.40
4.35	Waterloo **FO**	6-set (410)	10.8 Andover Jcn*	10.35
		3-set	10.54 Waterloo	1.24
4.56	Templecombe	3-set (770)	2.48 Basingstoke	4.0
		1 PMV (4)	Berth	
5.15	Waterloo	1 third	Berth	
		3-set	1.6 Exeter Central	4.32
		1 PMV (4)		
	Clapham Junction	1 Van B		
		Milk Tanks	Berth	
7.6	Yeovil Junction	3-set (770)	5.0 Waterloo F.P.	7.0
	thence 9.3 to Extr.	1 kitchen buffet car		
		1 refreshment saloon		
8.50	Waterloo	2 PMV (4)	4.52 Bournemouth	6.22
	Woking	3-set	4.5 Yeovil Town	5.42
9.55	Yeovil Town	3-set (770)	6.54 Waterloo F.P.	9.46
10.40	Waterloo **V**	1 News Van B	5.18 Sidmouth Jcn	10.25 **V**
		3 PMV (4)		
		1 Van B (stove)		
		1 PMV (4)		
		1 News Van B	8.55 Ilfracombe	1.49
		1 News Van B	4.5 Yeovil Town	5.42
		Milk Vans	5.18 Sidmouth Jcn	10.25 **V**

Key

* empty stock	**V** Van train
Van B bogie guards van	
F.P. front portion	**F** Freight train
BY 4 wheel guards van	
M.P. middle portion	**FO** Fridays only PMV (4)
4 wheel luggage van	
R.P. rear portion	
Cor.PMV bogie luggage van	

25.7.01 58030 with 9 loaded vans and container flat Ludgershall to Eastleigh

9.11.2002 66501, 66534, 57001 on diverted Freightliners, several diverted Virgin Voyagers

These are examples only, a full list would be far too long.

CARRIAGE WORKING DIAGRAMS

We concentrate here on carriage workings east of Salisbury. The formations of through trains from Waterloo to destinations west of Salisbury will be covered in Volumes Two and Three.

Waterloo to West of England
Train Formations

The formations of trains from Waterloo to Yeovil, Exeter and beyond will be covered in Volumes Two and Three, and were often complicated by the number of destinations served. Furthermore there were differences between Up and Down formations, for example the Down 11.0am Waterloo Atlantic Coast Express conveyed two brake compos detached at Sidmouth Junction for Sidmouth and Exmouth, which returned next day not on the 12.30pm Exeter Atlantic Coast Express but on the 10.30am Exeter instead. On arrival at Waterloo Up trains were worked empty to Clapham Yard for cleaning and re-marshalling into the correct formations for Down trains.

Top left. On 20th September 1947 Maunsell U class 2-6-0 No.1795 in Salisbury platform 5 with a three coach train which will provide a stopping service to Templecombe or Yeovil, connecting with a down express. H.C.Casserley.

Middle left. 4-4-0s at Basingstoke shed. Left is No.62663 *Prince Albert* a Director class of the Great Central Railway and right Schools class No.30901 Winchester. The Director was a most unusual visitor and 62663 had worked a Farnborough Air Special from Leeds to Basingstoke with Atlantic 251 on 12th September 1954. It is also a reminder that freight traffic between the LSWR and the Great Central was worked by way of Basingstoke, Oxford and Banbury.

Bottom left. The prolific Bulleid Pacifics, Merchant Navy, West Country and Battle of Britain, were used on all manner of work along the main line. Merchant Navy 4-6-2 21C1 *Channel Packet* receives some attention from the fireman at Salisbury shed in 1946. R.C. Riley, The Transport Treasury.

BR standard class 2-6-0 No.76011 passes Salisbury Milford Goods station running light engine towards Salisbury. This class was used on many duties in the last decade of steam traction. Paul Strong.

A notable visitor at Salisbury was BR standard class 2-10-0 No.92220 *Evening Star*, seen at platform 3 on a Bristol line train.

Ivatt 2-6-2T No.41320 shunting in Salisbury Milford Goods yard. One or two shunting engines were required here, sometimes round the clock. These LMR tank engines worked on a number of Southern lines in the last decade of steam. Paul Strong.

Western Region Warship class No.805 departs from Andover on 23rd July 1969 with the 1310 Waterloo to Exeter St David's train. John Scrace.

Class 33s Nos.33055 and 33035 depart from Basingstoke with the 1410 Waterloo to Salisbury train. John Scrace.

On 11th May 1993 class 47 No.47717 hauls the 1317 Exeter St David's to Waterloo train past the site of Oakley station, closed some thirty years previously. R.K.Blencowe Collection.